CW00531027

Strategic Survey 2022
The Annual Assessment of Geopolitics

published by

 Routledge
Taylor & Francis Group

for

The International Institute for Strategic Studies

The International Institute for Strategic Studies

Arundel House | 6 Temple Place | London | WC2R 2PG | UK

Strategic Survey 2022
The Annual Assessment of Geopolitics

First published December 2022 by **Routledge**
4 Park Square, Milton Park, Abingdon, Oxon, OX14 4RN

for **The International Institute for Strategic Studies**
Arundel House, 6 Temple Place, London, WC2R 2PG, UK

Simultaneously published in the USA and Canada by **Routledge**
52 Vanderbilt Avenue, New York, NY 10017

Routledge is an imprint of Taylor & Francis, an Informa business

© 2022 The International Institute for Strategic Studies

DIRECTOR-GENERAL AND CHIEF EXECUTIVE Dr John Chipman

EDITOR Dr Nigel Gould-Davies

ASSOCIATE EDITOR Katie Holland
ASSISTANT EDITOR Nicholas Woodroof
EDITORIAL Gregory Brooks, Daniel Edwards, Christopher Harder, Jill Lally, Jana Phillips
KEY EVENTS RESEARCH Birna Gudmundsdottir
DRIVERS OF STRATEGIC CHANGE RESEARCH Graham Ivory, Kevin Jewell
COVER/PRODUCTION/CARTOGRAPHY Alessandra Beluffi, Jade Panganiban, James Parker, Kelly Verity
COVER IMAGES Centre image Arsen Petrov; all other images Getty

British Library Cataloguing in Publication Data
A catalogue record for this book is available from the British Library

Library of Congress Cataloguing in Publication Data

ISBN 978-1-032-30441-0
ISSN 0459-7230

Contents

Chapter 1

Introduction

Editor's Introduction

Strategic Survey 2022 charts a geopolitical fault line marked by two decisions. The first was the West's withdrawal from Afghanistan in August 2021. This ended a 20-year military intervention that was the first act of the now-forgotten 'war on terror'. The second was Russia's invasion of Ukraine six months later. This began the biggest war in Europe since 1945.

These twin events will shape world politics for years. They have already thrown up surprises. Few expected that the Afghan government forces would collapse so completely, or that Ukrainians would stay and fight so hard and so well. Few expected, after the calamitous evacuation from Kabul, that a new war would restore Western unity and purpose, or lay bare Russia's weaknesses across every domain of power, so quickly.

They offer lessons too. On the hubris of power, which drove the West to try to remake a very different state and society, and which led Russia to try to dictate the identity – and deny the very legitimacy – of another people. And on the significance of choices that might have been different. President Vladimir Putin's invasion of Ukraine despite a visibly unhappy, if compliant, elite unleashed forces that could end his regime. President Volodymyr Zelenskyy's refusal to leave Kyiv in the first days of the war, against the advice of his aides and Western governments, instilled in state, army and country the will to resist. By preventing a Russian victory, and thus a fundamental change to the European security order, this single decision changed the course of history.

More surprises and lessons will follow as the war and its consequences ripple out into the future. These are not only geopolitical, but also geo-economic. The war has disrupted global commodities markets and fuelled inflation. More fundamentally, it is driving rapid innovation in the theory and practice of economic statecraft. Potent new instruments of coercion and constraint, such as an oil-price cap, are being honed and used against Russia, a systemically important oil exporter. Governments around the world are watching closely. And as states harness global markets for security ends, the private sector must reckon with – and better understand – a dawning era of political risk.

Beyond the war, wider forces are also shifting the landscape of world politics. Strategic rivalry between China and the West is deepening. AUKUS, an agreement between major democracies on three continents to develop and share military technology and research, is the most ambitious response so far to growing Chinese power. Islamic extremism continues to spread in Africa, especially in the Sahel and in Mozambique. An encouraging de-escalatory trend of Middle Eastern conflicts – with Israel–Iran relations the major exception – has set in. Conversely, a spate of violent episodes in Central Asian states point to rising instability.

There are growing signs, too, that the course of world politics, and especially of major rivalries, will be decided as much by the balance of domestic resilience as by the balance of power. Russia's late and reluctant decision to order a not-so-partial mobilisation is testing support for the war and loyalty to the regime that launched it. China's uncertain growth, against the background of a rigid zero-COVID policy, may test domestic stability. America's politics and society appear as polarised as they were during Donald Trump's presidency – and the revelations of the House of Representatives' Select Committee to Investigate the January 6th Attack on the United States Capitol show just how serious was the threat to democracy during his last days in office.

War is redefining Western security, may change Russia profoundly, and is influencing perceptions and calculations globally. Shifts in power are exposing unexpected strengths and weaknesses that will shape the international order. The rules and practices of political economy are being rewritten as globalisation – more market, less state – gives way to its opposite, economic statecraft. When the history of this era is written, the fault line of 2021–22 may run as deeply through it as that of 1989–91.

November 2022

Drivers of Strategic Change

Geopolitics is driven by changes in the ability of states to use and resist power. The first depends on power resources, and the second on domestic resilience. Our Drivers of Strategic Change measure and compare key trends in both areas. They illuminate recent shifts in geopolitics and sources of potential future change.

Geopolitics is a craft, not a science: judgement, skill, chance and other immeasurable factors also shape international relations. But they do so within a range of possibilities set by the underlying domestic and external capacities of states. We encourage you to explore the rich data in our Drivers and the insights they yield.

The Drivers begin each geographical chapter. Unless otherwise stated, they chart change over 20 years by plotting data from 2001, 2011 and 2021.

Regional Share of Global Population, GDP and Defence Budget
(Sources: United Nations Department of Economic and Social Affairs; IMF; IISS, Military Balance; IISS, Military Balance+)

The first Driver depicts the region's share of global population, GDP and defence budget. These are key power resources: the more of each that a country or region possesses, the greater its potential power, especially in combination. This Driver thus shows how the relative power of each region has changed over the past two decades.

The next six Drivers depict data for key selected countries in each region.

Population
(Source: United Nations Department of Economic and Social Affairs Population Division, World Population Prospects 2022)

The second Driver shows population, age structure and median age. These are important for several reasons. Population is a power resource. A high proportion of young people – a 'youth bulge' – is a strong predictor of civil violence. It also presages a 'demographic dividend' of higher economic growth through future workforce growth, especially if fertility rates subsequently fall. Conversely, an ageing population means a high dependency ratio of economically inactive to active citizens, creating fiscal and productivity challenges that can limit resources needed to sustain power.

GDP

(Source: IMF)

The third Driver shows GDP and global ranking. The larger a country's economy, the more of other forms of strength, including military hardware, it can procure.

GDP per Capita

(Source: IMF)

The fourth Driver shows GDP per capita, which has been shown to have a significant impact on the development of social values. Rising affluence leads to robust and predictable changes in political orientation – in particular, a decline in deference towards authority and a rise in demands for inclusion and participation.

Defence Budget and Active Military Personnel

(Sources: IISS, Military Balance; IISS, Military Balance+)

The fifth Driver shows defence budget and active military personnel, which are indicators of hard power.

Human Development Index (HDI)

(Source: UN Development Programme)

The sixth Driver shows Human Development Index scores, a composite measure of human well-being. This indicates a country's ability to provide well-being and life chances for its population, with positive implications for governmental legitimacy and stability – and, in foreign policy, for the soft power of attraction.

Political System
(Source: Freedom House, 'Freedom in the World')

The seventh Driver shows how democratic a political system is. Democratic legitimacy tends to produce stable and responsive government that is more resilient in a crisis. Conversely, the recent decline of democracy in some high-income countries, where the underlying demand for accountability remains high, may presage declining stability.

Regional Trends

The final Driver for each chapter uses a range of data to illuminate region-specific trends.

For Asia, Europe, Latin America and North America:

Trust in Government
(Source: Edelman Trust Barometer)

This Driver shows the general public's average percentage of trust in government. Falling trust in governmental institutions – a recent feature of many countries – implies a decline in stability and cohesion. Questions that afforded respondents the opportunity to criticise their government were not asked in China, Russia and Thailand.

For Russia and Eurasia:

Approval Rating for President Vladimir Putin, and Assessment of the Current State of Affairs in Russia
(Source: Levada Center)

This Driver shows approval ratings for Russian President Vladimir Putin and popular views about the state of affairs in Russia. Despite setbacks in the war against Ukraine, there has been a large rise in the number of Russians who say the country is going in the right direction. Putin's popularity has also risen sharply.

For the Middle East and North Africa:

Breakeven Oil Prices
(Sources: bp Statistical Review of World Energy 2022; IMF)

This Driver shows the oil price per barrel needed to ensure that planned government spending will not incur a budget deficit for 2016–22, together with the average annual oil price for 2015–21. It highlights the impact of the post-2014 oil-price decline on the fiscal sustainability of oil-export-dependent states.

For sub-Saharan Africa:

Adults with a Mobile-money Account
(Source: World Bank Global Findex Database)

In *Strategic Survey 2021* we showed how education – and thus human capital – is growing rapidly in sub-Saharan Africa. This year, we show the rapid rise in mobile-money payments, which support financial inclusion and drive growth. Sub-Saharan Africa accounts for two-thirds of the world's mobile-money payments.

Chapter 2

Key Events
July 2021–June 2022

July 2021

07 Haiti's president Jovenel Moïse is assassinated at his residence by foreign mercenaries.

08 United States President Joe Biden moves forward the deadline for withdrawal from Afghanistan to 31 August, due to the increased risk the Taliban pose to US personnel.

12 Russian President Vladimir Putin publishes a 7,000-word essay 'On the Historical Unity of Russians and Ukrainians', arguing that they are 'one people'.

August 2021

04 Mexico files a lawsuit against some of the largest US weapons manufacturers for contributing to illegal arms trafficking.

12 Opposition leader Hakainde Hichilema wins presidential elections in Zambia, leading to a more pro-business government and opening the way for debt renegotiations.

15 The Taliban enter Kabul and take control of Afghanistan.

24 Algeria severs diplomatic ties with Morocco as tensions rise over Western Sahara.

26 13 American military personnel are killed in a terrorist suicide bombing during the final effort to withdraw remaining Americans in Afghanistan.

September 2021

07 Poland imposes a state of emergency at its border with Belarus in response to a surge of migrants engineered by the latter. The order is lifted on 1 July 2022.

11 North Korea starts a new phase of missile tests.

15 President Biden, United Kingdom prime minister Boris Johnson and Australian prime minister Scott Morrison announce AUKUS, a trilateral security pact focused on the Indo-Pacific region.

16 The European Commission and High Representative present their Joint Communication on the European Union's Indo-Pacific strategy.

24 President Biden, Indian Prime Minister Narendra Modi, Japanese prime minister Suga Yoshihide and prime minister Morrison meet in Washington DC for the first in-person Quadrilateral Security Dialogue (Quad) Leaders' Summit.

27 The US and Mexico sign the 'Bicentennial Framework for Security, Public Health, and Safe Communities' to govern bilateral cooperation on security.

October 2021

Russia begins a new military build-up on Ukraine's borders.

04 Kishida Fumio is confirmed as prime minister of Japan, succeeding Suga.

25 Military elements dissolve Sudan's civilian-led transitional administration, effectively derailing the transition to democratic rule and setting off months of protests.

31 The UK hosts COP26 in Glasgow. Over 100 countries pledge to limit methane emissions.

November 2021

01 Algeria shuts down the Maghreb–Europe Gas Pipeline (MEG), cutting off Morocco's only source of natural gas.

07 Daniel Ortega wins a fifth term as president in Nicaragua's general elections. The election outcome is not recognised by most countries.

28 Xiomara Castro from the left-wing Libre party wins Honduras' presidential elections, ending 12 years of conservative National Party rule.

29 Senegal hosts the eighth Forum on China–Africa Cooperation. China reduces its headline financial pledge to the continent for the first time in the history of the summit.

December 2021

08 Olaf Scholz is sworn in as chancellor of Germany, ending Angela Merkel's 16-year tenure.

09 The US convenes the virtual Summit for Democracy.

17 Russia publishes draft security treaties with the US and NATO.

19 Gabriel Boric wins the run-off in Chile's presidential elections, beating José Antonio Kast.

23 Elections in Libya are postponed. Rival governments in Tripoli and Benghazi claim political authority.

January 2022

01 The Regional Comprehensive Economic Partnership (RCEP), a free-trade agreement between nations in the Indo-Pacific, enters into force.

02 Protests against fuel-price rises in Kazakhstan break out and escalate into mass violence. President Qasym-Jomart Toqaev prevails in the intra-elite struggle that follows.

06 Australia and Japan sign a Reciprocal Access Agreement intended to enhance military cooperation.

February 2022

11 The Biden administration releases its 'Indo-Pacific Strategy', which pledges to support regional connectivity, trade and investment and deepen bilateral and multilateral partnerships.

17 France and several other EU states announce the withdrawal of troops from Mali, effectively marking the end of *Operation Barkhane*.

21 Russia recognises the 'independence' of the Luhansk and Donetsk 'people's republics'.

24 Russia launches its second invasion of Ukraine.

27 Chancellor Scholz pledges to raise military spending to 2% of GDP as part of Germany's historic *Zeitenwende* in response to Russia's invasion of Ukraine.

28 Ukraine submits an application for EU membership. Georgia and Moldova do so the following week.

March 2022

09 Yoon Suk-yeol is elected president of South Korea.

13 Iran fires missiles at a site in Erbil, Iraq, claiming it was being used by the Israeli intelligence service Mossad.

21 The Council of the EU approves the 'Strategic Compass for Security and Defence', which aims to make the bloc a stronger security provider by 2030.

22 Canada's Liberal Party and New Democratic Party (NDP) broker an agreement that will keep Prime Minister Justin Trudeau in office until 2025.

24 Rebels in Tigray and the Ethiopian government agree to a cessation of hostilities, marking a major turnaround after a period in which the federal government looked to be under threat from the rebels.

27 The Negev Summit on security and cooperation begins in Israel, with Bahrain, Egypt, Morocco, the United Arab Emirates (UAE) and the US attending.

April 2022

01 The EU–China Summit ends with no joint statement and few clear deliverables. EU High Representative Josep Borrell calls it a 'dialogue of the deaf'.

02 The first nationwide truce in Yemen since 2016 takes hold.

05 The Biden administration confirms a major sale of defence equipment to Taiwan, the third since taking office.

06 Russian forces complete their withdrawal from around Kyiv, having failed to seize the Ukrainian capital.

07 Yemeni president Abd Rabbo Mansour Hadi is forced to resign and transfer his powers to a presidential council.

11 Shahbaz Sharif succeeds Imran Khan as prime minister of Pakistan.

17 Mexico's Congress rejects a major electricity-sector reform proposed by President Andrés Manuel López Obrador.

19 China announces the signing of a confidential five-year framework security agreement with Solomon Islands.

21 Following a seven-month hiatus, Saudi and Iranian officials hold the fifth round of direct talks in Baghdad since the meetings began in April 2021.

24 Emmanuel Macron is re-elected president of France. Weeks later, his party loses its majority in the National Assembly.

May 2022

09 Sri Lanka's prime minister Mahinda Rajapaksa resigns following protests against the economic crisis. Dinesh Gunawardena succeeds him on 22 July 2022.

12 The Emir of Qatar Prince Tamim bin Hamad Al Thani flies to Tehran to mediate the stalled talks on Iran's nuclear programme.

13 UAE president Sheikh Khalifa bin Zayed Al Nahyan dies and is succeeded by Sheikh Mohammed bin Zayed.

17 A day after relaxing certain sanctions on Cuba, the US eases some sanctions on Venezuela following the visit to Caracas in March of a high-level US delegation to discuss issues of energy security.

19 The US Congress approves US$40 billion in economic, food and military aid for Ukraine, supplementing an earlier US$13.6bn package.

23 President Biden says that the US would defend Taiwan militarily if the island were attacked by China.

23 President Biden launches the Indo-Pacific Economic Framework for Prosperity (IPEF), an attempt to regain US economic initiative in the region.

24 The leaders of the Quad nations – Australia, India, Japan and the US – meet in Tokyo for the second in-person Leaders' Summit of the grouping.

24 China and Russia conduct joint bomber flights around Japan and South Korea, which scramble fighter aircraft in response.

26 China and Russia veto tougher United Nations sanctions on North Korea – the first time in 15 years that members of the UN Security Council have done so.

June 2022

01 Canada's military accuses Chinese aircraft of harassing Canadian planes engaged in enforcement of UN sanctions against North Korea in April and May 2022.

05 Democratic Republic of the Congo (DRC) President Felix Tshisekedi states that Rwanda is backing a rebellion in the DRC's eastern territories, marking a new ramp-up in tensions between the two states.

06 The US hosts the 9th Summit of the Americas in Los Angeles amid controversy on the exclusion of Cuba, Nicaragua and Venezuela.

19 Gustavo Petro becomes the first left-wing president of Colombia, beating Rodolfo Hernández, a populist who had run on an anti-corruption platform.

21 Two China Coast Guard ships spend more than 64 hours in waters near the Senkaku/Diaoyu islands, which are controlled by Japan – the longest incursion in over a decade.

23 The EU grants candidacy status to Ukraine and Moldova.

28 At a summit in Madrid, NATO leaders agree a new Strategic Concept and invite Finland and Sweden to join the Alliance.

Chapter 3

Strategic Prospects

The geopolitical earthquake that resulted from Russia's invasion of Ukraine on 24 February 2022 will send further tremors and reinforce fault lines in global politics. At the close of 2021, the United States and most European countries were committed to the Indo-Pacific as the strategic theatre to which attention must shift. Asia's strategic primacy was a settled strategic consensus. Russian President Vladimir Putin's imperial adventure, however, pulled the West back into defending the security of its original area of strategic focus. The European security order is 'a core interest' of the West. Its fracture would make any more external security commitments unviable. Its successful defence would lend credibility to any Indo-Pacific tilt. A variety of residual security commitments made in the Middle East would also be shown to be more reliable if success were achieved. Nevertheless, the perceptions of the conflict remained diverse in these other regions, with the Russian narrative that its invasion was provoked getting much more purchase than the facts warranted. Reputationally, then, the strategic challenge for the West became dual: defeat Russia to both restore the European security order and regain the trust of the rest of the world in Western strategic objectives and ethics.

The early course of the conflict was conducted by the West with considerable military reserve. Concerns about providing so-called offensive weapons to Ukraine and fears of escalation blunted the strength of the initial response. Over time, as the extreme brutality of the Russian attacks was exposed and the extraordinary national will of the Ukrainians to repel the invaders became evident, many of these worries abated. With the delivery of NATO-standard equipment, Ukraine was able to mount counter-offensives. But a persistent fear of direct conflict with Russia prevented the US from delivering long-range artillery, first-class tanks and other equipment that may have more decisively shifted the balance of power at an earlier stage. A creeping escalation of military support, justified by persistent Ukrainian successes on the ground, became the preferred option.

The instinct was to treat Putin's Russia the way predecessors had treated Leonid Brezhnev's Soviet Union – do everything to avoid a direct conflict that could lead to the horrors of a strategic nuclear confrontation. That goal was wise overall but may have cut off reasonable military options that would have brought a faster end to the conflict on terms that were consistent with the maintenance of the European security order. One Cold War memory was judiciously recalled – avoid a direct US–Russia war and keep NATO out of conflict. Another Cold War memory was unstrategically forgotten – devise flexible responses and ensure escalation dominance. Escalation became a 'four-letter word' in Western geopolitical parlance. But defence is not escalation, and counter-offensives are necessary for victory. Thermostatically controlling the exact levels of military assistance given to Ukraine against an outdated Cold War gauge set to 'warm' but avoiding 'hot' gave the Ukrainians just enough to defend and persist, but not quite enough to repel and win.

Initially, US policy tried to distinguish between offensive and defensive weapons, and then sought to provide artillery that did not have the range to target inside Russian territory. Russia had attacked the largest country in Europe and ripped up the European security order, and yet an arms-control policy and end-use restrictions were imposed on the defending state. It was not just Ukraine that urged the delivery of 'more, faster' – soon the Northern European and Baltic states became the strongest advocates of a robust response. After all, it had been President Niinistö of Finland already on 1 January 2022 who had provided elements of this evolving strategic 'thought leadership' in his New Year speech. Then, he counselled that 'whenever avoidance of war has been the primary objective of a group of powers, the international system has been at the mercy of its most ruthless member'. By 24 February, this sorry prediction came true. A country that had long had a strategy of self-reliance in defence and a prudential foreign-policy approach towards Russia realised that its long-standing strategic posture was no longer tenable. Within weeks of the invasion, support for NATO membership had risen from around 20% to over 80% of the Finnish population.

A genuine fear of Russia's intentions and the complete loss of a minimal level of strategic trust made the argument in favour of NATO membership overwhelming. Careful to march in lockstep as much as possible with fellow European Union member state and neighbour Sweden, the two had their membership applications accepted. The fact that two Nordic states so quickly changed their long-standing foreign policies to seek NATO protection was an eloquent rebuttal to Russia's claim that NATO's 2008 'Open Door' policy was the 'legitimate security concern' for which an invasion of Ukraine was the appropriate palliative cure. No material effort had been made since 2008 to advance the interest of Ukraine or Georgia to join NATO, despite Russia's occupation of Crimea and its military engagement in eastern Ukraine supporting separatists in 2014.

The Baltic states, with an unhappy history of Soviet occupation, and now with long NATO borders with Russia, also became strong advocates for robust Western military support to Ukraine. Lithuania had special concerns, given its additional Russian border with the exclave Kaliningrad. The leadership in Vilnius had to show formal respect for Russian sovereignty by ensuring that EU sanctions operated properly against it, while being prepared for the military hardware that Russia might position within Kaliningrad. Latvia, like other states, spoke frankly about its disappointment at the level of support offered to Ukraine, especially by Germany, and strongly criticised the early assumptions held by some in Western Europe that a negotiated end to the conflict was desirable, or that a face-saving gesture should be offered to Putin. Prime Minister Kaja Kallas of Estonia quickly gained wide prominence for her crisp interventions calling for a clear-eyed and firm response to Russia. These front-line states, along with Poland and the Czech Republic, persistently argued that, based on their prior experience of Russia, their warnings of Russian strategic intent and appeals for a determined defence of Ukraine deserved special attention.

In many respects, they won their case. The June 2022 Madrid NATO Summit not only accepted Finland's and Sweden's applications but also agreed a new Strategic Concept that gave greater prominence to the defence of NATO front-line states. These states contributed proportionately high percentages of their GDP per capita to Ukraine's defence, and other European states began pledging to spend more money too. The influence of these states became stronger in both the EU and NATO councils. This was not just because they were speaking out more; or because two of them applied to join NATO; or because the Czech Republic took the presidency of the EU Council; or because Poland was taking so many refugees, was a key transit point for weapons, including their own, to Kyiv, and offered to be part of the US 'nuclear sharing' arrangements. It was because all these states were powerfully making the case that they were the new 'front-line states'.

Thus, an important impact of Russia's war on Ukraine was that the geopolitical centre of gravity in Europe moved to the east and the north. These present and future NATO members were all soberly making the case for the defence of Ukraine as a matter of both high principle and urgent security. While some Western European states were emphasising diplomacy over deterrence or withholding arms to avoid escalation, these new front-line states were arguing for robust military support to Ukraine and emphasising that defence was not escalation. Even with an enlarged EU, France and Germany can still argue that their cooperation is key to fuelling EU progress. But in an enlarged NATO, and with Russia having attacked Ukraine, it is the countries of the north and east which rightly have a key 'swing vote' on how NATO analyses risks to European security and decides on the principal instruments of defence and deterrence. In security terms, it may soon be the case that Western European leaders explaining the rationale for European defence structures will need to speak of 'Nordic centrality' just as they diplomatically defer to 'ASEAN centrality' when considering the regional security architecture of Asia.

The US, along with key Western allies such as France, Germany, the United Kingdom and others, possesses the preponderance of military and economic power on the continent. Without the military support offered by the US, and the economic sanctions organised especially by the EU with the US, Ukraine's war effort would not have been able to last. Slowly, the awareness grew that the balance of power between Russia and the West had radically changed. The fact that by the seventh month of the war, Ukraine was able to mount very substantial counter-offensives even though Russia had sent much of its best troops and materiel to the war, while the West had desisted from sending its best tanks, aircraft or longest-range artillery to Ukraine, was a testament to this. The US, and many NATO states, appeared to 'remember' Russia as an unapproachable behemoth. Yet it had become, as those in the north and the east had perceived, a weakened but violently neo-fascist state. And with this anachronistic memory in mind, it took too long for the US and NATO states to consider that the best way to end the war was to shift more radically the balance of power in Ukraine's favour.

One can only imagine what might have been the result in the early 1980s if the US had thought that, when the Soviet Union deployed RSD-10 *Pioneer* (RS-SS-20 *Saber*) intermediate-range ballistic missiles against Europe, it would have been 'escalatory' to place MGM-31 *Pershing* medium-range ballistic missiles and ground-launched cruise missiles (the BGM-109G) in Europe in response. Then, political-military training kicked in properly: balances of power that are changed need to be reset if stability is to be maintained. The administration of US President Joe Biden even referred in October 2022 to the risk of nuclear war as being greater than it had been since the Cuban Missile Crisis of 1962. Here was a case of a well-advanced war in Ukraine, where the competitors were not strictly Washington and Moscow but rather Moscow and a third large independent state that was prevailing on the battlefield, and conventional means were sufficient to support it. There was plenty of time for the right signalling. Yet commentators regularly spoke of the risk of World War Three if there were a strong conventional response to Russia's invasion, as if the US and the wider West could not shape that risk by their own clear deterrence strategies and statements.

Thus, Putin's nuclear threats were more effective than they might have been because there was at best a random application of deterrence messaging. Every weapons transfer was analysed through an ill-defined and smoky prism of 'escalation'. Arms-control measures were taken, with artillery transferred to Ukraine that could not strike attacking positions located in Russian territory. The presumption that there was only one rung on an escalation ladder was nearly universal. The idea that one could regularly adjust one's response – flexible response – to maintain escalation dominance was lost. A reluctance to reinforce success by Ukraine in combatting Russian brute force persisted even as the Ukrainians recovered territory burned to a crisp by the enemy. The levels of strategic illiteracy were at times shocking. At one point, some in Germany argued that it could not give more arms to Ukraine because it needed them to deter Putin, who only understood force. Yet it might have been wiser to assist more robustly the country fighting Russia so Germany did not have to and, if Putin only understood force, to give Ukraine what it needed. The hesitation to provide modern tanks for fear of some form of escalation later appeared even more ironic when Ukrainian forces captured intact some of the best Russian mechanised equipment and tanks, which they then used against the enemy.

Diplomatic efforts to end the war early understandably collapsed when it became evident that Putin's diplomacy was fraudulent in both form and substance. Since his aim was to deny Ukraine its status as an independent country, territorial concessions could play no useful part in a negotiation. A 'two-state solution' was far too little for Putin, and intolerably too much for Kyiv. And as the war carried on, the sense deepened that Ukraine not only could but must win. When asked at the inaugural October 2022 European Political Community (EPC) meeting in Prague to suggest a way out of the conflict, Finnish Prime Minister Sanna Marin's crisp reply was that 'the way out of the conflict is for Russia to leave Ukraine'. She did not say the West needed to moderate its support for

Ukraine for fear of Russian escalation. And by this time, few in Europe still thought that it was a diplomatic duty of the West to provide Putin with an off-ramp. The exit door was clearly marked. Eventually, in the autumn of 2022, the US sent a clear message to Putin that any nuclear use would have catastrophic consequences for Russia. It might have had more deterrent value if the US had specifically said that any nuclear use would mean that all the United States' conventional power would be put at the disposal of Ukraine to eject Russia from Ukraine's internationally recognised territory.

By this time, it was clear that Ukraine's war aims comprised, at a minimum, the recovery of all occupied territory, including Crimea. They could possibly extend to seeking full reparations from Russia and ensuring that Russian leaders are taken to international courts for war crimes. None of these aims could be contested as a matter of law or realpolitik. Once Ukraine had sacrificed so much to be able to mount counter-offensives, it was evident that they would wish to claim the independence and sovereignty that had been stolen from them. And it was difficult for Westerners to invite Ukraine to think of war aims that did not include regaining its own territory. For Kyiv, having suffered a rough stalemate from 2014–22, once the initiative was back in Ukraine's hands, even at a huge cost, the nation demanded more.

For Putin, it may have been both humiliating and unacceptable to be beaten on the battlefield by Ukraine alone. What pretensions of great-power status could then be retained? It would evidently be less embarrassing, and more explainable, if Western powers were seen to be key co-authors of a Ukrainian victory. Despite all the worries about escalation, Western states supporting Ukraine as de facto co-belligerents against him would give Putin the opportunity to blame the West for his retreat. As a military fact it should be self-evident that radically changing the balance of power in Ukraine's favour would bring a faster victory to Kyiv, while as a political fact, dictators can save face more easily if they can blame the outside world for a failure. Russian state TV began broadcasting regularly that many of the losses suffered by their troops were at the hands of the US, the UK or the 'collective West'.

Without this assistance, the propagandists argued, the mission would have been accomplished. When the so-called 'partial mobilisation' was announced in September, the difficulty of getting 300,000 people to the front was attributed mainly to incompetence and overzealousness, especially by local officials. In fact, massive corruption also played a major role in weakening the system. As a consequence, maintenance was poor, and the capacity to supply key support to new personnel was eroded by malfeasance.

A domestic reckoning was in the offing. The Kremlin clearly preferred to have some of the security forces criticised for not anticipating the capacities of Ukrainian resistance or the strength of Ukrainian national will. The military and general officers could be blamed for corruption and incompetence. The president could clearly protect himself for some time from general criticism. The central questions became for how long he could insulate himself from elite frustration and how completely he could trust his commanders to follow his orders, especially if they became escalatory in a way that would shock them. On this, the future of Russia and the European security order would rest. The probability of a Ukrainian victory over Russia appeared much more likely than either a Russian win or a prolonged stalemate.

For many countries in Asia and the Middle East the war raised questions about their alignments and hedging strategies. It is natural that countries engage in strategic hedging. There are few truly cast-iron guarantees in security. Some independence and autonomy of action are preferred by most states. Strategic self-determination may mean that interests do not always align with the same security partner. It is better to have many friends than only a few. Multi-alignment has its attractions. But strategic hedging, rather like its financial equivalent, requires active portfolio management. Russia's strategic currency was now in free fall. By the second half of 2022, it was perhaps not prudent to be too 'long Russia', to use the financial-markets term. Indeed, being 'overweight Russia', including for those countries that have traditionally had Russia as a major arms supplier, may prove costly in the medium term and perhaps rather sooner. Rebalancing will eventually be necessary, and countries in both Asia and the Middle East, perhaps too long in thrall to Russia's reputation as a great power, were slow to adjust themselves to the prospect of a Russian fall from the first rank of geopolitical status.

China will clearly have been irritated by Putin's failure to produce a quick win. Beijing will also have warned against the use of a nuclear device, as lowering the threshold of nuclear use would be very much against China's interests. Beijing was hardly a vocal supporter of the war. It appeared cautiously more on the military sidelines and in public a diplomatic abstainer, especially at the United Nations. It would benefit from buying discounted Russian energy, but it was not pressing ahead in taking ostentatious commercial advantage. In time, the probability is that Russia will continue to be an opponent of the West, but will be a weak and cracked pole in the multipolar world of Chinese strategic hopes. India's Prime Minister Narendra Modi brought himself to say to Putin that 'this was not a time for war', but India's multi-alignment pose still revealed a non-alignment attitude. For India, diversification would come most quickly perhaps in the military sphere, in which the realisation would dawn that Russia would not be a trusted source of reliable weaponry.

Leaders in the Gulf were unwilling to bend the decision-making of the Organization of the Petroleum Exporting Countries (OPEC) to America's will. Its October 2022 decision to lower production to preserve prices at around US$90 per barrel was probably less 'pro-Russian' and more inspired by a sense that they wished to maintain production levels just short of capacity and were reluctant to please the US 'on demand'. High prices, however, will also create economic pain for the global south proportionately more than for the West. Some Gulf states were encouraging their business leaders to buy distressed assets in Russia, in particular companies and factories from which Western firms were withdrawing.

By 2023, it is likely that more profound decisions will need to be made about geopolitical alignments. Few will likely see an advantage in close association with a depleted Russia. As the domestic crisis in Russia continues to unfold, and the anxiety over the war grows as 'partial mobilisation' turns into something fuller, Putin will have to think more about the stability of the home front. In the regions, the upset at mobilisation was palatable. Russia itself has an internal imperial quality. How to maintain national cohesion will become the Kremlin's priority in 2023 as decisions are made on how to explain the war's process and ultimate end.

What this war has additionally shown is that the Euro-Atlantic and wider Indo-Pacific strategic theatres are co-dependent. The largest importer of Ukrainian wheat is Egypt; the second largest is Indonesia. The impact of this war in Europe was felt internationally. For North Americans and Europeans who pledge their commitments to the Indo-Pacific region, success in Europe would also be vital to success in Asia. It is not simply a question of time commitment, but one of credibility. Put bluntly, how can one speak about helping to support a free and open Indo-Pacific, if it is not possible to ensure a free and open Black Sea? Had the West been able to find a way to reopen the Black Sea fully, sending vessels in for the protection of ships delivering grain and fertiliser to the global south, it would have lessened the food-security impact of the war on the rest of the world. That action would also have exposed the truth that Putin's war was not just a regional issue but also one with global implications. In the regional and wider interest, freedom of navigation in the Black Sea should rise as a priority in the European security agenda, at least as much as the question of energy independence from Russia.

The great strategic issues for 2023 will revolve around the best way to deal with falling, rising and rebel powers. Putin's Russia has evolved into a terrorist state, bombing civilians with casual, evil regularity. A revanchist Russia now threatening nuclear use must necessarily be opposed by European states with their North American allies if the Western security order is in any way to hold. A weakened, fragmented and possibly defeated Russia would pose a different sort of challenge. That possible outcome should not deter the West from winning the war in Ukraine, and European states will need to assess and be alert to the ancillary threats it would pose.

And, as Japanese Prime Minister Kishida Fumio said in June 2022 at the IISS Shangri-La Dialogue, 'Ukraine today may be East Asia tomorrow'. In Asia, there is alarm at the worsening relations between the US and China. Some blame China for 'overplaying its hand' and being too assertive; others blame the US for not appreciating China's core interests and finding too many other issues on which to confront China, including in the economic domain. The small Pacific Island states feel themselves caught up in a new US–China competition. Following the conclusion of the Chinese Communist Party's Fifth Party Congress, and as China finds its way out of its 'dynamic zero-COVID' policy, it will be desirable to see some moderation of the Chinese external stance and some lessening of US–China tension, but the path to this is not evident. None of this is helped by North Korea's regular testing of its missile capabilities. Its political noise may be muffled by the attention spent on the Russia–Ukraine war, but its strategic effect is still felt powerfully by the United States' East Asian allies.

In the Middle East, Iran's theocratic leadership was under attack from women seeking their independence and freedom. The regime was still assertive regionally through its influence operations and was resisting entreaties to curtail its nuclear programme within a modest extension of the Joint Comprehensive Plan of Action (JCPOA). Again, here the challenges were of different kinds: how to contain Iran's regional ambitions, and how to deal with an Iran that may also be subject to huge internal dissent, the suppression of which would have other consequences. In 2023, it will be necessary for the US, Europe and the Gulf Arab states to find a common policy on Iran. But the experience of the last two decades, when approaches were rarely synchronised, does not inspire optimism.

In this moment of intensified geopolitical competition and uncertainty, adding a further political-ideological battle into the mix is unlikely to result in strategic advantage. The US, the UK and others have defined the current struggle as one between democracies and autocracies. There is truth to this in many respects. Yet it would be a mistake to mount a new bipolar competition between so-called autocratic and democratic states. The West is not in the best position to launch a fresh global democratic mission. Democracy, in any case, is not a product that can be exported – the 'non-tariff' barriers are high. The Western example remains successful, and one that many in other countries will wish to follow, but in their own way and by their own means. The West still needs to work closely with states whose mode of government is not perhaps to its liking. Alienating them by putting them into an opposing camp will make needed cooperation more difficult. As the IISS has argued in these pages before, 'good governance without democracy is safer strategically than is democracy without good governance'. The political-military responsibilities to sustain global stability are huge. That 'pol-mil' professional competence must be carefully deployed in 2023.

Chapter 4

Strategic Policy

Russia's War in Ukraine
What are the emerging military lessons?

Major wars severely test armed forces. The Russia–Ukraine war is no exception. Although there are currently only two direct combatants, many other states are involved in the conflict: politically, diplomatically and economically, and by providing military and intelligence assistance to Kyiv. They have supplied Ukraine with considerable military support, including a wide variety of weapons, ammunition, spare parts and training. The international effort to prevent Russia from winning the war has also seen self-organised participation by international businesses in withdrawing from Russia and, in some cases, helping Ukraine.

At the time of writing, the outcome and duration of the war cannot be reliably forecast. But it has demonstrated some key features of modern war between states. It has reaffirmed that war is a highly dynamic contest of wills across multiple domains, where both sides seek to outfight, out-manoeuvre and out-adapt each other. The battle of the narrative is a key factor. The war reminds us that the prime military capability is competence and that numbers and mass still count, both on the battlefield and in logistics stockpiles. It also suggests that many current precision weapons are limited by cost, complexity and lead times to manufacture; and that it is increasingly difficult to hide forces from surveillance by satellites and uninhabited aerial vehicles (UAVs), the latter playing an increasing role in land warfare. Battles in the conflict have often revolved around urban terrain, demonstrating the need for competence in urban warfare.

The changing character of the war

Carl von Clausewitz, the German military theorist, outlined two dimensions of war: its nature, which is enduring; and its character, which changes as the ways and means used to fight wars change. War's nature is brutal and chaotic. It is an intensely human activity in which the enemy exercises its free will and its determination to fight to the death. Waging war is a political act. Aims can include gaining advantage, improving a situation or influencing the attitudes or behaviour of other parties.

Combatants can use a wide range of military and non-military ways and means, constantly seeking advantage over each other. This makes war a dynamic contest. Initiatives, such as the introduction of new strategies, technologies or tactics by a combatant, often result in attempts by other combatants to develop countermeasures. These can often prompt further adaptation by the enemy. So, wars often become contests of combatants' ability to 'learn under fire', as each side tries to gain advantage by adapting the ways and means of conducting the war. This means that most wars feature action–reaction dynamics that constantly change their character. This can result in conflicts changing direction as they evolve, often generating opportunities and setbacks that were unanticipated before the war.

These factors and dynamics can be discerned in the war between Russia and Ukraine and at all levels: the strategic, operational and tactical. Russian efforts to rapidly decapitate the Ukrainian government, followed by a speedy seizure of the capital Kyiv, both failed, largely due to considerable weaknesses in the planning, tactics, training and command of Russian land and air forces. But Russia adapted its strategy, seeking to eject Ukrainian forces from the Donbas by concentrating large amounts of artillery to inflict a high level of attrition. Ukraine then conducted counter-attacks and precision strikes around the Kherson *oblast*, seeking to threaten Russian control of the city of Kherson and draw Russian forces away from the Donbas. This proved, in part, an effective deception operation. In early September Ukraine launched an offensive around Kharkiv that liberated up to 6,000 square kilometres of territory that Russia had held for months. Neither Russia nor Ukraine has secured dominance of the air or maritime domains, which has constrained both sides' options. External supplies of weapons, ammunition, intelligence and military training have greatly influenced the war's dynamics on land, at sea and over Ukraine's airspace.

The battle of the narrative

War since 9/11 has featured considerable competition to influence the attitudes of combatants, national populations, their leaders and international supporters. From the outset this has been an important part of this war, applied at all levels – from the national and strategic to the tactical. For example, Ukrainian President Volodymyr Zelenskyy has played a major role in influencing Ukraine's international supporters by directly addressing a wide variety of bodies, ranging from national legislatures to the IISS Shangri-La Dialogue in Singapore and the Glastonbury Festival in southwest England. Zelenskyy tailors each message to his audience to maximise its impact. He has also made extensive use of social media, not least in showing walkabouts in Kyiv early in the war. Zelenskyy's constant presence in Western media and political and public fora has been a major factor in influencing attitudes in the United States, Europe and further afield.

Both sides have invested considerable resources in a wide variety of communication technologies. They have sought to use short videos and phone intercepts to influence international attitudes to the war. Ukraine has been much more successful at producing these (despite disruption from Russian kinetic and cyber attacks on Ukrainian government communications), reflecting the speed with which videos can be produced and released. Copious amounts of photographs, video and satellite imagery add credibility to Ukrainian allegations of war crimes committed by Russian troops against Ukrainian civilians. But Russia has adapted its diplomacy and messaging in the global south, claiming that the US and NATO were responsible for Russia's aggression and that Western sanctions are responsible for global economic harm (especially food insecurity). The lesson is that the battle of the narrative is a key element of modern warfare, as is the maintenance of legitimacy by the warring parties. Nations will need to plan for this battle with a wide variety of means, from traditional to modern social media, and to wage it among diverse global audiences, taking into account local differences (especially between societies with 'open' and 'closed' media environments).

The prime military capability is competence

In early 2022, many intelligence agencies and international military experts forecast that Russia would defeat Ukraine. It was seen as having the advantages of ten years' investment in military modernisation, relevant military experience from its 2014–15 war in Ukraine and its 2015 intervention in Syria, and considerable numerical superiority.

On the first day of the war Russian special-operations and airborne forces failed to seize control of Kyiv. This tactic had worked in Prague in 1968 and Kabul in 1979. Its failure must have come as a shock to Russian President Vladimir Putin, as must the failure of the two large Russian armoured formations advancing on Kyiv from the north and the west. Both columns advancing towards Kyiv were slowed down by Ukrainian infantry exploiting the wooded and urban terrain north of the city to ambush Russian armoured units, delay them and subject them to mortar and artillery fire. Despite the temporary capture of some outlying towns such as Bucha, Russian forces were not able to breach Kyiv's main defences, let alone advance into the city centre, as evidence emerged of logistical difficulties, low morale and weak standards of combined arms tactics and battlefield leadership. After the first month of fighting, Russian forces that had sought to capture Kyiv and Kharkiv withdrew to more defensible positions.

What explains these early Russian military failures? Over-optimistic planning certainly seems a major factor. The initial attacks displayed hallmarks of over-confidence and wishful thinking that the Ukrainians would not offer serious resistance. If the Kremlin thought sustained Ukrainian resistance was unlikely, expensive and time-consuming, Russian logistical preparations would not have seemed necessary. And there would be no requirement to concentrate force at a decisive point or points.

Other contributing factors appear to have been inadequate command and control, with a lack of a single Russian joint theatre commander supported by an empowered joint HQ. The failure of officers to properly brief and lead their men contributed to poor morale. The war has also exposed the weaknesses of Russian training in modern combined arms and joint operations. For example, neither the army nor the air force appears to have trained against a competent and agile opposing force, with many previous Russian field exercises being highly scripted. Many reports suggest that Ukrainian troops displayed much higher standards of initiative and tactical leadership, possibly as a result of training provided by the US and NATO states since 2015 that sought to enhance junior leadership.

Russian equipment has also exhibited weaknesses, especially in the apparent ease with which its tanks were destroyed by US *Javelin* and Anglo-Swedish Next Generation Light Anti-Tank Weapons (NLAW) that attacked the weaker armour on the top of tanks. And there are credible reports that about 40% of the cruise missiles fired by Russia have failed to strike their targets.

It may well be that the effectiveness of the considerable financial investment made by Russia in its military modernisation was eroded by the effects of the nation's authoritarian political culture, as well as of nepotism and corruption. These factors can undermine the institutional health and effectiveness of defence ministries and armed forces. The lesson is that, without investing in the capability of personnel – including the competence of commanders and adequate individual and collective training – such investments in hardware can be wasted.

These factors in combination have greatly reduced the overall effectiveness of Russian forces in Ukraine. The war reminds us that the prime requirement for armed forces is competence. This should be measured against the capabilities of a determined enemy. An armed force's effectiveness partly depends on the procurement of adequate military hardware supported by sufficient ammunition, spare parts and logistic capability. But all these are worth nothing if the force's intelligence, leadership, command, logistics and training are inadequate. Far too much analysis of armed forces, defence industries and military equipment defaults to equipment numbers and parameters without taking these other vital factors into consideration.

The cyber dimension

In early 2022, before the invasion, Russia attempted several major cyber attacks against key Ukrainian political and infrastructure targets. The most damaging was the successful strike on military command and control through the Viasat system on 24 February (the day of the invasion), an attack described by one US source as 'elegant and sophisticated'. But most other cyber attacks were defeated or mitigated quite quickly. Ukraine, working with substantial allied support and private-sector operators like Microsoft, was able to nullify most of Russia's ambition for a decisive advantage in cyberspace. Even the Viasat attack, though quite damaging, did not prevent Ukrainian victory in the battle for Kyiv. One mitigating factor was the immediate supply by the US government and the SpaceX-owned satellite internet constellation Starlink of several thousand portable, encrypted ground-communications links.

A US assessment of why Russia did not achieve its aims in these cyber operations pointed to three reasons: Russia probably made a number of incorrect assumptions (presumably about the cyberspace terrain); the US quickly introduced important defensive capabilities and worked with a number of Ukrainian partners; and coordination between different cyber actors in the chain in Russia was reported to be very poor. Russian failures may also illustrate that mounting cyber attacks to neutralise well-developed and robust military command-and-control networks with capable cyber defences may be more difficult than the Kremlin had imagined.

Numbers count

There is much about the war that is not new. In the early twenty-first century many Western military theorists, the leaders of the US armed forces and the Western defence industry argued that new precision weapons would reduce the requirement for mass on the battlefield, as greater effect could be achieved by modern land and air forces, reducing the need for size. The rapid success of US-led international coalitions in deposing the Afghan Taliban regime in 2001 and Saddam Hussein in 2003 was seen as confirmation of this theory. This war has pointed in the opposite direction.

Numbers have counted, showing that mass remains an important factor. Achieving mass at decisive points has depended on being able to move forces, concentrate them and sustain their key logistic supplies of fuel, ammunition and spare parts. Russia failed to achieve the necessary concentration of force in the first month of the war to capture Kyiv and Kharkiv, while Ukrainian forces were often able to concentrate anti-tank and indirect fire against Russian units struggling to cope with both unexpected resistance and the challenges of urban and wooded terrain.

Russia then adapted to achieve concentration of force in the Donbas. Its summer 2022 offensive saw it assemble considerable numbers of artillery guns and rocket launchers, firing up to 20,000 rounds a day. This was in concert with limited short-range attacks by Russian ground troops. These acted to fix Ukrainian defenders in place, making it difficult for them to withdraw out of the lethal footprint of Russian artillery. Unsurprisingly, the defending Ukrainian infantry suffered heavy casualties from the sustained bombardment.

From the outset of the war Ukraine appealed to its allies to supply not only weapons but also ammunition. It appears that both sides have been expending ammunition at prodigious rates. Evidence of this is the 411,000 155mm artillery rounds that by late July had accompanied the delivery of 126 US M777 howitzers to Ukraine – over 3,200 artillery rounds for each gun. The very high expenditure of ammunition throughout the war will give pause to many nations, particularly the US and its allies, who have previously economised on the size of their logistic stockpiles.

Limitations of precision weapons

This high expenditure of conventional unguided ammunition has been accompanied by an equally high expenditure of precision weapons. For example, Russia's inventory of land-attack cruise missiles appears to have been depleted and Ukraine has stated that on several occasions it has come close to running out of *Javelin* and NLAW anti-tank missiles.

The accuracy of precision weapons comes at a price. Their guidance systems contain sophisticated electronics and electro-optical sensors. Every time the missile is fired these expensive components are lost. Anti-armour warfare illustrates this: although tanks are expensive vehicles, the ammunition they fire against enemy vehicles is simple and much less expensive than anti-tank missiles. For an army's anti-armour defence to be resilient, expensive anti-tank missiles will need to be complemented by cheaper, simpler anti-tank shells fired by tanks. This illustrates a wider point: any future military capability that relies exclusively on precision weapons is not only likely to be expensive, but will also take a long time to resupply.

Battlespace manoeuvre

Fighting has reinforced the utility of combined-arms warfare on land. A major contributor to the failure of the initial Russian attacks on Kyiv and Kharkiv was Russia's inadequate coordination of the activities of its tanks, infantry and artillery, while Ukrainian defenders proved much more skilled at coordinating their infantry's use of anti-tank weapons with strikes by mortars and artillery. Subsequently, in the Donbas both sides have sought to wage combined-arms warfare against each other, with the Ukrainians increasingly using deep-precision attacks by guided rockets fired by US-supplied High Mobility Artillery Rocket System (HIMARS) rocket launchers. The war illustrates the continuing importance of the combined-arms approach to land tactics – albeit with drone and counter-drone capabilities increasingly integrated into land units.

Russia quickly neutralised Ukraine's navy and was able to use its Black Sea Fleet to assist its land attack on southern Ukraine. The rapid imposition of a de facto blockade of Odesa prevented exports of Ukrainian grain by sea, resulting in shortages in global grain supplies, rising global food insecurity and diplomatic pressure on nations supporting Ukraine. But successful Ukrainian attacks using anti-ship missiles, including the sinking of the Russian cruiser *Moskva* in April 2022, reduced the utility of Russia's fleet. This reminds us that while sea control can confer great advantages, warships manoeuvring within effective range of enemy coastal defences will continue to be vulnerable.

Many commentators had expected Russia to rapidly gain air superiority over Ukraine and were surprised when they did not. Ukraine appears to have fielded a distributed air-defence network with radar and missiles using guerrilla-style 'shoot and scoot' tactics. It has created a layered air defence in which man-portable missiles force Russian aircraft to operate at higher levels, where they are vulnerable to longer-range S300 missiles. It also seems that the Russian air force was inadequately prepared to coordinate its activities with Russian land forces, not least to overcome the challenge of aircraft being shot down in error by the Russian Army's own considerable number of organic air-defence units.

The lesson of Russia's apparent failure to achieve either maritime control or air superiority reinforces the importance of both domains in modern war, as well as the considerable potential of anti-access and area-denial approaches as asymmetric ways of countering enemy maritime and air capabilities.

A more transparent battlefield

The war has sometimes featured a very high degree of transparency that makes it difficult for land forces to hide. At the strategic level, in the months before the invasion the US and the United Kingdom made unprecedented use of declassified intelligence to support their narrative that Russia was surrounding Ukraine with mobilised formations. This position was reinforced when Maxar, a civilian satellite-imagery company, published photographs of Russian units deployed in Belarus and western Russia. Maxar has continued to publish imagery of Russian forces in and around Ukraine ever since. This should be assumed to represent only a small proportion of the imagery available from modern civilian and military observation satellites.

The war has also featured intensive use of UAVs by both sides. These have ranged from long-range systems and medium systems to large numbers of simple short-range commercial small UAVs ('drones') adapted for military use. Both sides have made extensive use of these to locate their opponents and to control strikes by artillery and rockets. For Ukraine, US-supplied *Switchblade* loitering munitions, essentially kamikaze drones with a small warhead, have proved especially effective, as have Turkish *Bayraktar* armed UAVs. The high utility of UAVs has resulted in great efforts to acquire more of them – for example, charities in Ukraine and Central Europe have crowdfunded some supply drones, while Russia is reportedly sourcing UAVs from Iran – and to shoot enemy UAVs down, with the reported life of a Ukrainian battlefield drone being about a week on average.

The lesson is that UAVs and drones are now key capabilities for land forces. This adds a degree of land–air integration to the lowest tactical levels, right down to company and platoon level, that was not achievable in earlier wars, including the recent conflict in Nagorno-Karabakh. This also means that counter-drone capabilities are similarly required by land forces, including at the lowest tactical level. And the threat from both UAVs and civilian and military satellite reconnaissance will require US and NATO forces to rediscover the art of camouflage, concealment and deception, which has been lost in recent decades.

Exploiting terrain

Terrain has had a considerable influence on the war. The Russian advance on Kyiv was hampered by woods and boggy ground. And Russian forces have been slowed down by having to cross rivers. Ukrainian troops have imposed further delays by demolishing bridges and successfully using artillery to attack Russian troops conducting river crossings – an operation that is difficult in peacetime and even more so in war.

Much of the fighting has revolved around the control of urban terrain. Initially this offered great advantage to Ukrainian troops defending against Russian armoured forces. The Ukrainian defenders of Mariupol imposed considerable delays on the attackers, with the Azov Battalion holding out so successfully in its underground redoubt below the Azovstal steelworks that a final assault by Russia and its allies from the Donetsk 'People's Republic' was not attempted; a surrender was negotiated instead. Much of the recent fighting in the Donbas has featured the attack and defence of towns, such as Severodonetsk. The war illustrates that the global mega-trend of ever-increasing urbanisation means that urban-combat capabilities are essential for armed forces.

'Big war' is back

Perhaps the most important facet of the war is that what was planned as a short 'special military operation' against an inferior enemy has turned into a large-scale conflict between states, in which prolonged fighting has been at a high intensity and over a wide geographical area. Both sides are finding it much more difficult to prevail than the US did against the Taliban in 2001 and Iraq in 2003, where it took little more than a month to accomplish regime change.

This war might be more like the wars in Korea (1950–53), Bosnia (1992–95) and between Iran and Iraq (1980–88). Its outcome, military dynamics and lessons will have a significant influence on global military thinking and planning as defence ministries contemplate possible future wars.

Managing Competition in Outer Space
Can a new agenda mitigate the growing threat of instability?

Introduction

Space, a critical security domain, is more contested than ever. New and emerging threats in space have grown exponentially in the past decade, exposing new vulnerabilities to assets supporting military capabilities, critical civilian functions and, increasingly, global commerce. These threats undermine strategic stability, raise the risk of miscalculation and rapid escalation in a crisis, and require new solutions. The international community needs an agenda to manage competition in space that embraces innovation and uses commercial capabilities to enhance resilience and transparency and to develop new rules and norms. If harnessed correctly, these capabilities will contribute to dissipating the 'fog of war', give decision-makers more time to make rational and informed decisions on conflict in space, and prevent inadvertent escalation.

The threat environment

Space warfare is highly asymmetric. Legacy space-based assets have traditionally been costly to develop, launch and operate, but remain vulnerable to kinetic and non-kinetic threats. Attack surfaces could include satellites but also ground stations. Countries that are heavily reliant upon space-based assets for commercial, civilian and military operations are particularly vulnerable to attacks that could disrupt them or their related Earth-based systems. These threats can manifest in different forms and vary in intensity from low-end, non-kinetic harassment to high-end kinetic attacks with permanent effects.

Among the easiest space threats to understand are Direct Ascent Anti-Satellite (DA-ASAT) missiles and co-orbital weaponry. DA-ASAT missiles are cheaper to develop and use than their targets and can be impact-based (destroying targets through kinetic force) or armed with conventional or nuclear explosives. Four states have demonstrated the ability to deploy DA-ASAT weaponry: China, India, Russia and the United States.

Space-based kinetic threats can also be developed under the guise of civilian or commercial space applications. Satellites intended for inspection, docking or repairs can be used to destroy nearby satellites. Russia and China have expanded their counter-space weapons, including sophisticated ASAT weapons, to hold US and allied space assets at risk. Russia is thought to have demonstrated a number of dual-use orbital satellites which could be used to damage other satellites in proximity operations. They include *Cosmos* 2504 and 2536, prototype ASAT weapons with kinetic kill capability in low Earth orbit (LEO); *Cosmos* 2542, launched in 2019; and its sub-satellite 'inspector' *Cosmos* 2543, which approached and followed a US national-security satellite. Russia also launched *Cosmos* 2558 in August 2022, which is suspected of matching the trajectory of a US satellite. It is also reportedly developing a satellite for operations in geostationary orbit (GEO). Its test of a DA-ASAT missile against its own satellite, *Cosmos* 1408, using an A-235 *Nudol* in November 2021, created thousands of pieces of dangerous debris. China is able to target satellites in LEO and probably intends to pursue weapons that can reach GEO. It is testing inspection and repair satellites that could also be used to damage other satellites.

Non-kinetic threats, including cyber attacks, electronic warfare and directed-energy attacks, are intended to blind, jam, spoof, hijack and otherwise disable satellites. They are a grave threat due to the vulnerability of satellites, the difficulty in attributing such attacks, the ability to launch them from Earth and the limited capability to repair satellites. China and Russia have pursued electronic-warfare and cyber-attack capabilities and directed-energy weapons.

Cyber attacks can include the use of sophisticated means of spoofing, taking over a satellite or attacking a ground station. Cyber threats are characterised by the anonymity and flexibility of attacks, ranging from high-end operations using space-based support infrastructure, to relatively simple attacks using phishing-derived entry points. Reports have also speculated that Russia may be researching obscurants to shield its satellites – which also could be used in jamming. Directed-energy interactions include attacks using land- or space-based energy generators to temporarily or permanently blind sensors. Lasers are used in space to detect and measure objects but could be adapted for attack. Using directed energy to disrupt or block satellite transmissions would create little or no debris and would be difficult to attribute. According to press reports, Russia has deployed satellites strongly suspected of such missions.

Satellite disruptions occur regularly because of debris impacts, design or manufacture flaws, or solar flares and other forms of space weather. Objects as small as 1 centimetre in diameter can cause severe to lethal damage to spacecraft, and it is estimated that between 300,000 and 500,000 objects of 1 cm or larger are currently in orbit. Debris can often remain in LEO for years, and debris in GEO can be permanent – endangering current assets and preventing the use of certain orbital bands. Satellite protection measures are limited and expensive due to the added weight they require. Satellites are also vulnerable to environmental phenomena including solar flares and Earth's magnetic fields. Many actors seek resilience to protect functions and mitigate vulnerability – such as by enabling a 'safe mode' or fielding more, smaller, manoeuvrable, less expensive and redundant satellite capabilities. Starlink by SpaceX is one example of a resilient network of thousands of satellites. Recently, SpaceX reported that its satellites were forced to conduct more than 6,800 avoidance manoeuvres between December 2021 and May 2022, including 1,700 just to avoid debris from the 2021 Russian *Nudol* DA-ASAT test.

Existing agreements and new initiatives

The international community has initiated several efforts to govern space activity, including draft treaties and codes of conduct. Most efforts have struggled due to the difficulty in designing effective mechanisms, especially to judge compliance. Instead, the most promising efforts have focused on transparency, codes of conduct, rules and responsible behaviours.

A legally binding 1967 agreement prohibits placing nuclear weapons or other weapons of mass destruction in orbit or outer space. The Treaty on Principles Governing the Activities of States in the Exploration and Use of Outer Space, Including the Moon and Other Celestial Bodies also encourages transparency. Related multilateral arrangements include the Convention on the Registration of Space Objects Launched into Outer Space (1976), an important transparency measure which creates the obligation to maintain a registry of all space objects that is shared with the United Nations. However, membership and compliance are limited, with only 73 states having ratified, and many commercial and military assets missing from the registry.

Russia and China in 2008 proposed a legal arrangement called the Treaty on the Prevention of the Placement of Weapons in Outer Space, the Threat or Use of Force against Outer Space Objects, which they submitted to the UN Ad Hoc Committee on the Prevention of an Arms Race in Outer Space (PAROS). Russia and China have long worked together to use PAROS to limit US space-based missile defence, efforts that the US has sought to block. Russia and China submitted an updated proposal in 2014, seeking to prevent the placement of weapons in space, but it contains no credible verification mechanism, includes vague definitions and excludes ground-based weapons.

The UN Group of Governmental Experts Report on Transparency and Confidence-Building Measures in Outer Space Activities was initiated in 2011. It produced a final report in July 2013, with a series of voluntary measures, including exchanging information on national space policies, military expenditures on space, a risk-reduction notification regime and visits to space launch sites and facilities. Many of these proposals overlap with the 2002 Hague Code of Conduct on Ballistic Missiles (HCOC), which itself has a mixed implementation record. A related effort by the European Union resulted in a non-binding draft International Code of Conduct for Outer Space Operations in 2014. It established a set of voluntary guidelines to address all space-based operations and objects. It also focused on mitigating risks and uncertainties, and on flexibility to grow into a legally binding treaty. But it was blocked at the UN by Russia and China, among others, during talks in 2015. In 2017, the UN agreed to revive the process of establishing transparency and confidence-building measures, and the UN Institute for Disarmament Research (UNIDIR) continues to facilitate discussions on the proposals, but without any significant progress.

At the same time, the UN Committee on the Peaceful Uses of Outer Space addresses the long-term survivability of space activities. It published a June 2019 report with policy guidelines and potential regulatory frameworks for space activities, safety of space operations, international cooperation, and scientific exploration and development. However, these are voluntary and non-binding, and implementation remains substantively unrealised.

In 2020, the United Kingdom spearheaded the latest and most promising development in using rules and norms to improve security in space. The UN General Assembly approved a UN Open Ended Working Group (OEWG) to identify responsible behaviours in space with the aim of developing rules of the road, modelled on those governing the high seas, such as the US–USSR Avoidance of Hazardous Incidents at Sea Agreement of 1972 (INCSEA). In support, the US announced on 18 April 2022 a new initiative to stop DA-ASAT testing in response to the Russian and Chinese ASAT tests. In addition, the US–Russian Strategic Stability Dialogue launched in 2021 included space as a potential topic for further work. However, these US–Russian talks halted after Russia invaded Ukraine in February 2022 and are not likely to resume soon.

Challenges and opportunities

There are three principal challenges to designing governance measures for space: verification, transparency, and setting and following rules. The primary difficulty of verifying any space arms-control agreement is designing effective tools. Longer-reach missiles and launch vehicles have inherent space-attack capabilities, and many dual-use kinetic and non-kinetic capabilities would be nearly impossible to discern. These capabilities include a repair satellite that could also sabotage, or a range-finding laser that could also be used to blind other satellites. Invasive inspections could reveal military or commercial secrets, further complicating verification. In many countries, civil, military and commercial applications are closely entwined, and commercial firms have objected to their inclusion in arms-control regimes such as the Chemical Weapons Convention (CWC) – a matter that was resolved only after extensive lobbying and congressional engagement.

Given the obstacles to effective verification, transparency measures are essential to mitigate risks. Transparency largely involves information exchanges, such as reporting policies, budgets, and research and development, as well as information on existing objects and their functions. However, compliance with existing measures, such as the UN Convention on Registration of Objects Launched into Outer Space and HCOC, is poor, especially regarding military objects. Any agreed measures of pre-launch notification or inspection can be supplemented by increased communication, information sharing and rules of the road. Agreeing definitions of acceptable behaviour in space would be a useful first step towards establishing norms and rules. The UK-inspired UN OEWG effort to do this is useful. The OEWG is working to define a set of prohibited behaviours, as well as a deconfliction and notification mechanism, and a post facto forum for the prevention of subsequent incidents, with potential models in other domains such as INCSEAs.

National-security officials have recognised that space is becoming more congested and competitive. In the past decade, many more countries have sought access and increased investments in capabilities, making space a focal point of their national strategies. In addition, national and commercial assets have grown exponentially. Starlink, OneWeb, Kuiper and China's planned StarNet mega-constellations are adding thousands of satellites in LEO, increasing the number of satellites from 1,500 a few years ago to more than 5,000 now, with thousands more projected. The growing number of state and commercial satellites will exacerbate congestion and debris. General John Raymond, the chief of space operations for the US Space Force, has called it a new 'wild, wild west'. While some private companies such as SpaceX have made a commitment not to add to space debris, ideas for domestic and international regulation on debris are just emerging. Given the challenging environment in space, no such commitment can ever be entirely successful.

This increased interest in space is also changing geopolitical dynamics. States that have relied on space for commercial and military purposes must now address the growing vulnerability of space satellites developed in an earlier era. This contributes to asymmetries where some states develop new systems as space becomes a war-fighting domain while other states with legacy platforms must replace these with less vulnerable systems.

Commercial players also have a strong interest in widening access to this domain. By introducing innovative solutions such as reusable rockets, more efficient launch designs and small launch capabilities, the commercial industry has reduced the cost of reaching LEO by a factor of 20 in the past two decades. Private-industry revenues, valued at more than half a trillion US dollars, are derived largely from commercial satellite services such as telecommunications, observation, and global positioning systems (GPS) and supporting space infrastructure. The space domain is thus highly interconnected economically, militarily and politically, and will become more so over the next decades.

The rapidly growing space industry presents challenges for governments. Industries such as commercial rocket manufacturing and solid-rocket-fuel production require international regulation to prevent proliferation. However, discussion of domestic safeguards to govern commercial dual-use industry is still in its infancy. In addition, commercial competition and espionage could extend to space, where commercial space-based systems may use illicit means of damaging or blinding other satellites for commercial ends, or they could become collateral damage in international conflicts. This raises the question of whether states have a responsibility to defend commercial satellites. When Russia reportedly jammed SpaceX Starlink terminals used by Ukraine soon after its invasion, SpaceX patched the software within a day to prevent further Russian jamming. If it had been unable to demonstrate such commercial agility, the US government would have been faced with the choice of whether to step in and try to restore the functionality of Starlink terminals in response to Russia's attack on a commercial entity.

Space is already changing the temporal and geographic dimensions of conflict. Beyond serving as an enabler of ground-based military, economic and civilian operations, space has been recognised by many states as a war-fighting domain. Destruction or disruption of space assets could drive simultaneous effects anywhere – or everywhere – on Earth. For example, targeting GPS satellites could have significant consequences that transcend military targets, affecting sectors such as agriculture, transportation and banking. Such attacks could produce deadly effects even before traditional kinetic military action begins.

Developments in technology and access to space will complicate these dynamics. The expansion of assets in cislunar space – that is, between the Earth and the moon – with the growing ubiquity of space transportation and on-orbit servicing, ensures that this sector will remain replete with commercial and civil benefits. However, these technologies could also be used to attack other satellites.

Implications for strategic stability

Space is a uniquely observable environment. Satellites follow highly predictable orbits and can be monitored by anyone with a lens or sensor of sufficient strength (infrared, radar, electronic or electromagnetic). This, together with the critical nature of the infrastructure housed on satellites, constitutes an asymmetric vulnerability and could create daunting dilemmas. With potentially slow assessment of satellite outages, states cannot be certain whether such an incident is an attack, natural event or technical malfunction. This underscores the importance of national and commercial space situational awareness capabilities. Even if attacks are identified, the difficulty of attribution may increase confusion and misperception, leading to rapid escalation.

These changing threat dynamics raise the prospect of a new arms race of risk acceptance that lowers the threshold for runaway escalation to nuclear war. This danger requires national and international attention.

Solutions: resilience, transparency, rules and norms

The international community should engage with the space industry now to shape an innovation ecosystem that can deliver stability and sustainability. Lessons from the eventually successful engagement with industry and government to develop and implement the CWC could serve as a useful precedent. Emerging technologies and capabilities can provide new solutions to address fundamentally changing deterrence requirements. They could do so by increasing transparency and providing resilient and survivable systems that deny an adversary the advantages of an attack. These solutions would give senior leaders more time to make decisions and thus more opportunities to de-escalate tensions or conflict.

Resilience plays a critical role in successful and sustainable space operations. A small number of large, expensive and highly capable legacy systems are vulnerable to attack early in a future conflict, and they are therefore no longer suited to effective deterrence. New distributed space architectures, including LEO populated by many, smaller and reconstitutable or replaceable satellites, are key to denying adversaries the benefits of an attack. The new US missile warning and tracking satellites being developed by the Space Development Agency, the US Space Force and the Missile Defense Agency offer a model for more resilient systems using different, less congested orbits and cheaper and smaller payloads. Increasing resilience through more satellites and multiple orbits is necessary across the board as new constellations of space-based capabilities are developed. While no orbit can remain completely safe from attack, adding redundancy and capacity to absorb attacks without catastrophic degradation or loss of critical capabilities is essential to effective deterrence.

Greater resilience is needed to stabilise the management of space. But space technologies can in turn help enhance broader strategic stability by offering greater transparency. Transformational increases in commercial capacity and capability in space have resulted in more imagery and information becoming available at greater speed and lower cost. Artificial intelligence and machine-learning tools enhance the speed of analysis of space data. These new tools are already changing the face of international security, from debunking Russian misinformation during its war on Ukraine to spotting the construction of hundreds of missile silos in China. The rapidly increasing spread and speed of delivery of satellite information can add decision time, options and opportunities to deter or de-escalate a crisis or conflict involving nuclear-armed states. For example, a better understanding of changes in patterns of human activity derived from space imagery and processed data could help predict proliferation, crises, conflicts or unintended escalation. In addition, disaggregating strategic and tactical communications with separate satellites (rather than co-mingling these on the same satellite) can also provide clearer signalling to allies and adversaries, and thereby reduce the risk of miscalculation.

Finally, rules and norms can help manage risks. By analogy, INCSEAs not only regulate behaviour on and over the high seas, but they also allow parties to understand the difference between an intentional and unintentional act by helping avoid accidents, providing instant communication during ambiguous incidents and providing a forum to discuss ways for the sides to improve the functioning of the agreement. States will still deliberately conduct hazardous activity from time to time to send political and military signals. But INCSEAs help both sides manage an incident and prevent miscalculation and unintentional escalation or conflict. The current UN OEWG has taken initial steps in this direction by identifying responsible and irresponsible behaviours in space. Further work on the current path, combined with improved transparency and resilience, can help avert escalation and manage risks of conflict.

Conclusion

Space plays a crucial role in fast-changing security environments. Threats are rapidly increasing, notably from Russia and China. As access to space for a wide range of commercial and military purposes becomes easier, the challenges posed by dual-use capabilities and attribution will exacerbate the risks of miscalculation and other sources of instability.

To reduce these risks and enhance strategic stability, national and international attention must prioritise effective governance and innovative capabilities and architectures to achieve greater resilience and transparency. Space can enhance effective deterrence, and reduce the risks of unnecessary and deadly conflict, if new approaches and tools are applied. Improved transparency and resilience, and new rules and norms, can mean better and more reliable information for leaders that will reduce risks of conflict, including precipitous escalation that could lead to nuclear war.

China's Military Modernisation
Will the People's Liberation Army complete its reforms?

Chinese President Xi Jinping has set three goals for the People's Liberation Army's (PLA) modernisation by mid-century (2049 or 2050) as part of China's larger ambition to become a strong country (强国 *qiáng guo*) with a strong military (强军 *qiáng jūn*). These goals were slated for completion between 2020 and 2050, with a fourth added in 2021 as a midway point between 2020 and 2035. The goals are: by 2020, mechanisation of PLA army forces and progress in 'informationisation' – the integration of information and communications technology (ICT); by 2027, army building and profession-alisation; by 2035, full modernisation and 'intelligentisation' – integration of artificial intelligence (AI) and autonomy into the PLA's command and control, weapons systems and platforms, and decision-making – through reform of theory, organisational structure, service personnel and weap-onry; and, by the mid-21st century, the ability to fight and win wars. These reforms will be implemented across all PLA service arms – army, navy, air force, rocket force and strategic support forces – and focus on developing efficient joint operations for theatre commands according to modern and future war-fighting concepts of network-centric and target-centric warfare.

While the PLA commissioned impressive military platforms and systems in 2021 and into 2022, modernisation is not just about 'heavy metal' (procuring hardware). The less visible aspects of reform, includ-ing institutional reform and restructuring, reveal greater variation in the PLA's progress towards modernisation. Though the PLA plays an impor-tant role in Beijing's regional assertiveness below the threshold of war, incomplete modernisation may limit the PLA's willingness to enter into state-on-state conflicts. While Washington points to the PLA's meteoric rise, the latter's own assessment of its capabilities is less confident. Lessons from Russia's invasion of Ukraine may further dampen any confidence.

Expanding the PLA's heavy metal

By 2022, the PLA had undergone significant change since Xi set forth his military-reform agenda in 2013. This is particularly true as regards the procurement of more (and more modern) military systems and platforms – an aspect of military reform easily visible to public audiences in China and abroad.

The past two years have also seen an impressive procurement of military heavy metal – platforms and systems that the Chinese leadership sees as central to building modern war-fighting capabilities in the maritime, air and land domains.

Between 2014 and 2018, the PLA launched naval vessels with a total tonnage greater than the tonnages of the entire French, German, Indian, Italian, South Korean, Spanish or Taiwanese navies. This momentum has continued. In 2021, the PLA Navy (PLAN) commissioned at least nine guided-missile cruisers and destroyers (two Type-055 and seven Type-052D), one Type-075 amphibious assault ship and one Type-094 nuclear-powered ballistic-missile submarine. By July 2022, they had commissioned two more Type-052D destroyers, three more Type-055 cruisers and a second Type-075 amphibious assault ship. In June 2022 in Shanghai, the PLAN launched its third aircraft carrier, the *Fujian* – fitted with a new electromagnetic catapult launch system.

The PLA Air Force (PLAAF) has now largely removed its inventory of ageing Cold War era combat aircraft from frontline service. Instead, it appears to be standardising on the modern multirole J-10C and J-16 designs and the advanced, low-observable J-20. In April 2022, it was reported that the 111th Air Brigade in the Western Theatre Command had received its first J-20s, and in September 2022, a PLAAF spokesman appeared to confirm that all five theatre commands now have at least one brigade equipped with the J-20. This rate of deployment suggests that over 100 such aircraft are currently fielded.

While the PLA Army has not been the priority recipient of platform modernisation, their armoured vehicle fleets have to a large degree been standardised with modern equipment. By 2022, roughly 70% of the PLA's 5,400 main battle tanks listed in service could be classified as modern, while the ZTQ-15 light tank has now also been fielded with at least four combined-arms regiments and brigades in southern and western China. By mid-2022, over 60% of the PLA Army's heavy and medium combined-arms brigades had also been equipped with modern tracked or wheeled infantry fighting vehicles (IFVs).

Modernisation, diversification and growth of China's conventional and nuclear missile forces continues apace. In addition to the three main services, the PLA Rocket Force has been equipped with several new strategic and theatre-range missile systems, some of which were unveiled at the 2019 National Day parade in China, including the DF-41 road-mobile intercontinental ballistic missile (ICBM), the DF-31A(G) ICBM, the DF-17 hypersonic glide vehicle/medium-range ballistic missile and the supersonic CJ-100 cruise missile. In 2021, reports also highlighted the construction of at least three new missile silo fields in northern and western China with the capacity for several hundred ICBMs. For the moment, Beijing is still mostly reliant on its land-based nuclear forces for deterrence, due to the limitations of its nuclear-powered ballistic-missile submarines and lack of credible air-launched systems. However, the PLA is looking to develop a complete nuclear triad, consisting of air-, ship-, and ground-launched missiles, initially by fielding a nuclear-capable air-launched ballistic-missile design.

In 2021, the United States' Department of Defense (DoD) reported in its annual China Military Power Report that the PLA was accelerating the expansion of China's nuclear arsenal to up to 700 nuclear warheads by 2027 and at least 1,000 warheads by 2030. While the DoD believes that China may potentially move away from its policy of no first use and intends to move to a launch-on-warning posture to improve the peacetime readiness of its missile forces, the position of Chinese officials has not changed. China's conventional-missile forces form an essential component of keeping adversaries at bay and preventing outside interference in key military contingencies – such as a war with Taiwan. The PLA's nuclear missiles also play an important role in China's strategy of deterring adversaries, using nuclear threats to prevent the escalation of a conflict and providing a counter-strike capability. At the 19th Shangri-La Dialogue held in June 2022 in Singapore, China's Defence Minister and State Councillor General Wei Fenghe confirmed that a

July 2021 launch had been a test of a weapons delivery system, and not a reusable spaceplane as it had previously been claimed. This weapon is believed to have the characteristics of a Fractional Orbital Bombardment System (FOBS), placing warheads in a fractional low-earth orbit, before de-orbiting them towards their targets. Since these warheads would use a different approach path to those deployed by traditional ballistic missiles, they could pose additional challenges to existing detection and early-warning systems. If China were to deploy a FOBS, this would likely complement rather than transform China's first- or second-strike options.

Slow progress on the softer sides of PLA reform

The PLA's modernisation will not be completed by acquiring modern weapons and platforms alone. Through reforms, the PLA intends to transform itself from a military that has operated in a highly siloed fashion for much of its history, and focuses on land campaigns, to one that can operate in a high-intensity war through integrated operations and network-centric warfare across all services and domains. The PLA thus requires structural changes appropriate for modern war fighting through joint operations across theatres, domains and services. This in turn demands new thinking, military education and command structures. The PLA's newly acquired advanced platforms will require greater efforts to recruit and retain highly skilled personnel, as (like other militaries) it has to compete for talent with the private sector. Lastly, the PLA has not fought in a war since 1979 and so has no modern combat experience. In order to turn its resources and structure into actual capability, it will have to train its personnel in a greater number of exercises and training scenarios that are also more realistic. This remains a formidable task with multiple obstacles. These include difficulty recruiting sufficient talent to fulfil PLA requirements, certain command structures remaining unclear, and slow progress on achieving a force capable of joint operations (reflected in leadership, practice and doctrine).

The Chinese military's structural reforms were addressed early on in Xi's reform effort during his first term in office. In 2016 the PLA was reorganised from seven military regions to five theatre commands, each broadly organised in accordance with specific missions. For example, the Eastern Theatre Command would be likely to have a leading role in any Taiwan contingency, while the Southern Theatre Command is structured to focus on South China Sea and other maritime contingencies. Secondly, the PLA was reorganised into brigades from a division- and regiment-led structure, and units within services were standardised across the PLA. Services were also reformed. The PLA Rocket Force was elevated to a service, and the PLA Strategic Support Force and Joint Logistics Support Force were created to enable the navy, army, air force and rocket force to work jointly and with greater efficiency. Military leadership structures were also reformed. The Central Military Commission (CMC), a Chinese Communist Party (CCP) body responsible for administration of the PLA and chaired by President Xi, was downsized from 11 to seven members. This diluted the influence of the army, traditionally the dominant service in the PLA, and its leadership and paved the way for reform progress.

However, areas of weakness remain that indicate that the PLA still has fundamental problems to resolve. In 2021, the National People's Congress Standing Committee adopted a revised Military Service Law which, among other things, aimed to recruit and retain highly educated university talent in the PLA. The law raised the recruitment age for those holding secondary-school and undergraduate qualifications from 22 to 24, and for those holding postgraduate degrees from 24 to 26. In order to incentivise recruitment and retention, the law set out rights for soldiers, but also increased penalties for those refusing to perform military service. Secondly, the military conscription cycle has increased from once to twice per year, suggesting that the PLA has to date not received enough volunteer enlistment to meet quotas. The PLA requires roughly 400,000 recruits annually to meet the force's needs, as approximately one-third of all active-duty personnel are two-year conscripts.

Command structures have been reformed to create a five-theatre command, but still require further fine-tuning. Firstly, while the PLA has moved towards a nuclear triad with the acquisition of sea-launched, air-launched and ground-launched strategic weapons, it is unclear how command structures have changed to take this into account. The PLA Rocket Force, which controls the PLA's ground-launched nuclear forces, falls under direct CMC command, but that of PLAN and PLAAF nuclear weapons is less clear.

Secondly, inconsistencies still exist within the theatre-command structure with regard to certain mission sets. In the PLA's new structure, the theatre commands focus on joint command forces and lead in the command of non-nuclear operations directly under the supervision of the CMC. Theatre commanders each lead their theatre command's Joint Operations Command Centre (JOCC, 联合作战指挥中心), which comprises representatives from each of the services present in their theatre. The Western Theatre Command, for example, is focused on an Indian border contingency and its JOCC is made up of representatives from the army, air force, rocket force, strategic support force and joint logistics support force. However, an Indian contingency may also include a naval component in the Indian Ocean. It is thus unclear how the Western Theatre Command's JOCC would coordinate with the PLAN in a two-front Indian contingency.

Lastly, achieving jointness is easier said than done. Over five years after reforms were started, in 2020 the CMC issued a new, classified operational guideline for PLA joint operations. However, as of September 2022, four of the five theatre commanders were PLA Army generals. Progress towards incentivising joint career paths seems to be slow and leadership positions in the PLA still do not reflect the desired joint force.

PLA training and exercises have also undergone significant change in order to provide personnel with more realistic and joint opportunities to hone modern war-fighting skills. In 2017, the PLA increased the intensity and difficulty of pilot training. In the past, exercises were executed according to highly scripted plans, and pilots received detailed instructions about where targets would be located and what tactics their practice opponents would employ in drills. High-level commanders would not accept risks that could emerge in fierce simulated confrontations, and losses in simulated drills were seen as reputational risks. However, Xi has instructed the PLA to address its 'peace disease' (a lack of war preparedness throughout the force after decades of peace) and develop a mentality of 'freestyle fighting, live-fire strikes and long-range sea patrols'. Exercises are now designed to test the weaknesses of participants in order to force them to keep improving. Similar changes can be seen across the PLA ground forces and PLAN.

These exercises have not immediately improved the PLA's warfighting ability. In a 2021 *PLA Daily* article, participants of a meeting at the PLAN's submarine training centre reportedly stated that 'research into maritime tactics isn't deep and lacks insight into methods of tactical command', while another meeting found that PLAN personnel were overly risk-averse and that 'battlefield training gives much consideration to safety, but gives little consideration to the enemy's circumstances'. Other problems included a lack of clear command and failure to train 'in the dark' (simulating an electromagnetic attack or power failure). Large-scale joint exercises across services and theatre commands are still nascent.

Impact on perceptions and reality

The PLA's ongoing reforms are incomplete. In the softer elements of reform related to personnel, it may need close to a decade to achieve its goals. This is logical, as the obstacles to the PLA's desired transformation from the outdated military it was in 2013 to a modern military by 2035 were always going to need addressing. However, the PLA's rapid procurement of modern and advanced platforms has led concerned Western and Indo-Pacific military leaders to conclude that modernisation has been sped up by eight years. Former US Indo-Pacific Command (INDOPACOM) Commander Admiral Philip S. Davidson said in 2021 that China's military modernisation was already changing the Indo-Pacific balance of power in China's favour, and that China could potentially 'forcibly change the status quo in the region' by 2026. The DoD's 2020 China Military Power Report stated that China had 'already achieved parity with – or even exceeded – the United States' in

PLA theatre-command commanders, February 2016–present

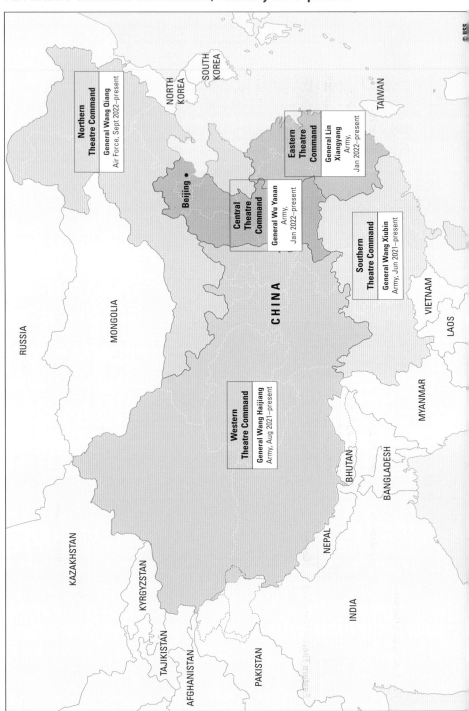

Northern Theatre Command
General Wang Qiang
Air Force, Sept 2022–present

Eastern Theatre Command
General Lin Xiangyang
Army, Jan 2022–present

Central Theatre Command
General Wu Yanan
Army, Jan 2022–present

Southern Theatre Command
General Wang Xiubin
Army, Jun 2021–present

Western Theatre Command
General Wang Haijiang
Army, Aug 2021–present

RUSSIA

MONGOLIA

KAZAKHSTAN

KYRGYZSTAN

TAJIKISTAN

AFGHANISTAN

PAKISTAN

NEPAL

BHUTAN

INDIA

BANGLADESH

MYANMAR

LAOS

VIETNAM

TAIWAN

NORTH KOREA

SOUTH KOREA

CHINA

Beijing

© IISS

Prevalence of army generals in PLA theatre commands

Theatre Command		Name		Service affiliation	Years in position
Western Theatre Command	Current	General Wang Haijiang	汪海江	Army	August 2021–present
	Predecessors	General Xu Qiling	徐起零	Army	June 2021–August 2021
		General Zhang Xudong	张旭东	Army	December 2020–June 2021
		General Zhao Zongqi	赵宗岐	Army	February 2016–December 2020
Eastern Theatre Command	Current	General Lin Xiangyang	林向阳	Army	January 2022–present
	Predecessors	General He Weidong	何卫东	Army	December 2019–January 2022
		General Liu Yuejun	刘粤军	Army	February 2016–December 2019
Southern Theatre Command	Current	General Wang Xiubin	王秀斌	Army	June 2021–present
	Predecessors	Admiral Yuan Yubai	袁誉柏	Navy	January 2017–June 2021
		General Wang Jiaocheng	王教成	Army	February 2016–January 2017
Central Theatre Command	Current	General Wu Yanan	吴亚男	Army	January 2022–present
	Predecessors	General Lin Xiangyang	林向阳	Army	August 2021–January 2022
		General Yi Xiaoguang	乙晓光	Air Force	August 2017–August 2021
		General Han Weiguo	韩卫国	Army	February 2016–August 2017
Northern Theatre Command	Current	General Wang Qiang	王强	Air Force	September 2022–present
	Predecessors	General Li Qiaoming	李桥铭	Army	September 2017–September 2022
		General Song Puxuan	宋普选	Army	February 2016–August 2017

Source: IISS

areas such as shipbuilding, land-based conventional ballistic and cruise missiles, and integrated air-defence systems. Chinese leaders, however, downplay their achievements, particularly when comparing the PLA with the US Armed Forces. China's 2019 Defence White Paper stated that 'the PLA still lags far behind the world's leading militaries'.

Although the United States' and China's military leaders may differ in their comparisons of relative military capability, the PLA is currently able to assert China's interests in the region below the threshold of war. In the South China Sea, the PLA continues to assert Chinese territorial claims against regional claimant states as well as foreign militaries operating in international waters. In the East China Sea, the PLAN and PLAAF still conduct routine exercises, some in conjunction with Russia. In 2021, PLAAF, PLAN and PLA Army aircraft flew a then-record number of sorties into Taiwan's Air Defence Identification Zone (roughly 900 aircraft were flown), using a variety of aircraft types flying in various flight paths and conditions. By the end of August 2022 this record had been broken again, with PLAAF, PLAN and PLA Army aircraft estimated to have made over 1,000 sorties since the start of the year. The sorties are likely intended to send political signals to Taiwanese and US leadership, hone PLA skills, test Taiwan's military response and impose a financial and maintenance cost on the Taiwanese military by forcing it to respond. President Xi has used strong language about the inevitability of reunification with Taiwan, and the PLA has conducted Taiwan-contingency-relevant exercises in China and around Taiwan. However, the PLA's capability does not immediately translate into political will. Taiwan's Defence Minister Chiu Kuo-cheng said in 2021 that the PLA 'has the capacity now, but it will not start a war easily, having to take many other things into consideration'.

What impact has Ukraine had on the PLA and Chinese thinking?

Russia's invasion of Ukraine, and the Russian military's surprisingly poor tactical and operational performance to date, have prompted questions about the military lessons China may learn, as well as those related to sanctions, intelligence-gathering and party loyalty. Firstly, PLA analysts will likely be watching how a more experienced military is faring operationally. They may reflect on lessons about the importance of air supremacy; electromagnetic, cyber and information warfare; the adversary's ability to resupply; the use of nuclear threats as deterrence; and the importance of logistics and maintenance.

Perhaps the most important lesson for the PLA is that, even for more experienced militaries, war fighting is difficult and even the best laid plans can go awry. Reports that some Russian soldiers have refused to fight in Ukraine may lead the CCP to double down on its call for party loyalty. The PLA remains the army of the CCP, not the state. Secondly, since Russia's failure to achieve its expected early victory has cast doubt on the quality of its intelligence on Ukraine, Beijing may consider how effective its own information flow to policymakers is, including from Chinese think tankers who have faced growing restrictions on their work in recent years, especially in regard to Taiwan's military and civilian response to a conflict scenario. Thirdly, Beijing will monitor the scale and longevity of Western sanctions against Russia, both by governments and the private sector. Beijing is already considering ways to 'sanction-proof' China's economy, such as building its own international payments system.

Conclusion

The PLA's modernisation reforms will take years to complete. Beijing's continued progress in hard power has been more visible to outside observers, and has already been leveraged by the CCP to project military power and assert Chinese interests in the Indo-Pacific region, particularly the South China Sea, East China Sea and around Taiwan. The modernisation of the PLA's strategic forces and missile technological developments have also raised concerns about the ability of China to put the assets of the US and other countries in the region at risk in a conflict. However, the PLA requires talented personnel, doctrinal changes, decision-making structures and practice to turn weapons and platforms into actual capability. Progress on the PLA's informationisation has fallen behind its originally envisioned completion date of 2020 with its current status still unclear, and the PLA continues to grapple with issues around command-and-control structures, operationalising the concept of 'jointness', recruiting and retaining highly skilled talent to the levels required, and training them in a realistic manner. Until it has done so, the PLA is not yet the military that Xi envisions will 'fight and win wars' on the CCP's behalf.

The Russia–Ukraine War: Wider Implications
What does it mean for geopolitics?

Russia's war against Ukraine has been the dominant feature of international relations in 2022 and will likely continue to be so well into 2023. It is arguably the most momentous single geopolitical action for two decades. What are its broader longer-term implications for Moscow and its principal partners and adversaries?

Deflating expectations about the Russian military

When Russia invaded Ukraine on 24 February, expectations of a quick victory for this so-called 'special military operation' were high, and not only in Russia. Since Russia's invasion of Georgia in 2008, Moscow had used its armed forces to considerable effect in a series of conflicts both in Russia's 'near abroad' (other former Soviet countries) and further afield in the Middle East and North Africa. A combination of willingness to use military force and the effectiveness of these operations served as a substantial force multiplier for Russian foreign policy. These successes created a widespread impression of competence and effective planning in Russian military operations.

Russia's campaign in Ukraine has so far turned out very differently. Despite (or perhaps because of) its presumed familiarity with its adversary, it made a host of planning errors that were compounded by manifold problems of poor tactics, equipment, communication and leadership. At the beginning of the war, Russia's plan was to quickly take control of Kyiv, impose a pliant regime and subordinate all or most of the country. But despite failing to kill or capture President Volodymyr Zelenskyy and other Ukrainian leaders, the Kremlin continued to deploy forces broadly across Ukraine in the early weeks of the war, in numbers completely insufficient for the task of defeating an army whose leadership and structure remained fully in place. Russia also failed to implement a combined operational plan that could have synergised its air- and sea-power capabilities with land operations, as well as cyber and information power, to achieve its strategic ends.

As a result, the most important early consequence of the Russia–Ukraine war has been the diminished reputation of Russian power across military and other domains. Moscow will pay a long-term price for this, even though the eventual outcome of the war remains uncertain. Although Western countries have been supplying Ukraine with increasingly sophisticated weaponry, Russia may still be able to bring a numerically superior military force to bear, especially if it is willing to risk expanded use of airpower and, in particular, to take the fateful step of ordering a general mobilisation. This would enable the Kremlin to compel – not just persuade, cajole and pay – its citizens to fight, thus releasing a far greater proportion of its potential manpower for the conflict. But it would also remove the last pretence that the 'special military operation' is anything less than a war by any other name, and would set a new and far more severe test of popular support for it. Whether or not Russian President Vladimir Putin crosses this Rubicon, and irrespective of the outcome of the war, the weaknesses the invasion has exposed will prompt a major reappraisal of Russian power, and even of the future of the Putin regime.

NATO strengthens as defence spending rises

Just as the war has exposed the limits of Russian power, so it has dramatically strengthened the West's unity and resolve, and enlarged its security commitments. In particular, by shifting the political calculus in Finland and Sweden it has catalysed the enlargement of NATO. Both countries' entry is now being fast-tracked. At the Madrid Summit in June 2022 NATO approved a new Strategic Concept – the first since 2010 – that focused on Russia as the principal security threat to the Alliance (and included new language on cyber activity potentially triggering the Alliance's collective-defence clause). The Concept also classifies China as a challenger to the 'rules-based international order'. Taken together, the addition of Finland and Sweden and the new Strategic Concept mark a sweeping change in Western security thinking.

The war has also triggered an expansion of defence spending within the Alliance. At the March 2022 NATO summit, the allies committed to accelerating efforts to fulfil the commitment to the Defence Investment Pledge and strengthening individual and collective capacity to resist attacks. German Chancellor Olaf Scholz declared the Russian attack to be 'a watershed' in the history of Europe and announced an additional €100 billion of military spending, which will put Germany over the 2% of GDP NATO norm for the first time since the end of the Cold War.

Has Russia's invasion of Ukraine achieved what every president of the United States since John F. Kennedy has sought without success: a breakthrough to full financial burden-sharing between the US and its European NATO allies? Only time will tell. But the tone of the discussion in Europe about 'strategic autonomy' is clearly evolving. This ambition is no longer about going a separate way from the Americans, but rather building sufficient capabilities to ensure European defence within the context of the transatlantic alliance. Worries about the United States' long-term political commitment that had been fuelled by the Trump administration are receding. The US is the single biggest provider of support for Ukraine and is ready to backstop defence production for European states.

At the same time, European states are aware that without the continuing expansion of US capabilities in Asia, a balancing coalition against rising Chinese military power cannot be sustained. And while the United Kingdom and France have clear national interests at stake in increasing their military (especially naval) presence in the Indo-Pacific, Russian aggressiveness clearly implies that most European states should double down on their principal geographic focus on the continent and its immediate periphery.

De-linking Russia economically from the West

A third set of implications concerns the global economy. The US, Europe and their major non-Western allies have imposed the most severe set of coercive economic measures ever inflicted against a major power in the absence of direct military hostilities between sanctioners and their target. The West has been putting into effect its own 'combined operation' that integrates financial and economic pressure on

Moscow, military and economic support to the Ukrainian government and a global information campaign to turn wavering public opinion, especially in the democracies of the developing world, against Putin. While the last of these efforts has not had a major impact, military and economic support for Ukraine is limiting Russia's ability to subordinate Ukraine to Moscow's ambitions of regional dominance. While economic sanctions are unlikely to change Moscow's behaviour in the short term, their longer-term impact is likely to be significant.

This state-sanctioned severing of economic ties between Russia and the world's advanced economies has been amplified by a large-scale (though not total) voluntary withdrawal of Western businesses. Many of these companies will struggle to sell or repatriate their assets. At the same time, most Russian oligarchs have been sanctioned and their Western assets frozen.

The most politically significant aspect of the economic relationship, for both Russia and the European Union, is the energy dimension. As of July 2022, the EU had put in place seven rounds of sanctions, including a phased oil ban that envisages a cut by over 90% of oil imports from Russia by the end of 2022 (with carve-outs for Bulgaria, the Czech Republic, Hungary and Slovakia to allow longer transitions). Shipping and insurance bans are also being discussed, which would effectively act as secondary sanctions that hinder Russian business with non-sanctioning states too. Europe is also expanding de-listings from the SWIFT payments system to include Russia's largest lender, Sberbank.

For its part, Russia is escalating economic pressure on Europe by restricting gas flows to several countries, presaging a possible full-scale cut-off in the winter, when gas consumption peaks. Gazprom further escalated this in late July 2022 by announcing its intent to halve gas deliveries to the EU via the Nord Stream 1 pipeline. In response to these threats, the EU agreed to a common response to potential shortages in the form of a voluntary 15% reduction in gas usage through to the end of March 2023.

Europe's search for alternative energy sources, including coal, will in the short term likely push back the EU's ambitious timetable for a transition to a post-carbon energy system. It is also scrambling to find other sources of natural gas, including from the US. This promises to add a further economic dimension to transatlantic common purpose on Russia policy. Under presidents Barack Obama and Donald Trump, the US rapidly expanded its production of shale oil and shale gas. The US became the world's leading oil producer, with output doubling between 2009 and 2019 from less than 6 million barrels per day (bpd) to over 12m bpd.

Russia's war against Ukraine is beginning to highlight the strategic value of this asset, not only in reducing US dependence on energy imports from geopolitically volatile regions – notably the Middle East – but also reducing the dependence of its key allies in Europe on another such region: Russia. In its first few months, the Biden administration steered away from highlighting the strategic significance of the US shale revolution, in deference to the progressive wing of the Democratic Party. But without the shale revolution, Putin's energy leverage over the West in this crisis would have been dramatically higher. The Russia–Ukraine war is shifting the political landscape in the US on energy, creating more space for the Biden administration to promote domestic shale oil and gas production and at the same time begin to rebalance its relationship with Saudi Arabia and other Gulf producers. US production will be a vital factor in enabling Europe to disconnect from Russian energy. In July 2022 European Commission President Ursula von der Leyen noted that liquefied natural gas (LNG) imports from the US had trebled over the past year. However, gaining access to LNG supplies in the necessary volumes from all sources will require more import terminals and greater connectivity across the continent.

Meanwhile, faced with the EU's embargo on most Russian oil, Russia seeks to deepen its energy relationship with emerging markets, most importantly China and India, which have taken up much of the slack from Moscow's lost markets in the West. China increased its oil purchases from about 750,000 bpd in the first quarter of 2022 to over 1.9m bpd in May, and at a discount. India went further: in June 2022 it imported approximately 950,000 bpd from Russia compared to none in January and February.

The long-term impact of economic decoupling from the West is likely to be severe for Russia. The most vulnerable sector of the Russian economy is advanced manufactured goods, which will lack access to key components and supply chains. The exit of hundreds of thousands of skilled workers from Russia in recent months will exacerbate these costs. This will become a particularly challenging issue for Moscow's defence industry, the second-largest sector in Russia's economy after commodity exports.

China's economic weakness limits energy-price increases

Russia's invasion of Ukraine coincided with a COVID-19 outbreak in China, especially in Shanghai. This lowered market expectations of Chinese economic performance in 2022–23 and put downward pressure on global energy prices. This is bad news for Moscow. Although China achieved great success in preventing major outbreaks over the past two years, the combination of limited natural immunity, ineffective domestically produced vaccines, highly infectious COVID-19 strains and continued commitment to zero-COVID in the run-up to the Chinese Communist Party's (CCP) 20th Congress meant that the coronavirus continued to spread. This led global markets to largely discount Beijing's 5% growth target for 2022. As a result, while oil prices rose by about 15% in the first half of 2022, the world did not experience the spiking prices that many observers thought would be an inevitable side effect of the EU's decision to wean itself off Russian oil supplies. The risk of an oil-price spike remains limited for the remainder of 2022, and probably well into 2023, given expectations of a global economic slow-down. This will ease Europe's decision to shift away from Russian oil imports – though it will not help it weather Russia's own decision to restrict gas supply.

Major developing countries seek to remain neutral

The US and its European allies have sought to isolate Russia from the wider international community. So far, these efforts have had mixed results. Although major developed Asian states, notably Japan, Singapore and Taiwan, have joined the Western-led sanctions coalition against Russia, many developing states, while criticising the invasion, remain wary of efforts to isolate Russia.

Brazil, India and South Africa, members of the BRICS grouping along with China and Russia, have tried to walk a diplomatic tightrope. In what was broadly seen as an effort to avoid publicity and potential disagreements over Ukraine, the BRICS leaders chose not to meet in person for their annual summit in June, despite the fact that the group had been unable to do so because of the pandemic since 2019. India has steered what it portrays as a neutral course on the war, while sustaining its close ties – including on defence purchases – with Moscow despite its increasing tilt towards US allies, especially in the Indo-Pacific zone, in recent years. It has abstained on UN votes condemning Russia's invasion. New Delhi refuses to publicly blame Moscow for the crisis, even as it emphasises India's traditional respect for sovereignty and territorial integrity. India received Russian Foreign Minister Sergei Lavrov on a diplomatic visit in April 2022.

In June, Brazilian President Jair Bolsonaro had a long phone call with Putin that focused on food security, in which Putin reaffirmed his commitment to supply fertilisers to Brazil as part of strengthening their 'strategic partnership'. Bolsonaro's electoral rival, former president Luiz Inácio 'Lula' da Silva, has also refused to criticise Russia, highlighting the wariness of the Brazilian political class to be seen supporting the US-led coalition against Moscow.

South Africa has long had sympathetic views towards Russia, dating back to the anti-apartheid struggle. President Cyril Ramaphosa has blamed NATO for the war in Ukraine, and claimed he had been asked to mediate in it. In June and July, both Russia and the US stepped up their efforts to shape African views on the crisis by sending several delegations to the continent.

Beyond the BRICS, Russia's partners in the OPEC+ arrangement have also worked to avoid becoming enmeshed in Western efforts to isolate Moscow. When President Joe Biden travelled to Saudi Arabia to meet with Crown Prince Muhammad bin Salman bin Abdulaziz Al Saud (MBS) in July 2022, their joint communiqué made no mention of Russia.

Looking ahead: implications of greater Russian dependence on China

While China has accommodated US sanctions, and some Chinese companies have suspended or scaled back their relations with Russia, Beijing still supports Moscow in important ways – not only by providing an alternative market for Russian raw-material exports but also closer military cooperation – especially in conducting further military exercises in the Far East. One major consequence of the war is likely to be even closer ties between Moscow and Beijing. These ties have already been strengthening for the past decade. But given the damage the war has inflicted on Russia's long-term status as a great power, there is a growing possibility that the relationship could undergo a qualitative shift. Moscow could become less autonomous and increasingly dependent on Beijing. This may not be the outcome that China wishes for. Even a weakened Russia would not be amenable to control by Beijing. China would much rather have a robust and predictable Russia as a partner.

While Russia and China share an interest in opposing what they both see as US dominance of the current international system, they have different aims towards that system. China is far more interested in both a broadly stable and an economically prosperous global order. Its goals are to gain greater influence over the system and to promote its evolution to one that accommodates regional spheres of influence by non-Western powers. Russia, on the other hand, is likely to continue to see instability as a source of opportunity and is not seriously invested in assuring global economic dynamism.

A closer Sino-Russian relationship will affect other key inter-state relationships in Asia. India will continue to see China as its principal challenge, and it is likely that Moscow's increasing dependence on China will further propel what are already moves by New Delhi to limit its military reliance on Russia. Meanwhile, Tokyo has emerged as a strong member of the sanctioning coalition against Russia, which will lead to the end of the decades-long effort to restore Japanese sovereignty over the Northern Territories through diplomacy with Moscow.

When Russia's war in Ukraine finally ends, there is little doubt that Russia will emerge as a diminished power more dependent on China. But it is far too soon to know in any detail what such a relationship would entail, just as the form of any new transatlantic security order – and its relationship to Russia – can barely yet be imagined. A war whose course has already confounded expectations, and is summoning new geopolitical forces, will continue to shape the future long after the guns have stopped.

CHAPTER 5

North America

CANADA

UNITED STATES

©IISS

Drivers of Strategic Change

REGIONAL SHARE OF GLOBAL POPULATION, GDP AND DEFENCE BUDGET

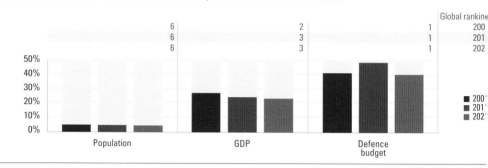

POPULATION

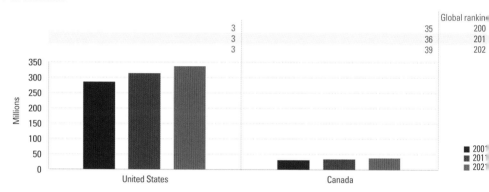

AGE STRUCTURE
(Percentage of national population)

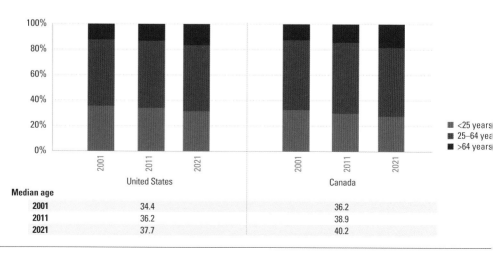

Median age	United States	Canada
2001	34.4	36.2
2011	36.2	38.9
2021	37.7	40.2

America's huge share of global defence spending has fallen over the past decade, but remains as high as it was before 9/11, despite a declining share of global GDP. For a high-income country, the population continues to grow impressively and remains young. But the quality of democracy, and relative ranking in human development, are in decline. Trust in government hovers below 40%, near the low end of countries surveyed.

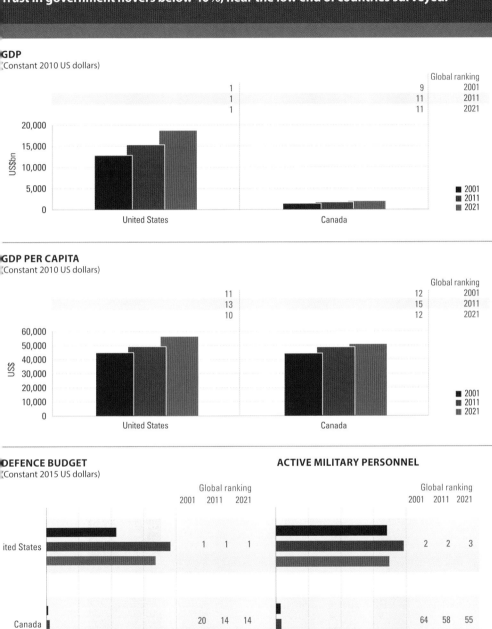

GDP
(Constant 2010 US dollars)

	Global ranking	
1	9	2001
1	11	2011
1	11	2021

USSbn — United States, Canada

■ 2001
■ 2011
■ 2021

GDP PER CAPITA
(Constant 2010 US dollars)

	Global ranking	
11	12	2001
13	15	2011
10	12	2021

US$ — United States, Canada

■ 2001
■ 2011
■ 2021

DEFENCE BUDGET
(Constant 2015 US dollars)

	Global ranking		
	2001	2011	2021
United States	1	1	1
Canada	20	14	14

US$bn

ACTIVE MILITARY PERSONNEL

	Global ranking		
	2001	2011	2021
United States	2	2	3
Canada	64	58	55

Millions

■ 2001 ■ 2011 ■ 2021

For explanation of drivers and sources, see page 8

HUMAN DEVELOPMENT INDEX (HDI)
(Score between 0 and 1, where 0 denotes a low level of development and 1 a high level of development)

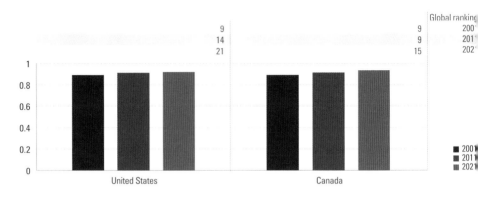

POLITICAL SYSTEM
(Score between 0 and 100, where 0 denotes no political freedom and 100 fully free)

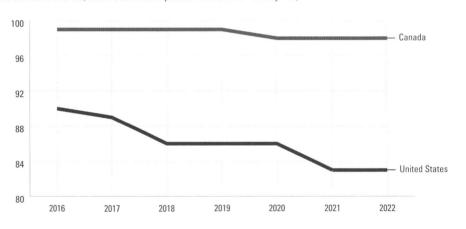

TRUST IN GOVERNMENT
(Average level of trust)

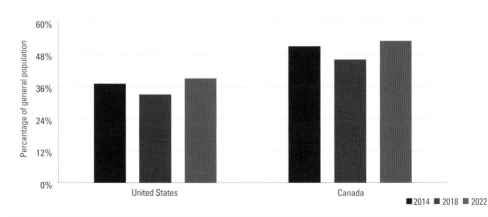

For explanation of drivers and sources, see page

2021–22 Review

At the start of his presidency, President Joe Biden framed his administration's mission as confronting anti-democratic trends at home and abroad. This would entail mobilising democratic allies against authoritarian challenger states while securing democratic values within the United States, including through attempting to reinvigorate its socio-economic model and bridge partisan splits. The chaotic fall of Kabul to the Taliban in the summer of 2021 marked the failure of two decades of investment in creating a stable and democratic Afghanistan. More broadly, though, Washington did enjoy some success in its alliance diplomacy, most notably in its leadership and mobilisation of NATO allies in opposition to Russia's invasion of Ukraine. But America's political, social and cultural polarisation remained entrenched and, if anything, reached new extremes. By mid-2022, Biden's hopes of healing the national wounds that his predecessor's presidency had inflicted appeared increasingly forlorn.

US domestic policy

By mid-2022, the House Select Committee investigating the 6 January 2021 attack on the US Capitol by supporters of then-president Donald Trump had made several disturbing claims. Evidence suggested that president Trump had been actively involved in attempts to overturn his defeat in the 2020 presidential election, despite being warned by several close advisers that his claims had no factual basis; that several Republican members of Congress had subsequently requested presidential pardons for their efforts to overturn the election, indicating an awareness that their actions were illegal; that at least one Republican representative gave a tour of the congressional complex to individuals later involved in the attempted insurrection; and that Trump himself had encouraged his supporters to march to the Capitol, despite knowing that some were armed. Indeed, allegations emerged that he had wanted to participate directly in the riot and had expressed approval of some of the insurrectionists' desire to murder his own vice president for failing to overturn the election results. The Committee's hearings were widely publicised, including on primetime television, and enjoyed a substantial audience. According to a June 2022 opinion poll, 58% of Americans believed that Trump should be criminally charged for his supposed role in the Capitol attack. Perhaps in part because of the hearings, as well as a broader fatigue with Trump's erratic behaviour, by the summer of 2022 there were early signs that his hold on the Republican Party could finally be loosening, if only slightly. The majority of Republican candidates that he endorsed in contested midterm elections lost their races. A poll released in late June 2022 suggested that Ron DeSantis, the governor of Florida, would win 39% of votes in a New Hampshire Republican presidential primary and Trump 37%. Nevertheless, Trump continued to lead most polls of likely Republican voting. Moreover, Trump's insistent narrative of election fraud remained dominant among the Republican electorate, with around 70% of Republicans continuing to believe that Biden's 2020 election victory was fraudulent and illegitimate. The core belief motivating the 6 January attack remained largely immune to contrary evidence, boding ill for any prospect of political reconciliation.

Another legacy of Trump's presidency was the Supreme Court's strong conservative majority, following his appointment of three conservative justices. The decision to overturn the *Roe v. Wade* ruling of half a century earlier, which had argued that a woman's right to an abortion was constitutionally protected, was unusually leaked some weeks ahead of its eventual announcement in June 2022. This advance notice did not soften the shock to progressive Americans or diminish the jubilation of many conservatives. While 61% of Americans believed that abortion should be legal in all or most cases, the Supreme Court's new appetite to overturn existing rulings, especially on particularly polarising issues, raised concerns that a minority view could continue to enjoy enormous influence for decades to come. During a year which looked set to break records for mass shootings, a rare instance of bipartisan political cooperation to tighten gun laws slightly, forged after yet another school massacre, was soon followed by a Supreme Court ruling that struck down a 1911 New York law restricting gun-carrying rights. This decision implicitly challenged similar restrictions in other, predominantly Democratic-voting, states. A ruling against the Environmental Protection Agency's efforts to transition to lower-carbon energy production further underlined the new activism and ambition of the court's conservative majority.

Some Democrats hoped that these judicial setbacks might at least serve to energise their voters in the 2022 midterm election. As Biden himself put it, 'this fall, Roe is on the ballot'. While such mobilisation remained possible, most electoral indicators looked discouraging for the incumbent party. By June 2022, annual inflation had hit 9.1%, its highest figure since 1981, largely eroding wage increases and presaging future interest-rate increases; stock markets had fallen; and business confidence was low, with widespread expectations of a recession. Despite controlling the White House and, in principle, Congress, the Democrats failed to make significant progress with their legislative agenda. This was largely because two of their senators from traditionally Republican states (West Virginia and Arizona) refused to support several bills or efforts to allow their passage through Congress, including the Build Back Better Act and legislation on climate change and voting reform, essentially negating the Democratic majority. Biden's approval rating in July 2022 averaged at below 39%, a record low since 1945 for any president 18 months after inauguration. While Biden was still narrowly beating Trump in the polls, only 24% of Democratic voters believed he should receive the presidential nomination in 2024.

Biden's unpopularity stemmed not only from figurative political or economic malaise, but at least in part from a persistent, literal malaise. While no longer prompting lockdowns or threatening to overload the health system directly, the coronavirus pandemic continued to kill Americans, with the cumulative death toll surpassing one million by May 2022. The majority of this figure, a tally which would perhaps have been unthinkable at the start of the pandemic, was composed of deaths occurring since vaccination had become widely available, and which were therefore largely preventable. The emergence of the Delta variant in the summer of 2021, with its more common 'breakthrough infections' despite vaccination, dashed hopes that the US could fully return to the status quo ante, and dented Biden's popularity. His approval ratings entered net negative territory, however, with the fiasco of the final US withdrawal from Afghanistan.

US foreign policy

Biden had long argued, largely in private before his presidency, that the US should withdraw its military forces from Afghanistan, and once in office confirmed a decision Trump had taken to do so late in his own administration. Most Americans agreed with the strategic logic of withdrawal after almost 20 years' investment of blood and treasure in what appeared to be a dysfunctional state mired in an intractable civil war. The nature of the withdrawal, however, revealed an abysmal failure to predict the rapidity of Kabul's collapse and to make adequate provisions for the evacuation of Afghan allies vulnerable to Taliban retaliation. The image of desperate Afghans clinging to US aircraft departing Kabul airport before inevitably plunging to their deaths will remain, alongside footage of helicopters evacuating the US embassy in Saigon 46 years earlier, a powerful symbol of the limits of US military power and the risks facing local actors who trust Washington's assurances. The withdrawal's proponents argued that it would not diminish Washington's strategic credibility in other theatres and could, in fact, allow for a wiser global distribution of US capabilities and attention.

In the aftermath of the war the Biden administration worked to reinvigorate, reshape and augment the post-1945 security architecture. This was part of a broader international tendency towards less formal, 'minilateral' groupings. Some of this trend was driven by the perceptions of regional actors that traditional partnerships, particularly with Washington, were no longer fulfilling their security needs. A unifying motivation, however, and one which extended to Washington, was the belief that established alliances and institutions were often failing to respond to challenger states such as China, Iran or Russia with sufficient agility. Perhaps the most prominent minilateral partnership was one brokered between Australia, the United Kingdom and the US in the autumn of 2021. Dubbed AUKUS, the partnership was immediately submerged in controversy due to Australia's abrupt cancellation of a naval contract with France and Paris's resentful, albeit temporary, diplomatic response. Along with additional diplomatic and rhetorical momentum behind the Quadrilateral Security Dialogue ('Quad'), AUKUS reflected a growing willingness in Washington and elsewhere to seek new mechanisms to balance a rising China. The Summit for Democracy, a virtual summit in December 2021, was another example, although its list of participants, which included a number of illiberal or unfree US allies, prompted accusations of hypocrisy.

The most significant international event, though, was Russia's invasion of Ukraine. Washington's efforts to forestall the war through active diplomacy and selective leaking of intelligence, and then after the invasion to mobilise international support for Ukraine's defence, underscored the enduring strategic significance of America's traditional alliances – especially NATO, which experienced a striking revitalisation of purpose and signed an accession protocol with Finland and Sweden. The Afghanistan quagmire and US withdrawal had highlighted the limits of Washington's power, at least in that context. But the response to Russia's invasion revealed that US willingness and ability to use its power to defend core national interests remained formidable, especially when employed in concert with its allies. Russian President Vladimir Putin's grave underestimation of American (and European) power brought dramatic strategic consequences.

In the war's early stages, some Biden administration officials had expressed concern that US support for Ukraine that was too overt or crossed various perceived thresholds could escalate to direct clashes between NATO and Russia, possibly with nuclear weapons. As the war progressed, and the Ukrainian state survived and then repulsed Russian forces on some fronts (partly thanks to Western anti-tank weapons, as well as remarkable national courage and cohesion), these fears appeared to diminish, and US provision of heavier weapons became more forthcoming. By late April, US Secretary of Defense Lloyd Austin stated that Washington's goal was 'to see Russia weakened to the degree that it can't do the kinds of things that it has done in invading Ukraine'. The US was the largest donor to Ukraine, with its military contributions dwarfing those of the European Union. In May 2022, Congress approved US$40 billion in economic, food and military aid for Ukraine, supplementing an earlier US$13.6bn package. By mid-summer, advanced US artillery appeared to be having a significant effect against Russian forces in the war of attrition in eastern Ukraine. Sanctions against Russia, unprecedented in their scale and scope, also underscored Washington's enduring economic strengths and ability to mobilise global geo-economic coalitions.

Given Putin and Chinese President Xi Jinping's declaration shortly before the invasion of Ukraine that their nations' relationship had 'no limits', the war and associated international sanctions prompted concerns that Beijing could attempt to bolster Moscow economically, provide it with more direct military support, or even take advantage of the international tumult to attempt to seize Taiwan. In May, Biden stated that the US would defend Taiwan militarily, a much more explicit posture than previous, more ambiguous, US formulations, although the White House later claimed that US policy was unchanged. In the same month, Secretary of State Antony Blinken declared that while the US did not seek a cold war with China, Beijing had both the intent and capability to 'reshape the international order'. Biden also launched the Indo-Pacific Economic Framework for Prosperity (IPEF), an attempt to regain US economic initiative in the region. While the IPEF contained provisions for international harmonisation of clean energy, tax and various digital economic policy areas, it did not allow for greater market access as an incentive to participants.

Biden had entered office seeking to marginalise Saudi Crown Prince Muhammad bin Salman bin Abdulaziz Al Saud (MBS), the de facto ruler of one of Washington's closest Middle Eastern allies, whom the CIA had judged responsible for the murder of Jamal Khashoggi in 2018. As a presidential candidate, Biden had suggested making Saudi Arabia 'pay the price, and make them, in fact, the pariah that they are'. Refusing for the first 18 months of his presidency to speak directly to MBS, Biden's efforts to ignore him were abandoned by mid-2022, when the deteriorating situation with both international energy supply and Iran's nuclear ambitions made more direct cooperation with Saudi Arabia, and with MBS himself, unavoidable.

Canada

Canadian Prime Minister Justin Trudeau, in power since 2015 and leading a minority government since 2019, gambled on a snap election in September 2021 but once again failed to secure a majority. Returned to minority government, in March 2022 Trudeau brokered an agreement with the New Democratic Party (NDP) in which the NDP would remain an opposition party out of government, but would support Trudeau's Liberals in return for various policy pledges. The agreement made it more likely that Trudeau would survive until the end of his current term in 2025.

Canada continued to maintain an active foreign policy, notably alongside NATO allies in support for Ukraine. This support included military equipment, as well as financial and humanitarian donations. Ottawa's long-running dispute with Beijing over the detention of its citizens Michael Spavor and Michael Kovrig – who were imprisoned following Canada's detention in 2018 of Meng Wanzhou, Huawei's CFO and daughter of its founder and the subject of a US extradition request – appeared to have been resolved after Meng and then Spavor and Kovrig were released in September 2021. The bilateral relationship remained unsettled, however, with Chinese aircraft harassing Canadian planes engaged in enforcement of UN sanctions against North Korea in May 2022. Trudeau described China's behaviour, which had endangered Canadian lives, as 'irresponsible and provocative'.

Political Polarisation and Institutional Strain
How fragile is US democracy?

Over the course of eight televised hearings during June and July 2022, the House Select Committee to Investigate the January 6th Attack on the United States Capitol released new evidence implicating former president Donald Trump in a plot to overturn the results of the 2020 presidential election. Much was already known. The former president's support for the insurrectionary attack on the Capitol had been manifestly clear on that day. Indeed, after voting to acquit Trump in his second impeachment trial 38 days later, Republican Senate Minority Leader Mitch McConnell had stipulated that Trump was 'practically and morally' responsible for the events, and added:

> The people who stormed this building believed they were acting on the wishes and instructions of their President. And their having that belief was a foreseeable consequence of the growing crescendo of false statements, conspiracy theories, and reckless hyperbole which the defeated President kept shouting into the largest megaphone on planet Earth.

But with the advantage of time and after conducting interviews with myriad witnesses, the Select Committee was able to construct a more detailed version of events from November 2020 through to the attack on the Capitol. This version showed that Trump's attempt to overturn the election, though scattershot and run according to his impulses, was also a sweeping effort, featuring a cast of enablers – powerful in their own right – who knew what they were doing was wrong and said as much to the president. The committee described the plan to overturn the election as proceeding in seven phases, beginning before the election and culminating with the siege of the Capitol. It provided convincing new evidence that, among other things:

- Top government officials, including the attorney general, told Trump on several occasions that he had lost the election;

- Trump was directly involved in the pressure campaign to compel the vice president, Mike Pence, and state and local officials to overturn the results;
- Trump knew that the crowd on 6 January was armed with knives, guns, bear spray, body armour and spears when he told them to march on the Capitol;
- The march was planned in advance;
- Trump thought arrangements had been made for him to accompany the rioters to the Capitol and was furious when he discovered that this would not be possible for security reasons;
- Trump took no action to stop the violence as it unfolded – he did not attempt to contact the defence secretary, the attorney general or the secretary of homeland security, for example – and instead waited to see if the situation would play out to his advantage, despite the risk to the lives of the vice president and members of Congress;
- Rioters came very close to Pence, and some members of his security detail feared they would die defending him;
- Trump knew about the physical danger to Pence when he tweeted additional condemnations of the vice president that further aroused the mob; and
- Prominent Republican officials, including the president's own chief of staff, sought pardons during the final days of the administration.

Though Trump's plot failed, the audacity of the effort portended a revolution in consciousness and expectations about whether future election results might be rejected and reversed. Such an outcome is conceivable only because of the extraordinary level of political polarisation driving behaviour among political elites in Washington and in state capitols across the US in 2021–22, and because Americans themselves have become more socially and politically differentiated from each other than at any time in recent memory.

Polarisation

One of the clearest signs of the polarisation of the American electorate is that majorities of voters in each main political party have questioned the legitimacy of leaders in the other party. In April 2001, a public-opinion poll indicated that 64% of Democrats viewed then-president George W. Bush as illegitimate, and in April 2017 a poll found that 56% thought the same of Trump. It should be noted, however, that both men lost the national popular vote (by 544,000 and over 2.8 million votes, respectively). Before the 2020 election, a Pew poll found that 89% of Trump supporters thought that electing Joe Biden would cause 'lasting harm to the US', and 90% of Biden voters thought the same in reverse. More recently, a June 2022 poll found that 73% of Republicans did not think that Biden was elected legitimately, even though he won 7m more votes nationally.

Most people join political parties not on the basis of agreement over matters of public policy, but because they personally identify with members of that party (or feel alienated by members of an opposing party.) This pull and push of identification and alienation has become stronger in recent decades because Americans have less in common now than they used to. Indeed, polarisation has increased as Americans have sorted themselves geographically and socially into more homogeneous groups, a trend amplified by the ease with which states have been able to create congressional districts to maximise partisan political advantage. Partisan primaries have thus become more competitive – and in many places more important – than general elections, with more extreme candidates emerging from the process.

In 2002, there were 124 'swing' districts in the US House of Representatives out of 435 that might plausibly elect a Democrat or Republican. In 2022, there are only about 30. This means that every two years the critical test for over 90% of House legislators does not come in a general election but in a partisan primary, where threats originate not from the centre but from the right and left according to the preferences of small numbers of motivated voters whose views diverge strongly from those of the median voter. The power of state legislatures to draw congressional districts for partisan advantage has made this problem worse. The result is that elected politicians have largely deserted the middle ground, with Republican legislators moving further right than their Democrat counterparts have moved left (see Figures 1 and 2).

This phenomenon is a major reason why cross-national surveys taken since the 1980s have found that 'affective polarisation' – the degree to which political-party members feel negatively towards other parties – has increased faster and risen further in the US than in 11 peer countries. A 2020 study led by Levi Boxell at Stanford University pointed to two other causal factors in addition to elite polarisation: racial diversity and, less significantly, the number of private 24-hour news networks operating in a country (which, not coincidentally, also encourages elite polarisation).

In an earlier era, it was much harder to predict a person's political affiliation on the basis of a single attribute – church attendance, residential geography, level of education or race. Today, however, these identities are much more strongly linked to each other and to political preference. Voters in urban areas are now overwhelmingly Democratic, and also tend to be non-religious, college educated and younger on average. Older voters in rural areas who are religious and did not attend college are overwhelmingly white Republicans. This social-sorting phenomenon is increasingly visible in presidential-election returns, with Democratic candidates since the 1990s winning national pluralities but fewer and fewer counties, which are linked more to land area than to population. Biden, for example, received the most popular votes ever while winning majorities in only about 500 of 3,000+ counties.

The extreme political polarisation of twenty-first-century America is partly a product of the period of civil-rights activism that crested with the passage of the Voting Rights Act of 1965, soon after Trump and Biden had reached adulthood. Biden provoked controversy during the 2020 Democratic primary campaign by recalling his friendly relations in the 1970s with segregationist senators from the South. He was alluding to a tradition of bipartisanship and comity in Congress that has since

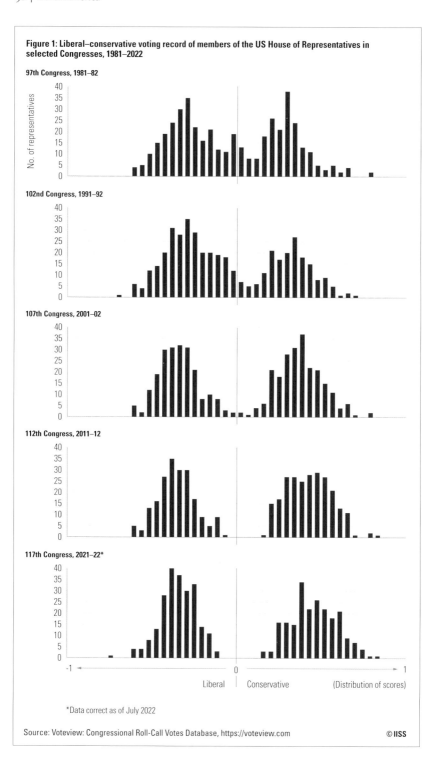

Figure 1: Liberal–conservative voting record of members of the US House of Representatives in selected Congresses, 1981–2022

97th Congress, 1981–82

102nd Congress, 1991–92

107th Congress, 2001–02

112th Congress, 2011–12

117th Congress, 2021–22*

Liberal | Conservative   (Distribution of scores)

*Data correct as of July 2022

Source: Voteview: Congressional Roll-Call Votes Database, https://voteview.com

© IISS

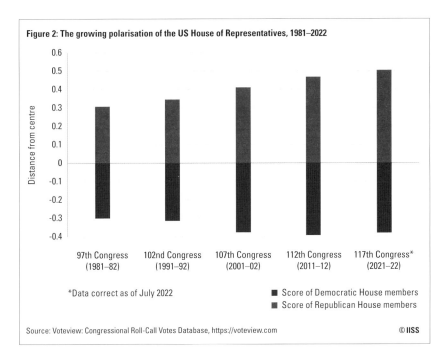

Figure 2: The growing polarisation of the US House of Representatives, 1981–2022

*Data correct as of July 2022

■ Score of Democratic House members
■ Score of Republican House members

Source: Voteview: Congressional Roll-Call Votes Database, https://voteview.com   © IISS

vanished. In that era, the two main political parties were heterogeneous: the Democratic Party included representatives and senators who were conservative – sometimes overtly racist – Southerners and Northern liberals, while the Republican Party included staunch conservatives in addition to moderates and liberals. This structure left space for bipartisan coalition-building in an era of progress on civil rights and other issues. The stability of governance in this period was underwritten by the willingness of politicians from both parties to adhere to norms of mutual deference and accept rule by political opponents. But this consensus has been fraying since the 1990s, and with the Republican Party still embracing Trump since he left office in the shadow of the 6 January melee – and refused to attend the inauguration of his successor – it may be irretrievable.

Constitutional fragility

While America considers itself the world's oldest democracy, the survival of some practices and institutions more than 230 years after they were established poses its own problems insofar as they predate contemporary ideas about popular sovereignty. The concepts and norms of modern democratic processes have essentially evolved, often in unwritten form, alongside a constitution that remains, in many respects, a pre-democratic document. Its eighteenth-century authors, despite being men of the Enlightenment, did not accept the idea of universal suffrage even for white males.

The evolution of American democracy has been inspired, to be sure, by the radicalism of Thomas Jefferson's Declaration of Independence, its vision of equality and its insistence that governments derive their power from the consent of the governed. More explicitly democratic language was added to the constitution in Civil War- and Reconstruction-era amendments. Yet Reconstruction was contested and, in the South, largely defeated until well into the late twentieth century. And the fact that US presidents are still not elected directly, but through an intermediary Electoral College that gives outsize influence to small rural states, is the clearest example that the tension built into the constitution between republicanism and democracy remains with us today. Indeed, the Electoral College was developed when the drafters of the constitution could not agree about whether the president should be elected by popular vote or by Congress, and each state has the freedom to administer its own process for appointing electors.

Before 2020, there had not been a major dispute regarding the Electoral College process itself since 1876, when questions about fraud, voter intimidation and arguments over the appointment of electoral voters marred the processes in Florida, Louisiana, Oregon and South Carolina. As a result, these states submitted two different slates of electoral votes for certification, which forced Congress to adjudicate. The 1877 Electoral Count Act was passed to prevent a future such crisis and continues to govern the presidential-election process through Title 3, Section 15 of the US Code of laws. The wording of this statute is archaic; among other problems, the role played by the vice president during the vote-counting process in the Senate is not described clearly. And when the law is applied in combination with the relevant provisions of the constitution, there are significant loopholes that partisan malefactors could use to flip a close election. This is precisely what Trump and his associates tried to do in the aftermath of the 2020 election.

In a forensic survey of 2022 primary-election results, the *Washington Post* found that in the six battleground states of Arizona, Georgia, Michigan, Nevada, Pennsylvania and Wisconsin, 'candidates who deny the legitimacy of that election have claimed nearly two-thirds of GOP nominations for state and federal offices with authority over elections'. This includes, for example, Pennsylvania gubernatorial nominee Douglas Mastriano, who joined the rally outside the Capitol on 6 January and attempted to organise an alternate slate of pro-Trump electors to replace the Biden electors chosen by the state's voters. Similar attempts in just two or three of the battleground states have the potential to change the national result in 2024. It is conceivable that the current Supreme Court, with its six–three conservative majority, could even endorse the so-called 'independent state-legislature theory', once a fringe view, which could result in a state legislature disregarding a state-wide popular vote and appointing its own electors. Such an attempt – or an election-theft effort perhaps better planned and organised than Trump and his allies were capable of – would almost certainly lead to constitutional and political chaos marked by violence on both left and right.

Anxiety and alienation

Trump's early forays into the political spotlight did not betray a discernible political ideology. They did, however, offer a preview of the appeals to violence and white-middle-class anxiety that would characterise his campaign and presidency and that accelerated the American right's transformation into a European-style right-populist movement. Trump was first quoted in the *New York Times* in 1973, when defending his family's real-estate company from a Department of Justice lawsuit alleging racial discrimination against renters. He later took out a full-page advertisement in the newspaper to demand the death penalty for the alleged rapists in the infamous 'Central Park jogger' case. The five men were African American and Latino and, after spending years in prison, were found to be innocent. Trump joined in the fashionable Japan-bashing of the 1980s, sounding nearly identical notes about trade and tariffs as he did towards China as president. And in the third year of Barack Obama's presidency, Trump became a chief propagator of the false 'Birther' allegation that America's first African-American president was illegitimate because he was supposedly born abroad, in Kenya or elsewhere.

Trump stoked right-wing fears and grievances throughout his presidency, and since leaving office in 2021 this has manifested itself in, for example, the promotion by the influential Fox News Network of the 'Great Replacement Theory' that sees Democrats (and, in some neo-Nazi versions, specifically Jewish Democrats) engineering mass immigration to replace whites with a new citizenry of colour that will dominate society with its voting power. And some prominent Republicans have attempted to tap into a strain of paranoia on the right by echoing the idea that the Democratic Party is promoting a paedophiliac agenda, a false and dangerous allegation tied to the QAnon conspiracy-cult.

'Great Replacement' anxieties are a clue to why both political parties now seem convinced that electoral stakes are existential. Demographic trends indicate that in the 2040s, whites will lose their status as the majority racial group in America (while retaining a plurality). Republican Party leaders have not made a sustained effort to broaden their base of voters, which is currently overwhelmingly white, to include non-white voters who hold moderate or even conservative views on cultural and economic issues. Instead, the party has worked America's constitutional levers of minority rule, or at least blockage, through measures such as the filibuster – an arcane Senate procedure used much more frequently in recent years that effectively imposes a super-majority requirement on the passage of most types of new laws. Hence, well before the 2020 election, grassroots activists, conservative intellectuals and many elected Republicans repeated the mantra that the US is 'a republic, not a democracy', implying that majority rule is both threatening to the party and not essential to the character of the country.

Republican officials have been taking steps to uphold what they see as 'election integrity'. Their efforts at the state and national levels to fight alleged voter fraud intensified before the 2018 midterm elections and again in the lead-up to and aftermath of the 2020 presidential election, and they have supported or implemented policies making it more difficult for citizens to vote. Their declared principle is that a single unlawful vote should be stopped, even at the cost of excluding many lawful votes from being cast. This is appealing to those who are concerned about, for example, the possibility that a US immigrant might vote illegally. Operationally, however, the problem of voter fraud is statistically non-existent, and these policies disproportionately prevent citizens who tend to support Democratic candidates from voting: those who are young, members of a racial minority, live in a city or for whom English is a second language.

On the Democratic side, there is an existential fear that the US could be governed by minoritarian institutions for the foreseeable future and that these might further entrench minority power, effectively neutering American democracy. Democratic presidential candidates have lost the popular vote only once since 1988, yet Republican presidents have appointed six out of the current nine justices on the Supreme Court. The June 2022 decision by the court to rescind the constitutional right to abortion, a right established by a previous ruling in 1973, went against the views of a clear majority of the population and has been a bracing reminder of the political minority's clout. There is clear potential for conservative members of the court, all of whom have lifetime appointments, to reconsider past decisions regarding other constitutional rights and to issue new judgments that would strip away the powers of the federal government as they have existed since the New Deal.

Democratic activists, meanwhile, have focused much of their energies on widening the circle of rights and social privileges available to women and to those marginalised because of their race, gender or sexuality. This has stoked anxiety on the right among those who feel that their status might be diminished as a result – a dynamic well known to observers of multi-ethnic democracies globally. There are also fears on the right about illiberal currents on the left that have emerged as part of what has been called the 'Great Awokening'. This phenomenon began taking shape in 2014 and has led young people and particularly white, college-educated

Democrats to express – sometimes in dogmatic fashion – new levels of awareness and concern about racial inequality and discrimination. Two events that year precipitated the shift in opinion: an influential essay on slave reparations written by Ta-Nehisi Coates in *The Atlantic* and the killing of a young African-American man, Michael Brown, by police in Ferguson, Missouri, that August, which was followed by waves of public protests. The ensuing debate over systemic racism in American society has continued for years and expanded to include gay rights, women's rights – particularly since the emergence of the #MeToo movement in 2017 – and transgender rights. By the late 2010s, 'woke' ideas had moved from universities where they long held sway and become live issues in mainstream-media outlets, human-resources departments and public schools. This is where many older and working-class Americans encountered 'wokeness' for the first time. Fox News has found that it can bolster ratings by fanning outrage about woke ideas and its exaggerated interpretations of them. These efforts have been aided by the tendency among some proponents of wokeness to engage in tinny and sometimes ponderous language policing on social media that has little practical effect on racism or discrimination. It is mainly those on the right, however, in Republican-run states such as Florida, who have used the powers of government to suppress the teaching of ideas about race and sexuality and to remove related books from public-school libraries.

Future implications: American democracy and its influence abroad

There is an academic debate about whether the US could face civil war in the coming decade. The answer may depend on definitions. Violence has re-emerged as a salient feature of American politics. In August 2022, the FBI raided Trump's Florida resort residence to recover documents relating to national defence, many of them highly classified, that he had removed from the White House. Trump supporters, including South Carolina Senator Lindsey Graham, stated that any attempt to hold the former president criminally accountable would unleash a violent reaction. Arch-conservative Rep. Liz Cheney, the co-chair of the January 6

Select Committee who was ousted from her leadership role in the House Republican conference in May 2021 after criticising Trump, was unable to make open public appearances in Wyoming while campaigning for renomination in 2022 because of the number of credible death threats she had received. Right-wing terrorists responsible for attacks in El Paso, Texas, and Buffalo, New York, in recent years have used the Great Replacement Theory to justify their actions. The 6 January attack – and the subsequent revelation by the Select Committee that Trump knew his supporters were armed and yet had still tweeted, after the attackers had taken control of the building, a condemnation of Pence that accused him of failing to protect the country – is a reminder that one side of the great American divide is armed, and has long cited Second Amendment rights to bear arms as a guarantee against the imposition of tyranny. If 'tyranny' comes to be defined as the other side winning a presidential election, America will face, if not civil war, then a severe threat to its democratic character.

The fraught and fragile state of democracy in the US causes anxiety among allies and encourages adversaries. The practical consequences for American credibility and power abroad are complicated. Russian President Vladimir Putin may well have reassured himself with a narrative of American decline and disorder that his invasion of Ukraine would encounter no effective Western opposition. This was obviously a mistake. Most Republicans in Congress continue to have a hawkish and interventionist outlook towards foreign policy, lending Biden's hardline Russia and China policies bipartisan support. That said, the new nationalist populism on the right includes a rising isolationist strand. A University of Maryland public-opinion survey conducted in June 2022 showed significantly less willingness among Republican than Democratic voters to accept sacrifices such as rising energy prices in support of Ukraine. And there is the prospect of Trump himself returning to the White House in 2025. Whatever course the war has taken by then, his return would raise questions about the future of US policy, given Trump's affinity for Putin and his attempt in July 2019 to pressure Ukraine's President Volodymyr Zelenskyy into providing him with information that might be politically damaging to Biden.

More broadly, a future of chronic electoral and constitutional disputes, even short of violence, where each side fundamentally rejects the other side's legitimate right to govern, would diminish the appeal of the American democratic example abroad and likely embolden democracy's adversaries. A fractured American polity would both reflect and amplify an increasingly fractious global system.

The US Withdrawal from Afghanistan
Have the lessons of failure been learned?

Early in President Joe Biden's presidency, hopes were expressed in *Strategic Survey* and elsewhere that his senior National Security Council (NSC) appointees would substantially reconstitute and implement the regimented and deliberate inter-agency national-security decision-making process that president Donald Trump had largely abandoned.

The United States' chaotic withdrawal from Afghanistan, involving tens of thousands of Afghan nationals clamouring desperately for scarce seats on aircraft departing from Kabul International Airport as the Taliban closed in on and seized Kabul and vicinity, cast some doubt on this prospect. Although the administration harboured a standing preoccupation of avoiding the optics of the 1975 American pull-out from Saigon, its conduct of the Afghanistan withdrawal ended up conjuring painful comparisons to it. Bipartisan consensus, however, supported a prompt withdrawal.

US officials going back to the Obama administration, both Democratic and Republican, had come to view the George W. Bush administration's determination to extend obligatory retaliation for the 9/11 attacks on the US homeland into optional US-engineered nation-building as ill-advised overreach. In 2010, when Biden himself was vice president, he had dissented from the Obama administration's continuation of full-blown counter-insurgency in Afghanistan, preferring a leaner 'counter-terrorism plus' approach. Furthermore, the withdrawal deal that the Trump administration reached with the Taliban on 29 February 2020 – known as the Doha Agreement – established deadlines that imposed a sense of urgency. Under the terms of the agreement, NATO would withdraw all its troops from Afghanistan, the Taliban would prevent al-Qaeda from operating in areas under Taliban control and talks on a 'permanent and comprehensive ceasefire' would be held between the Taliban and the Afghan government. The US agreed to initially reduce deployed forces from some 13,000 to 8,600 troops by July 2020, followed by a full withdrawal within 14 months (that is, by 1 May 2021) provided the Taliban met its obligations. The US also agreed to close five military bases within 135 days and to end economic sanctions against the Taliban by 27 August 2020.

Between 10 March 2020 and 20 January 2021, when Biden took office, the Trump administration had drawn down the number of US troops in Afghanistan from 13,800 to 2,500. A resolute US withdrawal, whatever its operational details, appeared overdetermined: any administration – Republican or Democratic – would have felt compelled to implement it for the sake of ending the 'forever war' that began after the 11 September 2001 attacks and had become a strategic and political liability for US leaders. Although some US officials hoped that the Afghan government would retain control over the country or reach an accommodation with the Taliban, most believed that the Taliban would eventually prevail. Sacrificing the gains for democratic governance and equal rights (in particular, those of women) that the Afghan people had won through US-led sponsorship and protection was viewed as unfortunate but unavoidable.

By 30 August 2021, the US had airlifted an estimated 124,000 people from Afghanistan, including 2,000 embassy personnel, 5,500 American citizens, 2,000 citizens of NATO countries, 3,300 citizens of other countries, 2,500 Afghans who had worked for the US holding US Special Immigrant Visas and their family members, and 64,000 'at risk' Afghans – that is, those who had helped the US and its allies in various ways and were therefore vulnerable to Taliban retaliation. More than a third of the total, however, left on private or non-US aircraft. The administration characterised the evacuation as a resounding success. But it was conducted in disarray and danger. The final effort to withdraw Afghan nationals and those Americans remaining as the Taliban took Kabul was an improvised, poorly organised undertaking involving private-sector and veterans' groups as well as the US government. 13 American military personnel died in a terrorist suicide bombing on 26 August 2021 that also wounded some 45 more US military personnel and killed at least 170 Afghans. Others were crushed to death in separate incidents. An errant US drone strike, intended to target terrorists from Islamic State in Khorasan Province (ISIS–KP), also killed ten innocent Afghan civilians as the withdrawal was being completed on 29 August. According to Human Rights First, a US-based organisation, about 90% of at-risk Afghans were left behind. The chaotic and perilous nature of the withdrawal appeared to be attributable primarily to the Biden administration's failure to anticipate the Taliban's rapid advance.

The role of US decision-making

On 14 April 2021, in a speech from the White House, Biden said that while it was 'time to end the forever war', the US withdrawal would not be 'a hasty rush to the exit' and would be done 'responsibly, deliberately, and safely'. Revising the Doha Agreement's 1 May 2021 deadline for US troop withdrawal to 11 September 2021, he expressed confidence that the 352,000-strong Afghan National Defense and Security Forces (ANDSF) trained and equipped by the US would fight the Taliban effectively. Reinforcing the president's sanguine view of the ANDSF's capabilities in testimony before the House Foreign Affairs Committee on 18 May 2021, Zalmay Khalilzad, the US special representative for Afghanistan reconciliation, downplayed the possibility of a rapid Taliban takeover after the departure of US forces. He stated that any Taliban attempt at military victory would 'result in a long war'. On the same day, however, the Department of Defense Office of the Inspector General released a quarterly report indicating that the Taliban and al-Qaeda were preparing for 'large-scale offensives'. Meanwhile, president Ashraf Ghani asked US officials not to start evacuating Afghan nationals too far in advance of final withdrawal for fear of signalling Washington's loss of faith in the Afghan government.

On 8 July 2021, Biden moved the withdrawal deadline forward again, this time to 31 August, because the Taliban's offensive was posing increased risks to US personnel. He continued to publicly manifest confidence in the ANDSF, though his words were more qualified and subdued. He merely stated that a Taliban takeover of Afghanistan 'was not inevitable' and denied that US intelligence had assessed that Afghan security forces would likely collapse. According to a senior White House official, 'there was nobody anywhere in our government, even up until a day or two before Kabul fell, that foresaw the collapse of the government and army before the end of our troop withdrawal at the end of August, and most of the projections were that there would still be weeks to months before we faced the very real prospect of the collapse of Kabul'. The city fell to the Taliban on 15 August.

Almost all intelligence assessments regarding Afghanistan are still classified. Based on open sources, US officials overall failed to accurately assess the Taliban's strength compared with that of Afghan government forces and gravely miscalculated how quickly they would take control of the country. Secretary of Defense Lloyd Austin and Chairman of the Joint Chiefs of Staff General Mark Milley expressed surprise at the Afghan security forces' abject failure. Milley's statement at an 18 August 2021 press briefing was especially telling. He said that the intelligence indicated that

> multiple scenarios were possible. One of those was an outright Taliban takeover following a rapid collapse of the Afghan security forces and the government. Another was a civil war. And a third, was a negotiated settlement. However, the timeframe of a … collapse … ranged from weeks to months and even years following our departure. There was nothing that I or anyone else saw that indicated a collapse of this army and this government in 11 days.

Milley's phrasing hinted that the array of possibilities presented to senior officials at NSC meetings may have obscured lower-level intelligence assessments that rated rapid collapse as the most probable. More broadly, the NSC might have held fast against contrary indications because Biden himself was averse to temporising and insisted on sticking to a set plan. National Security Advisor Jake Sullivan reportedly shared reservations that Pentagon and intelligence officials (including Milley himself) had lodged about the planned timetable months prior to the withdrawal, though Secretary of State Antony Blinken reportedly supported the timetable. Reported comments by intelligence officials implied that intelligence agencies had long harboured pessimism about the US train-and-equip mission.

By July 2021, the CIA was suggesting that the Taliban would likely control Kabul within weeks. But it is customary for the intelligence community to be more pessimistic than the rest of the inter-agency community, and for the Pentagon and the State Department to discount its assessments. Some embassy personnel, however, came around to a pessimistic assessment. On 13 July, the US embassy in Kabul transmitted a 'dissent cable' to Blinken, signed by around two dozen officials, warning that the Taliban were advancing quickly and that the Afghan government could collapse in a matter of weeks, and urging the Biden administration to start evacuating qualified Afghans.

Furthermore, the Special Inspector General for Afghanistan Reconstruction's (SIGAR) July 2021 quarterly report to Congress and SIGAR interviews with US military trainers published by the *Washington Post* confirmed that American personnel interacting directly with the ANDSF recognised significant flaws. These included a high incidence of desertion, police recruits' theft of US-provided supplies and salaries being allocated to non-existent Afghan soldiers in order for Afghan commanders to pocket them. The *Post* concluded that none of the trainers was confident that the Afghan security forces 'could ever fend off, much less defeat, the Taliban on their own'.

The intelligence community and Department of Defense and State Department personnel with the highest visibility on the ground in Afghanistan, then, had grown deeply sceptical of the ANDSF's ability to contain the Taliban by summer 2021. Classified notes from an NSC Deputies Small Group meeting in the White House Situation Room on 14 August – the day before Kabul fell – leaked to the press, however, indicated that basic assignments and taskings for mass civilian evacuation were then still under discussion and unexecuted. Although some US and allied troops were pre-positioned to facilitate secure evacuations, most American military personnel had already been withdrawn and resources for civilian protection were therefore minimal. The NSC had not tasked agencies to prepare for an evacuation under duress. It had not created an inter-agency task force to coordinate resources, involved NATO allies in planning, gathered the names and contact details of Afghans warranting evacuation, initiated a soft roll-out of the evacuation by organising flights on commercial aircraft, composed and rehearsed emergency plans, or explored ways to incentivise the Taliban – such as early sanctions relief and qualified diplomatic recognition – to ease the withdrawal.

Intelligence, defence and diplomatic officials may have discounted pessimistic assessments in developing analyses to inform inter-agency deliberations in NSC meetings. This would have nourished wishful thinking among policymakers about the independent capabilities of the Afghan government and security forces, and continued a pattern of bureaucratic politics distorting US decision-making. US officials were heavily invested in building an effective Afghan force. Over the course of 20 years, the US had spent US$88 billion on Afghanistan's security sector. For over half of that period, US policy focused on establishing conditions for the withdrawal of US forces and handing over the national-security mission to the ANDSF. Even so, many US officials were critical of the decision to leave. In Vietnam in 1975 and Iraq in 2014, civilian intelligence officers and lower-level military personnel were in fact sceptical that local forces trained and equipped by the US were adequately prepared to stand up to their adversaries on their own, but their superiors favoured rosier outlooks that were more consistent with White House policy, reinforcing rather than challenging confidence in that policy. A similar dynamic appears to have taken hold for Afghanistan.

The NSC's comparatively deft handling of the subsequent crisis created by Russia's aggression against Ukraine suggests that it has learned from its mistakes in Afghanistan. Although the intelligence community's assessments that Russia intended to invade Ukraine as it massed troops near Ukraine's border were daunting and unwelcome, senior officials in the inter-agency community heeded them. As a result, the US and its allies were able to help orchestrate a remarkably swift, cohesive and forceful Western response to Russia's invasion. Greater candour between US policymakers and the intelligence community also appeared to facilitate the Biden administration's innovative instrumentalisation of declassified intelligence to counter Russian propaganda and deception. After a serious and conspicuous stumble, Biden's national-security team appeared to re-establish a robust and effective inter-agency decision-making process. It is likely that senior NSC staff learned broad lessons from the Afghanistan debacle about managing the inter-agency process, and in particular, how best to present options to the president so as to promote the one they considered most advisable.

Afghanistan in retrospect

It was perhaps fanciful for US officials to expect the Taliban, having demonstrated a degree of resilience and persistence comparable to that of the Vietcong during the Vietnam War, to exercise self-restraint with a hostile power that had occupied their country for almost 20 years. Indeed, the group had demonstrated its defiance during the six weeks following the signing of the Doha Agreement by increasing its attacks on Afghan security forces by 70%, killing 900 national and local personnel, compared to 520 in the same period a year earlier. Slightly more understandable was the American failure to anticipate just how fast the Taliban would move or how precipitously the ANDSF – long abandoned by the ministries responsible for them and then by the Americans – would fold.

The evolved view of American leaders that taming the Taliban and remaking Afghanistan into a modern democratic state was futile, and that the US was compelled to cut its losses, appears to have been correct. The US also had other compelling reasons to disengage. It was in the early stages of a massive redirection of American military assets to the Indo-Pacific region that began during the Obama administration and continued under Trump. To carry forward this strategic shift, the US needed to extricate itself from Afghanistan. As for Biden's political calculations, he had the option not to honour Trump's deal and to delay the US withdrawal. But he seemed to regard the Doha Agreement as a kind of political cover for something he was going to do anyway, convinced that a US withdrawal in any circumstances would be unruly and inclined to tear off the Band-Aid.

There were several reasons the US could not succeed in Afghanistan. The salient factors are familiar from the lessons of the Vietnam War. These were obscured by the First Gulf War in 1991 and forgotten after 9/11, when US officials concluded that launching a global counter-insurgency against transnational jihadists was necessary to protect the US homeland. But most indigenous insurgencies are more committed to winning a war on home territory than outside parties are to preventing this. In addition, democracies like the US lack tolerance for expeditionary military engagements – especially protracted efforts like counter-insurgency and nation-building – that are costly in blood and treasure and do not implicate vital US strategic interests. Such interests are not at present vital in Afghanistan, which poses no major threat to US security.

Successful counter-insurgencies also require a level of brutality on the part of the victor that is at odds with the American military ethos and international standards. From case studies in *Bullets Not Ballots: Success in Counterinsurgency Warfare*, Jacqueline L. Hazelton convincingly concludes that insurgencies are defeated not by 'winning hearts and minds' through the provision of social services, economic assistance and democratisation, but rather by brute force in conjunction with the political cooperation of pro-government elites. The Taliban were not susceptible to these methods because the Pashtun tribe that composed them was so deeply rooted in Afghan culture and society. Simultaneously Afghan presidents Hamid Karzai and Ashraf Ghani could not secure the collaboration of Afghan regional leaders due to government corruption, ineptitude and lassitude.

Furthermore, the world was not the same in August 2021 as it was on 9/11. The alliance between the Taliban and al-Qaeda had fitfully survived the long US-led intervention, and both al-Qaeda and the Islamic State (ISIS) had a presence in Afghanistan. But al-Qaeda has been decentralised and diminished over the past 20 years, and ISIS, which had become more potent than al-Qaeda and may remain so, has been rolled back and may remain largely confined to the greater Middle East, even if it is resurging in parts of the region. Neither was now intent on staging mass-casualty attacks on the US homeland, US allies and partners, and American interests. The US-led intervention in 2001, disruption of al-Qaeda activity, ouster of the Taliban from power and subsequent counter-terrorism operations may have partially deterred the Taliban from proactively sponsoring any group with such aims.

At the same time, mutual accommodation between the Taliban and al-Qaeda remains viable. Although the Doha Agreement incorporates a Taliban pledge not to allow al-Qaeda to operate in areas under Taliban control, the US has relatively little leverage to enforce it even as it gradually moves away from the economic and political isolation it imposed immediately after the withdrawal towards limited engagement. The Taliban would not mount a sustained and proactive effort to suppress jihadist activity without additional inducements such as sanctions relief, some measure of diplomatic recognition and economic aid. Even if these were conferred, however, Taliban restrictions on jihadist groups' freedom of action in Afghanistan would tend to be grudging and regarded by its leadership as strictly transactional. CIA Director William Burns has told Congress that at some point al-Qaeda or a like-minded group would almost certainly find secure haven in Afghanistan and re-embrace Osama bin Laden's doctrine of engaging the 'far enemy' by targeting the US and attempting to use Afghanistan as a base. If this happens, the US may be compelled to take suppressive measures using proven counter-terrorism methods, including lethal targeting and regional law-enforcement and intelligence cooperation.

In the face of long, costly wars undertaken as part of a politically ambitious and geopolitically expansive post-9/11 US policy centred on the greater Middle East, impulses of selectivity and retrenchment initially motivated the United States' messy withdrawal from Afghanistan. Burgeoning great-power competition rendered it more urgent to end what had become strategically peripheral commitments and devote greater attention and resources to core ones in Europe and the Indo-Pacific. The US military campaign in Afghanistan was successful in diminishing the Taliban's capacity as a terrorist host and facilitator and in establishing a limited deterrent against its full resumption of that status. On balance, although some US officials considered a continued US presence in Afghanistan sustainable and advisable, the withdrawal reflected a painful American acceptance of the failure of its larger objective of building Afghanistan into a modern democratic state, and a belated acknowledgement that attempting to achieve it was unrealistic from the outset.

The Biden Administration and the Indo-Pacific
What challenges face the new US strategy?

Joe Biden is the third consecutive US president to declare the Indo-Pacific region his top priority. Shortly after coming into office, and following the publication of its 'Interim National Security Strategic Guidance' in March 2021, his new administration engaged in a series of region-centric efforts. These began with a high-profile trip by the secretaries of defense and state to the region in March and the hosting of key allies Japan and South Korea at the White House in April. The surprise announcement of AUKUS and a virtual summit of the leaders of the Quadrilateral Security Dialogue ('Quad') followed in the autumn. In early 2022, the administration released its 'Indo-Pacific Strategy'.

An assessment of three lines of activity – the Indo-Pacific strategy, bilateral-alliance relationships and the Quad – shows both the strengths and challenges of the Biden administration's approach to the region. Russia's war against Ukraine has the potential to make matters more difficult in the year ahead.

Indo-Pacific Strategy

Released in February 2022, the Biden administration's 'Indo-Pacific Strategy' advocates freedom and openness in the region by pledging to support regional connectivity, trade and investment and deepening bilateral and multilateral partnerships.

The strategy summarises the state of US–China relations, citing the 'mounting challenges' posed by the rise of China as a key driver of the 'intensifying American focus' on the region. Specifically, it refers to China's 'coercion and aggression [that] spans the globe' but goes on to highlight its use of economic, diplomatic, military and technological instruments to pursue a 'sphere of influence in the Indo-Pacific'. The strategy states that the US objective is not to change China but to build a 'balance of influence in the world that is maximally favorable to the United States, our allies and partners, and the interests and values that we share'. It sets out five objectives: 1) advance a free and open

Indo-Pacific; 2) build connections within and beyond the region; 3) drive regional prosperity; 4) bolster Indo-Pacific security; and 5) build regional resilience to transnational threats.

The strategy has two major strengths. Firstly, by being broadly similar to preceding strategic guidance, it ensures consistency in Washington's focus on the region. The Trump administration adopted the Free and Open Indo-Pacific (FOIP) strategy from Japan – with some changes – and the Biden administration maintained its language and core tenets even as it pivoted away from an 'America First' outlook to one that elevated allies and partners. The strategy's continued focus on the region, and advocacy of openness and the rule of law, helps maintain the support of regional countries which also adopted the FOIP concept. This is not limited to the Indo-Pacific: the strategy explicitly welcomes European engagement and commitment to upholding a free and open regional order.

Secondly, while the strategy maintains an emphasis on the centrality of the region, it puts greater weight on cooperation with regional allies and partners. The strategy's mix of deepening America's five regional-treaty alliances, strengthening relationships with leading regional partners, and efforts to 'manage competition' with China 'responsibly' (including finding ways to 'work with' Beijing 'in areas like climate change and nonproliferation') amounts to a more deliberate and strategic approach to the region. The Biden administration's resolution of contentious host-nation support agreements with Tokyo and Seoul, and continuation of a more visible outreach to Taiwan, shows that it recognises the value of sustained engagement.

But the strategy has two challenges. Firstly, though it identifies the region as a priority and advocates freedom and openness, several important areas appear to be lacking. For example, there is little detail about the Pacific Islands, leaving questions about how the US wants to engage with this part of the Indo-Pacific region. Similarly, while the strategy maintains the familiar US focus on the centrality of the Association of Southeast Asian Nations (ASEAN), it is unclear what the US wants to achieve by investing in US–ASEAN ties or committing to ASEAN-centric fora. And despite the administration's focus on the economic importance of the region, the strategy is silent on the Comprehensive and Progressive Agreement for Trans-Pacific Partnership (CPTPP). The strategy repackages existing programmes on supply-chain resilience, clean energy and infrastructure, but fails to show leadership in any free-trade agreements (FTAs). The administration's emphasis on the Indo-Pacific Economic Framework for Prosperity (IPEF), and lack of initiative to participate in the primary multilateral regional FTA, leaves the US without any voice in the growing web of trade agreements being created by regional actors.

Secondly, despite the changing nature of the Indo-Pacific region and its growing interconnectedness with other regions, the strategy appears to be centred on China rather than the region as a whole. Although the strategy maintains that it addresses more than US–China competition, it identifies Chinese activities as its primary concern and details Washington's intention to counter Beijing's growing clout through efforts to strengthen the collective capacities of US allies and partners. Less clear is what the US wants to achieve that is not defined by its response to a rising China.

Key regional relations

Despite claims that the Biden administration is taking a fundamentally different approach to the Indo-Pacific region from the Trump presidency, Washington's tough China policy has not changed much. But while the Trump administration can be criticised for taking a hard line with key allies even as it pursued a tough China policy, the Biden administration has sought to elevate its engagement with allies and partners as part of the ongoing strategic competition with China.

Key bilateral allies

The 'Indo-Pacific Strategy' emphasises 'alliances and partnerships' and the Biden administration has sought to reinvigorate its relations with Australia, Japan, the Philippines, South Korea and Thailand to repair the strains that each alliance experienced during the Trump administration.

As both candidate and president, Donald Trump criticised Japan and South Korea regularly and dismissed their value as allies. He also took a tough approach to negotiation of their respective bilateral Special Measures Agreements, which outline the host nation's burden-sharing costs. The Biden administration, by contrast, sought to reiterate the value of these allies and demonstrate US commitment to their defence, meeting with the leaders of both countries, engaging officials at different levels and working to resolve host-nation support agreements.

With Australia, despite a disparaging phone call between Trump and prime minister Malcolm Turnbull, bilateral ties were never bad. But Canberra was troubled by Trump's 'America First' turn from multilateralism toward more bilateralism or even isolationism. The Biden administration's task was to reassure Australia that America's commitment to the region was firm and to demonstrate US resolve to reinvigorate its alliances. This bore fruit with Biden's announcement in September 2021 of the AUKUS agreement promising closer military and technological ties between Australia, the United Kingdom and the US. The agreement will see Washington and London share nuclear-propulsion technology to help Canberra develop a nuclear-powered Australian submarine fleet.

With the Philippines, although president Rodrigo Duterte leaned closer to China early in his presidency, Chinese actions slowly led him to improve ties with the US. This was aided by Washington's donation of about six million COVID-19 vaccines, and its statement of US commitment (per Article IV of the Mutual Defense Treaty) to come to the Philippines' defence in the South China Sea. Both were welcomed in Manila. The restoration of the bilateral Visiting Forces Agreement in July 2021 testified to the significant improvement in ties. Perhaps Thailand, whose military government benefitted from Trump's de-emphasis of human rights and democratic norms in favour of geostrategic interests, may most regret his departure. That said, the Biden administration has sought to minimise friction even as it restores a values-based element to foreign policy.

The Biden administration's efforts to restore close alliance ties face two challenges. The first is to find objectives where the interests of the US and its allies overlap. More difficult than rebuilding regional-alliance ties will be agreeing a shared direction of travel for its diverse relationships, especially on issues relating to its China policy.

This will likely be easiest with Japan and Australia, where ongoing coercive Chinese activity in the region has encouraged both Tokyo and Canberra not only to beef up their own defence initiatives but also to assume more ambitious roles in the region. But challenges remain. It is still not clear in Washington how far Tokyo is willing to involve itself in a potential regional conflict that is not tied to Japan's defence. And there are still voices in Japan questioning US commitment to its defence, sparking domestic debates over nuclear sharing. For Canberra, there are questions over whether Washington's competition with Beijing can be managed in such a way that it does not isolate Beijing, given the latter's economic and diplomatic weight. And for both, continued US absence from the CPTPP undermines US credibility and leadership in the region.

With Seoul, the election of conservative Yoon Suk-yeol as president in March 2022 has raised American expectations that South Korea may be less inclined to appease China while also working to reinforce its alliance with the US, improve ties with Japan and increase its own regional role. Washington will also want to ensure that Seoul's North Korean policy is consistent with its own, and is not working at cross-purposes.

The new Philippine President Ferdinand Marcos Jr has also given rise to tempered expectations. It is unclear, however, how far the Philippines is willing to go to join the US in its competition with China, especially as Beijing has punished Manila several times for acting against its interests. Thailand could prove the most difficult case. Although ties have improved, the Biden administration did not invite Thailand to its democracy summit in December 2021. Should the US want to strengthen strategic ties, it will need to find the right balance between human rights and democracy concerns and security imperatives such as counter-terrorism and maritime-security issues.

The second challenge for the Biden administration is to ensure that key US allies work together. This is not new: historically, America's allies in its hub-and-spoke treaty system rarely worked together. But at a time when Australia and Japan have strengthened their bilateral ties and Japan and the Philippines are engaging in strategic dialogues and limited defence cooperation, friction between Japan and South Korea continues to frustrate Washington's approach to the region. Ensuring the US and its allies are in sync with their strategic objectives is challenging enough; Russia's invasion of Ukraine may exacerbate these difficulties if regional allies feel the US is distracted by competing priorities in Europe and may lose focus on the Indo-Pacific. This makes it more important not only for Washington to work with its allies, but also for its allies to work together.

The Biden administration has tried to foster this. Early on, it encouraged Seoul to strengthen trilateral cooperation with the US and Japan. This was followed by Biden's first face-to-face summit with an international leader at the White House when Japanese prime minister Suga Yoshihide visited in April 2021. A month later, he hosted South Korean president Moon Jae-in. Over the following year, the US supported meetings between officials of the two countries to discuss cooperation. In his first trip to the Indo-Pacific in May 2022, Biden visited both countries to deepen ties. With ongoing tensions with North Korea, continuing regional provocations by China and a host of non-traditional security challenges, US strategy would benefit from a more engaged trilateral relationship. Japan and South Korea have not yet been able to overcome their disagreements. And despite new leadership in both capitals, there is no guarantee that Seoul and Tokyo can agree a format to discuss their historical grievances while focusing on shared security concerns. The challenge for the Biden administration will be to find the right calibrated role to play to help its allies discuss their grievances, mend ties between them and focus on common strategic imperatives.

Quad

Like its outreach to its allies, the Biden administration is also engaged in minilateral endeavours. One of these is the Quad, which was revived under the Trump administration and has maintained its relevance under the Biden administration. The Quad's origin is rooted in the response of Australia, India, Japan and the US to the Indian Ocean tsunami in 2004. This attempt at a Quad 1.0 faded around 2008, only to be revived in 2012 by Japanese prime minister Abe Shinzo. But it was not until growing Chinese provocations against India and Australia combined with the Trump administration's eagerness to push back on China that Quad 2.0 found an interest among the four members once again. That meant that prior to the March 2021 virtual summit, the only recent meetings of the Quad were a 2017 gathering of member states on the sidelines of an ASEAN summit in Manila, and then ministerial-level meetings in 2019, 2020 and February 2021. Biden's agreement to push the gathering to the leader level for the first time was therefore critical in promoting it as a venue and elevating it to greater prominence.

Beyond this elevation, the Biden administration has sought to find ways to leverage the Quad's flexibility. Quad members share an interest in pushing back on Chinese influence that threatens their national interests and broader regional stability. But there are limits to what all Quad members are willing to do. The Biden administration has sought to sustain cohesion by focusing on broad objectives, such as securing the Quad Vaccine Partnership pledge to cooperate on the manufacturing and distribution of up to one billion doses of safe, accessible and effective vaccines to help end the coronavirus pandemic in the region.

But the administration faces the challenge of using the Quad more strategically. The grouping struggled to gain traction prior to 2017 because of the lack of common interest in pushing back on China due to its members' varying threat perceptions of, and relationships with, Beijing. More assertive Chinese regional behaviour has since provoked a stronger shared interest in resisting its growing influence. This enables the Quad to be used as a venue for more strategic dialogue and diplomatic endeavours. But interests and approaches to China may still change. This is particularly a concern for India, given its history of non-alignment. At the very least, it could make the Quad's involvement in the security domain rather limited.

Conclusion

By taking a firm line against China while elevating the importance of US partners, the Biden administration helps reassure anxious allies and partners that may be concerned about America's engagement in the region. But the lack of US participation in a trade agreement continues to be a weakness of its approach. Moreover, despite the strategy's use of terminology that regional countries appreciate – including references to a free, open, connected, prosperous and secure region – it remains unclear what the US wants from ASEAN centrality or greater engagement with the Pacific Islands. One of the biggest questions is how the Indo-Pacific strategy differs from a strategy meant to curb Chinese regional influence.

Furthermore, not every country views China primarily as a threat. Many see it as a major source of investment to grow their economy and build critical infrastructure. The US has to find a middle way that ensures that its regional interests are protected while not asking regional countries to choose sides. At the same time, the Biden administration's public comments about US commitment to Taiwan's defence show it is prepared to push the boundaries of strategic ambiguity. Less clear is how ready its allies and partners are to deepen their involvement in Taiwan-related issues.

Since February 2022, the Biden administration has faced the further challenge of implementing its Indo-Pacific strategy against the background of Russia's invasion of Ukraine. While the administration maintains that the US can sustain 'deep commitments' in both theatres simultaneously, its ability to do so will draw scrutiny. The length and severity of the war in Europe may be a decisive factor. Only time will tell.

©IISS

Drivers of Strategic Change

REGIONAL SHARE OF GLOBAL POPULATION, GDP AND DEFENCE BUDGET

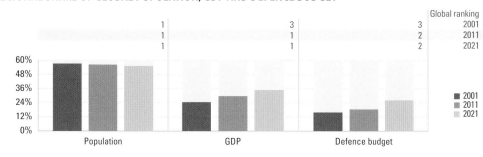

	Global ranking
1 3 3	2001
1 1 2	2011
1 1 2	2021

Legend: 2001, 2011, 2021

Categories: Population, GDP, Defence budget

POPULATION

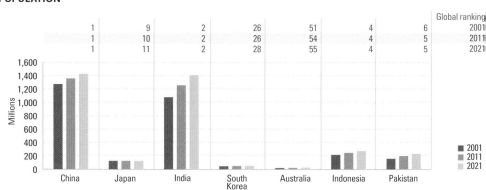

Global ranking							
1	9	2	26	51	4	6	2001
1	10	2	26	54	4	5	2011
1	11	2	28	55	4	5	2021

(Millions)

Countries: China, Japan, India, South Korea, Australia, Indonesia, Pakistan

Legend: 2001, 2011, 2021

AGE STRUCTURE
(Percentage of national population)

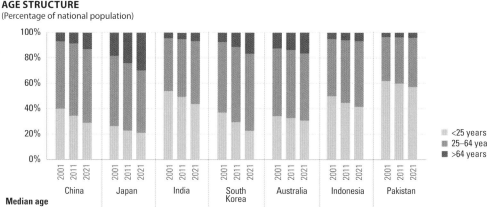

Legend: <25 years, 25–64 yea, >64 years

Median age	China	Japan	India	South Korea	Australia	Indonesia	Pakistan
2001	29.5	41.1	21.7	31.2	34.7	24.0	17.4
2011	34.5	44.5	24.3	37.3	36.2	27.0	19.0
2021	37.9	48.4	27.6	43.4	37.0	29.4	20.2

Asia has the biggest GDP and population of any region. It is also the most diverse, with huge variations in power, prosperity and governmental accountability. China's remarkable economic growth has fuelled huge rises in defence spending and living standards. But a rising median age – higher than America's – presages future population decline.

GDP
(Constant 2010 US dollars)

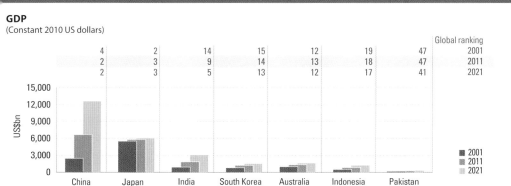

GDP PER CAPITA
(Constant 2010 US dollars)

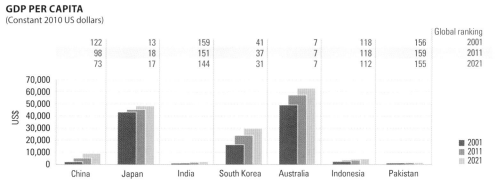

DEFENCE BUDGET
(Constant 2015 US dollars)

ACTIVE MILITARY PERSONNEL

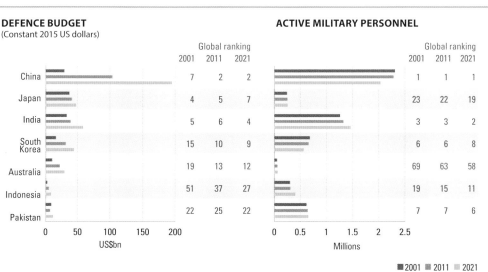

For explanation of drivers and sources, see page 8

HUMAN DEVELOPMENT INDEX (HDI)
(Score between 0 and 1, where 0 denotes a low level of development and 1 a high level of development)

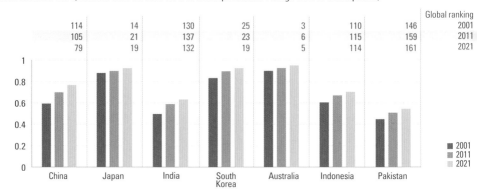

POLITICAL SYSTEM
(Score between 0 and 100, where 0 denotes no political freedom and 100 fully free)

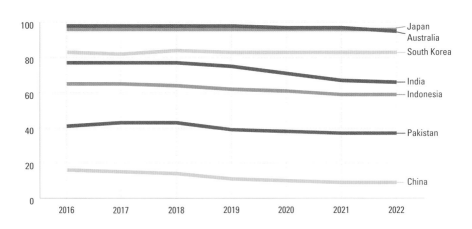

TRUST IN GOVERNMENT
(Average level of trust)

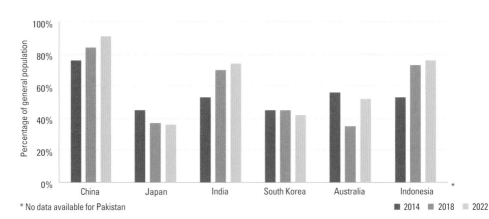

* No data available for Pakistan

For explanation of drivers and sources, see page

2021–22 Review

Indo-Pacific

As most Asian countries began their recovery from the economic, social and political impacts of the coronavirus pandemic, inter-state security concerns were prominent throughout the region. Russia's invasion of Ukraine in February 2022, widely viewed as a major blow to international order, only reinforced such concerns. The Indo-Pacific regional power balance remained in flux: China's economic and military power continued to grow, despite the continuing major domestic impact of the pandemic, and it maintained its quest for strategic advantage across the region. While some regional states – notably Australia and Japan – actively supported efforts led by the United States to counter China's growing power and influence, most Asian governments showed little enthusiasm for 'taking sides' despite Beijing exerting pressure on their geopolitical interests.

Unlike most countries in the Indo-Pacific and across the globe, China maintained a policy of attempting to eradicate COVID-19 rather than mitigate its impact. Fearing the potential toll on China's population of 1.4 billion of even a low mortality rate if it abandoned its zero-COVID policy (one study suggesting that 1.5 million deaths were likely), the leadership in Beijing chose to rely on mass-testing and quarantine measures to control the spread of the virus, despite 87% of the population reportedly having been fully vaccinated by June 2022. In early and mid-2022 there were protracted lockdowns in major cities, including Shanghai. These measures impacted China's economy adversely, challenging the country's ability to meet its 5.5% annual GDP growth target. More effective vaccines currently under development in China – including one employing mRNA technology – might ultimately give its leaders the confidence to move towards 'living with COVID', but such a policy shift seemed unlikely to occur during 2022.

Meanwhile, China's growing power and strategic extroversion continued to impact the Indo-Pacific. Taiwan, which Chinese Communist Party (CCP) leaders and People's Liberation Army (PLA) commanders alike stressed must be reintegrated with the People's Republic, was particularly affected. At the 19th IISS Shangri-La Dialogue in June 2022, for example, Minister of National Defense General Wei Fenghe reiterated China's core policy positions on Taiwan: China will 'definitely realise' reunification with Taiwan; any attempt to 'pursue Taiwan independence' would lead China to 'fight at all costs and … to the very end'; and 'foreign interference is doomed to failure'.

As well as firm statements from its leaders, Beijing ordered frequent flights into Taiwan's Air Defence Identification Zone by PLA aircraft, possibly in part to exert pressure on Taipei. Some of these missions, such as those in January and May 2022, involved 30 or more aircraft. While they may have had training purposes or, in some cases, have been intended to track US submarines as well as those of other countries, the flights were interpreted by Taipei as intimidatory and designed to erode the effectiveness of Taiwan's air defences through repeated alerts and scrambles. Other instances of what US Secretary of Defense Lloyd Austin, speaking at the Shangri-La Dialogue, called 'provocative and destabilising military activity' included PLA live-fire exercises near Taiwan in August 2021 and April 2022. The Biden administration was also reportedly perturbed by the assertion by Chinese officials in bilateral meetings during the first half of 2022 that the Taiwan Strait was not international waters, a position that a Chinese foreign-ministry spokesman reinforced in June 2022 when he said that Beijing exercised 'sovereignty' there.

There was much speculation by observers from the US and elsewhere over whether and when China might use its military power to force Taiwan's reintegration. In March 2022, Commander of US Indo-Pacific Command (INDOPACOM) Admiral John Aquilino told the House Armed Services Committee that Russia's invasion of Ukraine had reinforced concerns that China might attack Taiwan, and said that the US should 'look very closely' at whether its policy of 'strategic ambiguity' towards defending Taiwan should be more clear-cut. Austin noted that the US was maintaining its 'capacity to resist any use of force or other forms of coercion that would jeopardise the security or the social or economic system of the people of Taiwan'. However, ambiguity prevailed:

while President Joe Biden indicated in August and October 2021, and again in May 2022, that the US was willing to defend Taiwan militarily, on each occasion White House officials quickly denied that there had been any change to US policy. Nevertheless, the US was evidently increasing its efforts to strengthen Taiwan's capacity to defend itself. By April 2022 the Biden administration had confirmed three major sales of defence equipment to Taipei since taking office.

Japan also felt Chinese pressure. In May 2022, Tokyo protested to Beijing over China's attempts, including the positioning of drilling rigs, to develop natural-gas resources in an area of the East China Sea where a 2008 bilateral agreement had banned unilateral drilling and Exclusive Economic Zone (EEZ) and continental-shelf borders remained to be settled. Moreover, according to Tokyo, in June 2022 two China Coast Guard ships spent more than 64 hours in waters near the Senkaku/Diaoyu islands, which are controlled by Japan but claimed by China. This was the longest incursion in more than a decade. The PLA also continued naval and air activity close to Japan's home islands: in June, a task force of four PLA Navy (PLAN) ships sailed through the Tsushima Strait and then around the Japanese archipelago, while PLA bombers and electronic-warfare aircraft flew over the Miyako Strait to the Pacific Ocean. As with Chinese flights close to Taiwan, these may not have been intentionally intimidatory, but they nevertheless provoked Japanese air-defence aircraft to scramble and monitor the PLA aircraft.

The Japanese government led by Kishida Fumio, who became prime minister in October 2021, continued developing a tougher security posture intended to deter Chinese 'grey-zone' coercion as well as any potential larger-scale aggression. In November, Kishida's cabinet approved a supplementary budget that boosted annual defence spending to more than 6 trillion yen for the first time. The inclusion of equipment funding that had not been expected until the following fiscal year emphasised the urgency of Japan's defence build-up. During the same month, it was reported that Tokyo would adopt a new National Security Strategy – the first since 2013 – in late 2022, with the intention of fundamentally reinforcing Japan's military capabilities even if this required substantially increased defence spending. In his keynote address to the Shangri-La Dialogue, Kishida said that no military options, including 'counter-strike capabilities' to deter missile attacks, would be ruled out. Meanwhile, Japan's alliance with the US remained fundamental to its international security policy, with Biden's visit to Tokyo in May 2022 providing an opportunity to expand and deepen bilateral security and defence cooperation.

Under Kishida, Japan also continued to develop a more active economic and security role in its region. With the intention of promoting a 'rules-based' international order – and implicitly a regional environment conducive to Japan's economic and security interests – his administration promoted the Free and Open Indo-Pacific (FOIP) concept that Abe Shinzo had inaugurated when prime minister in 2016. FOIP had found favour with many of Japan's Western economic and security partners, including several European countries and the European Union as well as Australia and the US, which all adopted their own versions of the concept. Kishida emphasised his government's view that cooperating with Southeast Asia and the South Pacific was also vital to realising the 'grand vision' of the doctrine, announcing that Japan would increase its official development assistance to these sub-regions. He also revealed that Japan would set out a FOIP 'plan for peace' by early 2023, which would see Tokyo helping to strengthen the maritime law-enforcement capabilities 'of at least 20 countries' over the following three years.

The Quadrilateral Security Dialogue (referred to almost universally as 'the Quad') – involving Australia, India and the US as well as Japan – increased in importance as a vector for Tokyo's regional policies. In September 2021, Kishida joined Biden, the then-prime minister of Australia Scott Morrison and Indian Prime Minister Narendra Modi in Washington DC for the first-ever in-person Quad Leaders' Summit, which adopted wide-ranging initiatives relating to the production and regional distribution of COVID-19 vaccines, high-quality infrastructural development, climate-change mitigation and adaptation, critical and emerging technologies including 5G telecommunications, cyber security and exchange of satellite data. In late May 2022, the next Quad summit in Tokyo (involving Australia's new Prime Minister Anthony Albanese, who had only taken office the previous day) unveiled an Indo-Pacific Partnership for Maritime Domain Awareness (IPMDA), intended to promote information-sharing among regional countries, particularly in the Indian Ocean, Southeast Asia and the South Pacific. Japan also intensified its bilateral security cooperation with Australia; the two countries signed a Reciprocal Access Agreement in January 2022 with the intention of enhancing cooperative military activities involving visiting forces.

Together, these developments underlined the earnestness of Japan's response to its deteriorating regional security environment. However, Tokyo did not see the security threats it faced only in terms of a growing challenge from Beijing to regional order and Japanese interests. While Kishida referred to the lack of compliance with international law in the South China Sea, 'unilateral attempts to change the status quo by force' in the East China Sea and the challenge of maintaining peace 'across the Taiwan Strait', he did not explicitly identify China as the source of the threat. Indeed, he referred more directly to the unwelcome impact on international order of Russia's invasion of Ukraine and North Korea's nuclear and missile activities. This rhetorical restraint regarding a major Chinese security challenge, that was widely recognised not just among politicians from the government's Liberal Democratic Party (LDP) but also increasingly at the popular level, reflected an effort by Kishida's administration to assert a nuanced policy towards China. While wary of Beijing, this policy recognised the continuing importance of economic and diplomatic engagement. The Japanese government's economic agenda for 2022 included legislation that could lead to focused decoupling from China in critical and emerging technologies, but Japanese business sentiment remained favourable towards China. Tokyo's engagement in the Regional Comprehensive Economic Partnership (RCEP), which came into effect at the start of 2022, indicated the importance for Japan of maintaining overall economic cooperation with China.

The dilemmas inherent in managing relations with China were also felt in Southeast Asia. Economic links were more important than ever: China's total trade with the ten member states of the Association of

Southeast Asian Nations (ASEAN) almost doubled between 2013 and 2021. Yet growing economic power did not win it commensurate influence in the sub-region. One important reason was Beijing's continuing efforts to assert control over the South China Sea, which conflicted with the claims of several ASEAN members (most importantly the Philippines and Vietnam), impinged on the maritime interests of others and cast doubt on China's overall trustworthiness. In March 2022, US INDOPACOM's Admiral Aquilino claimed that China had 'fully militarized' at least three of the features in the Spratly Islands that it occupied, contrary to Chinese President Xi Jinping's assertion to former US president Barack Obama in 2015 that Beijing did not intend 'to pursue militarization'. Soon afterwards, a spokesman for Vietnam's foreign ministry criticised China's militarisation efforts and asked Beijing to desist. In March, Vietnam for the first time officially commemorated its 1988 battle with Chinese forces at Johnson South Reef, in which 62 Vietnamese sailors and marines died. Meanwhile, the Philippines remained in the front line of Chinese pressure, protesting in May 2022 over the China Coast Guard's alleged harassment of a research vessel operating within Manila's EEZ. Both the Philippines and Vietnam also protested against China's imposition of a fishing ban lasting three and a half months in waters partially within their overlapping EEZs.

Amid growing geopolitical pressures, most Southeast Asian governments nevertheless showed every intention of keeping their geopolitical options open. This was seemingly acknowledged in the Biden administration's policy towards Southeast Asia which, in contrast to its predecessor's, carefully avoided putting any pressure on governments to 'take sides' between the US and China as these two major powers tried to maintain and increase their influence. Kurt Campbell, the US National Security Council's (NSC) Indo-Pacific coordinator, said shortly before the US–ASEAN special summit in Washington DC in May 2022 that the US recognised that any initiative simply designed for competing with China was 'likely to have difficulty gaining altitude in Asia'. Reflecting this logic, the Joint Vision Statement for the summit emphasised that the US Indo-Pacific strategy and the ASEAN Outlook on the Indo-Pacific shared 'fundamental principles in promoting an open, inclusive, and rules-based regional architecture, in which ASEAN is central'.

During the first half of 2022, considerable regional and international attention focused on Cambodia, which had taken over ASEAN's rotating chair in October 2021. The country's previous turn as chair in 2012 had been marked by controversy: ASEAN's first-ever failure to issue its traditional joint communiqué following its annual foreign ministers' meeting that year led critics to accuse Cambodia of siding with China. Subsequently, Cambodia came widely to be seen as enjoying the closest relationship among ASEAN members with Beijing.

This time, Phnom Penh seemed determined to demonstrate its effectiveness and even-handedness as chair. This was evident in relation to Myanmar, where a coup by the armed forces' leadership in February 2021 had deposed the elected government effectively led by State Counsellor Aung San Suu Kyi, leading to the outbreak of widespread armed rebellion. As ASEAN chair, Cambodia continued to exclude Myanmar's military regime from the association's meetings. In his capacity as ASEAN's special envoy to Myanmar, Cambodian Foreign Minister Prak Sokhonn visited the country in March 2022 and again from late June to early July. The Naypyidaw regime denied Prak Sokhonn access to Aung San Suu Kyi, who had been detained since the coup, but he continued pressing for a meeting with her and for her return from solitary confinement in jail to her previous state of house arrest. However, ASEAN's approach faced criticism within Southeast Asia and internationally from those who wanted to see it adopt a tougher posture towards Myanmar's military regime. Disappointed by the regime's failure to implement a five-point peace plan agreed by all ten ASEAN member states, in May 2022 Malaysia's government called on the association to open informal channels to Myanmar's opposition National Unity Government.

In March 2022, Cambodia also demonstrated unexpected readiness to condemn Russia's aggression against Ukraine, with Prime Minister Hun Sen saying that he stood 'in solidarity with the Ukrainian people against the invasion'. At the US–ASEAN special summit, Cambodia supported the elevation of relations between the two parties to the level of a Comprehensive Strategic Partnership. However, in June regional and international observers expressed concern over the potential security implications for Southeast Asia of long-standing rumours, reiterated in a report by the *Washington Post*, that Cambodia planned to grant China's PLA exclusive access to part of a naval base at Ream, the renovation of which Beijing had paid for. At the Shangri-La Dialogue, Cambodian Deputy Prime Minister and Minister for National Defence General Tea Banh flatly denied the report.

Analogous concerns were provoked by China's policies in a different sub-region – the Southwest Pacific. In April 2022, Beijing signed a confidential five-year (and potentially extendable) framework security agreement with Solomon Islands. A leaked draft of the agreement revealed that its central provisions were the potential dispatch of Chinese police and military personnel to Solomon Islands to maintain order as well as provide humanitarian assistance and disaster response, if requested by the government in Honiara; Chinese ship visits and logistical replenishment; and the use of Chinese security forces to protect Chinese projects. In May, Chinese Foreign Minister Wang Yi visited seven of the ten island states in the Southwest Pacific that Beijing hoped would agree to a 'Common Development Vision', under which China would cooperate with them on 'traditional and non-traditional security' as well as law enforcement; jointly develop a plan for fisheries; collaborate on internet provision; and possibly establish a China–South Pacific free-trade agreement.

These developments prompted a bout of intense diplomatic activity that reflected considerable anxiety in Japan, the US and some island states as well as in Australia and New Zealand – traditionally the leading powers in the Southwest Pacific. Australia became particularly active. Meeting in Fiji with counterparts from the countries that China hoped to include in its multilateral sub-regional agreement, Wang encountered an ambivalent reaction to Beijing's regional vision, reportedly partly due to lobbying by Australia's new Foreign Minister Penny Wong. Consideration of the agreement was deferred pending further 'discussions and consultations'. Australia also urged Pacific leaders to make compromises to prevent a split in the Pacific Islands Forum, the sub-region's political grouping which had been in disarray since 2021 owing to a dispute over its leadership. In early June, Canberra provided a military aircraft to transport the leaders of three Micronesian countries to Fiji for a special meeting of the Forum, at which an agreement was signed restoring its unity. Later in June, as part of a regional tour, Wong visited Solomon Islands, where she announced that Canberra would expand the locally popular Pacific Australia Labour Mobility scheme. However, there was no sign that Solomon Islands Prime Minister Manasseh Sogavare would repudiate the security agreement he had signed with China.

Australia's concerns over the evolving regional balance of power were reflected not just in its response to developments in the Southwest Pacific and its enthusiasm for the revived Quad, but also in its signing in September 2021 of AUKUS, a trilateral security agreement also involving the United Kingdom and the US. The initial focus of AUKUS will involve Australia's partners helping it to develop a nuclear-powered submarine capability. The three governments immediately began an 18-month effort to find 'an optimal pathway' to that end.

China's growing power and strategic activity were by no means the only source of security-related anxiety in the Indo-Pacific. North Korea remained a looming security concern, particularly for Japan, South Korea and the US. In September 2021, it began a new phase of missile tests, which included a new submarine-launched ballistic missile in October. In March 2022, it conducted a series of land-based intercontinental ballistic-missile launches. At the end of May the US Ambassador to the United Nations, Linda Thomas-Greenfield, said that during the first five months of 2022 there were 31 missile tests compared with only eight during the whole of 2021. Moreover, she claimed that North Korea was 'actively preparing' to conduct a seventh nuclear test, its first since 2017.

As North Korea's behaviour became more worrying, US policy toughened. In response to North Korea's missile tests, the US submitted a resolution to the UN Security Council in May 2022 that condemned Pyongyang and aimed to strengthen existing sanctions. However, China and Russia vetoed the resolution, the first time in 15 years that Security

Council members had used their vetoes to obstruct punishment of North Korea. Some observers criticised the poor timing of the resolution and argued that the US should have waited until North Korea's next nuclear test, which by mid-2022 was expected 'at any time', according to US officials.

South Asia

As South Asia tried to recover from the impact of the coronavirus pandemic on lives and livelihoods, it was struck by political and economic turmoil resulting in a change in regime in Afghanistan and Pakistan and a prospective regime change in Sri Lanka, alongside severe scrutiny and challenge of India's 'multi-alignment' policy following Russia's invasion of Ukraine.

Afghanistan

By the end of July 2021, the Taliban had surrounded most major provincial capitals and on 6 August the first provincial capital Zaranj, located in the south of Afghanistan, fell to the Taliban. By 13 August, the Taliban had captured 26 out of 34 provincial capitals including Herat and Kandahar – the domino effect was clear and Kabul was all but surrounded. On 15 August the eastern city of Jalalabad surrendered without resistance to the Taliban. The decision to abandon Kabul the same day by president Ashraf Ghani and his inner circle effectively allowed the Taliban to monopolise power and gave them the legitimacy to enter Kabul and seize full control of the country. The humanitarian consequences of the violence that ensued prior to the collapse of the government and after were devastating. According to the UN High Commissioner for Refugees (UNHCR), over 3.4m Afghans were internally displaced, 24m were in need of urgent humanitarian relief and over 5.7m Afghan refugees were living in neighbouring countries alone. The intervening months saw the Taliban attempt and fail to normalise their rule.

India

With India's policy of non-alignment challenged by the end of the Cold War and the onset of a multipolar world, India began to emphasise 'issue-based alignment' or 'multi-alignment'. This was an attempt to build meaningful ties on specific issues with different partners, short of an alliance relationship. This had worked well even during tense political situations. But since Russia's invasion of Ukraine in February 2022, India's multi-alignment policy has come under severe scrutiny and challenge. India's attempt to balance ties between the US and Russia, amid the aggressiveness of its largest and more powerful neighbour China, led to its decision to abstain from voting on UN resolutions condemning the invasion of Ukraine. Although India did not condemn Russia's actions, it did not condone them either.

Pakistan

On 10 April, Imran Khan became the first Pakistani prime minister to be ousted by a no-confidence vote following weeks of stand-off with an unusually united parliamentary opposition. This marked the end of Pakistan's first experience with an overtly populist leader since the return of competitive parliamentary politics in 2008. Having been elected prime minister in July 2018 on a reformist, anti-corruption platform with the tacit support of the army, Khan failed to govern effectively and exacerbated tensions with the army chief General Qamar Javed Bajwa due to his initial opposition to the transfer of a loyalist Inter-Services Intelligence (ISI) chief. Shahbaz Sharif, the younger brother of the exiled Pakistan Muslim League (N) leader and former prime minister Nawaz Sharif, then formed a coalition government with the Pakistan Peoples' Party (PPP) and others.

This dramatic transition opened a new period of domestic turmoil. Amid divergences with the PPP and a defiant Khan, now conspiratorially alleging the army's role in his ouster (in collusion with the US), Sharif had to contend with an acute balance-of-payments crisis, forcing Pakistan to return to talks with the IMF which began in May 2022, and inflation that stood at a 13-year high of 21.3% by June 2022. Amidst a rise in terror attacks, including the high-profile killing of Chinese teachers in Karachi on 26 April, Pakistan's security leadership remained divided over whether to engage with the anti-Pakistan Tehrik-e-Taliban (TTP), which used 'safe havens' in neighbouring Afghanistan. After four years of slow progress on tackling terrorist financing, in June Pakistan entered the final stages of being taken off the 'grey list' of international sanctions of the Financial Action Task Force (FATF).

Sharif sought to re-engage meaningfully with Washington following the refusal of presidents Trump and Biden to engage with Khan. The visit of new Foreign Minister Bilawal Bhutto Zardari to the US in May followed his first bilateral visit to Beijing. Nevertheless, this orientation marked a change from Khan's controversial meeting with Russian President Vladimir Putin in Moscow on the day Russia invaded Ukraine in February 2022. Relations with India remained tense over their dispute over Kashmir. Sharif also had to contend with the likely appointment of a new army chief by the end of November and general elections to be held by the summer of 2023.

Sri Lanka

In the first half of 2022, Sri Lanka experienced its worst economic crisis since independence nearly 75 years ago. This was due to a combination of several factors, including mismanagement of the economy and a substantial decrease in tourism following the April 2019 terrorist attacks and the coronavirus pandemic. This led to a massive reduction of foreign-currency reserves, from US$7.6bn in 2019 to less than US$50m in May 2022. Russia's invasion of Ukraine and the consequent rise in fuel and food prices was the tipping point. Sri Lanka soon lacked sufficient foreign currency to pay for vital imports.

Shortages of fuel and food caused inflation to reach a record 55% in June 2022, with expectations that it would rise further. Regular power cuts also took place which, along with a lack of access to medicines, impacted the country's health system. Large-scale protests from March 2022 against president Gotabaya Rajapaksa and his elder brother prime minister Mahinda Rajapaksa led to the latter's resignation in May and the re-appointment of Ranil Wickremesinghe as prime minister for a sixth term.

In April the Sri Lankan government suspended external-debt payments, and the following month defaulted on its debt for the first time.

Sri Lanka sought a US$3bn financing programme from the IMF to keep its economy afloat and attract further assistance from regional countries.

As of June, India had provided assistance of over US$3.5bn to Sri Lanka in the form of economic assistance including through currency swaps and lines of credit, along with humanitarian assistance through the supply of food, medicines and fuel. Wickremesinghe stated in May that China had offered a 'few hundred million dollars' in lending, but this had not been completed by June 2022. China announced assistance of 500m RMB for the supply of essential goods, but did not respond to Colombo's request to defer its loan repayment or to president Rajapaksa's request for a US$1bn loan to buy essential goods. Sri Lanka was also unable to utilise a proposed US$1.5bn line of credit from Beijing, as China was concerned that Colombo's loan repayments to Beijing would be delayed if Colombo entered an IMF deal.

But political unrest continued, sustaining much of the uncertainty in Sri Lanka's outlook. President Rajapaksa fled the country after protestors overran the presidential palace on 13 July. Wickremesinghe became acting president on 15 July, and was officially elected as president on 20 July, winning the votes of 134 of the 225 members of parliament. Wickremesinghe's primary challenges were to tackle Sri Lanka's economic crisis and to conclude a financing programme from the IMF.

Afghanistan: the Return of the Taliban
What prospects for domestic policy and foreign recognition?

The agreement between the United States and the Afghan Taliban signed in Doha on 29 February 2020 was expected to serve as a template for a political settlement between the Afghan parties and a road map for the orderly and responsible withdrawal of foreign forces from Afghanistan – the key demand of the Taliban.

However, the return of the Taliban to power as a result of a successful political-military strategy and the collapse of the Afghan government on 15 August 2021 marked the end of both the peace process and the young democratic republic that had been established with the support of the international community following the removal of the Taliban regime in late 2001. Meanwhile, the US-led military coalition's chaotic pull-out ended its two-decade-long armed conflict, which had already become the longest war in the United States' history.

Although the Taliban had been expanding their territorial control gradually for some time, the militant group intensified its military campaign in mid-2021 by starting a series of countrywide attacks aimed at capturing district headquarters. The Taliban were emboldened by the lack of substantial resistance from the government forces as they marched on to seize dozens of district centres in just a few weeks. Their next target was provincial capitals, which they achieved with a speed and ease that not even the Taliban themselves expected. On 6 August, Zaranj, the centre of Nimroz province on the border with Iran, became the first provincial capital to fall to the Taliban. Within ten days the Taliban had captured all the other cities, including the country's capital, Kabul, on 15 August.

A number of factors contributed to the sudden collapse of Afghanistan's security forces and the rapid return of the Taliban. These included the reduction of US military and logistical support to Afghan security forces, the failure of the Afghan government to develop and implement a national-security plan for after the US/NATO withdrawal, mismanagement of the Afghan security sector and lack of leadership from high-ranking Afghan officials.

Suspicion and mistrust between the Taliban and the Afghan government led by president Ashraf Ghani, as well as lack of flexibility on both sides, were key reasons for the failure of the intra-Afghan dialogue. Meanwhile, the gradual reduction of US/NATO forces from Afghanistan as well as the Afghan government's aforementioned failings meant that time was on the Taliban's side. In addition, US domestic politics, including the November 2020 presidential election, also contributed to the reluctance of the two Afghan parties to make meaningful concessions and progress in peace talks because both wanted to see who would win the election and what the new US administration's Afghan policy would be. Although the US–Taliban agreement had set 1 May 2021 as the date for the 'conditions based' withdrawal from Afghanistan, the Biden administration extended the deadline by four months following a thorough review of the United States' military engagement in Afghanistan. At the same time, Ghani and his close circle hoped that the US and its international partners would not pull out their forces completely. By the time of the Afghan government's fall, Ghani and his associates were increasingly seen by US officials as less than willing to make the necessary compromises and agree to the formation of an interim government as part of the political settlement with the Taliban.

More importantly, the sudden secret departure of Ghani, his closest advisers (including his national security adviser), head of the presidential security unit and a few other government officials – who, on 15 August, flew in helicopters from the grounds of the presidential palace in Kabul to Uzbekistan (and then to the United Arab Emirates [UAE]) – scuppered the last chance for a deal with the Taliban, which had been designed just days earlier with the mediation of the US to secure a political settlement as well as a more orderly transition of power and withdrawal of foreign forces. The plan was to send a delegation of prominent politicians from Kabul – including the former president Hamid Karzai and Dr Abdullah Abdullah, who was the chairman of the High Council for National Reconciliation – to Doha to talk to the Taliban's negotiation team in a last-ditch effort to save the peace process and agree on a relatively inclusive set-up.

However, as soon as the news that Ghani had fled the country spread, all the government institutions, including security and intelligence departments in Kabul, collapsed, with government officials, including the army chief, head of intelligence as well as defence and interior ministers, desperately looking for ways to get out as well. Although most of the high-ranking officials and politicians left the country, Karzai and Dr Abdullah took the risk of staying in Kabul. They have since been living in their own houses in Kabul and can meet each other and other Afghan dignitaries generally, as well as foreign officials and diplomats visiting Kabul. But they are not allowed by the Taliban authorities to move freely in the country or travel abroad, with one exception when Dr Abdullah was allowed during the occasion of the Muslim festival of Eid al-Fitr in early May 2022 to travel to India, where his family lives, for a few weeks.

The Taliban announced the formation of their 'caretaker' government in September 2021 and reinstalled the emirate system, in which the supreme leader (which they call the *amir ul-momineen* or 'leader of the faithful') of the Islamic Emirate of Afghanistan has ultimate power. An absolute majority of ministers and deputy ministers, provincial and district governors as well as security commanders are members of the Taliban. It is not clear how much power they would be willing to share with non-Taliban Afghans, or when. It is clear, however, that the Taliban want to keep absolute power in their own hands for now. Thus it looks unlikely in the short term that they will accept a political mechanism (such as elections, a representative Loya Jirga or the traditional 'grand council') under which non-Taliban Afghans from various backgrounds could have the opportunity to influence the political system or obtain a share of power by peaceful means.

In an effort to show to the Afghans at home and the international community abroad that their government and system has internal legitimacy and public support, the Taliban convened a three-day 'grand gathering of the religious scholars of Afghanistan' in Kabul from 30 June to 2 July

2022, in which around 3,000 clerics and a few tribal elders and traders declared their support for the Taliban's government and pledged their allegiance to the Taliban leader, Mullah Hibbatullah Akhundzadah. The 11-point declaration issued at the end of the gathering also called upon the international community to recognise the new regime as the legitimate government in Afghanistan.

The Taliban's reclusive supreme leader, based in the southern city of Kandahar since the takeover and not seen or filmed in public, also joined the gathering and delivered an hour-long speech which, like that of the other speakers, was streamed live. He underlined the country's 'independence' from 'foreign occupation', adding that foreigners should not interfere in the domestic affairs of Afghanistan or try to give them orders.

The resolution also stated that the Islamic State (ISIS, called 'Daesh' in the resolution) was a seditious and deviant group and any cooperation with it was religiously forbidden. It said that defending the Islamic Emirate of Afghanistan was obligatory and that any armed opposition to the Taliban-led political system and government was also against sharia law. The declaration also announced support for a Taliban government decree banning drugs, including opium. As the members of the all-male gathering were handpicked and approved by the Taliban, it was criticised for not being representative and inclusive.

Security challenges

For most countries, especially in the West, their vital national interest in Afghanistan remains the prevention of a terrorist attack on their homeland originating from Afghan territory. Since the US/NATO withdrawal from Afghanistan and the Taliban takeover, overall violence has drastically reduced but the security situation remains complicated and volatile. According to US official estimates, the number of al-Qaeda operatives in Afghanistan has increased since US/NATO forces withdrew in August 2021. Both al-Qaeda and ISIS are trying to grow in strength, which, if left unchecked, could pose a threat beyond Afghanistan.

Since the military withdrawal, US officials have spoken about an 'over-the-horizon' counter-terrorism strategy to monitor militant groups and, if needed, strike targets to degrade their capabilities and disrupt their operations. However, the US has not conducted any airstrikes in Afghanistan since the withdrawal of its troops.

Meanwhile, the Taliban have repeatedly emphasised that, as outlined in the Doha deal, they will not allow any individual or group to use Afghan territory as a base for hostilities against another country. However, questions have been raised about their capability and commitment to fulfil their promises. On the one hand, the Taliban have maintained links with 'friendly' groups, such as al-Qaeda and the Tehrik-e-Taliban (TTP) – the Pakistani Taliban – and have not taken any meaningful and visible action against them. On the other hand, they have been fighting against the Islamic State in Khorasan Province (ISIS–KP), an extremist militant group active mainly in the Afghanistan–Pakistan region.

Militarily, the Taliban are faced with two immediate challenges: ISIS–KP and the armed 'resistance' groups. Both have targeted the Taliban and vowed to topple the regime. Since its establishment in January 2015, ISIS–KP has frequently attacked the Taliban and remains the only major Islamist militant group to challenge them ideologically and military. Though much weaker than the Taliban in resources and manpower, remains a bitter foe.

Since regaining power, the Taliban have applied a heavy-handed approach against ISIS–KP, killing and imprisoning members as well as forcing them to abandon ISIS and pledge obedience to the Taliban. ISIS–KP has been diminished in Afghanistan, but this falls far short of the total annihilation claimed by several high-ranking Taliban officials. The Taliban have been successful in preventing ISIS from holding territory in Afghanistan, but ISIS–KP still has sleeper cells and the capacity to carry out attacks in certain parts of the country. ISIS–KP has targeted the Taliban in several parts of the country, including Kabul, and also killed and injured hundreds of civilians in deadly attacks since the Taliban takeover.

ISIS–KP's main goal is to challenge the Taliban ideologically and destabilise the situation so it can operate and recruit with relative ease. Compared to 2021, ISIS–KP is much weaker and under immense pressure, but it will continue its efforts not only to survive but also to thrive. This will largely depend on the overall stability in Afghanistan and the Taliban's ability to govern and maintain security. ISIS–KP's capacity to carry out external attacks remains questionable at this stage.

The second military challenge the Taliban government faces is from armed 'resistance' groups. Since early 2022, about a half-dozen of these groups have emerged, claiming responsibility for various attacks in a few provinces, including Panjshir, Baghlan and Takhar. However, the armed opposition has yet to gain momentum. It must overcome a number of challenges, especially logistical, and lacks an external supporter that can offer sanctuary, training and medical treatment against the dominant, better armed and numerically larger Taliban. As of June 2022 there had been no public pledges of military and financial support for anti-Taliban resistance by any state actor. In fact, the US special representative for Afghanistan, Tom West, said at a public event in February 2022 that 'we are not supporting organized armed opposition to the Taliban and we would discourage other powers from doing so as well'. In mid-June 2022, Hugo Shorter, chargé d'affaires at the United Kingdom's Mission to Afghanistan in Doha, made a statement setting out a similar position: 'The UK does not support anyone, including Afghan nationals, seeking to achieve political change through violence, or any activity inciting violence for political purposes, in Afghanistan, and will not allow UK soil to be used to plan or prepare it, and we strongly discourage others from doing so.'

However, any future support that states in the region give to the armed opposition will depend on their relations with the Taliban's government and its policies. Neighbouring countries do not want instability in Afghanistan that would harm their own national security. However, this calculation might change depending on the Taliban's policies and governance style as well as the degree of their tolerance and accommodation of the demands and aspirations of various segments of Afghan society.

Humanitarian crisis and human rights

In the wake of the Taliban takeover, Afghanistan's economy collapsed and the country was cut off from international banking systems and funding. Almost all countries suspended or significantly cut funding to Afghanistan, a country that was already heavily dependent on foreign aid and financial assistance. Under Ghani, about 75% of the country's annual budget had been funded by external aid.

In addition, the Biden administration, blaming the Taliban for violating the Doha agreement and capturing power by force, froze Afghanistan's US\$7 billion in banking reserves held in New York. The economic situation for ordinary Afghans and businesses deteriorated. Half (US\$3.5bn) of these Afghan reserves are still earmarked for possible provision to a group of families of victims of 9/11 who had previously filed lawsuits against the Taliban. Humanitarian aid continued to flow from a number of countries, with the US the largest donor, followed by the European Union, but overall levels of aid have fallen. This, coupled with the Taliban's policies, their lack of capacity to run institutions and their inability to formulate a viable economic policy, meant that hunger and poverty further increased. The UN announced in early 2022 that the worsening humanitarian situation – exacerbated by a severe drought – had left over 20 million of Afghanistan's estimated 36m population in need of assistance. A major earthquake in the southeast of the country in June 2022 only worsened matters.

Many countries have argued that aid (except to address humanitarian needs) should be linked to the behaviour and policies of the Taliban and to the degree to which they respect human rights. However, restrictions on aid or financial sanctions on the Taliban government or Afghanistan in general risk making the humanitarian crisis even worse and forcing many people to leave the country. Therefore, it will be a challenge for many donor countries and organisations to decouple the Taliban's domestic policies and behaviour from the needs of ordinary Afghans, the vast majority of whom depend on international aid and assistance.

Meanwhile, in another major development, the Taliban issued an order in early April 2022 banning poppy cultivation, the manufacturing of narcotics and the transportation and trade of heroin, hashish and alcohol. The decree added that violators would be arrested and 'tried according to Sharia law'. Afghanistan has long been the world's biggest opium producer and a major source of heroin in Europe and Asia. Drug production spiralled upwards in the country over the past 20 years despite billions of dollars spent by the US to stop drug cultivation. In May, the Taliban began a campaign to eradicate opium-poppy fields in some parts of the country, mainly using tractors, to show that they were making a serious attempt to tackle the drug problem. However, in the absence of a viable alternative livelihood strategy, the drug ban seems certain to serve as another heavy blow to millions of impoverished farmers and day labourers who rely on proceeds from the crop to survive, especially at a time when the flow of international development money has stopped.

The Taliban imposed a number of social and political restrictions after taking power. There was a crackdown on journalists and activists, leading to an erosion of the country's once-thriving media landscape. Civil society and political activism were put under immense pressure. The Taliban increasingly restricted the rights of women and girls, announcing that only boys would be allowed to attend school from grade 6 and above. However, they have so far allowed girls to attend university while sitting in separate classes from boys. Contrary to their announcement of a general amnesty, the group's fighters carried out reprisals in several provinces against some former officials and security-force personnel.

Although many countries and organisations, including the United Nations, the EU and the Organisation of Islamic Cooperation (OIC), have spoken out against such abuses, especially the violations of the rights of women and girls, there have been calls from human-rights groups for more coordinated action to show to the Taliban that the world is united in defending the rights of Afghans.

Recognition and foreign relations

The Taliban expected that at least those regional countries with whom they had 'friendly' relations would recognise their government within weeks, if not days. However, no country or international organisation, including the UN and the OIC, has so far done so. Nonetheless, many countries in the region and beyond have engaged with the Taliban. Of Afghanistan's six neighbouring countries, five (China, Iran, Pakistan, Turkmenistan and Uzbekistan) have good relations with the new government, despite not formally recognising it. Unlike most other countries, these neighbours kept their embassies open during the Taliban takeover of Kabul, as did a few other states, notably Qatar, Russia and Turkey.

Many regional countries – including China, Iran, Pakistan, Qatar, Russia, Turkmenistan and Uzbekistan – have accepted and accredited diplomats appointed by the Taliban government. These countries have allowed these 'diplomats' to serve in official capacities in Afghanistan's embassies in their countries without any official recognition of the Taliban government. Although it is an awkward situation for both sides, the Taliban have lobbied for more countries to do the same, as they see this as a path towards formal recognition of their government by other countries. It is expected that a few more countries will do so in the near future. In addition, foreign ministers and/or special envoys of several countries, including Iran, Pakistan, Russia and Uzbekistan, have visited Kabul for meetings with Taliban officials. Special envoys from several European countries, including Germany, the Netherlands and the UK, have also visited Kabul, while a number of others, including the US special representative for Afghanistan, Tom West, have met with Taliban officials in other countries.

One of the most high-profile visitors to Afghanistan in the months after the Taliban takeover was the Chinese Foreign Minister Wang Yi, who met the Taliban government's co-Deputy Prime Minister Mullah Abdul Ghani Baradar as well as his counterpart, in Kabul on 24 March 2022. The Taliban statement said that the two sides discussed 'political, economic and transit issues, air corridor, dried fruit export, educational scholarships, visa issuance, commencing work in the mines sector, Afghanistan's role in BRI [Belt and Road Initiative] and other matters of significance'. High-ranking officials of the Taliban government, China and Pakistan also agreed to extend the China–Pakistan Economic Corridor (CPEC) to Afghanistan – a move that, if implemented, would further increase China's influence in Afghanistan.

Only one neighbouring country, Tajikistan, remained critical of the Taliban and did not engage with the Taliban government. Officials from the two sides have not met since the Taliban takeover. Tajikistan is hosting several officials of the former Afghan government and some of the leaders of the armed resistance to the Taliban. India, a major regional player, initially kept a distance, before signs began to emerge that it wanted to engage with the Taliban in a variety of ways.

In early June, an Indian delegation led by a joint secretary of its external affairs ministry visited Kabul, the first such visit by Indian officials since the Taliban's takeover. Senior Indian diplomats met the Taliban government's foreign minister, deputy foreign minister and other officials. This was the most high-level meeting between the two sides since the emergence of the Taliban movement in 1994. These discussions were expected to pave the way for India to resume a diplomatic presence in Afghanistan (which ended after the Taliban takeover of Kabul last August). On 23 June, India's Ministry of External Affairs disclosed in a statement that New Delhi had deployed a 'technical team' to its embassy in Kabul 'to closely monitor and coordinate' the delivery of humanitarian assistance. Both sides seem eager to build trust and further develop bilateral relations.

The Taliban are generally keen to develop good relations with the outside world for three reasons. Firstly, they hope that close political and economic relations will bring foreign investment and increase regional trade, and thus much-needed government revenues. Secondly, the Taliban want to neutralise any threat to their rule. In particular, they do not want any regional player to provide military and financial support to Afghans opposing their regime, as India, Iran and Russia did in the 1990s. Thirdly, the Taliban also hope that recognition by and good relations with the outside world, especially Western donor countries and organisations, will bring humanitarian aid and developmental assistance to the country.

The Taliban government has repeatedly asked the international community to grant it diplomatic recognition, arguing that it has fulfilled all the criteria for this. But at the time of writing, even Pakistan, which had been seen as the main supporter of the Taliban, had not recognised the Taliban regime. In general, the structure, composition and policies of the Taliban government will determine the future course of action in foreign capitals. Three concerns dominate. Firstly, foreign governments want the Taliban government to cut ties with, and support to, transnational violent extremist groups – and, above all, prevent them from using Afghan territory to threaten their national security. Different countries are concerned about different such groups. For the US and the West in general, it is ISIS and al-Qaeda; for China, it is mainly the East Turkestan Islamic Movement (ETIM); for Pakistan, it is mainly the TTP; for Iran, Central Asian countries and Russia, it is mainly ISIS/ISIS–KP; and for India, it is regional groups (such as Lashkar-e-Taiba [LeT] and Jaish-e-Mohammed [JeM] in Kashmir) as well as al-Qaeda.

The second major concern of foreign countries is the nature and system of the Taliban government. They want the new Afghan government to be inclusive and broad-based, not a Taliban monopoly. Their third concern, which is particularly shared by Western countries, is the Taliban government's policies towards human rights, such as female education, the right of women to work and freedom of expression. However, some regional countries, including China and Russia, are less concerned by the Taliban's gender attitudes and human-rights record.

In general, countries in the region and beyond have been reluctant to grant full recognition to the Taliban. It is now a matter of who will take the lead so at least some others can follow. It is likely that a few countries will come together to jointly announce their recognition of the Taliban government. However, given the Taliban's violent record and poor reputation for upholding human rights, it is now largely up to them to make it easier for countries to grant them recognition by changing their behaviour for the better and moderating their policies.

Many countries, especially in the West, will find it hard to recognise the Taliban regime as long as it allows foreign militants to operate in the country and does not show flexibility on social freedoms, human rights and political inclusion. However, engagement with Taliban officials by foreign governments, including Western ones, will continue.

The Chinese Communist Party at 100
What domestic and foreign-policy choices face it now?

On 1 July 2021 the Chinese Communist Party (CCP) celebrated the 100th anniversary of its founding. On the face of it, the celebration was amply justified. When the CCP held its first congress in July 1921, just 13 delegates attended. Before it took power in 1949 at the end of a civil war, the CCP had several times come close to annihilation at the hands of Chiang Kai-shek's Nationalist forces. Thereafter China – and by extension the CCP – was riven by internal instability due to Mao Zedong's obsession with class struggle and the Leninist imperative of constant party rectification and renewal. In 1989, a democracy movement that erupted as Eastern Europe was poised to abandon communism seemed to presage the CCP's demise.

Not only did the CCP survive these vicissitudes but it went on to preside over the most remarkable economic transformation the modern world has seen. At the time of Mao's death in 1976 China was mired in – largely self-inflicted – poverty, accounting for just 1% of global economic activity. 50 years later a predominantly agrarian society has been transformed into a modern industrial and economic powerhouse with global reach and with military capabilities second only to those of the United States. Meanwhile, an ideology which by the late 1980s had seemed destined for the dustbin of history has acquired a new lease of life.

By the time of the centenary celebration, China appeared to be on top of the world, having seemingly outperformed the US and the West in both pandemic management and economic growth. 'The East is rising, the West is in decline' *(dong sheng, xi jiang)* became a widely used trope in leadership speeches and articles in China's state-controlled media. China looked on course to achieve its second centenary goal of becoming a strong, democratic, civilised, harmonious and modern socialist country by 2049. But since then, China's party-state leadership has faced a series of growing headwinds that, short of calling into question their ability to deliver this vision, have undoubtedly made it much harder.

How well the CCP responds to these challenges will have significance not just for China but for the world at large.

The CCP: a complex and contradictory hybrid

The CCP is a hybrid and in many ways contradictory entity. It purports to be a Marxist-Leninist organisation. As such, the Marxist concept of historical determinism dictates a conviction that its success is preordained because it has achieved an understanding and mastery of the forces that shape history. As President Xi Jinping observed in a speech to mark the CCP's centenary, 'the Communist Party of China and the Chinese people, through tenacious struggle … have shown the world that China's national rejuvenation has become a historical inevitability'. But it is also a Leninist organisation that came into being in a climate of conspiracy and paranoia, and as such is driven by a persistent sense of insecurity that requires it constantly to be scanning the horizon for threats. And it is a nationalist organisation infused with a sense of Chinese exceptionalism that makes it a difficult model for other states to emulate.

The CCP cannot escape the influence of China's past and indeed has sought selectively to draw upon it, in particular from Confucian thinking, to shape a distinct form of socialism 'with Chinese characteristics'. Traditional Chinese concepts of statecraft have always accepted that ruling dynasties were time-limited and would in due course lose the 'Mandate of Heaven' and be replaced after a period of turmoil. This perception is encapsulated in the opening lines of the mediaeval Chinese classic *The Romance of the Three Kingdoms*: 'It is said that the empire, long divided, is bound to unite; and, long united, is bound to divide.' This impending sense of impermanence was also shaped by the fate of the Soviet Union, the subject of obsessive analysis that has been turbocharged by the Ukraine crisis.

There are many contradictory aspects to the way the CCP operates. It is at once egalitarian and a meritocracy whilst at the same time led by a member of the hereditary 'red aristocracy' – the offspring of the founding fathers of the People's Republic, a status that confers great privilege and rent-seeking opportunities. Initially a party of workers and peasants, it now increasingly recruits from China's intellectual and entrepreneurial elites. The leadership is riven with factionalism, and corruption is still rife despite an anti-corruption campaign that has been running since 2012 and has seen some 900,000 party members sanctioned. It demands high levels of performance, as well as absolute loyalty and obedience, from its members – but, under the rubric of democratic centralism, also permits wide-ranging intra-party debate up to the point when a decision is made. It is unapologetically authoritarian and ready to use brutal methods to enforce its authority, while simultaneously placing great emphasis on understanding and responding to popular concerns – what Mao referred to as the 'mass line'.

What has thus far ensured the CCP's success is a degree of pragmatism and flexibility that has enabled it to draw extensively on a range of policies, many borrowed from the capitalist West, giving rise to a characteristically Chinese eclecticism that has been described as market socialism. Together with this has been its ability to engage in long-term strategic planning and to mobilise on a whole-of-nation basis to deliver strategic objectives. Another key to its success has been the CCP's ability to harness the power of modern information and communications technologies (ICTs) without allowing these to become a vector for introducing potentially subversive ideas to the Chinese population. These technologies have been developed in ways designed to minimise the risks of social disorder and enforce obedience to the CCP's will. At bottom, the CCP is an organisation dedicated to getting and keeping political power. These technologies may prove to be the 'secret sauce' that enables it to succeed in the long term where other authoritarian regimes have failed.

A return to ideology

China's rise owes much to a unique conjunction of circumstances, unlikely ever to be repeated, that enabled it to ride the wave of globalisation that grew after the end of the Cold War. But its leadership now confronts a more complex and less permissive environment, both domestically and internationally. The high economic growth rates that attended China's early success now lie in the past and the country is facing the challenge of avoiding a middle-income trap. Meanwhile, relations with the West, still a major export market and a source of both key technical inputs and financial investment, have grown more fraught. This new environment is the product of structural factors but also of choices driven by a combination of politics and ideology, and these latter are becoming more salient in determining China's responses to a new set of challenges.

Key to all of this is the role of CCP Secretary-General Xi Jinping, who, since his appointment in 2012, has progressively centralised power in his own hands, in the process creating a cult of personality comparable to that of Mao. The cumbersomely named 'Xi Jinping Thought on Socialism with Chinese Characteristics for the New Era' – likely soon to be rebranded as simply 'Xi Jinping Thought' – which all CCP members are expected to study both via an online app and a newly published Maoist-style little red book, has been incorporated into the CCP's constitution, making Xi the only CCP leader other than Mao to achieve this accolade. To date Xi has sedulously avoided designating a successor – indeed, he has sidelined a number of potential contenders for this role – and, at the forthcoming 20th Party Congress scheduled to begin on 16 October 2022, is expected to secure an unprecedented third term in office, paving the way for him to become leader for life. As part of this process, he has overseen a sustained propaganda campaign that has sought to make him coterminous with the CCP by emphasising the overriding imperative of protecting the core of the party leadership, that is, Xi himself.

It is clear that not all Xi's CCP peers are happy about this centralisation of power. It is, for example, noteworthy that, following the sixth party plenum in late 2021 which approved a contentious Third Historical Resolution – the main aim of which was to entrench Xi's claims to party leadership – Xi felt obliged to appear before the Central Committee and offer a 'clarification' – *shuoming* – in which he affirmed his belief in the concept of collective leadership established by Deng Xiaoping after the Cultural Revolution. But the direction of travel is clear. And although Xi has had difficulties asserting control over

China's security agencies – there have even been suggestions of plots against him from within these agencies – the pervasive nature of China's techno-surveillance society makes it unlikely that he will fall victim to a leadership putsch.

As Xi has consolidated his power, he has demonstrated an intolerance of any form of dissent or of any organisation or grouping that might constitute an alternative pole of power to the CCP. And although he has periodically been obliged to heed the reservations of his peers and make tactical concessions, he has demonstrated a clear determination to reshape Chinese society and in doing so to take significant risks to address the challenges China faces, in particular the issue of extreme inequalities through the promotion of the concept of common prosperity – the creation of a so-called olive-shaped economy. The result has been another set of contradictions. On the one hand, China asserts its commitment to globalisation and open markets. At the same time, Xi has emphasised the importance of indigenous innovation through programmes such as Made in China 2025: greater reliance on domestic consumption in preference to a reliance on exports, an approach that bears the title Dual Circulation; and greater self-sufficiency in key areas such as energy and food.

This turn inward has been accompanied by a significant shift in attitudes towards the private sector. In recent years the Chinese party-state has repeatedly asserted that the market should play a decisive role in the economy. Under Xi the reality has been an increasingly uneasy coexistence between communist dirigisme and private enterprise. Although the latter accounts for 60% of China's GDP, 70% of its innovation and 80% of its urban employment, China's state-owned enterprises (SOEs) continue to occupy a privileged position in the economy. Meanwhile, Xi has taken dramatic steps to constrain 'the disorderly expansion of capital' through a raft of legislative and administrative measures designed to contain the excesses of the private sector. So far, this assault has brought to the brink of collapse some of China's largest property-development companies, effectively obliterated a lucrative private-education sector and seen the stock-market valuation of China's top technology companies fall by US$1.5 trillion at the beginning of 2022.

It is becoming ever clearer that, as a convinced Marxist-Leninist, Xi thinks of the economy in terms of production and distribution and views consumption and wealth creation in a negative light. His vision for the future is an industrial IT economy based on small- and medium-sized enterprises (SMEs) located in China's inland provinces rather than on the eastern seaboard that has been the engine of Chinese economic growth. The result has been a rush by provincial and municipal administrations to attract such enterprises through a variety of subsidies and other incentives, with predictable results in the form of waste, corruption and the creation of excess capacity.

At the beginning of 2022 China confronted additional headwinds in the form of a deeper-than-expected drop in economic growth due to a surge in COVID-19 cases. Xi's determination to persist in a zero-COVID approach – the precise term of art is 'dynamic clearing', *dongtai qingling* – led to the effective closure of many major cities including Shanghai, causing severe hardship for residents and having a devastating effect on economic production. Xi's prestige is so bound up with zero-COVID that he cannot resile from it at least until after the 20th Party Congress. The pressure on the economy has led to some backtracking on Xi's redistributive and dirigiste agenda, but that is likely to be more in the way of a tactical pause than a strategic shift. Xi appears to have decided that China's economy is sufficiently developed to enable him to pursue his agenda, and that his authority is strong enough to impose a COVID strategy that has given rise to significant expressions of dissent.

Xi seems to be driven by a sense of urgency based on a fear that if China does not now take urgent steps to achieve its centenary goals, it may never do so, due to a combination of internal and external challenges. Many of the internal challenges were set out in 2020 in the communiqué of the CCP's fifth plenum. They include unbalanced and inadequate development; slow progress in achieving reform and innovation; high levels of inequality and weak social-security systems; a backward agricultural sector and environmental degradation; and weakness in social governance – this last being code for the propensity of local administrations to ignore central directives.

Added to these are a severe demographic crunch meaning that China, with 15% of its population over the age of 65, has already become an aged society; and an education system that at the top produces more graduates than there are graduate-level jobs, while at the bottom sees only 30% of the population graduating from high school – a particular problem as China aspires to move up the value chain. A further significant complication is the marked deterioration in relations with the US and the West more generally. This has been some years in the making, and inter alia has limited access to critical technology inputs such as advanced microprocessors, which China cannot produce for itself.

It's all about America

During the high-growth era of the 1990s and 2000s China was content to appear as a status quo power within the US-led global order and to benefit from the international security goods this provided. But as China has grown wealthier and more powerful it has increasingly chafed under US global hegemony and has become convinced that the US will use its still-considerable power to frustrate China's rise. This perception was powerfully reinforced by the Trump administration's trade and technology wars, which restricted China's access to US and other Western markets and to advanced technologies, notably in the field of microprocessors, on which China remains dependent. Hopes that the Biden administration would relax these restrictions proved unfounded.

Moreover, the US and its allies have orchestrated a collective response to Chinese assertiveness in the South and East China seas and in the Taiwan Strait through arrangements that include the Quadrilateral Security Dialogue ('Quad') and AUKUS, while engaging more proactively and visibly with Taiwan through the provision of political, economic and military support. This latter is of particular concern to Beijing in the light of Xi's assertion that the 'great rejuvenation of the Chinese nation' – his signature vision – is contingent upon completing the process of national reunification that began with the recovery of Hong Kong and Macao. In effect, China has to recover Taiwan – preferably by peaceful means but if not, through the use of military force – if it is to put its Century of

National Humiliation behind it and take its place on the world stage as a major civilisational power.

This raises the question of what kind of civilisational power China aspires to be and what its vision of a global order might look like. China has become increasingly vocal in its denunciation of the US-led order as one designed to entrench the privileges of the US and its Western allies to the detriment of nations in the global south. It has advanced an alternative vision that is notably lacking in specifics through formulations such as the Community of Common Destiny for Mankind and the Global Security Initiative, which purport to be both inclusive and capable of accommodating different cultures and value systems. Such nostrums are easily dismissed precisely because of their lack of definition. But they resonate with a Global South that perceives the US as disengaged and disinterested.

In a 2013 speech, republished in the CCP theoretical journal *Qiushi* (*Seeking Facts*) in 2019, Xi spoke of the necessity of demonstrating the superiority of socialism and, in the context of international relations, the importance of China 'winning the initiative, winning the dominant position and winning the future' – *yingde zhudong, yingde youshi, yingde weilai*. This has been interpreted within US policy circles as an indication that China aspires to replace the US as the global hegemon. In reality this formulation is widely used within CCP narratives in relation to all aspects of policy, both domestic and foreign, and as with many such formulaic expressions is to be taken seriously but not literally. China sees the cost of the US model of hegemony, involving major overseas commitments that include maintaining large numbers of overseas military bases, as expensive and unsustainable.

China's own vision, by contrast, is of a world dominated by a small number of major powers, each with its own sphere of influence in which it can act unconstrained by international humanitarian law. This explains why China, though maintaining an official stance of neutrality, has in practice been supportive of Russia's invasion of Ukraine. However, the prolongation of that conflict is not in China's economic interests and has exacerbated relations not just with the US but also with the European

Union, where China had – as it transpires, erroneously – assumed that its failure to condemn the Russian invasion would not adversely impact relations. Events in Ukraine have called into question Chinese assumptions about the fragility of Western cohesion. But far from inducing a course correction, this has intensified a zero-sum Chinese approach to relations with the US and the West more generally. There is within leadership circles a growing belief that a rising nation such as China must undertake a decisive action at the correct historical juncture if it is to succeed in asserting itself, even at the risk of failure. For some years now Xi has spoken of the need to promote a spirit of struggle within both the CCP and the population more generally. And commentators associated with the CCP leadership have begun to talk of preparing the population psychologically for war.

The CCP is at a crossroads and the decisions that it takes in the lead-up to the 20th Party Congress will determine which of two directions it will take. The first is to ease off on a dirigiste and redistributive economic approach and create an enabling environment for the private sector, while simultaneously adopting a less overtly confrontational stance in relations with the US and its allies – though, given the extent of anti-Chinese animus in US political circles, this will be a challenge. The other is to reinforce the approach in which Xi appears to be invested, with the attendant risks that this may inadvertently discourage domestic entrepreneurship and innovation while deterring foreign inward investment; and to double down on the CCP's efforts to discredit and subvert the US-led global order while intensifying pressure on Taiwan.

In the short term the latter looks to be the more likely outcome, resulting in a China that is more inward-looking, more ideologically rigid, harder to deal with and more inclined towards a more adventurist foreign policy that could in the worst case go kinetic. In doing so, the CCP would hope to leverage a carefully nurtured nationalism and sense of grievance to secure popular support and shape a domestic narrative that would not face serious challenge. How soon this might occur is impossible to predict. But the odds on it happening are shortening.

India's Foreign Policy: towards Multi-alignment and Minilateralism
How is it navigating the new complexities of great-power relations?

India's policy of non-alignment during the Cold War sought to avoid involvement in the power politics of groups aligned against each other – which, according to India's first prime minister and foreign minister Jawaharlal Nehru, had led to two world wars. This did not mean an inflexible posture of equidistance between the two power blocs of the United States and the Soviet Union. But it involved some tightrope walking as the shadows of the Cold War came closer to India.

For example, India received US military assistance during and after its 1962 war with China. US-sourced aircraft supplied India's forward bases, and spare parts were delivered to the Indian air force. After the war, the US and India signed an air-defence agreement and increased intelligence-sharing. In August 1971, India signed a friendship and cooperation treaty with Moscow that provided reassurance for its war four months later with Pakistan, which enjoyed US political backing and military support. India's ability to take these contrary decisions on the basis of independent judgement demonstrated its strategic autonomy.

But India's policy of non-alignment was challenged by the end of the Cold War and the onset of a multipolar world. In response, India began to emphasise 'issue-based alignment' or 'multi-alignment'. This was an attempt to build meaningful ties on specific issues with different partners, short of an alliance relationship. This worked well during tense political situations. India was one of a few countries that deftly balanced relations with both Iran and Saudi Arabia/the Gulf states, with Israel and the Palestinian Authority, and with Qatar and the United Arab Emirates (UAE)/Saudi-led group in the Gulf Cooperation Council (GCC) during the 2017–21 Qatar diplomatic crisis. India is a member of the Shanghai Cooperation Organisation (SCO) and the BRICS grouping, both of which include China and Russia, as well as the Quadrilateral Security Dialogue ('Quad'), alongside the US and two US treaty allies, Australia and Japan.

India's former foreign secretary, Jyotindra Nath Dixit, aptly noted that 'in Indian diplomacy, sometimes, you need to do a bit of Bharat Natyam', referring to an Indian dance form with multiple representations. Essentially, Indian diplomacy may appear in different forms to others but only after India secures its own interests.

India's role in the 2017 revival of the informal grouping of the Quad indicated a stronger foreign-policy and security 'tilt' towards the US and its partners in the Indo-Pacific region than before. But since Russia's invasion of Ukraine in February 2022, India's multi-alignment policy has come under severe scrutiny and challenge. India's attempt to balance ties between the US and Russia, amid the aggressiveness of its largest and more powerful neighbour China, led to its decision to abstain in the votes on UN resolutions condemning the invasion of Ukraine. Its stance of neutrality appeared to surprise the West.

As part of India's new focus on regional relationships, India has engaged in minilateral arrangements in the Middle East and the Indian Ocean. In October 2021, India's foreign minister participated in the first virtual India–Israel–UAE–US quadrilateral meeting. This was primarily an economics-focused meeting, where the four countries decided to establish a four-member international forum for economic cooperation. In-person meetings of the grouping, christened I2U2, are planned, after meeting virtually at summit level in July 2022.

India is also part of an expanded (originally trilateral) security grouping in the Indian Ocean region, based on meetings of the national security advisers of India, the Maldives and Sri Lanka and known as the 'Colombo Security Conclave'. In March 2022, Mauritius joined this grouping to form a new quadrilateral, with Bangladesh and the Seychelles as observers. Its focus included maritime safety and security, counter-terrorism and radicalisation work, and cyber security and protection of critical infrastructure and technology. In November 2021, the navies of India, the Maldives and Sri Lanka conducted their first joint exercise in the Arabian Sea.

Most importantly, the Quad in the Indo-Pacific has been bolstered. Its first two in-person Leaders' Summits were held in Washington DC in

September 2021 and Tokyo in May 2022, and a virtual Leaders' Summit was held in March 2022. At the May 2022 Leaders' Summit, the group announced a new maritime initiative: the Indo-Pacific Partnership for Maritime Domain Awareness (IPMDA).

India has emphasised that the Quad is not a security organisation but a broad partnership focusing on non-security issues, and indeed at the 2021 summit the four countries discussed cooperation over the coronavirus pandemic, vaccine production, emerging technologies, space, cyber security and 5G deployment and diversification. However, this skirts the fact that the US has emphasised the security aspects of the partnership. In March 2021, US Secretary of State Antony Blinken referred to the 'first ministerial meeting of the Quadrilateral Security Dialogue' during remarks before the Foreign Affairs Committee in the US House of Representatives. The US State Department website also used the term 'security dialogue' until 20 February 2022, when it began using 'Quadrilateral Ministerial Meeting' instead.

In practical terms, the navies of the Quad countries gather annually to participate in the *Malabar* naval exercise. This began as a bilateral exercise by India and the US in 1992, with Japan and Australia joining in 2015 and 2020 respectively. While all four countries have stated officially that *Malabar* is unrelated to the Quad, it is unclear whether this is a meaningful distinction in practice. The first phase of the 2021 *Malabar* exercise took place in August off the coast of Guam, followed by its second phase in the Bay of Bengal in October. There have also been Quad meetings on cyber security, with the Quad Senior Cyber Group Meeting in Sydney in March 2022; and on intelligence, with a leadership-level meeting of the Quadrilateral Strategic Intelligence Forum in Washington DC in September 2021.

Yet India's response to the formation of AUKUS, a new minilateral security grouping in September, was mixed. At one level, it was supportive of a stronger military strategy by other countries as a counterbalance to China. But it was worried that AUKUS would detract from the Quad's significance and that the snub to France, an important strategic partner of India, would weaken the Western response. India was also concerned that AUKUS may lead to an increase in the number of nuclear-powered attack submarines (SSNs) operating in the Eastern Indian Ocean from the 2030s onwards, an issue aggravated by the fact that the Indian Navy would like to acquire these types of vessels but has not received political approval to do so.

Engagement with Afghanistan, tensions with Pakistan

The US administration's view, prior to the Russia–Ukraine war, that its withdrawal from Afghanistan provided an opportunity to focus on countering China in the Indo-Pacific region received a mixed reaction from India. The chaotic exit of US/NATO forces and the Taliban's victory over Afghanistan represented a huge loss of influence for India, which had been a major development partner for Afghanistan, but had not previously engaged with the Taliban in a significant way. As a result, India closed its embassy in mid-August and evacuated its diplomatic staff, but several hundred civilians, including Afghan Hindus and Sikhs, were not evacuated.

In June 2022, a terror attack against a Sikh gurudwara (temple) in Kabul was carried out by Islamic State in Khorasan Province (ISIS–KP), killing two people. India also had serious concerns that Afghanistan could be used as a staging post for terror attacks against its interests. Anti-India terror groups, including the Pakistan intelligence-supported Lashkar-e-Taiba (LeT) and Jaish-e-Mohammed (JeM), continued to be present in Afghanistan and were reportedly active in the Taliban's military campaign.

But, as a near neighbour, India had no 'exit policy'. Decades of investment in infrastructure and capacity-building, and resultant soft power, were not easily eroded. India's support to the Afghan people and efforts to stabilise Afghanistan through a regional consensus continued. At the end of August, India's ambassador to Qatar met the head of the Taliban's political office in Doha to discuss the safety and early return of Indian nationals from Afghanistan; and in October, Indian diplomats met Taliban co-Deputy Prime Minister Abdul Salam Hanafi in Moscow and offered humanitarian assistance. In February 2022, the first batch of wheat was sent to Afghanistan via the Pakistani land route; by the end of June, 33,500 metric tonnes of wheat had been sent in partnership with the World Food Programme (WFP). In June, it deployed a 'technical team' in its embassy in Kabul to engage on humanitarian and developmental assistance, short of granting diplomatic recognition to the Taliban.

Although India–Pakistan tensions over the Kashmir dispute continued, a ceasefire on the Line of Control (LoC) largely held. The Kartarpur corridor for Sikh pilgrimage, closed since March 2020 because of the pandemic, reopened in November 2021; for the first time, Pakistan allowed the overland transit of wheat from India to Afghanistan in February; and the Indus Water Treaty commissioners met in New Delhi in March. But on 9 March an 'accidental firing' of a high-speed unarmed Indian missile took place, with the missile crashing 124 kilometres inside Pakistani territory, reportedly due to a 'technical malfunction' during maintenance. Although this did not escalate into a crisis, two things were apparent: firstly, that another crisis between the two nuclear powers was highly probable given the disputes and tensions between them and the absence of a peace dialogue for nearly a decade; and, secondly, that neither country wanted uncontrolled escalation, including to a nuclear level. But, at the same time, the possibilities of misperceptions and miscalculations remain high, with terrorism in Kashmir escalating tensions between India and Pakistan.

A new coalition government in Pakistan, formed in April 2022 and led by Prime Minister Shahbaz Sharif, appeared to be more inclined to ease tensions with India than the previous Imran Khan government. But its main priority was to overcome the ongoing domestic political and economic turmoil. India remained adamant that talks with Pakistan could only begin when terrorist attacks ended. With India preferring to await the outcome of looming general elections in Pakistan, and ambiguity over whether Kashmir would be part of the talks if they began, discreet contact and communication on crisis management, as in the case of the accidental firing of an Indian missile, appeared to be a pragmatic option.

Deterioration of relations with China

India has serious security concerns about China, even if it is often loath to discuss them in multilateral settings. In June 2020, 20 Indian and four Chinese soldiers died during violent clashes in the Galwan Valley, according to official accounts. These were the first fatalities in 45 years in the vicinity of the long, undemarcated land border between the countries known as the Line of Actual Control (LAC), and resulted in the deterioration of relations between Asia's two largest nuclear-armed countries to their lowest point since the 1962 Sino-Indian war. India responded by imposing minor punitive trade measures against China – its largest trade partner – and by increasing the size of its military forces and defence-related infrastructure in the border regions. Although soldiers are no longer actively fighting, the situation remains tense despite several bilateral military and political meetings to de-escalate the situation.

In March 2022, China's Foreign Minister Wang Yi flew to New Delhi to suggest that the boundary issue be put to one side and not be allowed to impact other aspects of the relationship in his meetings with India's External Affairs Minister Dr S. Jaishankar and National Security Adviser Ajit Doval. But Jaishankar subsequently stated that 'frictions and tensions that arise from China's deployments since April 2020 cannot be reconciled with a normal relationship between two neighbours'. The 24th meeting of the Working Mechanism for Consultation and Coordination on India–China Border Affairs (WMCC), between the two countries' foreign ministries, was held in May 2022. This followed the 15th round of the India–China Corps Commander Level meetings in March 2022. In both meetings, the two sides agreed to continue diplomatic and military discussions. Jaishankar and Wang also met virtually during a meeting of foreign ministers from the BRICS countries in May 2022. Yet by the end of June the full disengagement of troops in the Galwan Valley had not been completed, nor the de-escalation of forces begun.

India's 'neutral' stance on the Russia–Ukraine war

The US and other Western powers had naively expected India to join in the international condemnation of Russia. This was based on the assumption that, as the largest democracy in the world, India would oppose the actions of an autocratic leader, and that as a major beneficiary of a rules-based international order, India would challenge the blatant violation of its principles. It was also expected that India would condemn Russia in order to send a strong signal to China to desist from an attack against Indian territory after their June 2020 clash in the high Himalayas.

Despite this, India chose to take a longer-term view of its ties with Russia, especially in the defence sector. As Jaishankar subsequently stated in parliament, India's foreign-policy decisions 'are made in Indian national interest'. When challenged at the Munich Security Conference in February in relation to India's pre-invasion abstentions on Ukraine in the United Nations Security Council, on the specific question of whether values such as adhering to a rules-based order and international law should apply uniformly across the Indo-Pacific as well as Europe, Jaishankar responded that 'principles and interests are balanced'. In June 2022, he stated that 'Europe has to grow out of the mindset that Europe's problems are the world's problems. But the world's problems are not Europe's problems.' This reflected a strongly felt Indian view that, while Europe expected India to show support to Ukraine, European governments had been slow to show support to India against China in June 2020. Indian commentators also argued that India need not take sides in what was essentially a 'European conflict', far from the Indian mainland and island territories, when its own security priorities lay in the Indo-Pacific region; and that Russia had 'legitimate security interests' to defend.

India's diplomatic stance on Russia's invasion of Ukraine was also driven by three further factors: the presence of about 22,500 Indian students in Ukraine; India's strategic dependence on Russia for arms and, to a far lesser extent, energy; and concern over China's aggressiveness against India. At the start of the war in February, India's overriding priority was to ensure the safety and safe evacuation of all its nationals from Ukraine. As over half of them were studying in universities in eastern Ukraine, India was concerned that Russia would be likely to hamper their evacuation if India were to publicly condemn Russia in the UN. India's government-led effort to ensure the safe evacuation of all students included the personal intervention of Prime Minister Narendra Modi with the Russian and Ukrainian presidents to ensure a temporary ceasefire in Sumy in northeast Ukraine. The evacuation of all Indian students was successfully completed in March, except for the death of an Indian student when Russia shelled the Ukrainian city of Kharkiv.

In the absence of substantive trade or people-to-people relations, defence and security ties are key to India's relationship with Russia. The Soviet Union provided arms to India after its defeat in the war against China in 1962 and emerged as India's principal defence supplier until the 2000s. It also used its veto power in the UN Security Council to enable India to launch a decisive military action to secure the independence of the then-East Pakistan, now Bangladesh, in December 1971, and has continuously supported India in the UN Security Council on the Kashmir dispute with Pakistan. Following the Indian government's sudden and controversial move on 5 August 2019 to revoke the special 'semi-autonomous' constitutional status of the Indian province of Jammu and Kashmir, Russia stated that the Kashmir dispute was a bilateral matter for India and Pakistan to resolve. India perceives Russia as a 'special and privileged strategic partner'. It did not condemn President Vladimir Putin's annexation of Crimea in early 2014. The 21st annual India–Russia summit on 6 December 2021 resulted in a 99-point joint statement.

India is estimated to depend on Russia for 55% to 85% of its arms, along with critical defence technology denied to it by the West. But the emerging paradox is that these arms are largely procured to be used in a conflict against China, with which Russia apparently now has a 'no limits' partnership. According to IISS data, the Russian-origin Sukhoi Su-30MKI *Flanker* makes up more than half of the Indian air force's fighter ground-attack fleet. The Indian army is, if anything, even more dependent on Russian equipment than the air force. Almost all its main battle tanks in its operational fleet are Russian, either the T-72M1 or T-90S.

The Indian navy's sole aircraft carrier, INS *Vikramaditya*, was supplied by Russia, along with Russian *Sindhughosh*-class *(Kilo)* conventional submarines, destroyers and frigates. India has begun to acquire Russian S-400 missile-defence systems, despite the continued threat of US sanctions, with the first of five units with eight launchers arriving at the end of 2021. India reportedly received Russian assistance in miniaturising the nuclear reactor to fit within the hull of its first strategic ballistic-missile submarine (SSBN).

Although the Indian armed forces publicly have defence stores for up to six months due to contingency planning, in the longer term Western sanctions on Russia and Russia's loss of military equipment in Ukraine are likely to delay or disrupt supplies of arms, spares and equipment to India. This has provided an inflection point for India. It has raised questions about whether India should re-energise its efforts to 'Make in India' arms and equipment through co-development and co-production, combining the transfer of Western technology with India's production base, or whether it should continue to acquire short-term arms and equipment from defence partners in the West, including France, Israel, the United Kingdom and the US.

Both options are complicated. The former is long-term, dependent on the transfer of technology from the West, which has long been concerned over the possibility of 'leakage' of technology from India to Russia, the sharing of intellectual property and liability issues for military equipment built in India with Western technology. The latter, although short-term, will not be applicable to spare parts, maintenance and refurbishment, and advanced defence technology, for which there is no credible, affordable or immediate alternative to Russia.

Furthermore, India has strongly pushed back on what it perceives as European hypocrisy on Russian energy supplies to India. In April 2022, Jaishankar pointedly noted that 'probably our total purchases for the month would be less than what Europe does in an afternoon'. But media reports in May stated that imports of Russian crude oil were nearly nine times higher than in the previous year, while in June Russia's share of India's total oil imports rose to just under 25%, compared to around 2%

of the total in 2021. However, in June Jaishankar stated that India's oil imports from Russia had 'gone up nine times from a very low base, because at that time the markets were more open'.

A final driver of Indian policy towards the Russia–Ukraine war is diplomatic. Since China is India's primary security challenge, a key diplomatic priority is to ensure that Russia is not isolated diplomatically to guarantee continued Russian support for India in a multipolar world. India also fears that if Russia becomes a 'junior partner' of China, Beijing could gain a veto on Russian arms supplies to India.

As a result, India has not condemned Russia's aggression against Ukraine; will not unilaterally impose sanctions on Russia; continues to purchase arms and energy from Moscow; and has not publicly described the conflict as a 'war' in any official government statement. Its initial position on 21 February, three days before Russia's invasion of Ukraine, in the UN Security Council called for 'restraint on all sides', widely perceived by the West as giving Russia a pass, with India stating that the 'de-escalation of tensions' should take into account the 'legitimate security interests of all countries'.

Yet India has not condoned Russia's aggression against Ukraine. Its diplomatic stance and statements have also changed as the war has intensified, suggesting not that its attitude was 'neutral' but that it was 'in favour of peace'. Since Russia's invasion of Ukraine on 24 February, India has criticised Russia in its explanatory votes in the UN, albeit not by name. It condemned the killing of civilians in the Ukrainian town of Bucha in March, but not Russia directly, calling for an international investigation; called for an immediate cessation of violence and an end to all hostilities; highlighted 'respect for territorial integrity and sovereignty of all states'; provided humanitarian assistance to Ukraine; and urged a return to the path of 'diplomacy and dialogue' between the Ukrainian and Russian leaderships for resolution of the conflict.

In March, addressing party workers in Hindi during a political speech at the Bharatiya Janata Party's (BJP) headquarters in New Delhi, Modi used both the Hindi *(yudh)* and Urdu *(jung)* words for 'war'.

He stated that 'war has also increased the worries of the world … two years on, the supply chain was badly affected and the war added to it … the war which is going on at this time is directly and indirectly affecting every country in the world … inflation is increasing all over the world due to war'. He added that regarding 'the countries which are directly fighting the war, India is related to them economically, in terms of security, in terms of education, politically'. India's Ministry of Defence also stated on 17 April that its Army Commanders' Conference would assess 'any impact of the Russia–Ukraine war'. In May, Modi stated that he believed there 'will be no winning party in this war, everyone will suffer'.

Although India's position on Ukraine has introduced a 'trust deficit' with European partners, it has not affected the enhancement of bilateral security ties. During former British prime minister Boris Johnson's visit to India in April 2022, the UK announced an India-specific Open General Export Licence (OGEL) for the export of equipment and emerging technologies to India. During the visit of the President of the European Commission Ursula von der Leyen to New Delhi days later, the two sides launched the EU–India Trade and Technology Council, to 'allow both partners to tackle challenges at the nexus of trade, trusted technology and security'. In June, the first India–EU Security and Defence Consultations took place in Brussels. The two sides discussed cooperation in co-development and co-production of defence equipment, including India's participation in the EU's Permanent Structured Cooperation (PESCO).

The 2022 US Indo-Pacific strategy, published in early February 2022, also recognised India as a 'like-minded partner and leader in South Asia and the Indian Ocean'. Initially US President Joe Biden had called India's response to the Russia–Ukraine conflict 'shaky', as India was the only Quad member that had not condemned Russia's invasion. However, the two Quad leaders' meetings in early 2022 highlighted the fact that, despite their divergences, India and the US would continue to engage, primarily over their implicit key strategic priority of countering China's influence in the Indo-Pacific region.

AUKUS: New Capabilities for Old Allies
What are the strategic implications of this path-breaking deal?

On 16 September 2021, United States President Joe Biden, flanked by television screens for a virtual address with the United Kingdom's former prime minister Boris Johnson and then-prime minister of Australia Scott Morrison, launched AUKUS, a tripartite agreement to cooperate on strategic technologies. Negotiated over months in ultra-tight secrecy and revealed under a global media spotlight, AUKUS instantly became one of the most dramatic international security developments of 2021, in the midst of a global pandemic and only weeks after the chaotic US/NATO withdrawal from Afghanistan. AUKUS has the potential to augment defence capabilities among three close traditional allies in the coming decades, with particular significance for Australia and the Indo-Pacific region. Given the ambitious objectives AUKUS has set itself, it is a high-risk, high-gain endeavour. For Australia, the chief instigator of AUKUS, it stands out as a striking exercise in entrepreneurial statecraft without obvious precedent.

AUKUS pursues two related lines of effort. Its *raison d'être* is a project to provide Australia with 'at least' eight conventionally armed nuclear-powered attack submarines (SSNs), drawing on special assistance from the US and UK. The three countries aim to deliver this step change in Australia's military capability as soon as possible, while adhering to Nuclear Non-Proliferation Treaty (NPT) obligations. Although there has been no public commitment to a delivery date, and many variables remain in play, the first of Australia's new boats may not arrive until the late 2030s or even later. In tandem, AUKUS aims to co-develop and share a range of advanced technologies directed at military applications. In addition to four focal areas identified at the launch – undersea, quantum, cyber and artificial intelligence (AI) – AUKUS has since branched into hypersonics and electronic warfare.

Mixed motives

The members of AUKUS do not call it a defence alliance or pact, but describe it as a partnership to enhance defence capability. Although not tied exclusively to a region, its main focus is the Indo-Pacific. Its primary, if unstated, purpose is to counterbalance China's growing military and technological power by enhancing technological collaboration among all three countries, leveraging their comparative advantages and economies of scale.

There are some gradations in national interests amongst its members. For the US, AUKUS binds two of its closest allies and Five Eyes intelligence partners into a new trilateral mechanism. The Indo-Pacific emphasis within AUKUS is consistent with Washington's designation of China as its primary strategic challenge. While the US stands to gain from technology transfers from the UK and Australia and a potential expansion of the allied defence-industrial base, reciprocity between AUKUS members needs to be gauged in conjunction with the likelihood of future augmentations to the US force posture in Australia and enhanced basing access, including for nuclear submarines from the US and UK (to a more limited extent, given the relatively small size of the Royal Navy). Australia has the least to contribute to AUKUS in technology terms, but it can offer access to an increasingly important location in America's priority theatre. AUKUS supports the UK's pursuit of an enhanced security role in the Indo-Pacific that was formalised in the 2021 Integrated Review. The UK broadly shares the United States' aim of counterbalancing China's growing power. But its interests in AUKUS and in jointly developing advanced technologies reflect wider commercial and economic imperatives, as well as military ones.

For Australia, the agreement is aimed primarily at improving its military capability to deter China, strengthening its alliance with the US and leveraging close security links with the UK, partly to access US technology. AUKUS originated in the Australian government's decision, gradually reached since 2020, to jettison a A$90 billion contract with France's Naval Group to build conventionally powered submarines (which had yet to progress beyond the design stage) in favour of acquiring SSNs. Canberra had earlier concluded that its strategic environment was deteriorating faster than expected, based on sharpening threat perceptions of China and increasing doubts that conventional submarines would be able to meet the Australian navy's future needs. A defence-strategic update, issued in July 2020, identified the need to boost Australia's combat power, including long-range strike capabilities, with the aim of honing a conventional deterrent posture currently lacking in the Australian Defence Force. This was the strategic context that gave rise to AUKUS.

Personal 'buy-in' from all three leaders has ensured that AUKUS is being resourced as a strategic priority at a time of fiscal overstretch, bypassing bureaucratic and political barriers to a level not seen since the Cold War. AUKUS was consistently high up the policy agenda for both Morrison and Johnson when they were in office. Senior UK officials regard it as one of the most consequential alignments in British foreign policy for decades. Biden's consistent backing of AUKUS has been essential to overcoming inertia and resistance within the US government, including those parts of the US Navy that jealously guard the secrets of nuclear propulsion. The political opposition was consulted in all three countries, on the assumption that bipartisan support would be essential to ensure the long-term viability of AUKUS. In the US, this included former members of Donald Trump's administration (2017–21). In Australia, the Morrison administration did not brief the opposition until after AUKUS was announced. The new Labor government in Canberra has signalled continuity by backing AUKUS, though it may be tempted to introduce fresh requirements to mitigate the risks of a submarine 'capability gap' before the SSNs are delivered and offer additional pledges on non-proliferation, given Labor's past activism on this. The British Labour Party has backed AUKUS, but attitudes within the party towards the agreement are somewhat opaque, with some MPs expressing concerns that AUKUS will destabilise the region.

Nuclear step-up

Australia's defence department has established a nuclear-powered-submarine task force to lead the submarine project. SSNs represent a leap in capability over even the largest diesel submarines. They provide a combination of speed, range, large weapons payloads and sensor capacity, packaged within a stealthy platform that can operate with a high degree of autonomy. Their essentially unlimited endurance will enable the Australian navy to operate SSNs across the Indo-Pacific littoral, including Northeast Asia. Land attack has reportedly been identified as a key capability requirement for Australia's future SSNs. A force of eight nuclear boats will add significant offensive potency to Australia's anti-ship and strike capabilities, whether operating independently or as part of a US-led coalition. Although modest in comparison with Asia's largest navies, Australia would marginally exceed both the British and French SSN inventories.

France also builds SSNs, but the option of converting the French submarine contract from diesel to nuclear was rejected because France's naval reactors run on low-enriched uranium, requiring mid-life refuelling. Australia would either have had to establish its own civil nuclear-energy programme from scratch – an option ruled out by the Morrison government – or send its submarines to refuel in France, taking them offline for extended periods. US and UK naval reactors use highly enriched uranium, meaning their boats can run on a single fuel load for their operational life. The US has shared its nuclear technology only with the UK since 1958. Crucially, access to US and UK reactor technology means Australia can operate SSNs without having to control the nuclear fuel cycle, enabling Canberra to remain in compliance with the NPT. This was an important consideration for Australia, given its diplomatic commitment to non-proliferation, but it was also a condition of the Biden administration's support for AUKUS. AUKUS therefore offers a pathway to acquiring SSNs that circumvents the political and economic costs of starting up a domestic nuclear-energy industry in Australia. This was persuasive for Morrison, even though a civil nuclear-energy programme would reduce the overheads of nuclear-submarine propulsion and deliver broader policy benefits.

Australia is the first country without nuclear weapons or nuclear energy to acquire SSNs. Prime Minister Anthony Albanese's new Labor government is unlikely to change this. But neither of these forbearances will necessarily obtain by the time Australia's last SSN enters the water in the 2050s. Morrison said emphatically that Australia had no intention of arming the new submarines with nuclear weapons and would continue to be bound by its obligations to the NPT. AUKUS includes a robust 'nuclear stewardship' framework to make this possible. The three governments have worked closely with the International Atomic Energy Agency (IAEA) to ensure that Australia can acquire SSNs while remaining compliant with the NPT and IAEA safeguards. Nevertheless, even assuming that future Australian governments maintain their commitment not to acquire nuclear weapons, the technical task of modifying an SSN equipped for conventional land attack into a platform capable of delivering nuclear-armed cruise missiles would not be too challenging and also would be hard to detect – provided such missiles were available. As a form of recessed deterrence against nuclear-armed adversaries, SSNs could serve as a latent 'breakout' platform for a basic nuclear deterrent *if* in future Australia felt sufficiently threatened and had lost confidence in America's extended-deterrence guarantees.

In November 2021 AUKUS members signed a three-way Exchange of Naval Nuclear Propulsion Information Agreement (ENNPIA). Its rapid ratification in February 2022 demonstrated the level of political support that AUKUS enjoys. A further agreement will be necessary to support the transfer of nuclear equipment upon expiry of an 18-month consultation period that was announced at AUKUS's launch. With continued support from the Biden administration, it is likely that AUKUS-related exports from the US will be shepherded through the State Department's onerous International Traffic in Arms Regulations. In this way AUKUS could help to break down persistent regulatory and political barriers to greater defence technology sharing between the US and even its closest allies.

It remains unclear what SSN design Australia will opt for at the end of the 18-month period, beyond a commitment from the outset to build them in South Australia. Australia's chief of navy made an exploratory approach to his UK counterpart in February 2021. The navy is thought to favour a British design partly because they require smaller crews. Other parts of the Australian system are more disposed towards choosing a US design and combat system. Despite early indications that a mature model would be preferred over the risks involved in building bespoke designs, Australia is not likely to select the US *Virginia*-class or British *Astute*-class SSNs 'off the shelf', as these will be obsolescent by the 2050s. The British-made reactor for the *Astute* is already out of production. There are reliable indications that Australia's submarine task force is looking at the British Submersible Ship Nuclear Replacement (SSNR) or the American Next-Generation Attack Submarine (SSN-X) future designs, or a mix.

Observers have expressed doubts about Australia's ability to construct nuclear submarines because of their complexity and a mixed record with the existing *Collins*-class build. But neither the US nor the UK has spare production capacity available for Australia because of existing commitments to replace their own SSNs and ballistic-missile submarines (SSBNs). A 'composite' production model, partially internationalising the future SSN build, has been floated as one possibility to compress timelines, thereby also facilitating a distributed workshare among the three countries. A winner-takes-all solution between the UK and US to supply Australia's submarine design would not be politically viable within AUKUS. At a minimum, overseas production of the reactor compartments seems assured, given Australia's lack of experience in nuclear engineering, as well as for security and safety considerations.

The nuclear-submarine plan has been criticised in Australia on the grounds that it increases Australia's exposure to a potential 'capability gap' in the 2030s, as the ageing fleet of *Collins*-class diesel submarines is progressively retired and before the new SSNs enter into service. This could coincide with a zenith of strategic danger, as China's military modernisation peaks and Taiwan faces an accelerated threat of invasion. AUKUS could help to alleviate any gap by boosting 'undersea' capabilities, including autonomous underwater vehicles. Australia's *Collins* submarines are also due to receive service-life extension upgrades from the mid-2020s. The introduction of a new submarine class as a bridge between *Collins* and the SSN is not currently planned for, but a growing possibility for Australia's new government, which is keeping its options open. However, forward basing of US and possibly UK SSNs appears to be the most obvious way of advancing AUKUS's timelines and bolstering Australia's submarine capability over the next 10–15 years.

US and UK officials have visited Australia to determine its infrastructure, workforce and industrial-capability needs for the nuclear-submarine project. The previous government announced a plan, in March 2022, to establish a second submarine base at a site to be determined on Australia's Pacific coast, at an estimated cost of A$10bn. Currently, Australia's submarines are all based in the west, near Perth. The new base is partly intended to boost recruitment and retention for the submarine force, but extra capacity would facilitate forward deployment of American and British SSNs to Australia, while also expediting nuclear-submarine training for the Australian navy through joint crewing. AUKUS seems likely to resurrect the close submarine-training relationship that previously existed between the Australian and British navies, as well as establishing a submarine training pipeline with the US Navy.

The cost of building Australia's nuclear submarines has been estimated as high as A$171bn. The real costs are likely to go higher, given Australia's need to educate a nuclear workforce and build up supporting infrastructure without the scale benefits of a civil nuclear industry. Nuclear-waste management is a major consideration, including decommissioning, even if the reactors themselves remain sealed and are disposed of in the UK or US.

Advanced technologies

Submarines aside, AUKUS members claim to have made trilateral progress on the advanced-technologies front, for example, in 'undersea warfare' – a broad descriptor that includes underwater sensors and autonomous vehicles. The lead project under way in the latter category is the AUKUS Undersea Robotics Autonomous Systems (AURAS), which was described as a force multiplier in the April 2022 AUKUS joint statement. This points to the growing importance of the seabed as a contested space, including in peacetime. Submarine cables, although not classed as a military capability, are already a locus for undersea competition between China and the US and its Pacific allies: China has made advances in deep-sea submersibles. AURAS is expected to commence trials as early as 2023.

In quantum computing, the lead project – dubbed the AUKUS Quantum Arrangement (AQuA) – is meant to spur investment in quantum-capabilities technologies specifically for positioning, navigation and timing, over a three-year period of trials and experimentation, to 2025. Quantum-enabled guidance systems hold out the promise of pinpoint accuracy independent of GPS, which can be spoofed or jammed. Joint work in AI will help to improve the speed and precision of decision-making processes, with the initial focus on strengthening resilience in contested environments. Cyber activity within AUKUS is labelled 'advanced', though based on the limited public information available it is difficult to distinguish this from existing initiatives, such as the new UK–Australia Cyber and Critical Technology Partnership announced at the January 2022 '2+2' AUKMIN meeting of foreign and defence ministers.

The inclusion of counter-hypersonics in addition to hypersonics, in April 2022, is a reminder that AUKUS is in part a reaction to the technological advances of potential adversaries. China tested a hypersonic missile over the South China Sea in November 2021, while Russia has invested heavily in this area. AUKUS has also created an innovation working group to help capture technological advances by private industry as well as government R&D efforts. It is not clear, though, how effectively AUKUS can foster greater collaboration between defence and technology companies that are commercial competitors.

One constraint common to all three AUKUS members, including the US, is the availability of human capital. AUKUS has expanded to a total of 17 working groups: nine in nuclear propulsion and eight in advanced technologies, including a catch-all category of 'information sharing'. The challenge of staffing AUKUS is most acute for Australia, given its smaller population base and requirement to stand up a nuclear-qualified workforce from a very limited base (Australia operates a solitary research reactor at Lucas Heights). Recruiting submariners has been difficult for the Australian navy, even with a force of just six conventional boats. The move to nuclear propulsion means recruiting more people and adds considerably to the length and complexity of training, including nuclear qualification for a large proportion of the crews. AUKUS poses a basic 'supply' challenge for its members, given the existing intense competition for science, technology, engineering and maths (STEM) graduates, and is likely to require comprehensive investments in education. There are also opportunity costs to consider.

International reactions

AUKUS met a mixed international reception. The fact that it was announced before Canberra had communicated its decision to abort the French submarine contract badly strained relations with France. President Emmanuel Macron and his principals reacted furiously, recalling France's ambassadors to Australia and the US. Macron accused Morrison of lying and downgraded France's strategic partnership with Australia. Biden, who claimed to have been blindsided by the French fallout, mounted a rapid rapprochement campaign. French odium towards London and Canberra has been more open-ended, though the change of government in Australia in May 2022 provides an opportunity to reset relations.

The fact that AUKUS groups together three 'Anglosphere' countries, but has no Asian member, has not helped to 'sell' it to the region. China's reaction was predictably hostile, alleging that AUKUS was fuelling a regional arms race and weakening non-proliferation regimes. India has tacitly welcomed AUKUS, while Japan has openly embraced it. Initial responses in Southeast Asia varied. Singapore declared itself 'not unduly anxious', while the Philippine Foreign Ministry lauded AUKUS as a positive contribution to the regional balance of power. Malaysia and Indonesia initially echoed China's criticisms of AUKUS. Privately, though, Malaysia was more equivocal, while Indonesia's

Defence Minister Prabowo Subianto said he respected Australia's decision to acquire nuclear submarines.

In an effort to allay regional concerns about AUKUS and repair relations frayed by Canberra's lack of prior consultation, the US and Australia jointly announced their firm commitment to Southeast Asia and the centrality of the Association of Southeast Asian Nations (ASEAN). Canberra also swiftly dispatched a special envoy to Southeast Asia in the wake of the AUKUS announcement. Australia has remained at pains to reassure its regional partners that AUKUS is intended to supplement, not supplant, the existing regional architecture and that it will continue to abide by its non-nuclear commitments, including adherence to Southeast Asia's Nuclear Weapon-Free Zone.

Over time, regional criticism of AUKUS has ebbed. A recent exception was Solomon Islands, whose prime minister defended his government's lack of transparency, after it was revealed that Honiara and Beijing had concluded a secret security deal in April 2022, by comparing this with the secrecy surrounding the launch of AUKUS. Wider interest in AUKUS may be limited by the fact that there is currently no appetite to expand its membership, although it could yet evolve to engage other countries where additional benefits are identified. Japan, a close ally of the US and bilateral defence partner of Australia and the UK, is the obvious choice for some form of 'AUKUS plus' partnership in the future. But Australia's focus remains squarely on delivering nuclear propulsion, which places practical limits on membership.

AUKUS has had an eventful debut, originating from a failing submarine contract to a high-profile launch and diplomatic fallout, only to recede from public view. Occasional joint statements have served as a reminder that AUKUS remains active and has, in fact, expanded close to the limits of strategic coherence and available capacity. Looking ahead, the high-level political backing that made AUKUS possible could become harder to sustain as the agreement matures, and if perceptions begin to diverge among its membership, a political risk that remains despite broader strategic alignment. It is more likely that AUKUS will slowly stratify as another layer of 'deep state' architecture among the

Anglosphere allies, just as the Five Eyes network has endured and evolved. Cooperation on advanced technologies provides a rationale for AUKUS beyond midwifing the nuclear-submarine project, and could eventually overtake it in importance. But AUKUS's effectiveness will be judged primarily on its ability to deliver an Australian SSN fleet in time to deter threats to Australia and its regional interests and, if this fails, to equip it for a credible military response.

The Milk Tea Alliance
What are the prospects for Asia's online activism?

In April 2020, an online movement taking its name from a popular drink in Asia was born. The Milk Tea Alliance (MTA) originally stemmed from an online argument in which Thai actor Vachirawit 'Bright' Chivaaree, supporting the Hong Kong protests of 2019 on Twitter, faced a nationalist backlash from Chinese netizens. The disagreement escalated to a trans-national social-media battle in which supporters of Vachirawit protested against China's encroachment into the rest of Asia and its support for authoritarian rule, forging solidarity among online grassroots democracy activists and birthing an informal alliance.

From bubble tea in Taiwan to Royal brand milk tea in Myanmar, over ten million tweets, the pan-Asian pro-democracy platform of netizens has persisted for over two years through scores of protests (and crackdowns) from Hong Kong, Taiwan and Thailand to Myanmar. While the movement has reached as far as Belarus, India and Iran, and has been copied by protesters in Russia and Ukraine through the use of their fermented milk drink *ryazhenka*, the MTA is distinctly Asian; it speaks to changing power relations of a more powerful and assertive China, new nodes of contention and an enduring struggle for democracy in East Asia.

From meme to movement

The MTA has attracted attention for its distinctive features. Foremost is its structure, a virtual, leaderless set of loose online networks. Unlike earlier transnational activism tied to concrete personal relationships between individuals and organisations, the MTA lacks distinctive personalities and is more amorphous. The movement has had its own Twitter symbol since April 2021 and has spawned numerous accounts, with its hashtag in use from Canada to the Philippines. Just as it appears to wane, it comes alive again with renewed vigour after arrests or protests.

Its core message promotes democracy, with themes of freedom and justice the most common. It has served to mobilise, inspire and represent democratic alternatives in the face of growing authoritarian rule. Even in comparatively more politically open environments such as Malaysia and the Philippines, the MTA symbol has been appropriated for democratic activism. In the four main locations where it has taken root, the focus varies. In Hong Kong it centres on the 2019–20 Umbrella/Occupy Movement protests and the takeover of democratic space by the Chinese Communist Party (CCP). In Thailand, mobilisation centres on the youth anti-royal protests that lasted for six months in 2020. In Myanmar, Milk Tea hashtags channel opposition to the military, which seized power in February 2021. And in Taiwan, the alliance embodies the democratic political culture of Taiwanese identity, marking its differences from authoritarian China. With democratic space in Asia contracting, the MTA has served to symbolise and reinforce the struggle for democracy, even during some of the region's most brutal crackdowns, as in Myanmar from March 2021 and in Hong Kong from July of the same year.

In part, this is due to how the MTA works. Dissent is expressed through humour and performance, allowing wider participation. Messages, repertoires and even games are created, spread, copied, commented upon, morphed, recirculated and re-enacted in a transnational democratic theatre. Images and symbols facilitate imagined connections of camaraderie and resistance. Playfulness mixes with pragmatic how-to learning guides, such as the HK19 Manual detailing tactics for protesters. In a powerful psychological cocktail of emotions, the MTA evokes empathy with experiences of everyday resistance near and far. Cross-regional connections are forged through digital conversations.

The MTA is tied to Asia's high internet penetration and social-media use, concentrated among the young, who comprise the heart of the movement. It parallels global social-media activism such as Black Lives Matter and #MeToo, yet due to the comparatively high risks of openly participating online in Asia, the MTA movement is less personalised, except in the sharing of stories of martyrs arrested or killed.

Political mobilisation through social media in Asia has expanded almost as rapidly as the technology itself. Thailand's Future Forward party, founded in 2018, used this trend to gain national prominence in just weeks ahead of the country's elections in March 2019. Rather than garner support or promote awareness within the formal politics of parties and policies, as had been the case before 2020, the MTA embraces informal practices and participation that openly challenge the legitimacy of existing elites and political structures, be it the royalty in Thailand, China's control of Hong Kong or Myanmar's military. This reflects how Asia's Zoomers (Generation Z, currently under 25, or 'Gen Z' for short) are participating in politics. Like their cohorts elsewhere, they engage less with voting, opting instead for protests, boycotts and symbolic expressions of resistance. The MTA's youthful activists are imbued with a moral sense of righteousness. Phrases like 'We Will Win' in Myanmar and the song 'Glory to Hong Kong' illustrate the core belief of rightfulness of those supporting the movement. Their political engagement embraces sharing experiences and democratic values on social media.

Yet there are underlying social conditions for Zoomers that reinforce the MTA. Many increasingly feel that their futures are being jeopardised. This is most apparent in Hong Kong and Myanmar, where thousands have been forced into exile and those that remain have had their options for free expression and education shut down. With extensive lockdowns and education disruptions, COVID-19 intensified the pressures Gen Z faced across the region, increasing youth unemployment (in some cases to record levels), limiting the avenues for social advancement and undercutting traditional safety nets of family support.

Weaknesses of soft power

The common enemy that binds the Milk Tea movement is Beijing, initially China's rabid nationalistic social-media 'wolf warriors' and its expansionist ambitions. But as the movement gained traction, China's crackdown in Hong Kong and support for authoritarian leaders in Thailand and Myanmar also began to be targeted for criticism. There is also deep resentment of China's alliance with oligarchic elites, many of whom are seen as corruptly using ties to China for their economic enrichment rather than inclusive development. As a consequence, perceptions of China have become increasingly negative, especially among younger Asians. Survey research in Southeast Asia shows that, with the

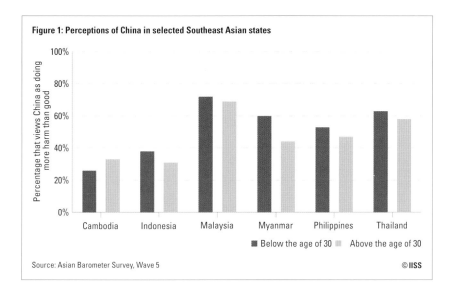

Figure 1: Perceptions of China in selected Southeast Asian states

■ Below the age of 30 ▓ Above the age of 30

Source: Asian Barometer Survey, Wave 5   ©IISS

exception of Cambodia, views of China are more negative among those under 30 than those over 30. The rise of the MTA has both reflected and reinforced these views.

The fact that suspicion of China is highest among Asia's young suggests that its ability to exercise soft power on East Asian populations will decline.

The MTA has portrayed China effectively as Asia's authoritarian mothership. Lacking formal institutionalisation and official signatories, the MTA is not a regional actor in a traditional sense. Yet the core centres of the MTA – Hong Kong, Myanmar, Taiwan and Thailand – comprise their own 'quad', connected in solidarity, and arguably wielding greater influence on their respective societies than the more formal Quad alliance of India, Indonesia, Japan and the United States. Unlike the formal Quad, the MTA allows ordinary citizens to be a part of their informal community and has greater influence on those on the front line of the struggle for democracy across East Asia.

Importantly, the MTA has gained influence without openly embracing the West. While support from the West, particularly in granting political asylum to persecuted activists and in providing funding for resistance/activism, is important, the MTA has maintained its 'Asianness' in its use of symbols and mobilisation. It has become the defender of

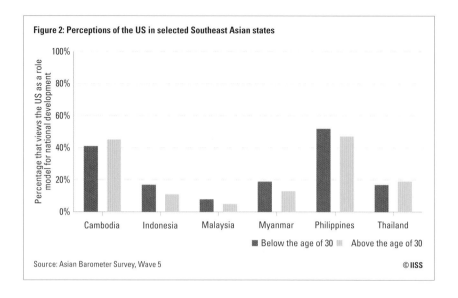

Figure 2: Perceptions of the US in selected Southeast Asian states

Source: Asian Barometer Survey, Wave 5

© IISS

democracy in East Asia by using local forms of legitimacy. In Myanmar, for example, protesters embrace *yadeya* (traditional rituals to delay misfortune) in their repertoires, such as banging pots and pans to drive evil from homes and stepping on images of those who bring bad luck (in this case General Min Aung Hlaing, the self-appointed head of the military's State Administration Council). In Thailand, the protesters propagate their own view of Thai identity by memorialising the important date of the Siamese Revolution of June 1932 and prioritising the central role that people (rather than elites) should play in bringing about democracy. This continues long-standing different interpretations of the role of royalty and citizens in Thai political life and reflects how pro-democracy activists have contextualised their struggle in their country's history.

The MTA has also avoided being drawn into the US–China rivalry, instead focusing on democracy at home in East Asia. The decline of democracy in the US, most notably illustrated by the attack on the Capitol on 6 January 2021, has contributed to a distancing between the MTA and the West. Survey data shows that younger Southeast Asians are not embracing the US as a role model, even as their views of China also grow increasingly negative. The US, like China, wields limited soft power among many Southeast Asian populations.

In contrast, Taiwan has gained soft power from the MTA. Its solidarity with the region's democracy struggle has marked its uniqueness, reinforcing the distinction between Taiwan and China. The rise of the MTA has coincided with Taiwanese President Tsai Ing-wen's New Southbound Policy. Introduced in 2016, the policy aimed to reduce Taiwan's economic dependence on China and to enhance economic, educational and people-to-people ties with Australasia, South Asia and Southeast Asia. With a focus on 18 countries, including Thailand (the original source of the MTA), the policy has driven an increase in trade with Southeast Asia from US$78 billion to US$89bn between 2016 and 2020. The growing number of students from countries that are the focus of the New Southbound Policy studying in Taiwan – from 32,000 in 2016 to 53,000 in 2018 (30,000 of whom were from Southeast Asia) – has been crucial in facilitating this. Even through COVID-19, many on Taiwanese government-funded scholarships continued to come to study there. These connections with young people from member states of the Association of Southeast Asian Nations (ASEAN) have been an investment in Taiwan's future, strengthening support as tensions rise with China as well as deepening MTA ties.

Protests and prison: authoritarian crackdowns

Over the past year East Asia has experienced democratic backsliding, with only Australia, Japan, Mongolia, New Zealand, South Korea, Taiwan and Timor-Leste ranked 'Free' by Freedom House in 2022. Hong Kong is 'Partly Free', while Myanmar and Thailand are ranked 'Not Free'.

The Milk Tea movement has become an integral part of the fight against the region's democratic decline and gained international prominence through pro-democracy street protests from 2020. Whether it was activists speaking out against arrests in Hong Kong, continued demands for monarchical reform in Thailand or youth behind barricades on Yangon roads, the MTA has maintained a persistent visible defiance in 2022. But public pro-democracy protests across East Asia have declined somewhat in 2022. They do still occur in more sporadic form in Myanmar, with many MTA supporters also a part of the People's Defence Force (PDF).

Three drivers account for the retreat of protesters from the streets. First is the pandemic, both the lockdowns and the severity of the virus. Asia experienced its greatest number of COVID-19 deaths in 2021, with over one million officially recorded deaths from the virus. Second is the failure of public protests to achieve concrete concessions from those in power; after months on the streets of Bangkok and Hong Kong and persistent protests across Myanmar, public demands were either deflected or rejected outright. Third, and perhaps most important, those in power have engaged in broad crackdowns, targeting activists and student leaders.

By the time the MTA emerged, protesters in Hong Kong were already on the defensive. The Umbrella/Occupy Movement protests reached their peak in 2019–20. In June 2020, Beijing introduced a draconian national-security law effectively criminalising the protesters. It also overhauled the electoral system, reducing competition to ensure the dominance of pro-Beijing candidates in the legislative assembly and restricting voting rights. In the same year, Hong Kong officials were required to implement a strict zero-COVID policy, limiting meetings in public space. The activists were not spared for their dissent, with 170 arrested under the national-security law by May 2022, and thousands more either arrested for protesting or forced to leave their homes. Those arrested include students, journalists and former lawmakers. The hardline former deputy police commissioner and Beijing loyalist John Lee is now the chief executive.

Myanmar's democratic contraction is similarly deep, with severe consequences for those opposing military rule. After rejecting the National League for Democracy's (NLD) election victory in 2020 and seizing power in February 2021, Myanmar's military has fought to hold on to power, engaged in brutal crackdowns and become embroiled in an expanding civil war. According to the Assistance Association for Political Prisoners Myanmar (Burma) the regime arrested 14,883 citizens and political opponents from February 2021 to July 2022. While accurate figures of deaths caused by the military are not known due to the scope of the fighting, they are believed to exceed 3,000 in the same period. This includes four pro-democracy activists who were brutally put to death in July 2022. Those targeted include artists, students, journalists and lawmakers. The NLD has been especially persecuted. By mid-July 2022, 917 members (98 of them lawmakers) had been arrested. One NLD lawmaker, U Kyaw Myo Min from the southern Mon State, was brutally murdered in early July 2022. One of the four activists recently executed was the former NLD parliamentarian Phyo Zayar Thaw. Yangon NLD member Ko Hla Htoo was tortured to death in a military interrogation centre. Another 19 NLD members have also been killed in detention through torture or inadequate access to healthcare.

Thai Prime Minister Prayuth Chan-ocha has also carried out a crackdown, albeit less violently. According to Thai Lawyers for Human Rights, from November 2020 through to June 2022, 201 individuals, including 16 children, were charged under the *lèse-majesté* provisions of Article 112 and face potentially long sentences.

Spyware and surveillance: technology and cyber control

The important role that social media and digital connections play in pro-democracy activism has expanded into another arena of political contestation: cyberspace. While battles have been waged over the internet for some time, in recent years governments across East Asia have ratcheted up their use of software and surveillance technology to target pro-democracy protesters.

Thailand is illustrative of this trend. The government uses the usual tools to protect itself, including cyber troopers, artificial intelligence (AI) algorithm searches, monitoring and tough laws on users to control dissent. After the 2020 protests and emergence of the MTA, Pegasus spyware was reportedly used to hack into the phones and computers of 30 activists. The authorities also launched a campaign labelling the activists 'nation haters' and 'foreign servants' to undermine pro-democracy narratives.

Next door in Myanmar, the military is also working to control access to the internet. The junta has reportedly procured Chinese facial-recognition cameras as part of its policing to make ten cities 'safe'.

It has also invited Chinese internet technicians to help replicate the 'Great Firewall of China' to control the use of VPNs within Myanmar. After the February 2021 coup, it blocked access to Facebook, Instagram and Twitter. The junta is now following the pattern elsewhere in the region of tightening laws and has proposed a draconian cyber-security law that would allow it to access data, block websites, shut down the internet and prosecute critics and those not seen as compliant, including companies. This broadening of digital repression has made the internet the front line for protecting democracy. Autocrats are going all out to break digital connections in order to undercut the MTA and similar pro-democracy networks.

Resilient democrats

There is a perception that the MTA has waned along with the region's public protests in the face of crackdowns and digital repression. This is not the case. The alliance continues to take strength from events beyond the borders of any one country. The Thai protests drew experience, support and inspiration from Hong Kong, as the Myanmar protests did from Thailand. Each week the MTA publishes an events calendar, reinforcing the momentum of the alliance and keeping the pan-Asian democracy community alive. The MTA has sustained itself through its use of social media, which allows individuals to participate in private.

The salience of the MTA's digital connections has increased as repressive conditions have intensified, especially in Hong Kong and Myanmar. There is now a broader Asian community watching, surveying what is happening next door and sharing knowledge. There is greater solidarity across the region with those being repressed. The digital conversations continue, with dialogues on and with alternative governments in Myanmar, notably the National Unity Government, and survival strategies for those opting to brave the crackdowns. In short, the MTA allows hope to stay alive and Asia's pro-democracy movement to imagine a better future – virtually.

Drivers of Strategic Change

REGIONAL SHARE OF GLOBAL POPULATION, GDP AND DEFENCE BUDGET

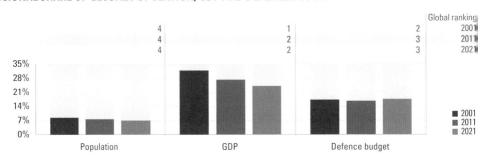

POPULATION

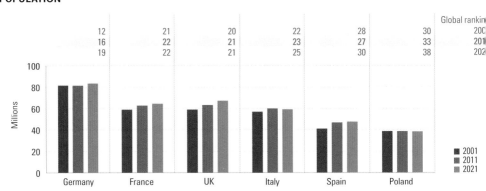

AGE STRUCTURE
(Percentage of national population)

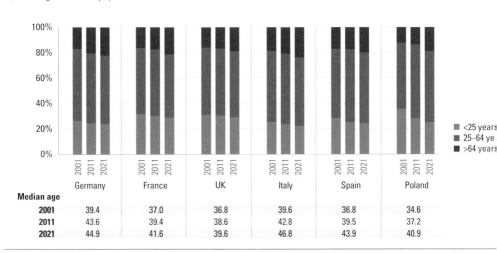

Median age	Germany	France	UK	Italy	Spain	Poland
2001	39.4	37.0	36.8	39.6	36.8	34.6
2011	43.6	39.4	38.6	42.8	39.5	37.2
2021	44.9	41.6	39.6	46.8	43.9	40.9

Economic and demographic trends chart relative decline. But there is headroom to meet the challenge of war and insecurity in Europe with higher defence commitments. As a rich, free continent, it wields soft power – though Poland's doubling of GDP per capita in two decades has been followed by the erosion of democratic governance.

GDP
(Constant 2010 US dollars)

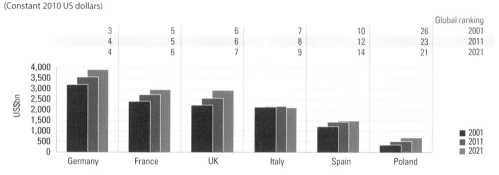

GDP PER CAPITA
(Constant 2010 US dollars)

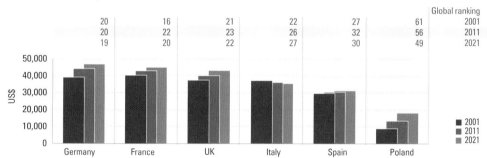

DEFENCE BUDGET
(Constant 2015 US dollars)

ACTIVE MILITARY PERSONNEL

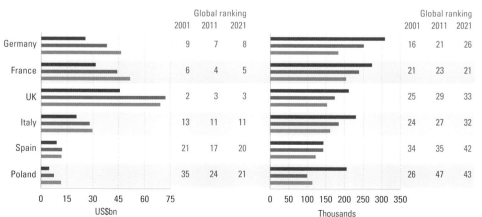

For explanation of drivers and sources, see page 8

HUMAN DEVELOPMENT INDEX (HDI)
(Score between 0 and 1, where 0 denotes a low level of development and 1 a high level of development)

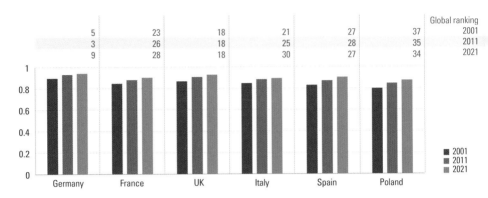

POLITICAL SYSTEM
(Score between 0 and 100, where 0 denotes no political freedom and 100 fully free)

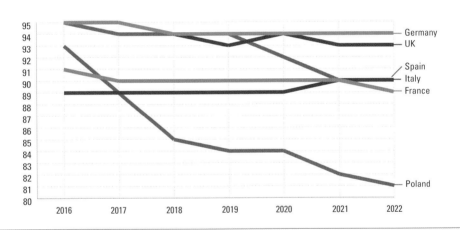

TRUST IN GOVERNMENT
(Average level of trust)

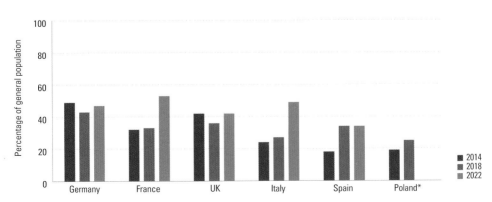

* No 2022 data available for Poland

2021–22 Review

For much of the second half of 2021, European politics was still dominated by the coronavirus pandemic. Efforts at the national and European Union levels focused on containing further waves of the virus and managing the challenging diplomacy of vaccine roll-outs. Several countries faced large-scale domestic protests, with demonstrators denouncing what they saw as repressive rules. Their anger focused on policy decisions such as the introduction of vaccine passes in many countries, or a doomed push (in the case of a few) for mandatory vaccinations. EU–United Kingdom relations, already strained by the process of Brexit, were again damaged by months of disputes between the EU and the UK-headquartered AstraZeneca over the slow pace of the company's delivery of COVID-19 vaccines to the EU. Relations were then further strained by implied threats to UK vaccine deliveries from the EU as countries raced to vaccinate their respective populations. However, initial disparities in vaccine roll-out rates rapidly decreased. By the end of 2021, 68.84% of the EU's total population and 70.50% of the UK's had been fully vaccinated (compared with 63.08% for the United States).

Europe's part in the global vaccine roll-out was substantial, with the EU becoming the world's biggest exporter of vaccines. By June 2022, the EU had exported more than two billion doses of COVID-19 vaccines to 168 countries. A controversial export and transparency authorisation mechanism, introduced to ensure that there were enough vaccine supplies for Europe, was allowed to expire at the end of the calendar year. However, a pledge to donate 700 million doses by the middle of 2022 was undoubtedly helped by initial European over-ordering and the depleting shelf lives of vaccines stocks.

Managing old challenges

From mid-2021 to mid-2022, several enduring policy challenges continued to plague Europe and the EU without notable resolution. Migration, for instance, continued to be a key issue for the continent. This was

evidenced by divisions over the policing of the EU's common external borders and the ongoing challenge of reforming EU migration and
asylum rules. Pressures here were further exacerbated by the humanitarian crisis at the EU's borders that developed from mid-2021, following
Belarus's efforts to bring in thousands of migrants from the Middle
East and send them to its borders with and Lithuania. EU Commission
President Ursula von der Leyen labelled it a 'hybrid attack'. The EU
accordingly updated its sanctions regime to permit it to respond to the
instrumentalisation of migrants for political purposes. Unprecedented
migratory pressures following Russia's invasion of Ukraine spurred the
adoption in June 2022 of a voluntary solidarity mechanism supporting
member states on the front line of migratory pressures, which could
prove to be a first step forward in the long-stalled reform of EU migration and asylum rules.

European economies were forced to revise their growth forecasts
downwards, as the outbreak of war in Ukraine curtailed the anticipated economic rebound from COVID-19. The war also complicated
the ongoing debate, already exacerbated by the pandemic-induced
deterioration of public finances, over reform of the EU's fiscal rules.
In May 2022, the European Commission confirmed its intention to
prolong the temporary suspension of the 1997 Stability and Growth
Pact (which requires member states to aim for a balanced budget and
not exceed a public deficit of 3% of GDP or national debt of 60% of
GDP) until the end of 2023. Plans to reactivate these fiscal rules in
2024 are likely to be contingent on, amongst other things, the evolution of the war in Ukraine. Public investment looks set to expand
in critical areas such as energy security, the green transition and
digital transformation.

The EU continued to face rule-of-law challenges. In February 2022,
Hungary and Poland lost their legal challenge against an EU mechanism
that permits the withholding of EU funds for member states consistently
breaching principles of the rule of law. Two days after Viktor Orbán
won a fourth term as Hungary's prime minister in April 2022, the EU
announced it would formally trigger a conditionality mechanism to

make the reception of EU common funds conditional on a country complying with the rule of law. While the procedure ahead is long, complex and unprecedented, the mechanism has the potential to suspend some or all of the EU's annual disbursements to Budapest.

Europe's continuing struggle against the forces of populism remained mixed. Whilst Orbán extended his autocratic rule, populist billionaire and Czech prime minister Andrej Babiš narrowly lost his grip on power following the October 2021 legislative election, and his Slovenian counterpart Janez Janša suffered a heavy defeat in April's 2022 national election. French President Emmanuel Macron fought off a challenge from the far right in the April 2022 presidential election, only to find his alliance losing its parliamentary majority in France's legislative elections two months later.

Italy's political system remained characterised by instability through to June 2022, even as its key institutions were headed by three highly respected public servants: Sergio Mattarella was re-elected as president, former prime minister Giuliano Amato was nominated as head of Italy's supreme court and Mario Draghi continued to serve as prime minister. Indeed, in December 2021, *The Economist* magazine chose Italy as its 'country of the year'. 'Not', as the magazine hastened to add, 'for the prowess of its footballers, who won Europe's big trophy, nor its pop stars, who won the Eurovision Song Contest, but for its politics'.

Russia's invasion of Ukraine, and President Volodymyr Zelenskyy's subsequent call for Ukraine to be given candidate status, gave fresh impetus to debates on EU enlargement policy. The EU fast-tracked the granting of this status to Ukraine and Moldova (but not Georgia) at its June 2022 European Council meeting. But the process from this first official step towards EU membership is well known to be long and tortuous. German Chancellor Olaf Scholz highlighted a further challenge with his call for EU institutional and voting reform, including the extension of qualified majority voting to EU foreign- and security-policy decisions prior to the EU being ready to admit any further member states.

Confronting new threats

Russia's invasion of Ukraine brought war to the border of four EU states: Hungary, Poland, Romania and Slovakia. Von der Leyen labelled it 'a moment of truth for Europe'. In close coordination with the UK and US, the EU imposed a series of unprecedented sanctions packages aimed at isolating Russia diplomatically, militarily, technologically and economically. Whilst individual European states offered more significant support for Ukraine's efforts to defend itself, for the first time in its history the EU jointly financed the provision of weapons to a third country. EU member states also expelled an unprecedented number of Russian intelligence officers. Europe-wide efforts to reduce energy dependency and build a more resilient economic base also gained new momentum even as they highlighted past policy failures. In June 2022, after a series of difficult discussions, the EU unanimously agreed to a partial ban on Russian oil imports, and the EU and the UK coordinated sanctions banning the insurance of ships carrying Russian oil. The delayed activation of the embargo (which, for example, impacts crude oil after six months and oil products after eight months), and the exemptions that were negotiated for this, risked short-term counter-productive effects, as tightening global oil markets pushed prices ever higher. Nonetheless, the decision will have a significant impact on Russia from 2023 and was important for demonstrating European determination to reduce its energy dependency. High Representative Josep Borrell suggested that European responses in the weeks that followed Russia's invasion represented 'the belated birth of a geopolitical Europe'.

While the change in geopolitical and geo-economic thinking was certainly dramatic, there were limits to European responses, especially concerning the difficulties of cutting dependence on Russian hydrocarbons and providing heavy weaponry to Ukraine. Russian gas supplies remained unsanctioned, and Gazprombank was exempted from the exclusion of other major Russian banks from SWIFT. Only in mid-June 2022 did Germany begin to deliver heavy weapons to Ukraine.

The UK offered among the strongest and most consistent support for Ukraine. However, tensions with the EU sharpened over the implementation of the Northern Ireland Protocol and UK attempts to renegotiate or replace the protocol in light of the practical difficulties being experienced by businesses moving goods between Great Britain and Northern Ireland. Signed as part of the UK–EU Withdrawal Agreement, the protocol was designed to prevent a hard border on the island of Ireland. Even as it allowed Northern Ireland to maintain frictionless access to the EU, though, it required goods entering Northern Ireland from Great Britain to prove they complied with the relevant EU laws. After months of failed negotiations with the EU following a July 2021 UK Command Paper that set out the UK's views on the required amendments, in June 2022, the UK tabled a bill that would allow it to unilaterally override the protocol.

Defence developments

In a speech in December 2021 ahead of a European Council meeting discussing security and defence, European Council President Charles Michel prophetically branded 2022 as 'the year of European defence'. Russia's invasion of Ukraine soon ensured this would be the case, although it also critically underlined the centrality of NATO to European defence. The invasion prompted Finland and Sweden to apply to join the Alliance. Their substantive and modern defence capabilities and defence-related industries will strengthen the Alliance, even as enlargement doubles the length of NATO's border with Russia (adding 1,340 kilometres). In June 2022, NATO allies agreed to a new Strategic Concept, defining the security challenges the Alliance faces and the political and military tasks that NATO will carry out to help address them. Working in parallel to NATO, the UK Joint Expeditionary Force (consisting of Denmark, Estonia, Finland, Iceland, Latvia, Lithuania, the Netherlands, Norway and Sweden and led by the UK as the 'framework nation') was notably active in bolstering European support for Ukraine as well as reinforcing the credibility of European defence and deterrence.

Russia's invasion contributed to a change in the trajectory of European defence and security. On 1 March 2022, von der Leyen claimed that 'European security and defence has evolved more in the last six days than in the last two decades'. Several European countries announced increased levels of defence spending. The first and most significant to do so was Germany. Just four days after Russia's invasion, Chancellor Scholz announced, as part of his *Zeitenwende* ('turning point') address to the German Bundestag, increases in German defence expenditure including a €100bn fund to bolster the German armed forces. Over the next three weeks, Belgium, Romania, Poland, Italy and Norway announced increases, and others followed. On 1 June 2022, Denmark voted in a referendum to end its opt-out from EU defence and security policy. Questions remained, however, over how new defence spending would be invested and how sustainable it would be.

A May 2022 report by the European Commission highlighted a €160bn European defence-investment shortfall resulting from a decade of inadequate defence funding. Recommendations included increasing weapons and munitions stocks, removing Soviet-era kit from EU member state inventories, and investing more in air and missile defence. Challenges of defence-industrial cooperation continued – according to the same report, only 11% of defence investment was spent collaboratively, against a target of 35%. Complex joint projects like the trinational Future Combat Air System stalled over issues between two of the three prime contractors. More encouragingly, in June 2022, France, Germany, Greece, Italy, the Netherlands and the UK signed a memorandum of understanding to cooperate on a next-generation helicopter.

In March 2022, the EU adopted its Strategic Compass for Security and Defence. While this offered the first-ever agreed common EU threat assessment, the practicality of some initiatives appeared questionable. For example, a 5,000-strong EU Rapid Deployment Capacity commanded by the EU Military Planning and Conduct Capability seemed unlikely to materialise any time soon. The history of European defence is littered with unfulfilled initiatives. Thus, even as Russia's invasion of Ukraine strengthened Europe's political will to work more closely together, nation-states remained hesitant to subordinate national-level decision-making on defence issues.

Implications for European foreign-policy engagement

Russia's invasion highlighted concerns about European strategic dependencies more broadly, including in relation to China. Indeed, the risk of China weaponising its economic ties was evident after China imposed punitive restrictions on Lithuanian trade following Lithuania's establishment of a Taiwanese Representative office in November 2021. A fraught EU–China summit in April 2022 further highlighted diverging paths. There would be no revival of discussions on the doomed Comprehensive Agreement on Investment. Attitudes hardened further following the leak of Xinjiang police files that documented the mass internment of Uighurs in China's northwestern province. In June 2022, the European Parliament adopted a resolution labelling the Chinese Communist Party's (CCP) actions in Xinjiang as 'crimes against humanity' providing 'serious indications of a possible genocide'.

The EU's release of its Strategy for Cooperation in the Indo-Pacific in September 2021 was somewhat usurped by the announcement of the AUKUS security pact between Australia, the UK and the US the previous day. Nevertheless, in February 2022, as part of its six-month rotating presidency of the Council of the European Union, France hosted an Indo-Pacific ministerial meeting. The forum brought together European institutions and foreign-affairs ministers (or their representatives) from the 27 EU member states, around 30 of their Indo-Pacific counterparts, and representatives of regional organisations from the Indian Ocean and the Pacific Ocean. Boosting engagement with partners in the Indo-Pacific remains a key part of European strategy in responding to China, diversifying economic ties and supporting a rules-based order.

In December 2021, the EU also set out its 'Global Gateway' plan for investment in major infrastructure projects around the world, billed indirectly as an alternative to China's Belt and Road Initiative (BRI). It aims to mobilise up to €300bn in investments in connectivity projects between 2021 and 2027. Critics were quick to point out that this was largely a repackaging of pre-committed funds. However, the plan's defenders noted that because the EU and its member states are already the world's largest development donors, the challenge was not to commit new resources but to deploy existing resources more strategically.

India attracted notable diplomatic investment from several European countries – most significantly France in the wake of AUKUS but also Germany and the UK. While there were evident frustrations with the country's diplomatic positioning following Russia's invasion of Ukraine, this spurred European enthusiasm for engagement, not least due to India's longer-term pre-invasion trend of attempting to reduce its own dependencies on Russia.

Transatlantic relations took a knock following the US-led withdrawal from Afghanistan, which served as another unwelcome reminder of Europe's limited capabilities for autonomous action. Speaking at the Bled Strategic Forum in September 2021, Michel suggested that Europe needed to 'strive for greater decision-making autonomy and greater capacity for action in the world'. However, Russia's attack on Ukraine soon reinvigorated the transatlantic partnership, with the US playing a critical role in the provision of military equipment and heavy weapons to Ukraine, whilst also underlining its centrality for the defence of Europe. Positive transatlantic dynamics were further supported by the closer sense of alignment on China, although this should not be overstated. The inaugural meeting of the EU–US Trade and Technology Council took place in September 2021, with ten working groups established to deepen EU–US cooperation across areas including artificial intelligence, semiconductors and export controls. Outcomes from the second ministerial meeting in May 2022 included the agreement to create an EU–US Strategic Standardisation Information Mechanism to work together on international-standards development.

Elsewhere, the countries of the Western Balkans moved back up the priority lists of many European countries. There was growing concern over the region's stability as the forces of secessionism strengthened with the influence of Russia and China. Both the UK and the new German government appointed special envoys to the region. But with European influence closely tied to the credibility of its offering further European integration, the EU struggled to persuade Bulgaria to drop its veto on the start of EU accession talks with North Macedonia and, by extension, with Albania.

Although in late June Bulgaria's parliament did finally approve the lifting of the country's veto on accession talks, paving the way for a deal, the EU's failure to accelerate the accession process for countries of the Western Balkans at the June 2022 European Council continued to undermine its credibility and influence, leaving a vacuum that others could exploit.

In February 2022, the EU held its sixth summit with the African Union (AU), with Brussels keen to recover ground lost to Beijing, which has become Africa's largest bilateral lender and a major investor and financier of infrastructure on the continent. South African President Cyril Ramaphosa was blunt in his scepticism concerning European follow-through on the panoply of commitments announced there. In Mali, France's relationship with the military junta continued to deteriorate as both sought to stem the ongoing jihadist insurgency. The arrival of the Wagner Group, the so-called 'private military company' closely linked to Russian military intelligence, further soured relations. In February 2022, after nine years of French anti-terrorist operations in Mali, President Macron announced the total withdrawal of French forces from the country, even as he emphasised France's ongoing commitment to fighting terrorism across the Sahel. The EU similarly suspended its military training mission in Mali, and Niger stepped in to help host French and European special forces pushing back against jihadist insurgency across the Sahel.

Concerns over energy security helped invigorate European engagement in an increasingly multipolar Middle East, albeit with limited success, as European powers continued to struggle to translate economic weight into strategic influence. For example, energy partnerships featured prominently in the EU–Gulf Cooperation Council Joint Action Program for 2022–27. Europeans were, however, at the forefront of global diplomacy on climate change. The UK hosted COP26 in Glasgow in November 2021, where the EU and US pushed, amongst other initiatives, a Global Methane Pledge to limit methane emissions that was eventually signed by more than 100 countries. The European Commission continued work on its July 2021 announcement of a package of proposals aimed at reducing emissions by 55% by 2030, with the intent of making Europe the world's first climate-neutral continent.

Germany's New Government
How has the coalition responded to war in Europe and other challenges?

On 8 December 2021, Germany's second-longest-serving chancellor finally had a successor. Olaf Scholz, Angela Merkel's finance minister through her fourth and final term in office, took over as leader of Europe's largest economy.

The September 2021 federal elections that called time on Merkel's political career also marked the end of her centre-right Christian Democratic Union's (CDU) 16-year grip on power. Uninspired by its chosen heir, Armin Laschet, and undermined by infighting with its Bavarian sister party, the Christian Socialist Union (CSU), the CDU was narrowly beaten to first place by Scholz's centre-left Social Democratic Party (SPD). The 24.1% of support recorded by the CDU represented the party's worst-ever federal-election result. In five years, it had lost the support of 6.5 million voters.

Speculation that subsequent coalition negotiations would leave Germany without a government into the start of 2022 and beyond proved unfounded. In the end, it took just 73 days to agree a three-party 'traffic light' government, working to a 177-page coalition agreement. (By contrast, following the federal elections of September 2017 over five months passed before a coalition government was formed.) Between them, the coalition commanded 416 of the 736 seats in Germany's increasingly unwieldy federal parliament. Germany's Green party entered national office for the first time, as the junior coalition partner to the SPD, supported by the Free Democratic Party (FDP).

Merkel's time in office saw her outlast three US presidents, three French presidents, four British prime ministers and seven Italian prime ministers. It will be hard for Scholz to do the same. As the campaign trail highlighted, the new German chancellor heads a three-party coalition with some conspicuous differences on key policies, most notably over the fiscal future of Europe's Economic and Monetary Union. Impressive displays of party leadership and discipline have been required to prevent policy differences from becoming more apparent following Russia's invasion of Ukraine and the challenges of arms-exports policies and hydrocarbon dependencies that this highlighted. Differences were also evident elsewhere. In April 2022, a draft bill that would have made coronavirus vaccination compulsory from the age of 60, which was supported by Scholz and Health Minister Karl Lauterbach, was defeated in the Bundestag after they failed to build a cross-party consensus.

The coalition embodied a desire for both continuity and change that was always going to be difficult to balance. During his election campaign, Scholz embraced large parts of Merkel's legacy, both in substance and in style. (In a campaign photo shoot for the *Süddeutsche Zeitung*, he even posed with Merkel's trademark rhombus hand gesture as he sought to present himself as the continuity candidate.) Yet a matter of months into office, and in response to Russia's invasion of Ukraine, Scholz found himself pronouncing a *Zeitenwende* (a 'turning point'). The legacy of the former government, in which he had been a key figure, took on a different hue. Persistent underfunding of the German armed forces, broken procurement processes, the wilful failure to think strategically about energy security – most obvious in its misguided fealty to Nord Stream 2 – and the poor progress made on a green transition all stood exposed.

Examining the *Zeitenwende* …

Scholz's Bundestag address was a watershed speech in response to a watershed event. It followed on the heels of what was already a watershed few days in German policymaking. That it was all overseen by the leader of a party that invented Ostpolitik and where traditions of detente still ran deep made it sound all the more remarkable.

But the revolution was relative. The starting point was, after all, underwhelming. Even as more than 100,000 Russian troops gathered on Ukraine's borders, the new chancellor was reaffirming positions that only days later he would be forced to repudiate. Germany, Scholz said, had a 'clear policy of not delivering arms to crisis regions, and that includes not sending lethal weapons to Ukraine'. This extended even to refusing permission for Estonia to export old German howitzers to

Ukraine. The best that the government could offer militarily at this point was 5,000 protective helmets and a field hospital. Scholz again defended Nord Stream 2 as a 'private commercial project', rejecting allied concerns about the pipeline's unwelcome strategic implications for Ukraine and Germany.

Then, on 22 February, following Russia's formal recognition of Ukraine's breakaway republics of Donetsk and Luhansk, the new German government finally announced that it was halting Nord Stream 2. On 26 February, it announced it would supply Ukraine with 1,000 anti-tank weapons and 500 *Stinger* surface-to-air missiles. Finally, Scholz's speech on 27 February presented a package of measures that appeared to mark the most fundamental of shifts in German security and defence thinking. Underlining Germany's unconditional commitment to its NATO defence obligations, Scholz announced, amongst other initiatives, that Germany would immediately spend 2% of its GDP on defence. A €100 billion extra-budgetary fund focused on procurement would be made available to help bridge, through to 2025, the funding gaps the 2% commitment presented.

Unprecedented developments followed. In March, the government placed an order for 35 F-35 fighter jets to enable it to continue its nuclear-sharing obligations beyond the lifecycle of its ageing *Tornado* fighters. It approved the purchase of 140 armed drones from Israel. (This acquisition was decided under the previous government but was held up by SPD objections that have now disappeared.) A bill aimed at anchoring the €100bn fund in Germany's constitution in order to prevent any future diversions of this money as a part of usual budgetary negotiations was passed in parliament. Germany's annual spending on defence could increase by as much as 50% in 2022. While the transformation will take years to deliver substantive effects, these commitments, in theory, currently put Germany on course to become the world's third-largest defence spender after the United States and China.

Albeit consistently slightly late and under pressure, the Chancellery repeatedly pushed back its own red lines. For most of April, Scholz insisted that Germany would not deliver tanks or other heavy weapons to Ukraine. Germany's armouries were, he suggested – somewhat surprisingly, and perhaps conveniently – bare of usable equipment. Furthermore, he argued, he was concerned about triggering an escalation of hostilities that could lead to nuclear war. Yet just four days after the interview in which he expressed these concerns was published, Germany agreed to send 50 of its decommissioned *Gepard* anti-aircraft tanks to Ukraine. Then, when it became clear that Germany could not, by itself, supply sufficient ammunition for Ukraine immediately to be able to make use of this commitment, in May Germany was seemingly almost embarrassed into joining the growing ranks of allied nations supplying Ukraine with self-propelled armoured howitzers. Germany offered a modest but respectable seven such artillery pieces, which it said would arrive in theatre in June and which came with prior German-Dutch training provision. Further promises in June that Germany would, in the months ahead, supply Ukraine with one IRIS-T Air Defence System and three *Mars* II multiple rocket launchers, while welcome, were hardly the swift deployment of capability that Ukraine urgently sought.

Vice Chancellor and former Green party co-leader Robert Habeck oversaw contingency measures that slowly eroded government resistance to quicker sanctioning of Russian hydrocarbons. By the advent of discussion on the European Union's sixth package of sanctions, Germany was no longer leading the opposition to the prohibition of Russian oil imports, and had instead declared its ambition to end all Russian oil imports by the end of the year. Having initially blocked SWIFT sanctions from extending to Russian banks, by March Germany had agreed to the inclusion of seven Russian banks in SWIFT sanctions, with notable exemptions for Gazprombank and Sberbank, Russia's largest bank. By May, its objection to the inclusion of Sberbank had also been dropped. As plans were hastily drawn up to help Germany move away from its dependency on Russian hydrocarbons, the government signed contracts worth €3bn for the lease of four floating liquefied natural gas (LNG) terminals, as well as ramping up plans for two new LNG import terminals in Wilhemshaven and Brunsbüttel. Nevertheless, by the end of June 2022, the extent of Germany's strategically inept dependence on

Russian hydrocarbons stood painfully exposed, as gas supplies from Russia continued to fall and concerns about access to sufficient and reliable supplies of energy for industry and private households through the winter ahead continued to rise.

… and its domestic challenges

In Germany's conventional domestic political context, much of this is remarkable. Indeed, some of the chancellor's reluctance to break with old shibboleths even after his announcement of the *Zeitenwende* reflects the substantive party-management challenges its delivery entails. Party leaders found themselves required to confront, or at least quieten, their respective bases. For the SPD, this meant selling to the base the idea that isolating Russia rather than engaging with it was now the only viable policy option. For the Greens – the most hawkish of the three coalition partners on Russia policy – this meant encouraging the party to step further away from its pacifist roots, supporting the restarting of coal-fired power plants in order to help conserve natural gas and accepting Germany's role in nuclear-sharing. Lastly, for the fiscally conservative, pro-business FDP, it meant enabling off-budget expenditure and agreeing to sanctions against which many German businesses were at least privately lobbying.

The scale of the challenge was also reflected in civil society. As Russian forces gathered on Ukraine's borders, Germany's naval chief had to resign when he argued, in extreme terms, that Vladimir Putin 'probably' deserved respect and that anyway Germany needed Russia to counter China. Once the invasion was under way, several open letters, albeit often signed by public figures well past their point of peak influence, urged the German government to do everything possible to achieve a ceasefire, even if this meant pushing territorial compromises on Ukraine that rewarded Russian aggression. Public support for the delivery of heavy weapons to Ukraine, which had been showing a clear majority, threatened to wane. A poll by DeutschlandTrend published on the day of the Bundestag vote to supply heavy weapons suggested a drop of 10 percentage points in support for such deliveries within a month, as concerns over conflict escalation grew. As Scholz addressed a rally of trade unionists on 3 May, the tension between where he appeared to want to lead the government and the resistance he needed to overcome in order to bring his base along with him was on full display. To choruses of boos, chants of 'warmonger' and banners calling to 'de-escalate instead of provoking', Scholz pushed back: 'It must' he snapped, 'seem cynical to a citizen of Ukraine to be told to defend himself against Putin's aggression without weapons'. Polling supported a graduated end to Russian oil and gas imports over a hard stop.

But still, what's missing?

Nevertheless, as remarkable as what Germany announced in those heady few days in February was what it still seemed unable to do in the weeks that followed. Even as German politicians lined up to denounce Russia's aggression, they struggled to find ways to limit the flow of US$850m a day that Europe still sent to Russia for its energy resources. Their speedy support for the EU to stop Russian coal imports by August 2022 represented a relatively small part of these revenues, and the least challenging hydrocarbon adjustment for the German economy. Even as Germany shifted position on sanctioning Russian oil, Russian gas remained firmly off limits. German dependence was simply too great, and the associated infrastructure requirements too complex.

Notably absent from the debate on German arms exports was the German defence ministry. The new minister, the SPD's Christine Lambrecht, who had been justice and family minister in the Merkel government, struggled to use her platform to push policy forward. She quickly became the easy scapegoat for slow weapons deliveries that were more likely the consequence of years of systemic defence-ministry underspend.

There was no apparent desire within the Chancellery even to try to lead European responses to Russian aggression. Instead, the aim was to stay firmly within the pack of NATO allies. Repeated justifications of actions on the basis of the need for 'unity' and the emphasis on being 'in concert' with other NATO allies implicitly suggested that decisions were being driven as much by the need to maintain Western unity as they were by a strategic appreciation that it was also in Germany's security interests for Ukraine to repel Russia's invasion.

There were notable exceptions to the desire to stay inconspicuously within the mainstream. Even before coming into office, the leadership of the German Green party had campaigned both for an end to Nord Stream 2 and for the export of weapons to Ukraine. Indeed, when in July 2021 Habeck argued that Germany should send arms to Ukraine to help the country prepare its defences against further Russian aggression, Merkel's spokesman dismissively responded that the government would stick to 'responsible policies regarding arms exports'. One month after entering office, German Foreign Minister and senior Green party figure Annalena Baerbock travelled to Moscow for her debut meeting with Sergei Lavrov, highlighting a range of issues on which 'our opinions differ hugely, in part fundamentally'. In reviewing the visit, Russia's Rossiya-1 state broadcaster commented: 'She is set on a confrontation course with Russia … she behaved as if she was from the US Congress, not from the Bundestag.' When, in May, Baerbock became the highest-ranking German government official to visit Ukraine since the invasion, she was commendably clear in her statements. Germany would cut its imports of Russian energy to zero, and it would then 'stay that way for ever'. Marie-Agnes Strack-Zimmermann, the FDP head of the Bundestag's defence committee, was equally outspoken in pushing for Germany to do more to aid the defence of Ukraine.

International attention on the limitations of Germany's *Zeitenwende* was intensified by the Ukrainian ambassador to Berlin, Andrij Melnyk, who took on a very public role in upbraiding Germany for its past and present policy failings. These failures were further magnified by the understandable outspokenness of Ukrainian President Volodymyr Zelenskyy himself, whether through his address to the Bundestag in March, or his disinterest in playing host to the only recently re-elected German President Frank-Walter Steinmeier. (Steinmeier had previously played key roles in governments supporting years of what Zelenskyy saw as clearly misguided German policies towards Russia, dating back to Steinmeier's time as chief of staff to former chancellor Gerhard

Schröder.) The notable transparency of the German system also played a part in perpetuating and highlighting the drama: a German chancellor cannot quietly command arms exports in ways afforded to a French president or a UK prime minister.

The consequences for Germany's position in Europe

There were signs of European unease with German thinking even before the crisis broke. In June 2021, leaders from other EU member states intervened to thwart efforts by Merkel and French President Emmanuel Macron to hold an EU summit with Putin. In January 2022, as Russian troops gathered, with little apparent course correction from the new government in Berlin, Latvia's defence minister warned that Berlin's actions (and inactions) were 'driving a division line between west and east in Europe' as a result of its 'immoral and hypocritical' relationship with Russia and China. A coalition that appeared, on paper and at the outset, potentially to be the most committed pro-European German coalition in years found itself inadvertently highlighting European divisions, to potentially damaging longer-term effect.

As Germany hesitated, the United Kingdom, Baltic countries, Poland, the Czech Republic and Slovakia were among those spearheading and coordinating European policy responses. Their agenda was clearer: military support for Ukraine, strong sanctions on Russia with a focus on immediate implementation, a meaningful framework for Ukraine's future cooperation with the West and the provision of accompanying security guarantees. Leadership, Germany learnt to its cost – given the reputational damage its position incurred in Central and Eastern Europe in particular – could come from sources other than the Franco-German axis.

Foreign policy beyond the *Zeitenwende*

Germany's new government was ready to change course on China even prior to Russia's invasion of Ukraine. But just six months into the government's four-year term, it is perhaps clearer what the new government has changed away from, than what it is changing towards.

The Greens and the FDP took office with no illusions of *Wandel durch Handel* ('change through trade'). Baerbock warned China of 'fundamental differences', even as her Chinese counterpart urged Germany to avoid 'megaphone diplomacy' and to continue to find quiet routes for productive cooperation.

How the new government's China policy, and its foreign- and security-policy thinking more generally, will evolve should become clearer as Germany, under Baerbock's supervision, draws up its first-ever National Security Strategy (NSS), and an accompanying China strategy. The government has set itself the target of publishing this by the end of 2022. Both the NSS and Germany's new China strategy will inevitably be informed by thinking set out in the EU's Strategic Compass and NATO's new Strategic Concept.

Germany's coalition agreement continued the line of the previous government's Indo-Pacific guidelines. Both notably emphasised the importance of deepening relations with India, even as gaps between ambition and reality continued and arguably widened after Russia's invasion of Ukraine. In March 2022, the German frigate *Bayern* returned from its seven-month tour of the Indo-Pacific. But capacity for defence engagement in the Indo-Pacific will remain limited, with increased funding for the Bundeswehr taking time to improve the situation of the navy, the German military's smallest branch.

On 1 January 2022, Germany's new government took over the rotating chair of the G7. Policy priorities, at least initially, focused on climate change, COVID-19 and China. This included the formulation of plans to develop a club of the willing on climate within the G7 framework, aimed in part at compensating for the lack of enforcement mechanisms in the Paris agreement, while protecting club members from competitive disadvantages in international trade. Russian actions sharpened further the G7's identity as a values-based group of democratic market economies, handing Germany a central role leading up to important G7 and NATO meetings in June.

Baerbock played a critical role embracing Germany's transatlantic and NATO commitments. Together with Habeck, she put forward a new transatlantic agenda for the two countries to work closely together to offer a 'democratic alternative' to the 'authoritarian hegemonic ambitions' of others, most notably China. And at a joint press conference with NATO Secretary-General Jens Stoltenberg in May 2022, Baerbock said that 'we are now seeing – unfortunately in the most brutal fashion – precisely why we need NATO, a security and defence union'.

Another priority area for the new German government looks to be the Western Balkans. In March 2022, Germany appointed its first special envoy to the region in order to ensure, in Baerbock's words, that the 'concerns of this region are on the very top of the agenda in Berlin'. The government has been clear in its support for beginning EU accession negotiations with Albania and North Macedonia and voluble in its concern about Russian destabilisation efforts in the region, most notably in Bosnia-Herzegovina.

Conclusion

The first Länder elections of 2022 appeared to confirm challenges ahead for the new government. Whilst in March 2022, in the small western German state of Saarland, the SPD took the majority away from the CDU (now under the leadership of veteran right-winger Friedrich Merz), the May elections in Schleswig-Holstein and North Rhine-Westphalia (NRW) turned out very differently. In Schleswig-Holstein, the CDU defeated the SPD by a humiliating 25 points, whilst in Germany's most populous state the SPD sank to an all-time low of 26.7%. Support for the FDP also dropped; in Saarland the party failed for a second time to pass the threshold to enter the state parliament, whilst in NRW, the home state of Christian Lindner, the party's leader and the country's finance minister, the FDP fell from 12.6% in 2017 to 5.9% in 2022. This left the Greens as the only coalition partner consistently to have performed better at the polls since taking office. This positions Baerbock or Habeck as serious challengers for a move into the Chancellery in 2024.

It is still early days for the government's *Zeitenwende*. Germany's hesitant positioning may have cost it reputationally in Europe, but part of the fixation with critiquing German approaches lies in the fact that the country remains such an influential and potentially powerful actor. Germany's government has been too quick to dismiss any criticism as a problem of 'communication' as opposed to substance, when it is both. But the *Zeitenwende* can still be substantive, though its impact is unlikely to be immediate or comprehensive. To achieve this will require consistent intellectual justification, bureaucratic facilitation and structural support – all of which Germany and its government is well equipped to provide should it so decide.

The Western Balkans
Transformation deferred?

For over two decades the Western Balkans have been at peace. NATO has enlarged to the region and all countries wish to become members of the European Union. Yet policymakers ought not to be complacent. Russian aggression in Ukraine has brought back memories of conflict across the former Yugoslavia and laid bare entrenched divisions. Though it is unlikely to reignite violence, the war highlights the obstacles hindering Western policy aimed at promoting democracy, the rule of law and reconciliation. Stalled democratisation, pervasive state capture and nationalism all blunt the EU's influence. Aleksandar Vučić's re-election as Serbian president on 3 April 2022 appeared to confirm the resilience of semi-authoritarianism. Non-Western actors such as Russia and China as well as Recep Tayyip Erdoğan's Turkey have all expanded their influence, taking advantage of their ties to Balkan elites and appeal to local publics.

The Western anchor

Since the end of the Yugoslav wars, the Western Balkans have made considerable progress towards institutional consolidation and integration into the EU and NATO. Following Croatia's accession to the EU in 2013, the six remaining countries – Albania, Bosnia-Herzegovina, Kosovo, Montenegro, North Macedonia and Serbia – are at different stages in their journey to the EU. Currently, Montenegro and Serbia are holding accession talks. By contrast, in late 2020 Bulgaria blocked North Macedonia's potential accession over a dispute to do with history and language. (Albania was likewise blocked, as member states were unwilling to 'decouple' it from its eastern neighbour.) By this time North Macedonia had already gained membership in NATO, however, after it had resolved a similar quarrel with Greece. It followed in the footsteps of Montenegro, which joined NATO in 2017, and Albania and Croatia, which did so in 2009. In June 2022, a proposal tabled by the Council of the European Union's French presidency offered a formula to resolve the Bulgarian-North Macedonian dispute. The Bulgarian parliament endorsed this and, on 19 July, the EU opened accession talks with North Macedonia and Albania. Thus, Bosnia-Herzegovina and Kosovo are trailing far behind the pack. Worse still, Kosovo has been denied visa-free travel to the EU, in contrast to its neighbours as well as Ukraine, Georgia and Moldova. All in all, the EU remains a long-term objective, not an immediate prospect, for the Western Balkans.

Though the collective West has shifted gears from post-conflict stabilisation to integrating the region, the institutional legacy from the interventions in the 1990s is still in place. In Kosovo, NATO is still running the KFOR peacekeeping mission. The EU has deployed EULEX, its largest civilian mission under the Common Security and Defence Policy (CSDP), comprising judges, prosecutors, police and customs officers. In Bosnia-Herzegovina, the EU is in charge of peacekeeping, with EUFOR *Althea* taking over from NATO in 2004. The Office of the High Representative (OHR) oversees the implementation of the 1995 Dayton Peace Accords. In 2021, Germany's Christian Schmidt replaced Valentin Inzko (Austria), who had served in the job since 2009. Though it uses them more sparingly than in the past, the OHR wields special powers, including sacking elected officials, striking down laws and passing legislation by decree.

In contrast to other countries, such as Afghanistan, where the West has intervened, its security commitment to the Western Balkans remains firm. The EU is clearly in the lead when it comes to diplomacy and especially economic affairs, yet the United States continues to play a key role. The deputy high representative in Bosnia is an American citizen. NATO, and by extension the US European Command, supports EUFOR *Althea* through the so-called Berlin Plus arrangement. In September 2021, the Biden administration appointed Gabriel Escobar, Deputy Assistant Secretary at the State Department, as its special representative to the region. The United Kingdom, which sits on the Peace Implementation Council (PIC) overseeing Dayton, is involved too. In December 2021, London appointed Sir Stuart Peach as its envoy in the Western Balkans. Even if troop numbers deployed in the Balkans are a fraction of the levels in the 1990s, their presence has a stabilising effect.

The Western Balkans are important for transatlantic relations. As on so many other issues, the Trump administration offered a stress test. For instance, the US and Europe diverged on the issue of partitioning Kosovo between Pristina and Belgrade. Trump's team flirted with the idea for a period in 2019–20. This put into question the EU policy of keeping the country together while granting local Serbs a measure of autonomy, the cornerstone of the 2013 Brussels Agreement concluded by Serbia and Kosovo – whose sovereignty Belgrade disputes – under the auspices of then-high representative for foreign affairs and security policy Catherine Ashton. Elsewhere, however, the EU and the US acted in sync. Washington facilitated NATO membership for Montenegro and North Macedonia as a response to Russia's as well as China's growing presence in Southeast Europe. The Europeans welcomed the Alliance's enlargement as stabilising a territorial enclave surrounded by EU territory. NATO enlargement is likewise a partial substitute for the frustratingly slow pace of the EU's own expansion, with the appetite for bringing in new members at historic lows. Joe Biden's presidency and Russia's war in Ukraine have resulted in even closer coordination between the transatlantic partners.

Europeanisation gone wrong

The base assumption of Western policy has long been that the six Western Balkan countries would follow the example of Central and Eastern Europe. They would build robust democratic institutions protecting individual and minority rights, reform their economies to achieve growth and, slowly but surely, converge with advanced countries in the West. The promise of EU membership, first extended during the 2003 summit in Thessaloniki, and eventual accession was expected to catalyse positive change, notably the resolution of conflicts inherited from the turbulent 1990s.

Some of that agenda has been fulfilled. Even without membership, the Western Balkans Six (Albania, Bosnia-Herzegovina, Kosovo, Montenegro, North Macedonia and Serbia, or the WB6) have become part of the EU's marketplace. Two-thirds of the region's trade is with the

27-member-strong bloc, a share which went up after Croatia's accession. The EU is by far the most important source of foreign direct investment (FDI) and financial assistance, a fact highlighted by the funds allocated to the Western Balkans as part of the COVID-19 recovery package. Montenegro and Kosovo use the euro as their national currency. Citizens of the region, except those of Kosovo, have travelled freely to the EU since Schengen visa requirements were removed in 2009–10. Many have moved to Western Europe, which has been home to substantial diasporas from the region since the 1960s. The EU has also extended parts of its legislation and policy templates into the region, for example, in areas such as the regulation of energy markets. For all intents and purposes, the Western Balkans form part of what some experts call the 'Eurosphere'.

However, Western policy has not delivered in full. Democratic stagnation or backsliding is the norm. The WB6 have not made any significant gains in complying with the EU's conditions of transparent governance and the rule of law. Some countries have actually gone backwards. In 2019, the international watchdog Freedom House reclassified Serbia from 'free' to 'partly free'. Vučić has amassed significant powers in his hands, even though constitutionally Serbia is a parliamentary republic. Control over the public sector coupled with influence over the economy and the media has enabled Vučić to outmanoeuvre political opponents and civil society. He also benefits from international support, having built strong ties to Russia, China and Western capitals at the same time. His policies, emphasising the role of the state as a provider of jobs and investment, along with the savvy manipulation of nationalist sentiments, have earned him genuine popular backing as well. Many Serbs who are at odds with their president vote with their feet and seek a better life abroad.

There are other examples of only partly democratic regimes with populist leaders in the region. Milorad Dodik's rule in Republika Srpska, the Serb-majority entity in Bosnia-Herzegovina, illustrates this. In Montenegro, Milo Djukanović has held power almost continuously since the early 1990s, switching between the presidency and the prime minister's office. Edi Rama has governed Albania since 2013, having won an unprecedented third term in 2021. Elites talk the EU talk but their primary concern is to stay afloat in a political environment where transparency and accountability are in short supply, corruption and state capture are institutionalised and clientelism is strong. In the 2000s, it was fashionable to debate 'member-state building' as a way forward for the Western Balkans. But now, the EU states that some in the region appear to be emulating are those in Central and Eastern Europe where the rule of law is under severe strain and democratic backsliding poses a serious concern.

Democratic stagnation is compounded by the strong influence of nationalism over Balkan societies and politics. Political actors tap the media and social networks to galvanise popular support by demonising neighbouring nations, minorities and, in some cases, the US and the EU. The narrative of the Balkans as the fulcrum of geopolitical competition between China, Russia, Turkey and the West and other external players is yet another tool elites wield to stir fears and passions. Those aligned with the EU and NATO – such as Djukanović or the political elite in Kosovo – point at Russia as a threat, often seeking to divert attention away from their failures on the domestic front. Others tap into the resentment against the West, common amongst ethnic Serbs but also in other communities. In Bosnia, Dodik has gone a long way in eviscerating central state institutions and turning Republika Srpska into his fiefdom by defying Western states and threatening to hold an independence referendum. The Bosnian Croat leadership is colluding with Dodik in the hope of wresting more power in Sarajevo too (e.g., by redrawing electoral rules). The EU-led normalisation talks in Kosovo have been at an impasse for years, with both Vučić and Kosovar Prime Minister Albin Kurti, leader of the radical Vetëvendosje (Self-determination) party, preferring to play to their respective galleries back home.

Regional countries are considering short- to medium-term alternatives to EU membership as well. In autumn 2019, Albania, North Macedonia and Serbia launched the so-called Open Balkan initiative aimed at building a regional market. Governments are also diversifying relations away from the West. Russia controls strategic assets in Serbia's energy sector, with the 2008 transfer of NIS, its national oil company, seen as a pay-off for Moscow's support in fighting against Kosovo's independence. With the Belt and Road Initiative (BRI), China has extended loans to fund infrastructure and energy projects carried out by its own state-owned corporations, as well as providing FDI to Serbia. Turkey, too, has made inroads through Erdoğan's cultivation of strong personal bonds with the likes of Vučić, Rama and the Bosniak leader Bakir Izetbegović. Downtown Belgrade boasts a swanky housing and commercial development bankrolled by the United Arab Emirates (UAE), which for a time also held a majority stake in the national air carrier. These financial flows generate rents for local power-holders and enhance their influence in domestic politics; buy China, Russia, Turkey and the UAE influence; and limit the West's clout.

However, despite the uncertain prospects for further democratisation, authoritarian consolidation is not a viable prospect. Politics in North Macedonia, Kosovo and even Montenegro remain highly competitive. Complex ethnic power-sharing in Bosnia as well as North Macedonia is likewise a constraint on leaders with authoritarian ambitions. Even in Serbia, the president has to reckon with a resurgent civil society. Popular mobilisation spanning the entire political spectrum from hardcore nationalists to urban liberals against the Jadar lithium mining project operated by the multinational Rio Tinto forced a U-turn by Vučić, who froze the venture. The decision helped the president secure a fresh term. Vučić was re-elected on 3 April 2022, without having to go through a run-off, while his Serbian Progressive Party (SNS) remained the largest grouping in parliament and is sure to lead the next governing coalition. But the opposition, which had sat out the previous elections held amid the coronavirus pandemic in June 2020, made some gains too, notably denying the SNS an outright parliamentary majority. Most importantly, Serbia, as well as the rest of the neighbourhood, is dependent on the West. The EU has been reticent in holding local leaders to account, prioritising stability over clean and transparent government. It has the political and financial muscle to sanction and curb transgressions if it musters the political will.

The fallout from the war in Ukraine

Russia's aggression against Ukraine has inevitably raised fears of spill-over into the Balkans. Kosovan Prime Minister Kurti told *Le Monde* that the Balkans were facing the same threat from the Kremlin as Moldova and Georgia. President Djukanović of Montenegro, too, warned of an impending conflict given Serbia and the Serbian Orthodox Church's close links to Moscow. Šefik Džaferović, the Bosniak member of the tripartite state presidency, called on the West to prevent a spread of the war to Bosnia.

There are several reasons why Ukraine resonates in the former Yugoslavia. Firstly, the memories of the devastating conflict in the 1990s are still raw, and tensions remain high in the political and informational arena. In July 2021, outgoing high representative Inzko used his extraordinary powers to pass amendments to the Bosnian criminal code to penalise the denial of genocide and the glorification of war criminals. In response, Dodik threatened to withdraw Serb representatives from the state-level Indirect Tax Administration, the common army and the judiciary. With Republika Srpska receiving Russian support in upgrading and rearming its police force over recent years, there are fears among Bosniaks that a replay of the conflict from three decades ago cannot be ruled out.

The second reason is that Russia has become increasingly visible in regional politics. It is developing security and defence cooperation with Serbia, for instance, having donated MiG-29 fighter jets and other equipment to Belgrade and engaged in joint annual exercises. In Bosnia, Moscow has been providing diplomatic cover for Dodik. Russia faces accusations of being behind a coup attempt in Montenegro in autumn 2016, aimed at preventing the country's accession to NATO. Russian money and disinformation networks allegedly amplified the nationalist protests against the Prespa Agreement in both North Macedonia and Greece. Across Southeast Europe, Russia has leveraged connections with political parties, business elites and opinion-makers to oppose the EU and NATO. In early March, Belgrade saw thousands rallying in support of Moscow's 'special operation' in Ukraine. In addition, Serbia and

Bosnia-Herzegovina have thus far refused to align with Western sanctions against Russia.

While Moscow has not been successful in blocking either NATO's or the EU's Balkan enlargement, it can throw sand in the wheels. The destabilisation of Bosnia-Herzegovina, where general elections in October 2022 are at risk of postponement because of a legislative fight, is a palpable prospect. Montenegro, too, could suffer from ripple effects. There, Russia-friendly parties united in the Democratic Front coalition left the governing coalition. Another flash point is the Serbian-populated municipalities in northern Kosovo. In an ill-advised move, the Kosovo authorities banned voting in the April 2022 Serbian general election in this disputed territory. Even if Russia has no capacity to project military force to the Balkans, it can take advantage of all those issues to foment trouble.

This is why the West took proactive measures to ensure stability. Days after Russia's incursion into Ukraine, the EU announced it would be reinforcing the EUFOR with 500 extra troops, a move aimed at deterring Dodik. The Union added personnel to EULEX in Kosovo as well. Senior officials such as EU High Representative Josep Borrell and German Foreign Minister Annalena Baerbock toured the region in mid-March to reassure it and voice support for the EU's continued enlargement. A bipartisan delegation from the US Senate paid a visit to Serbia, Bosnia and Kosovo in April. The critical piece in these diplomatic overtures appears to be Serbia, which has leverage in both Republika Srpska and Kosovo. The EU is hopeful that Vučić will rein in nationalist forces and eventually adopt some of the Western sanctions. Significantly, Serbia as well as Bosnia supported all UN General Assembly resolutions condemning the Russian aggression and suspending Moscow from the UN Human Rights Council.

The risk of an all-out conflict remains low. The potential troublemakers in Belgrade or Banja Luka, the capital of Republika Srpska, do not have the means to engage in all-out conflict, nor do the putative political benefits outweigh the tremendous costs of a military confrontation. There is little evidence of willingness to reignite the wars of the 1990s.

On the contrary, Vučić and others are exploiting the fears of violence to present themselves as guarantors of peace and stability.

Ukraine will undoubtedly have longer-term implications for Western policy in the Balkans. Sceptics fear that, because of the security challenge, the EU will be fixated on the east, neglecting its Western Balkan neighbourhood. On 28 February 2022, Ukraine submitted its EU membership application. Moldova and Georgia did so the following week. Adding those countries to the queue may slow down the accession process even further for Western Balkan aspirants. At the same time, the crisis on the EU periphery makes enlargement even more urgent. The historical record shows that the EU has taken major steps towards expansion when faced with security challenges. In 1993, the war in Yugoslavia informed its decision to open the door to the countries of Central and Eastern Europe. Kosovo was instrumental to the launch of membership talks with Romania and Bulgaria in early 2000. The French presidency of the Council of the European Union (January–June 2022) was committed to starting accession talks with Albania and North Macedonia, which began in July. In the best-case scenario, Montenegro could join before the end of this decade.

But it is far from certain that the best-case scenario will materialise. There is strong opposition within the EU to opening the gates wide. On 9 May 2022, Europe Day, French President Emmanuel Macron proposed the creation of a 'European political community' involving the EU and its neighbours. That implies that Paris sees the future of the WB6, along with Georgia, Moldova and Ukraine, as in an outer circle where some of the benefits of European integration apply but not the rights derived from full membership. Some EU member states oppose this limited vision – which harks back to François Mitterrand's proposals for a 'European Confederation' in the early 1990s – and favour a more ambitious approach to engagement with the Western Balkans.

Macron's speech is symptomatic of the mood in the parts of Western Europe where internal consolidation takes precedence over enlargement. The French position rests on the premise that expanding the boundaries of the EU puts at risk its internal cohesion at a time when Europe needs to assert its 'strategic autonomy' in an increasingly competitive world. On the other end of the spectrum are the member states in Central and Eastern Europe for whom enlargement is a means of stabilising the EU's periphery, driving out Russian influence as well as strengthening their own voice in Brussels institutions – on account of the close political and business ties with the WB6 and the Eastern Partnership countries. As ever, Germany sits in the middle and plays the arbiter in this intra-EU debate.

Irrespective of whether enlargement or retrenchment wins the debate, the EU is committed to enforcing more strictly its membership criteria. In 2020, the European Commission introduced the so-called 'new accession methodology', an idea originally proposed by France, allowing for policy chapters to be reopened in the course of membership talks. Given the democratic and institutional flaws in the Western Balkans, this decision makes membership an even more remote prospect for the region.

Conclusion

The Western Balkans exemplify both the resilience and the discontent of the European political order. The region is at peace and a return to the 1990s is hard to conceive. At the same time, the bold vision of transforming states and societies, modernising institutions and economic systems and fostering convergence with advanced countries in Western Europe has not been fulfilled. The West remains the dominant actor in the region, yet rivals such as Russia and China will seek to deepen their presence.

This is a classic case of 'half full, half empty'. Seen from Kharkiv or Mariupol, prospects for the Western Balkans look positive. Seen from Pristina or Sarajevo, however, the picture is less encouraging. The region's aspirations from the 2000s, when the EU originally promised membership, now contrast starkly with political and socio-economic realities, and the completion of Western Balkan accession to the Union remains elusive. The EU faces a choice in its approach over the next decade. It could continue with business as usual in the hope that the status quo, though imperfect, is sustainable. Or it could take a less economic, more geopolitical approach and seek to bring the region into its fold. Or it could experiment with new forms of political association. The war in Ukraine has brought this debate back into the spotlight, which will no doubt shape the EU's policy over its entire neighbourhood.

Europe and the War
Between aspiration and transformation?

There was little sense of a looming strategic crisis in Europe in the closing days of summer 2021. US–European relations were on the mend as the civil and familiar figure of Joe Biden replaced the psychodrama of the Trump years. While the chaotic US withdrawal from Kabul in August disturbed those European governments which had wrongly assumed that the United States would not actually close down its military operations in Afghanistan as intended, this did not cause a broader crisis.

Within Europe, the Brexit saga continued unabated even as it had ceased to be a front-page issue for the European Union. Like its partners, the EU was bracing itself for the onslaught of the lethal Delta variant of the coronavirus pandemic. The EU was also deeply split by rule-of-law issues in Hungary and Poland.

Russia's proxy war in the Donbas dragged on, but no more and no less than it had since 2014, causing some 14,000 deaths in eight years. In parallel, the so-called Normandy format (France, Germany, Russia and Ukraine) stumbled onwards, getting no closer to an accepted negotiated conclusion. The EU and the United Kingdom continued to renew the sanctions first implemented since the annexation of Crimea – which remained unrecognised – even as the corporate sector and many capitals were otherwise conducting business as usual with Russia: 'Londongrad' prospered and the German-curated Nord Stream 2 gas pipeline was being completed. The project was assisted by the Biden administration's early decision not to impose sanctions on Nord Stream 2's German industrial partners.

Although a Russian military build-up had occurred along Ukraine's borders in early 2021, this was seen less as a threat than as a device to catch the incoming American administration's attention. With the apparently successful Geneva summit between the US and Russian presidents in June, things seemed to settle down. President Vladimir Putin's seminal July 2021 article 'On the Historical Unity of Russians and Ukrainians' drew little political attention in Europe.

When Russian forces congregated again along Ukraine's borders from October onwards, there was initially little sense that this time it was going to be different. Gradually mounting worry rather than acute crisis was the climate.

Germany held general elections in September which led to the establishment of a new government by mid-December: as planned, after 16 years as chancellor, Angela Merkel left the scene. With a novel 'traffic light' Social Democratic Party (SPD)-led coalition including the Greens and the Free Democratic Party (FDP), and an untried chancellor in Olaf Scholz, Berlin was not in a position to take the lead. In the meantime, a rancorous dispute broke out in September between France on one side and Australia, the UK and the US on the other. The so-called AUKUS affair was driven by what the French perceived as diplomatic malpractice related to the secrecy-enveloped establishment of a new security pact between the three anglosphere partners in the Indo-Pacific region and France's loss of its huge 2016 submarine sale with Australia.

Presidents Biden and Emmanuel Macron immediately decided to limit the damage done to French–American relations and actually raised them to a new level before the end of 2021, but this was not a foretold outcome.

As such, a preoccupied EU, a Brexit-obsessed UK, a politically inchoate Germany, an AUKUS-distracted France, and two EU member states, Poland and Hungary, straining the rule of law, were to face what was to become the most severe strategic and military crisis in Europe since the end of the Second World War.

Russian revisionism hits Europe

Until mid-December, Russia's ambitions appeared to be mainly focused on Ukraine, albeit in a more muscular and threatening manner than had been the case after the first war of Ukrainian partition in 2014. Statements concerning the need to reorder Europe as a whole were no doubt prominent, but they were not particularly new. Ever since Putin's speech at the 2007 Munich Security Conference, a steady drumbeat of Russian revisionism played out, with Foreign Minister Sergei Lavrov as the most constant drummer.

Then, in mid-December, came an unexpected crescendo, as Russia handed to the US and NATO two draft 'security treaties' purporting to roll back the strategic and military situation in Europe to its pre-1997 dispensation and forbidding any new enlargement of NATO. These texts were presented in a form close to ultimata, an impression which was confirmed in the following days and weeks as Russia refused any substantive discussion outside the parameters set in those drafts.

At that stage, it was this Europe-wide challenge, rather than Ukraine's uncertain plight, which prompted Europe's and NATO's reaction. The Western response was both sharp and consensual. No NATO country could contemplate ratcheting the strategic geography of Europe back to Germany's eastern border, and this was true most obviously in the countries which had been part of the Soviet empire. Even Hungary, whose Prime Minister Viktor Orbán was sympathetic to Putin, avoided breaking ranks on this set of issues. Finland, a member of the EU but not of NATO, reacted bluntly as President Sauli Niinistö denounced the attempt to limit his country's sovereignty. In previous decades, Finland had refrained, of its own volition, from seeking NATO membership: accession was supported by only 25–30% of the population. By demanding that the country transform a free choice into a formal obligation, Russia had fatally undermined Finland's decades-old policy of keeping open the option of joining NATO but without exercising it.

Russia did not help its cause among the Europeans by refusing to bring them into the conversation: Dmitry Medvedev, former president of Russia and, since January 2020, deputy chairman of the Security Council, stressed that his country preferred to settle Europe's fate with the 'boss' (i.e., the US). On the continent, the prospect of a new Yalta Conference had few fans.

The US made a point of insisting that the Europeans are full partners in all formats, whether in NATO, the EU, the G7 or bilaterally. In many European capitals, not least Brussels but also AUKUS-scarred Paris, American diplomacy was held in high regard.

In practice, this meant that there was a firm European as well as a transatlantic consensus on rejecting the key Russian demand to put an end to NATO's open-door policy. Thus, when Macron and Putin met at the Kremlin on 7 February 2022, it was clear that there would be no room for manoeuvre between what were irreconcilable positions. Macron's toughness on that occasion also demonstrated that he had lost at least some of the illusions he had entertained when he launched his fruitless 'strategic dialogue' with his Russian counterpart from August 2019 onwards.

Although Russia's revisionism at the pan-European level was radical, it remained basically diplomatic in nature and was countered by the Europeans at that same level: economic issues were not, or not yet, of the essence.

The road to war

By December 2021, it had become clear that Russia was moving beyond mere sabre-rattling and was threatening Ukraine with a new war, though there was great uncertainty about the probability and scope of hostilities. The US and the UK were increasingly expecting war to break out some-time in February, whereas most continental Europeans, but also Ukraine itself, were somewhat more sceptical. This led to a divergence in plans to provide military equipment, notably portable anti-tank weapons, on an emergency basis, with the Baltic republics, Poland, the UK and the US in the vanguard, while at the other extreme Germany initially confined itself to protective equipment.

Conversely, all found it appropriate to try to persuade or deter Russia from considering war. Persuasion, such as attempts to revive the Minsk agreements, came to an impasse, with Putin paying mere lip service to such a prospect at his Moscow meeting with Macron. By 11 February, at its Berlin meeting the Normandy format faded into irrelevance, Russia having made it clear that it had other plans.

Deterrence took the form of the threat of economic and financial sanctions going well beyond those imposed after Russia's annexation of Crimea in 2014: there was broad agreement between the US and its European allies, and among their relevant organisations, notwithstand-ing the uncertainty about Nord Stream 2's future, which was awaiting certification by Germany's regulatory authorities. Part of the transatlantic sanctions package was not made public, thus limiting controversy. The fact that many Europeans believed Russia was unlikely to launch a war on Ukraine made it politically easier for some of them to agree on sanctions that were not expected to be put to the test. Less noticed was the amount of upstream work being done, notably between the US and the EU, on the technical implementation of the sanctions, a fact which was to speed up implementation when war came.

Deterrence failed.

24 February: war returns to Europe

For most in Europe, war was simply not expected. The searing memories of the role played by US and UK special intelligence during the Iraq crisis some 20 years ago did not help. That President Volodymyr Zelenskyy himself was not beating the drums of war even as late as 19 February at the Munich Security Conference enhanced the shock.

For those who took the threat of war seriously, there was a widespread sense that Putin's war aims would be limited and that his July 2021 vision of a Ukraine reunited within the Russian civilisational sphere was aspirational rather than strategic in nature.

Many Europeans, and notably those invested in the EU as a peace-building project, could hardly imagine that major inter-state war could return to the continent. The notion that interdependence would make war unthinkable was particularly rooted in Germany, with *Wandel durch Handel* – 'change through trade' – being a widespread belief system. That energy interdependence could become a tool of war had bypassed the political leadership of Europe's most important economy. Beyond Germany, the position was widely held that business as normal could be conducted with Russia without consideration of its revisionist and imperial ambitions, notably in France and Italy – not to mention Britain's 'Londongrad'.

These assumptions were brutally torn asunder on 24 February. The war produced an immediate transformation of European policies. But the lack of psychological, political and economic preparation for such a shock also set the uncertain bounds of that transformation.

Within days, the EU took on the geopolitical role which European Commission President Ursula von der Leyen had put forward in her maiden press conference in December 2019, by setting up a fund of up to €2 billion to help member states provide military assistance to Ukraine. In early April 2022, she visited Zelenskyy in a beleaguered Kyiv, as did President of the European Council Charles Michel and the EU's High Representative of the Union for Foreign Affairs and Security Policy Josep Borrell. This high-visibility militancy by the commission, better known for its normative role than for its operational acumen, is in large part due to its success in devising and implementing the EU's vaccine strategy during the pandemic.

Between late February and late May, six successive EU sanctions packages were unanimously adopted – more quickly, on a broader spectrum and on a much larger scale than after the annexation of Crimea in 2014. Halting oil imports from Russia was finally agreed on 31 May, albeit with a temporary exemption concerning pipeline oil to landlocked Central European countries. The sanctions would cover some 90% of Russian oil exports to the EU by the end of 2022.

The EU's shift from setting norms to framing strategies, including in what the French call '*domaines régaliens*' (areas of sovereignty, notably defence and foreign affairs), was still modest, but the trend was clear. Even the French, not normally known for their federalism, began to speak about extending Qualified Majority Voting to much broader areas of decision-making in the EU.

However, this broad push encountered limits. There was no agreement to remake the so-called EU recovery fund of some €800bn established during the pandemic, or to endorse a diversion of part of the fund to cope with the consequences of the war. Yet an increased EU role in defence procurement, the need to help economies cope with the collateral effects of energy sanctions and aid to Ukraine would normally call for an EU-wide effort. The EU's decision on 30 May to pledge an additional €9bn to Ukraine in 2022 met short-term needs only. Much more would be required. Nor was it clear that the French presidency of the EU Council would succeed in broadening the Union's defence role before the end of the French term on 1 July. A so-called Strategic Compass was agreed by member states in March, but its drafting pre-dated the war and its ambitions were correspondingly modest.

More generally, the EU remained at pains to define a common future. On 9 May, the EU's 'Europe Day', newly re-elected President Macron gave a speech which suggested treaty change to establish a three-speed Europe, with a hard core of full members embracing new areas of European sovereignty, notably in defence, while a 'political community' would accommodate an outer circle of former or future members of the EU, such as the UK and Ukraine respectively. Like François Mitterrand's similar proposal three decades earlier to create a 'European confederation' for the newly democratic countries of Central and Eastern Europe, Macron's speech was greeted by many with dismay, not least in Kyiv, as a device to counter full membership of the EU.

As things stood in Europe, nation-states continued to be the prime producers of defence and security policy. Initially, the Russian invasion prompted a unanimous push to raise defence spending, with practically every NATO and/or EU member stating its determination to spend at least 2% of GDP on defence. Most spectacularly, Germany's Chancellor Scholz pledged to raise an extra €100bn for defence, that is, the equivalent of two years of pre-war spending.

Arms transfers to Ukraine became the new normal in Europe, eventually involving crewed weapons systems such as heavy artillery, anti-ship missiles, tanks and armoured vehicles. At the popular level, opinion polls showed generally strong, and often massive, support for Ukraine as long as it did not extend to direct participation in military operations.

By the end of May 2022, the EU, in contrast to the UK's reticence, had welcomed almost nine million Ukrainians seeking refuge from the war, mainly women and children. A 'protected person' status crafted by the EU within hours of the war's beginning helped matters considerably.

However, as the war and its stresses stretched into months, something akin to the 'old Europe, new Europe' divisions of the Iraq crisis threatened to re-emerge. In May, Scholz proposed an immediate ceasefire, which would have left Russia in possession of its gains since 24 February. Italy came forward with its own plan. Macron talked about an outcome which would not humiliate Russia. On 28 May, Scholz and Macron pressed Putin to open direct talks with Zelenskyy, based on an immediate cease-fire to be followed by a Russian troop withdrawal. Macron's repeated recommendation that Russia not be humiliated produced particular resentment in Ukraine and in Central and Eastern Europe.

By 3 June, 100 days after the Russian invasion had begun, neither the French, German nor Italian leaders had visited Kyiv, unlike many other EU national and institutional leaders as well as former British prime minister Boris Johnson. This absence could only reinforce suspicions that the three leaders were ready to act over Zelenskyy's head. Furthermore, Macron was also exercising the presidency of the European Council, and therefore had an additional reason to meet Zelenskyy sooner rather than later.

Germany's and Italy's practical difficulties in reducing their gas imports from Russia did not help, nor did Germany's difficulties with the delivery of heavy weapons: by day 100, none of the armoured vehicles, field artillery or *Gepard* self-propelled anti-aircraft guns promised by Germany had managed to surmount the technical and bureaucratic obstacles which lay in their path to the battlefield.

Conversely, Poland and the Baltic states were prompt and effective in their substantial arms deliveries. In their political discourse, the war in Ukraine sometimes appeared primarily as a device aimed at decisively weakening Russia, with the restoration of Ukraine's territorial integrity serving as a means to that end.

If left unattended, this rift could entrench a damaging polarisation between those who were running the risk of appearing to 'fight to the last Ukrainian' in order to provoke regime change in Moscow, and those 'accommodationists' who would seek peace for its own sake while leaving unchecked Putin's neo-imperial Russia at the expense of Ukraine's integrity and sovereignty. Intemperate language amplified by social media, often directed at Germany and France, has not helped, not least when it includes officials.

However, lasting disaffection is not an inevitable outcome. Indeed, the divisions among the Europeans are not as stark as the caricatures made of them on social media. The hardliners have been more prudent than they sometimes have let on. They avoided the appearance of co-belligerence in the war and of 'jumping the gun' in terms of transferring crewed weapons before a wide consensus had emerged on that account. For their part, Paris and Berlin stress the territorial integrity of Ukraine no less than other allies do. French and Italian heavy artillery, like Poland's, was present in the field by May, no later than America's howitzers, albeit in more modest numbers. Germany's heavy weaponry began to arrive from late June onwards.

France's style has been cramped by its presidential and parliamentary elections. Macron had cause to recognise the fruitlessness of his efforts to open a bilateral mediation with Putin, except in humanitarian affairs such as the evacuation of Ukraine's soldiers from the Azovstal plant in Mariupol in May. France has been punching beneath its weight in terms of both war and peace. This may yet change, as Macron appears to have dropped his controversial attempts to position himself as a 'mediator' between Russia and Ukraine, as well as his strictures about the need to avoid humiliating Russia. These ceased in the wake of his 16 June visit to Kyiv with Scholz, then Italian prime minister Mario Draghi and Romanian President Klaus Iohannis.

Germany's leadership was initially quick to grasp the revolutionary impact of the war on its own choices, when Scholz gave his *Zeitenwende* ('turning point') speech on 27 February. The difficulties of managing trans-formative change, rather than a refusal to recognise its implications, are the problem here: an inexperienced coalition, a political system originally designed to hamper decisiveness, the effects of a quarter of a century of misguided energy policy, a hamstrung bureaucracy and an underfunded and rudderless Bundeswehr all constrain a more decisive shift.

Finally, Europe's unanimous reaction to the Russian 'security trea-ties' serves as a reminder that there is a broad understanding in the West that Russia's war against Ukraine is indistinguishable from the Kremlin's neo-imperial revisionism with its broader designs aimed at Europe as a whole. This reality should underpin the West's deeper unity, rather than give way to the divisive here-and-now of Twitter-fuelled point-making.

The words unspoken

The return of war in Europe, specifically one with a clear and present nuclear dimension, has unsurprisingly transformed the terms of the European security and defence landscape.

As a nuclear superpower, Russia's menace can only be credibly met by a countervailing force, in the form of the US and NATO, including its nuclear members. The EU, as such, is not part of that picture. Under these circumstances, EU strategic autonomy is hardly mentioned. Strategic unity and effectiveness, not doctrinal debates, are at a premium.

Even before it began, the war also had a Chinese dimension. Putin had secured an expression of 'limitless friendship' from his Chinese counterpart, President Xi Jinping, on 4 February 2022 at the Winter Olympics in Beijing. By establishing this direct connection, the Kremlin may have reinforced America's decision to engage fully in favour of Ukraine and Europe in general: limitless friendship turned out to be a reality within NATO rather than between Moscow and Beijing. By the same token, Europe is more fully aware than ever that there is a connection between the transatlantic theatre and the Indo-Pacific one: if domestic US political circumstances change, or resource constraints reduce its ability to handle two theatres simultaneously, choices may be different in the future. Strategic autonomy in the era of China's own revisionist journey will necessarily figure in the Euro-American discussions flowing from this war's consequences. The place China occupies in the agenda of NATO's June 2022 summit in Madrid is a harbinger to that effect.

In the meantime, NATO itself is already changing militarily and strategically. By insisting in his 'security treaties' on the cancellation of the 1997 Founding Act of the NATO–Russia Council, Putin has facilitated deep changes in NATO's force dispositions. Tripwire deployments are already giving way to deterrence-by-denial and forward defence in Central Europe. When NATO adopted its new strategic concept at its June 2022 summit, it announced plans to increase the size of its rapid-reaction forces earmarked for assignment to its command structure from 40,000 to 300,000.

Strategically, the Russian 'security treaties' prompted Finland to reconsider its options. By the time NATO held its summit, both Finland and Sweden were on the road to NATO accession, having dealt with Turkey's attempts to extract concessions in other fields as the price for accepting their accession. Finland is also notable for actively seeking a stronger defence role for the EU.

In parallel, on 1 June, Denmark held a referendum which yielded a stunning two-to-one vote in favour of abandoning its opt-out from the security and defence portion of the EU treaties. The signal from these Nordic countries is clear: in security and defence terms, being a full member of both the EU and NATO is deemed to be better than being only a member of one. These decisions will necessarily change the European defence order: 23 out of 27 EU members will be part of NATO. The other four (Austria, Cyprus, Ireland and Malta) represent barely 3% of the EU's population or territory.

The effects of the war on Europe in every dimension have already been considerable. Because this war is vast in scale and unpredictable in terms of its twists and turns, it must be assumed that much more is yet to come. Under these conditions, inspiration should be sought in those virtues contributing to long-haul success: adaptability, Finnish-style, rather than holding on to the comfort of the now-bygone post-Cold War era; consensual unity, along December 2021 lines, rather than snarky Twitter-trolling impatience at slow-moving Germans; and exemplary resilience as displayed by Ukraine, rather than the quest for instant gratification offered by half-baked diplomatic initiatives.

CHAPTER 8

Russia and Eurasia

RUSSIA

BELARUS

UKRAINE

KAZAKHSTAN

GEORGIA

UZBEKISTAN

KYRGYZSTAN

ARMENIA

TURKMENISTAN

TAJIKISTAN

AZERBAIJAN

©IISS

Drivers of Strategic Change

REGIONAL SHARE OF GLOBAL POPULATION, GDP AND DEFENCE BUDGET

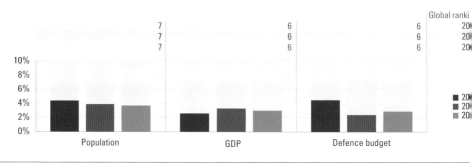

POPULATION

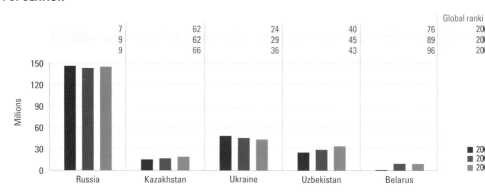

AGE STRUCTURE
(Percentage of national population)

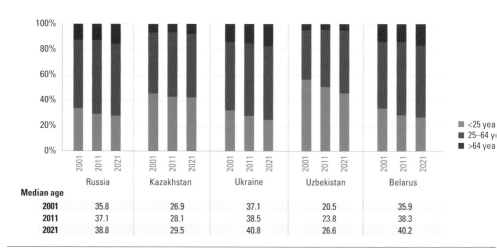

Over the past decade, Russia's global influence has been greater than its share of GDP, population and defence spending would imply. The data suggest it is poorly placed to prevail in a broader contest of strength with the West. Though Russia's war against Ukraine has laid bare weaknesses, approval of President Vladimir Putin, and belief that Russia is on the right path, have risen sharply.

GDP
(Constant 2010 US dollars)

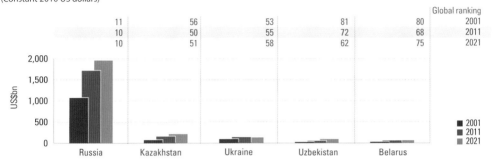

				Global ranking	
11	56	53	81	80	2001
10	50	55	72	68	2011
10	51	58	62	75	2021

US$bn

Russia · Kazakhstan · Ukraine · Uzbekistan · Belarus

■ 2001 ■ 2011 ■ 2021

GDP PER CAPITA
(Constant 2010 US dollars)

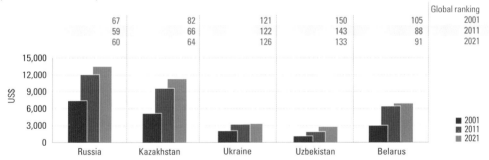

				Global ranking	
67	82	121	150	105	2001
59	66	122	143	88	2011
60	64	126	133	91	2021

US$

Russia · Kazakhstan · Ukraine · Uzbekistan · Belarus

■ 2001 ■ 2011 ■ 2021

DEFENCE BUDGET*
(Constant 2015 US dollars)

ACTIVE MILITARY PERSONNEL

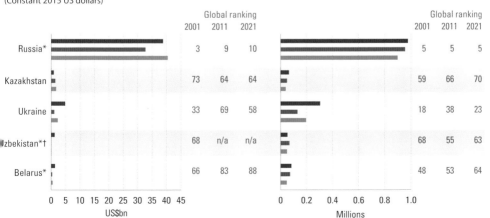

DEFENCE BUDGET*

	Global ranking		
	2001	2011	2021
Russia*	3	9	10
Kazakhstan	73	64	64
Ukraine	33	69	58
Uzbekistan*†	68	n/a	n/a
Belarus*	66	83	88

0 5 10 15 20 25 30 35 40 45
US$bn

ACTIVE MILITARY PERSONNEL

	Global ranking		
	2001	2011	2021
Russia*	5	5	5
Kazakhstan	59	66	70
Ukraine	18	38	23
Uzbekistan	68	55	63
Belarus	48	53	64

0 0.2 0.4 0.6 0.8 1.0
Millions

■ 2001 ■ 2011 ■ 2021

*2001 defence budget values for Belarus, Russia and Uzbekistan are estimates, and may be distorted by high inflation rates. † No 2011 or 2021 data available for Uzbekistan

For explanation of drivers and sources, see page 8

HUMAN DEVELOPMENT INDEX (HDI)
(Score between 0 and 1, where 0 denotes a low level of development and 1 a high level of development)

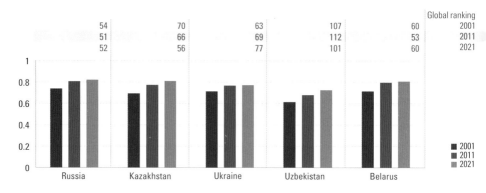

POLITICAL SYSTEM
(Score between 0 and 100, where 0 denotes no political freedom and 100 fully free)

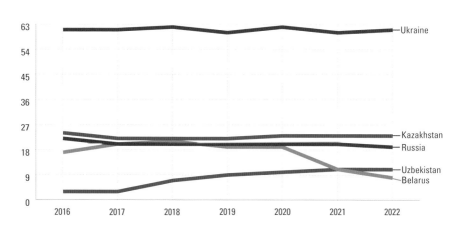

APPROVAL RATING FOR PRESIDENT VLADIMIR PUTIN, AND ASSESSMENT OF THE CURRENT STATE OF AFFAIRS IN RUSSIA

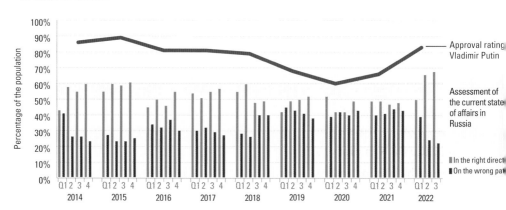

For explanation of drivers and sources, see page

2021–22 Review

Russia's invasion of Ukraine, and its political, economic and security consequences, dominated the geopolitics of Eurasia over the past year. But several other developments drew attention to further sources of regional instability and change, notably in Central Asia's two largest countries, Kazakhstan and Uzbekistan. Three decades after the break-up of the Soviet Union created 15 new states, Russia's war against Ukraine propelled a further decline of its influence across the region.

On 24 February 2022 Russia launched its second invasion of Ukraine, eight years after its first. This began the biggest land war in Europe since 1945, and an international geopolitical crisis. It followed a year of escalating efforts by Russia to exercise its last remaining elements of influence over Ukraine beyond the territories it did not already control. By mid-2021 Moscow had concluded that the 2015 Minsk-2 agreements that largely ended its first war against Ukraine had failed to constrain Kyiv's policies, and that Ukraine's President Volodymyr Zelenskyy was neutering Russia's major political allies in the country, notably by freezing the media and other assets of Viktor Medvedchuk, the veteran pro-Moscow party leader personally close to President Vladimir Putin. Ukraine's deepening relationship with the West, and robust national identity, also undermined Russia's aspirations to dominate a weak, pliant and dependent Ukraine.

On 12 July 2021 Putin published a 7,000-word essay titled 'On the Historical Unity of Russians and Ukrainians'. Surveying a millennium of history, Putin argued that Russians, Ukrainians and Belarusians comprised a 'triune nation', and specifically that Russia and Ukraine were 'one people'. He condemned contemporary Ukraine as a Western-inspired 'anti-Russian project', and insisted that the country could only secure its 'true sovereignty … in partnership with Russia'. He warned that those who 'allowed our historical territories … to be used against Russia' would 'destroy their own country', and implied that Russia was prepared to act to prevent Ukraine from developing in a way that did not conform to his view of its past.

In August 2021, Russia appeared encouraged by the limits of American resolve that the Taliban's rapid takeover of Afghanistan, and chaotic withdrawal of Western forces, demonstrated. Secretary of the Security Council Nikolai Patrushev drew a parallel with Ukraine, arguing that 'the country is going to disintegrate, and the White House at a certain moment won't even remember its supporters' in Kyiv.

In October, Russia began a huge military build-up on Ukraine's eastern and southern borders. The United States and United Kingdom began to release intelligence warning that Russia was preparing a major invasion, which was repeatedly denied by Moscow. In November Putin called on the Foreign Ministry to prepare security treaties with the US and NATO. Published in December, these proposed a series of unfulfillable demands that amounted to the rolling back of three decades of European security developments.

By mid-February 2022, Russia had amassed around 120 battalion tactical groups, some 75% of its principal combat units. On 21 February, in an unprecedented televised meeting of his Security Council, Putin berated, and at times humiliated, his inner circle into supporting his proposal to recognise the independence of the Donetsk and Luhansk 'people's republics', the two entities in eastern Ukraine that Russia had dominated since 2014. Evidently unprepared, most members of the council betrayed their anxiety throughout the meeting. The two entities declared 'independence' later that day. Russia recognised them (as, soon after, did North Korea and Syria), and sent further troops into their territory.

On 24 February Putin announced a 'special military operation' against Ukraine. The chief stated goals of the operation were to 'denazify' and 'demilitarise' the country. It quickly became clear that Russia sought to occupy Kyiv and overthrow the government. Russian forces advanced along five axes, including from Belarus where 30,000 Russian troops had remained after military exercises earlier in the month. It launched missile attacks, including on Lviv in the far west of the country. Special forces and other units infiltrated Kyiv and made several attempts to detain or kill Zelenskyy.

Ukraine declared martial law and a general mobilisation. Its fierce resistance, especially in preventing Russian airborne forces from holding Hostomel airport outside Kyiv, thwarted Russia's attempt to surround the Ukrainian capital. However, Russian forces gained territory along Ukraine's southern coastline as far west as Kherson, having secured a land bridge from occupied Crimea early in the war.

Russia's failure was the result of a bad plan poorly executed. At its root lay a basic misunderstanding of Ukraine's political-military circumstances. Russian planners appeared to believe that much of the Ukrainian population would welcome, or at least not resist, Russian forces. Logistics and equipment failures, and poor operational security (including the use of insecure mobile phones in the field), compounded this error. Crucially, Russia failed to gain air dominance. Only on 8 April did Putin appoint a theatre commander, Anatoly Dvornikov, who was in turn replaced by Gennady Zhidko six weeks later.

Facing strategic failure, and having incurred severe losses, Russia began to withdraw its forces from central Ukraine to more defensible positions around the Donbas in late March. But there was no sign that Russia had abandoned its primary goal of subordinating the whole country. It reverted to operations more consistent with its core military doctrine, concentrating its forces and using intense artillery and missile barrages to support advances in areas of the Donbas that it did not already occupy. In the south, Russian forces extended their grip on Ukraine's coastline on the Sea of Azov, notably by capturing – having largely destroyed – Mariupol in April.

There appeared little prospect of peace. Talks in the first weeks of the war, later renewed in Istanbul, broke down. In July Russian Foreign Minister Sergei Lavrov declared that 'the geography has changed' and that his country's territorial ambitions now extended to large areas of Ukraine's southern coastline. An eventual peace process would anyway have to address other issues beyond territorial ones. These include the question of future security guarantees for Ukraine; the fate of its citizens – over 1.5 million by mid-2022 – who had been forcibly deported to Russia; the terms (if any) on which the

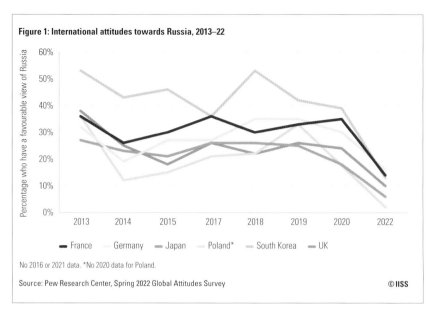

Figure 1: International attitudes towards Russia, 2013–22

No 2016 or 2021 data. *No 2020 data for Poland.

Source: Pew Research Center, Spring 2022 Global Attitudes Survey

© IISS

West and its partners would ease sanctions on Russia; and how those responsible for war crimes would be held accountable.

In summer 2022 the war entered an attritional phase, with the two sides locked in gruelling artillery battles. Ukrainian forces began to mount partisan activity in areas recently occupied by Russia, audacious attacks on Crimea, and even what appeared to be actions in Russia itself. In early September a dramatic Ukrainian breakthrough led to the recovery of up to 6,000 square kilometres of land around Kharkiv. This confirmed the superiority of Ukrainian forces and leadership, and demonstrated the war's unpredictability.

Domestic consequences of the war

The war had immediate and profound consequences for Russia and Ukraine. The Russian authorities intensified their repression of civil society, which had been gathering pace. In the months before the invasion they had continued their crackdown on supporters of imprisoned opposition leader Alexei Navalny. Many fled abroad to avoid arrest. According to Memorial, Russia's oldest and most respected human-rights organisation, by late October 2021 there were at least 420 political prisoners. Two months later, Memorial itself was closed down by the authorities.

Despite a highly authoritarian system, and widespread reports of electoral fraud, the ruling United Russia party won less than 50% of the vote for the first time in the September 2021 parliamentary elections – the last major electoral test before the 2024 presidential election. Nonetheless, United Russia secured a comfortable majority of seats in the parliament. The Communist Party of the Russian Federation (KPRF) was the main beneficiary of United Russia's declining popularity. But the arrest soon after of one of its senior officials, Valery Rashkin, allegedly for illegal hunting, added to pressure even on the officially sanctioned 'systemic opposition'.

The authorities repeatedly denied any intention to attack Ukraine, and did not prepare the population for it. The invasion therefore came as a shock and prompted demonstrations in several major cities. Some prominent influencers expressed their opposition. Several hundred thousand Russians, many in the IT sector, fled abroad. But when the state propaganda machine began to mobilise support (using, for no clear reason, the Latin letter 'Z' as its symbol), a majority of public opinion swung behind the war. It remained strong even as the regime escalated its rhetoric, portraying the conflict as an existential war against the West. According to the Levada Center, between November 2021 and June 2022 popular approval of Putin jumped from 63% to 83%.

Views of elites appeared more mixed. As the country faced growing sanctions, some technocrats in government and major business figures expressed anxiety. Security officials faced difficulties too. Unconfirmed reports suggested that senior personnel in the Fifth Service of the Federal Security Service (FSB), responsible for operations outside Russia, were arrested in March. Roman Gavrilov, deputy head of Rosgvardia, the Russian national guard created by Putin in 2016, was fired the same month. In March, May and June, Putin also reportedly fired several generals as Russia's senior officer corps suffered severe losses on the battlefield. Amplifying the growing sense of insecurity across elites, Vladimir Mau, rector of the Presidential Academy of National Economy and Public Administration, board member of state gas giant Gazprom and one of Russia's leading economists, was arrested on 30 June, ostensibly for corruption. Several senior officials in the oil and gas business died in mysterious circumstances. As battlefield setbacks multiplied, militant pro-war commentators, and prominent figures like Chechen leader Ramzan Kadyrov (who sent substantial forces to the war), grew increasingly critical too. All this suggested unprecedented turbulence and strain within the regime.

As Russia's invasion faltered, the authorities tightened the use of 'foreign agent' laws, forcing the last remaining independent news outlets to close or leave Russia. Censorship intensified: disseminating 'fake news' about the military – which covered anything unwelcome to the Kremlin, including calling it a war rather than a 'special military operation' – became punishable by up to 15 years in prison. The state extended its ban on foreign social media to Facebook and Instagram, which it labelled 'extremist'. Subscriptions to virtual private networks (VPNs) to evade online censorship surged.

Russia's economy was hit by successive waves of severe sanctions, and voluntary private-sector withdrawals, by Western countries and their major Asian allies. In response to these, and to the rising costs of a much longer war than the Kremlin had expected, the state began to impose creeping economic mobilisation. While state finances, buoyed by oil sales, were stabilised, there were increasing signs that the real economy was suffering from growing stresses due to loss of essential imports. In September an internal government report forecast a probable 8.3–11.9% fall in GDP.

The most significant domestic consequence of the war was Putin's announcement in September of a 'partial mobilisation' – which soon began to be implemented more comprehensively. This was a measure he had previously promised he would not take and had done everything to avoid. Knowing they could be called up, ordinary citizens could now no longer ignore the war. This provoked widespread anxiety, renewed protests and flight abroad – mostly to post-Soviet states, which faced the challenge of absorbing a large influx of mainly wealthy Russians.

The war also transformed Ukraine. The normal politics of anti-corruption struggles and other controversies – which had notably led to the adoption of an 'anti-oligarch' law in November 2021 to curb the influence of powerful business leaders – were submerged by the collective response to Russia's invasion. In a remarkable display of national unity, all important political and social forces rallied around Zelenskyy, whose popularity rose from around 27% to over 80% as he proved an inspirational wartime leader. His decision to stay in Kyiv, against the advice of Western states and his own advisers, played a key role in steeling resistance to Russia. This, together with the ingenuity and adaptability of Ukrainian forces, was decisive in driving back the assault on Kyiv.

War and occupation disrupted Ukrainian society. By summer 2022, over 6m Ukrainians, mostly women and children, had fled abroad. Military and civilian casualties, war damage – epitomised by the destruction of the huge Azovstal factory in Mariupol – and Russia's blockade of Ukraine's Black Sea coastline took a severe toll on Ukraine's economy. The IMF forecast a 35% decline in GDP. Nonetheless, a vibrant daily life continued in cities out of range of Russian artillery, if not missile attacks. A summer 'parade' of captured and abandoned Russian military vehicles in Kyiv symbolised Ukraine's morale, resilience and defiance after six months of war.

Regional consequences, responses and wider instability

The effects of Russia's war and Western sanctions were felt across Eurasia. Other, more local sources of tension and instability also drove change in several countries.

Belarus's relationship with the West, already dire following the repression of nationwide peaceful demands for change after rigged presidential elections in summer 2020, deteriorated further. In July 2021 Belarus began to bring migrants, mainly from the Middle East, into the country and transport them to the borders of its three European Union neighbours, Latvia, Lithuania and, especially, Poland. Migrant attempts to cross into the EU, abetted by Belarusian border guards, provoked a political and humanitarian crisis. This reached a peak in November before subsiding. The EU imposed further sanctions on Belarus in response to the crisis.

Belarus, the only post-Soviet state to support Russia's invasion of Ukraine, became a co-belligerent but not a combatant. While Russia sent ground forces and launched missile attacks into Ukraine from its territory, the Belarusian military did not directly intervene – contrary to Ukrainian and Western expectations. But the possibility that Russia would pressure Belarus into deeper involvement as part of a wider escalation remained live. Three days after the invasion, Belarus amended its constitution to allow nuclear weapons to be deployed on its territory. At a meeting with Belarusian leader Alexander Lukashenka in June, Putin said Russia would transfer nuclear-capable *Iskander*-M tactical missile systems to Belarus. Meanwhile, Belarusian citizens disrupted Russia's war effort by carrying out sabotage and cyber attacks on the local railway network transporting troops and materiel.

In Moldova, the pro-European Action and Solidarity party (PAS) won a resounding victory in the July 2021 parliamentary election, strengthening domestic support for President Maia Sandu's bid to seek EU membership. In September, Russian state gas company Gazprom, which supplied 100% of Moldova's gas, threatened not to renew its contract two days before it was due to expire unless Moldova agreed to less favourable terms. Moldova declared a state of emergency, began to source some of its gas from Poland, and negotiated a compromise with Gazprom. But the crisis rumbled on; Moldova declared a further state of emergency in January 2022.

Moldova's border with Ukraine, and Russian influence (including an estimated 1,500-troop presence) over the breakaway region of Transnistria, meant that Russia's invasion of Ukraine created immediate security concerns. These were heightened by a series of mysterious explosions in Transnistria in April 2022, and by a statement by acting head of the Central Military District Rustam Minnekaev, suggesting that Russia sought to establish a land corridor to Transnistria.

Russia's invasion of Ukraine triggered wider geopolitical developments in the region. Within days, Ukraine, Moldova and Georgia applied for EU membership. In June 2022 the EU accepted Ukraine and Moldova as candidate members, but not Georgia due to concerns, in particular, over excessive political polarisation and oligarch influence, and insufficient democratic oversight and judicial reform.

Central Asia felt the economic impact of Russia's war in Ukraine, and the West's sanctions response, through trade disruption, higher commodity prices and exchange-rate volatility. The World Bank forecast that Kyrgyzstan, Tajikistan and Uzbekistan would be particularly hit by a decline in remittances from labour migrants in Russia. Kazakhstan, which shares with Russia the longest continuous land border in the world, also faced more specific security concerns. Russian hints that it did not fully accept Kazakhstan's sovereignty over its northern territory were amplified by a social-media post from Dmitry Medvedev, former president and deputy head of the Security Council, that claimed Kazakhstan was an 'artificial state' comprising 'former Russian territories'. Medvedev blamed hackers for the post.

Kazakhstan's President Qasym-Jomart Toqaev publicly distanced himself from Russia to an unprecedented degree following the invasion of Ukraine. This departed from the cautious Russia policy of his predecessor, Nursultan Nazarbayev, and was especially surprising in light of the political crisis that the country had gone through just a month before the invasion. Following a price rise in liquefied petroleum gas that triggered demonstrations in several cities, elites close to Nazarbayev made an apparent attempt to remove Toqaev. When they orchestrated mob violence in Almaty, Kazakhstan's former capital and its largest city, Toqaev sought help from the Collective Security Treaty Organization. Russia promptly sent troops to Almaty and, although these saw no action, their dispatch sent a decisive signal of support for Toqaev, who prevailed in Kazakhstan's most serious political crisis since the early 1990s. Over 200 people were killed by the rioters and government forces that quelled them.

This marked the end of Kazakhstan's experiment in managed leadership transition following Nazarbayev's retirement in 2019. Nazarbayev lost his remaining titles, notably as head of the Security Council, while family members and allies were stripped of their positions or, like security-service chief Karim Massimov, imprisoned. Official rhetoric of a 'New Kazakhstan', constitutional amendments approved by referendum in June, and plans for early presidential and parliamentary elections all consolidated Toqaev's position and signalled his intent to set out a new path of development for the country.

Russia's support in the January crisis led many observers to assume that he had incurred a political debt he would be obliged to repay in loyalty. The opposite proved true. Kazakhstan did not support the war and sent humanitarian aid to Ukraine. In June Toqaev publicly refused, in Putin's presence, to recognise the independence of the Luhansk and Donetsk 'people's republics'. Soon after, a Russian court threatened to shut down the Caspian Pipeline Consortium that transports most of Kazakhstan's oil – on which its economy depends – to world markets.

Domestic unrest also hit Central Asia's only two autonomous regions. In November 2021 protests flared up in Tajikistan's Gorno-Badakhshan region over acts of state violence. Tensions continued to simmer until a brutal government crackdown in May 2022. In late June, violent unrest swept Nukus, the capital of Karakalpakstan, in Uzbekistan. The protests were triggered by proposed constitutional amendments, subsequently withdrawn, to remove Karakalpakstan's autonomous status.

Inter-state conflicts also flared up. Border clashes between Armenia and Azerbaijan continued to claim lives following the ceasefire that had ended their war in November 2020. Azerbaijan maintained military pressure and periodically cut its energy supply to the enclave of Nagorno-Karabakh. The EU's search for non-Russian sources of energy after the invasion of Ukraine also strengthened Baku's hand. European Council President Charles Michel played a growing role in mediating talks on a peace agreement. But these efforts suffered a severe setback in September when Azerbaijani forces made incursions into Armenia, igniting the most severe fighting since the end of the war. Relations between Kyrgyzstan and Tajikistan remained tense after a border clash in April 2021. In September 2022 these flared up again, leading to further loss of life.

In March 2022, 40-year-old Serdar Berdymukhammedov became president of Turkmenistan, replacing his father Gurbanguly who retired after 15 years in power. Speculation grew that his Tajik counterpart, Emomali Rahmon, would also bequeath power to his son, Rustam.

Russian State Power, Civil Society and War
How, and how successfully, is the regime managing public opinion?

Vladimir Putin has concentrated more power in the Kremlin – and achieved greater political control – than any Russian or Soviet leader since before Mikhail Gorbachev launched his reforms of *glasnost* ('openness') and *perestroika* ('restructuring') in the mid-1980s. This dominance, pursued as a reaction to a set of political challenges that began to emerge in 2019, was achieved well before Russia invaded Ukraine in February 2022. But while the Russia–Ukraine war has in many ways tightened the Kremlin's control even further, it has also exposed the degree to which Putin remains constrained by public opinion.

By the time the war began, the Kremlin had successfully deployed a series of measures – including the coercive policing of protest, constitutional reform, electoral manipulation and increasing media censorship – to ensure that the country's faltering economy would incite neither mass discontent nor elite anxiety, either of which could have destabilised Putin's rule. This success enabled him to pursue an initially unpopular war and suppress the early waves of discontent that it provoked. As the war grinds on into what looks likely to be a protracted conflict, however, Putin's domestic political challenges will take on new contours. With the liberal opposition effectively marginalised, threats may instead emerge from previously loyal swathes of Russian society and from pockets of deprivation caused by the war itself. It is not clear whether the Kremlin's existing arsenal of social and political control will be sufficient to see off these threats.

Consolidating domestic control

For most of the three years leading up to the invasion, the Kremlin's core focus was on shoring up the structures of its domestic political power. The 'rally around the flag' following the 2014 annexation of Crimea – which pushed Putin's approval ratings to stratospheric highs and, for a time, severed the connection between his soaring popular support and the country's faltering economic performance – had, by late 2018, faded in the face of a continuing decline in real disposable incomes, driven by chronic structural inefficiencies, corruption and sanctions.

For the Kremlin, however, the connection between economic performance and political fortunes is indirect. In the absence of genuine electoral competition, the primary function of popular legitimacy – whether expressed through election results, polling numbers or public quiescence in the face of impoverishment – is as a tool for managing elites, who pose a much more immediate threat to the longevity of any autocrat. If Putin's service to the elite is the maintenance of broad social compliance, then any sense that this compliance may be slipping gives elites a powerful incentive to find a new leader. Preventing such an incentive from emerging, or mitigating it if it does emerge, was therefore the Kremlin's priority from mid-2019 into early 2022.

The Kremlin began this period with a show of force. Between July and November 2019, it cracked down violently on public protests provoked by the barring of anti-Kremlin candidates from local and regional elections. Some 2,500 participants were arrested, and hundreds of fines and prison terms were doled out. This sent a message not only that protests would no longer be tolerated, but also that the elite could count on the Kremlin to put the full force of the Russian state behind the defence of its material and political interests.

Aggressively policing protest has since become a mainstay of Putin's politics. The state has also tightened its control over civil society by expanding the application of laws on 'undesirable organisations' and 'foreign agents', especially against the country's remaining independent media outlets, journalists and activists. Broadly, these measures failed to achieve the desired result, as political activists and critical journalists learned to cope with the state's harassment. The poisoning of Alexei Navalny with the military-grade nerve agent Novichok, and his arrest and sentencing after his return from treatment in Germany, deprived the opposition of its most high-profile and effective organiser. The state then declared Navalny's network of organisations to be 'extremist', opening up anyone with a formal or informal affiliation to prosecution on national-security grounds. Most of the core activists who were not already in prison fled the country, as did an increasing number of journalists and academics.

When Russians headed to the polls to vote in the September 2021 State Duma elections, they did so without any genuine opposition candidates on the ballot or even a modicum of independent election monitoring or journalistic oversight. These were the least-free nationwide elections since the Supreme Soviet election in 1984. The onslaught on the democratic opposition had a chilling effect on the rest of the political system. Accusations of extremism, disloyalty and treason were levelled at independent civic organisations and media outlets en masse. State-run media and Kremlin-backed political leaders even directed such accusations at the usually docile Communist Party of the Russian Federation (KPRF), many of whose candidates benefitted from anti-regime protest voting.

For all the extraordinary effort that went into them, the results of the 2021 Duma elections were underwhelming for the Kremlin, delivering Putin's United Russia party 49.8% of votes (down from 54.2% five years earlier). As a result, while United Russia retained control of the Duma, it lost 19 seats. The nationalist Liberal Democratic Party of Russia (LDPR) – most closely associated with Vladimir Zhirinovsky, until his death in April 2022 – also lost 18 seats, while the KPRF gained 15 seats and the Kremlin-loyal centre-left party A Just Russia – For Truth (SRZP) gained four seats. New People, a new Kremlin-backed political project created for the 2021 Duma election to capture the votes of the urban upper-middle classes, garnered 13 seats. Turnout was reported at 51.7%, up 3.8% from the previous parliamentary election in 2016, though independent analysts believe the turnout was inflated as part of an effort to manipulate the results in key races and regions.

Significantly, there was no noteworthy protest after the elections, and street-level politics in Russia remained quiet up until late February 2022. It would be difficult to overstate how remarkable this development was. For most of Putin's two decades in office, public compliance has been obtained through a combination of persuasion and co-optation, with only rare recourse to violence. By the close of

2021, however, the Kremlin had demonstrated to itself, the elite and Russian citizens that coercion – once an occasional supplement to its softer efforts at political persuasion – was now its core instrument for achieving compliance.

The impact of the war

The battle lines had been drawn in Russian domestic politics – labelling all opposition activity as treasonous and deploying the full force of the state against any pockets of significant resistance – well before Putin plunged the country into a full-scale invasion of Ukraine. Anti-war protesters mounted demonstrations in several major cities in the early days of the war. Some 15,000 were arrested, but they were only a remnant of a largely spent social and political force. Ordinary Russians were not clamouring for war. A Levada Center poll conducted in November 2021 showed that a plurality of respondents had a positive opinion of Ukraine, with fewer than 20% sharing Putin's apparent conviction that Russians and Ukrainians should be united into a single state. There is no indication that those figures changed before the invasion in February 2022, as Kremlin-controlled media, including all terrestrial television channels, insisted that the prospect of war was a figment of the West's paranoid imagination. Moreover, Putin's evident expectation of a quick and decisive victory, akin to the annexation of Crimea in 2014, may have led him to believe that political mobilisation at home would not be necessary. As a result, he took an unwitting and unprepared population to war.

That unpreparedness manifested itself not only in the scale of anti-war protests. As the war, and then sweeping Western sanctions, hit the rouble and Moscow's financial markets, ordinary Russians rushed to withdraw their savings and then spend a portion of them at Ikea, McDonald's, Starbucks and other Western retailers that soon began to withdraw from Russia. The inability of Russia's armed forces to achieve the swift victory that Putin expected meant that the Kremlin needed, once again, to worry about public opinion.

The Kremlin's initial response was a further escalation of coercion. The government rushed a law through the Duma that imposed fines and prison terms on journalists and private citizens for 'discrediting Russia's armed forces'. Its enforcement helped put an end to large-scale street protests and even to one-person pickets: lone protesters were arrested for holding up blank pieces of cardboard. The last stalwarts of Russia's above-ground independent media – the radio station *Ekho Moskvy*, the Nobel Prize-winning newspaper *Novaia gazeta* and the online broadcaster *Dozhd* – were all closed down or forced abroad. Internet censors blocked access to Facebook, Twitter, the BBC and the *New York Times*, as well as leading overseas and underground Russian-language media.

The war also pushed control and coercion more fully into the private lives of ordinary citizens. Taking advantage of the new law, prosecutors opened cases against people who posted about the war on social media or were overheard talking about it in a coffee shop. Pressure to support the war – whether symbolically, rhetorically or materially – began to be exercised through schools, universities, workplaces, churches and other social institutions. One result has been the beginning of another 'rally around the flag', as Russians come together to support their leader in the face of war. This, however, has had neither the scale nor the depth of genuine enthusiasm that greeted the annexation of Crimea in 2014.

Low-level protest and civil disobedience have continued, including a proliferation of anti-war graffiti and attacks on military recruitment centres. An estimated 36 buildings belonging to the country's Ministry of Defence, the majority of which are recruitment centres, have been targeted with Molotov cocktails, arson attempts, potshots from rifles and other acts of vandalism, causing damage but no casualties. These attacks have been accompanied by a 50% increase in the number of freight-train derailments around the country, leading some to suspect a coordinated campaign of anti-war sabotage. There is, however, no evidence of such a movement as of yet, and most of the attacks appear to have been carried out by individuals acting without any obvious organisational structure.

Yet another result of the invasion has been the emigration of many of those who either cannot support a war fought in their name or do not want to be caught up in the economic, political and social consequences that they fear it will bring about. Reasonable estimates put the number of new exiles at as high as 500,000. Much of this emigration came in the early days and weeks of the war, as people fearing a broadening political crackdown and the potential closure of borders – as well as conscription – sought to wait things out from the relative safety of exile. While some of those people have since returned to Russia, the exodus has continued, including a growing community of IT specialists and other white-collar professionals. Furthermore, many Western companies and even some Russian enterprises – including the Russian tech giant Yandex – have moved much of their Russia-based staff abroad.

The state's strategy of mounting pre-emptive strikes against the media infrastructure of urban liberal opposition, while also reinforcing incentives for compliance among the broader population, appears to be based on the assumption that the public-opinion challenges caused by the war are structurally similar to those the Kremlin has faced in recent years. That assumption may well be mistaken. For one thing, as already noted, the infrastructure of the political opposition had been dismantled and much of its constituency was in exile before the start of the war. Moreover, the opposition was already morally opposed to the current regime; while the war sharpened their sense of danger and moved them to act, it did not substantially add to their grievance or disaffection.

Rather, the greater danger for the Kremlin is that the war will increase disaffection among parts of the population that had previously been inclined towards compliance. This disaffection could emerge as the result of a moral shock – such as that which drove Channel One journalist Maria Ovsiannikova to protest against the war on air – or a material shock, as the isolation and decline of the Russian economy diminishes the quality of life of millions of ordinary Russians. Countermeasures designed to deal with marginal communities and pockets of discontent may struggle to succeed in the face of large-scale swings in public opinion.

A third way in which the current public-opinion challenge differs from others the Kremlin has faced stems from the uneven distribution of suffering and loss caused by the war. Documented casualties and journalistic reports suggest that the toll of the war in terms of lives lost is being borne disproportionately more by disenfranchised socio-economic and ethnic groups, as is often the case in military conflicts around the world. In particular, minorities including the Buryats of eastern Siberia and various ethnic groups from Dagestan in the North Caucasus, as well as the residents of Slavic rust-belt cities in central Russia, seem to be heavily over-represented among casualties. The economic costs are also falling disproportionately on many of the same communities, particularly in the form of food-price inflation. Per official Central Bank statistics, prices for fruit and vegetables have grown as much as 10 percentage points more quickly in the North Caucasus and 5 percentage points more quickly in Siberia than in central Russia.

Throughout the past eight years of economic malaise and fiscal austerity, the Kremlin has largely managed to prevent the emergence of pockets of relative deprivation in a deliberate attempt to mitigate the kinds of grievances that often lead to popular uprisings around the world. This had been done by ensuring that the pain of contraction and austerity was felt more or less equally across the country (with a few notable exceptions of outsized largesse). Thus, the uneven distribution of the negative impacts of the war – and the discontent it has caused in Buryatia and Dagestan – represents a challenge which the Kremlin has not seen since the regional unrest and strikes of the 1990s. This has contributed to a growing wave of social protest in the North Caucasus and the emergence of a Free Buryatia Foundation that is mobilising explicitly against the war and for a revisiting of Russian 'colonialism'.

Looking ahead

The Kremlin finds itself in a perplexing position. On the one hand, it enjoys a degree of control over Russian political life – including electoral politics, street-level mobilisation, the media and civil society – that is both unparalleled in Russia's post-Soviet history and almost entirely unchallenged. On the other, public opinion remains a significant constraint on the Kremlin's actions.

The Kremlin's continued unwillingness to call the war a war – which would enable it to mobilise far more of Russia's human and material resources – is the clearest evidence of the constraints imposed by public opinion. The Kremlin's ambiguous formulations to justify the war – such as the 'denazification' and 'demilitarisation' of Ukraine – and thus ambiguity about the degree of sacrifice that Russians will be asked to make, is part of the formula that has yielded quiescence. If Russians – particularly those who have already paid a disproportionate price – come to believe that the burdens of the war will increase, their patience may diminish. And while the state's coercive capacity has proven effective against a relatively small (if growing, until recently) urban intelligentsia, it has not been tested against a wider section of the population.

What Russians think of the war is a matter of considerable controversy. Surveys of varying degrees of depth and quality, and using different measurement techniques, have shown levels of expressed support for the war anywhere between 60% and 80%, with most estimates tending towards the upper end of that range. Given the scale of initial anti-war protest and the lack of an immediate public response, the galvanising of public opinion in support of the war – or at least *evident* support for the war – is remarkable and reflects a degree of success for the Kremlin. How deep that shift in sentiment really is, however, is another matter. In the context of rampaging coercion and blatant propaganda, when expressing the wrong opinion can bring jail time, it is not unreasonable to assume that many people may lie to pollsters. Indeed, research by Philipp Chapkovski and Max Schaub in early April suggests that as many as 15% of survey respondents may be lying about their support for the war.

Whether a person is willing to speak openly about the war is only part of the analytical conundrum. There remains a deeper question about what public opinion means, and how it is formed, in an environment as repressive as Russia's has become. For many, if not most, opinions even about things as consequential as the war are shaped in a social context; people's views are thus in large measure a reflection of how they read their social surroundings and what they understand to be the distribution of sentiment. The fact that it is not only the state and its television propagandists speaking in support of the war, but also the Russian Orthodox Church and the leaders of most of the country's major universities and cultural institutions, is particularly important. It communicates to ordinary Russians that opposing the war puts them at odds not only with Putin, but also with Russian society as a whole.

The problem for Putin, then, is not only how to keep that 15% of the population from revealing their real views, but also how to maintain the social consensus that currently binds a great many other Russians to pro-war sentiment. Throughout most of Putin's time in power, this consensus – and the compliance that it engenders – has been built on a foundation of strong horizontal ties between and among ordinary Russian citizens. Coercion, by contrast, relies on vertical relationships between citizens and the state to create compliance. As a result, the coercive turn that has so clearly bolstered the Kremlin's political domination may not deliver the social dominance that Putin needs to win his war.

Putin's announcement of 'partial mobilisation' in September 2022 imposed significant new strains on mass support for both the war and the regime that launched it. Citizens could no longer afford to ignore the conflict: they now knew they could be forced to fight in it. The initial chaotic and indiscriminate drafting of recruits – in practice, far less 'partial' than the official reassurances – only stoked popular worries, fuelling a new wave of protest and exodus. The fact that the Kremlin had long avoided mobilisation, despite the growing need for it revealed by Russia's failures on the battlefield, testified to its awareness of the challenge this could pose to its legitimacy. It promised to test the regime's methods of mass control more severely than ever.

Upheaval in Central Asia
What is driving change in Eurasia's heartland?

The past year has been one of the most momentous in Central Asia since the countries in this region gained independence in December 1991. The year featured protests and political violence in Kazakhstan and Uzbekistan – two countries that have prided themselves on political stability – as well as unrest in Tajikistan. In addition, tensions flared up between Kyrgyzstan and Tajikistan, as their military forces clashed over undemarcated borders in the Ferghana Valley in late spring 2021 and September 2022.

The prospect of the Taliban's return to power had caused trepidation in Central Asia, with Tajikistan and Uzbekistan conducting joint military exercises with Russia near the Afghan border at short notice in early August 2021. Once the Taliban's takeover was complete, Central Asian states developed proactive policies, rather than waiting on events – either engaging with the Taliban or standing up to them with surprising confidence. Russia's invasion of Ukraine six months later placed additional stress on the region. It heightened security concerns, transmitted adverse economic effects – especially through its impact on labour migration and remittances – and created diplomatic dilemmas. As a consequence, some Central Asian states sought to distance themselves from Russia.

Tajikistan–Kyrgyzstan conflict

Despite 30 years of independence, several borders between Central Asian states remain undemarcated. Border issues remain most acute in the strategically important Ferghana Valley. Although it is just 5% of Central Asia's territory, it holds one-quarter of the region's population. It is densely populated and divided between three countries: Kyrgyzstan, Tajikistan and Uzbekistan. Low-level skirmishes between citizens and border officials, alongside a history of large-scale ethnic conflicts – such as those in the city of Osh in Kyrgyzstan in 2010 – generate a simmering tension. Kyrgyzstan has more unresolved border issues than any other country in the region, especially along the Tajikistan–Kyrgyzstan border. Since independence, only half of this 1,000 kilometre-long border has been delimited.

These tensions rose to boiling point in April 2021. The immediate trigger was reportedly the placement of surveillance cameras by the Tajikistani authorities on an irrigation canal on a disputed part of the border: the authorities alleged that farmers in Kyrgyzstan had diverted water from the canal. The farmers began hurling small rocks and sticks at Tajikistani border guards. As the conflict escalated, local police and military became involved, which led to greater casualties when these forces used guns, artillery and other heavy weapons. Within two days, the security services of both countries announced a complete ceasefire and both sides agreed to joint patrols of the border and to ensure free flow of traffic between the countries. The violence reportedly claimed 36 lives on the Kyrgyzstani side of the border and 19 on the Tajikistani side and led to the displacement of approximately 58,000 residents in Kyrgyzstan. The border issues remain unresolved. Since this episode, there have been periodic skirmishes in the same area. In April 2022, a Tajikistani border guard was killed and two Kyrgyzstani border guards were injured in clashes, while in September approximately 100 people were killed in two days of fighting before a ceasefire was signed.

While low-level violence has characterised this border region for decades, the inter-state nature of the recent violence was the result of several factors. Firstly, Kyrgyzstan is in an increasingly vulnerable position in the Ferghana Valley. These skirmishes occur largely in Batken province, which is the poorest in Kyrgyzstan and heavily dependent upon livestock. Secondly, residents of Tajikistan are much more likely to be engaged in agriculture, and are thus heavily dependent upon water flows for irrigation that come through canals from Kyrgyzstan. Adding to tensions over water, birth rates among Tajikistani families are far higher than those of Kyrgyzstani families, which puts increased pressure on land in this densely populated region. Pastoralists and sedentary farmers often find themselves at odds with one another, and these differences map onto distinct ethnic groups.

There is an acute sense of insecurity among Kyrgyz residents in this region as they fear growing numbers of Tajiks encroaching on their land. In addition to structural factors such as birth rates and land use, the region has seen growing nationalism. This has been most noticeable in Kyrgyzstan. Since coming to power in early 2021 after the overthrow of the government in 2020, Kyrgyzstan's President Sadyr Japarov has relied on his populist appeal to unleash Kyrgyz nationalism. Such fervour is also embodied in his political party Mekenchil ('patriot').

In April 2021, Kyrgyzstan approved a new constitution that changed the political system from a parliamentary to a presidential system: the size of parliament was reduced and the powers of the president increased. The new constitution was also infused with elements of Kyrgyz nationalism by including a defence of 'moral values' and through the creation of a 'People's *Kurultai*', which is an advisory council designed to emulate customary forms of decision-making at the national level. It is unclear what role such a council plays under a democratic constitution. As a populist and nationalist, Japarov was able to rally support for constitutional reform in order to solidify his role as a strongman leader. This idea became popular in Kyrgyzstan because the parliamentary system had proved unstable, leading to almost annual rotations of prime ministers and their governments. In Japarov's nationalist vision, the country needed strong, centralised leadership to bring order.

Tajikistan emerged from the April 2021 clash emboldened. Its military appears to have been stronger and was more willing to use force. While Kyrgyzstan has seen a rise in nationalism, the war also generated nationalism among Tajiks as well. Unleashing stronger nationalist sentiments on both sides of the border does not bode well for prospects of peace nor for the work of demarcating state borders, which is essential to securing peace and overcoming Soviet-era legacies.

The rise of the Taliban in Afghanistan

The withdrawal of the United States from Afghanistan and the Taliban takeover did not lead to chaos in Central Asia, as many analysts had predicted. Except for Tajikistan, the region viewed this as an opportunity to begin afresh with a government that they hoped could restore order.

When the US moved to a support-and-assist role in Afghanistan in 2014, northern Afghanistan, which borders Tajikistan, Turkmenistan and Uzbekistan, descended into chaos. It was plagued by high levels of violence and mass displacement: over one-third of the population had already been displaced because of violence in the north in the previous decade. From the perspective of Afghanistan's northern neighbours in Central Asia, the longer the US was in Afghanistan, the more unstable the country became.

Neighbouring countries and regional powers began looking for alternative security strategies. Russia and China, who had once supported US military involvement in Afghanistan, turned against the US as bilateral relations between them soured. Similarly, they were concerned that the US was not able to bring stability to the region, as terrorist groups such as the Islamic State in Khorasan Province (ISIS–KP) and Tajikistani, Uighur and Uzbekistani militants were increasingly active in the north. By 2020, China, Russia and Uzbekistan found themselves in direct talks with the Taliban. All parties seemed to want to hedge their bets against a failing US strategy.

When the Afghan Republic led by Ashraf Ghani collapsed, China, Russia and Uzbekistan immediately embraced the Taliban. Although none of these countries formally recognised the new regime, they developed strong relations with it. Uzbekistan did so in the hope of developing trade routes and transport networks from Central Asia to South Asia, offering a new geo-economic option as it looks away from Russia. Unlike Uzbekistan, Tajikistan remained more reticent. It had historical ties with the Republic's chief executive officer Dr Abdullah Abdullah and the Northern Alliance. Tajikistan hosts the leader of the anti-Taliban National Resistance Front, Ahmad Massoud (son of the deceased Northern Alliance commander Ahmad Shah Massoud).

It remains unclear how Uzbekistan's big bet on the Taliban will play out. In spring and summer 2022, rockets launched from Afghanistan began falling on southern Uzbekistan and Tajikistan. It is unclear who was behind these attacks, but they are most likely to have been carried out by ISIS–KP. These attacks reminded Uzbekistan of the limits of Taliban control of Afghanistan, which offers a sobering counterpoint to hopes that a peaceful Afghanistan can facilitate trade and provide an economic corridor to South Asia. They are also significant because they represent the first time that Central Asian republics have been attacked from Afghanistan since 2001. These small-scale attacks did not cause casualties. But they undermined the narrative that the Taliban could provide a better security alternative to the Western-supported Ghani government – the issue of primary concern to Central Asia.

Upheaval in Kazakhstan

For decades, Kazakhstan had been the most stable and prosperous country in Central Asia. Although it had seen some protests, it had not suffered widespread violence. That changed in January 2022 when small-scale demonstrations over hikes in fuel prices led to nationwide protests. Price increases for liquefied petroleum gas, a fuel used in many cars, sparked the first protests in western Kazakhstan. They began in the town of Zhanaozen, which had just marked the tenth anniversary of the killing of 17 protesters in clashes with police.

Demonstrations gathered steam around the country across many major cities, though not in the capital, Nur-Sultan. The protests were a leaderless movement that expressed discontent with the corruption of the ruling elites. Large protests in Almaty, the country's largest city, turned violent. Peaceful protesters reported that their demonstrations were hijacked by groups of men intent on violence. Mobs of protesters then stormed and burned down the mayor's office among other buildings. As violence escalated, President Qasym-Jomart Toqaev requested the help of the Collective Security Treaty Organization (CSTO) to help restore order in the country. The CSTO's response was swift but limited. Its forces guarded facilities but did not see action. The arrival of Russian troops led many to fear that Kazakhstan was sacrificing some of its sovereignty in order to maintain political control. It is unclear how many people died in the violence. More than 10,000 were detained.

It is also unclear who was behind the violence. But there are clues that the violent mobs intended to weaken the government of President Toqaev and strengthen the hand of his predecessor, Nursultan Nazarbayev, who had remained influential after stepping down in 2019, notably by retaining his role as head of the country's Security Council. In the months after the violence, Toqaev removed Nazarbayev's family members and close associates from both government positions and their roles managing large enterprises. It thus appears that the violence was triggered by Nazarbayev supporters seeking to undermine Toqaev during a period of vulnerability. Instead, Toqaev prevailed in this intra-elite struggle and consolidated power. The CSTO intervention played a politically significant role in enabling him to do so.

Although the violence subsided, Kazakhstan continues to grapple with the consequences. In response to the protests, Toqaev promised sweeping governance reforms. In June, the country voted on a new constitution in a national referendum. This reduced the role of the president, increased the power of the parliament and completely erased the powers that Nazarbayev still enjoyed under the previous constitution. It did not introduce elections for regional governors, however, something Toqaev had long promised and a key demand of protesters.

Unrest in autonomous regions

After the events in Kazakhstan, Central Asia continued to see political violence as bloody protests swept across two autonomous regions with significant ethnic minorities. In Tajikistan, the government used significant force to suppress violence in the Gorno-Badakhshan Autonomous Oblast (GBAO) in spring 2022, continuing a period of repression in that region that has spanned the past decade. In Uzbekistan, the autonomous region of Karakalpakstan witnessed unprecedented protests in response to constitutional changes.

Violence in GBAO was caused by protests after the killing of an activist in police custody in November 2021. Mobile-phone videos that went viral on social media showed he was executed by security forces, sparking protests and clashes between the authorities and local citizens. Most of the latter are from the Pamiri ethnic-minority group and are distinct in language and culture from Tajiks. The government shut down the internet in most of the region after this, cutting this remote area off from the outside world. Violence returned to the region in May 2022, when renewed clashes between authorities and locals left perhaps as many as 40 people dead, resulting in an increased security presence by Tajikistani authorities in the region. The internet cut-off meant that it was impossible to know the extent of state violence.

Uzbekistan also witnessed violence in its semiautonomous region, Karakalpakstan. This comprises almost 40% of Uzbekistan's territory, but only two million of its 35m people. It is one of the poorest regions in the country, and has suffered from the severe shrinking of the Aral Sea due to Soviet-era irrigation policies. At the end of June 2022, the Uzbekistani parliament shared drafts of constitutional reforms with the public, who were given 10 days to deliberate the proposed changes. The most anticipated change to the constitution were amendments that would allow current President Shavkat Mirziyoyev to reset his tenure and stay in power for another two terms (he is currently serving his second term under the old constitution). These constitutional reforms also proposed extending the president's term in power from five to seven years. But the trigger for protests was a proposal to remove Karakalpakstan's autonomous status. Essentially, these reforms would have demoted the quasi-autonomous republic within Uzbekistan to provincial status.

The proposed changes were met by peaceful protests over the course of two days on 30 June and 1 July, but escalated into violence perpetrated by both protesters and the police. After the worst of the violence had subsided, Mirziyoyev flew to the regional capital Nukus and promised he would eliminate the proposals to change the status of the republic. By the time the violence finally ended, the authorities reported that 21 people had been killed, including several law-enforcement officers. More than 200 were injured.

It is unclear what prompted Tashkent to promote this constitutional change. Nationalism had never been a serious concern in Karakalpakstan, as ethnic Karakalpaks constitute only 40% of the population, with the rest made of up ethnic Kazakhs and Uzbeks. Karakalpaks had not been clamouring for increased independence or autonomy. In other words, the move by Tashkent to change the status of Karakalpakstan seemed to draw attention to the issue of separatism. One explanation is that Tashkent felt insecure about the autonomous status of Karakalpakstan after major gas reserves were discovered in the region in 2018. This made even the smallest risk of secession seem dangerous. Similarly, there has long been concern that outside powers such as Russia could foment nationalism and separatist movements inside the region and weaken Tashkent. In the past, newspapers in Russia had promoted greater autonomy for Karakalpakstan – just as they had promoted separatist movements in other parts of the post-Soviet space.

The violence in Nukus is the most significant test of the Mirziyoyev government so far. After the last major episode of violence, in Andijan in 2005, Uzbekistan turned inwards for more than a decade, and only emerged from autarky and isolation when Mirziyoyev succeeded Islam Karimov as president. How he responds to this latest unrest will set the course for the country's politics for the next decade.

Consequences

The Russian invasion of Ukraine cast a long shadow over Central Asia. Initially, there was great concern that the collapse of the Russian economy due to Western sanctions would severely affect the region – and in particular that it would force hundreds of thousands of Central Asian labour migrants back to Kyrgyzstan, Tajikistan and Uzbekistan, depriving these countries of flows of remittances.

Although inflation across the region soared, the initial economic impact was not as significant as many had feared. Fewer migrants have returned to Central Asia. Exchange rates in Kazakhstan and Kyrgyzstan – which are also members with Russia of the Eurasian Economic Union (EAEU) – fell sharply after the invasion, however. The greatest economic challenge posed by the conflict is growing inflation, especially of food and fuel prices.

Central Asian republics, most notably Kazakhstan and Uzbekistan, have expressed their concern about the invasion. In March 2022,

Kazakhstan said it would not recognise the independence of the Luhansk and Donetsk 'people's republics' – a striking move, given the debt he had apparently incurred to Russia during the January unrest in Kazakhstan. A few weeks later, Uzbekistan's then-foreign minister Abdulaziz Kamilov followed Kazakhstan's lead, endorsed Ukraine's territorial integrity and refused to recognise the two Russian-backed separatist republics. Like Kazakhstan, Uzbekistan has also sent humanitarian assistance to Ukraine.

Against the background of rising domestic expectations and a shifting international environment, Central Asian states face important domestic and foreign-policy decisions. They are not passive objects of 'Great Games', but active players developing a distinctive statecraft that seeks opportunities as well as managing threats amid new uncertainties. To the north, Russia's invasion of Ukraine, and to the south, the return of the Taliban to Kabul, are shaping a new environment in which Central Asia is making surprisingly confident choices. A domestic environment of growing civic demands on authoritarian governments and development challenges in a landlocked region may present the greater long-term difficulties.

Russia's War and Western Sanctions
A new era in economic statecraft?

Introduction

Russia's invasion of Ukraine in February 2022 triggered two responses from the West. The first was to provide military equipment, intelligence and training to Ukraine. The second was to design and implement sanctions and other forms of coercive economic statecraft to impose costs on Russia and constrain its capacity to wage the war.

The war has thus been fought on two fronts: on the battlefield by kinetic means and on the home front by economic ones. While Russia forbids the use of the word 'war' to describe the former, President Vladimir Putin uses this very term to describe Western sanctions against his country – even as he applies his own form of economic coercion, principally by restricting the gas supply to Europe.

This marks an important moment in the history both of Russian–Western relations and of sanctions themselves. Policy thinking and practice in this area have undergone significant and rapid evolution since the invasion began, and continue to do so. New economic and financial weapons are being honed, and older ones – some themselves relatively new – are being applied to an unprecedentedly large, dangerous and resilient target. Other states, notably China, are watching closely, drawing lessons and considering the implications for their own future. In short, the war has ushered in a new era not only of geopolitics but also of economic statecraft.

The past as prologue

Western sanctions on Russia are not new. During the Cold War, they were part of the strategy to contain the Soviet Union. Their main goals were to restrict Soviet access to advanced technology (especially militarily useable ones) and, periodically, to punish the Soviet Union for unacceptable behaviour, such as the invasion of Afghanistan in 1979 and the imposition of martial law in Poland in 1981. Conversely, Western states granted selective access to trade and investment to incentivise more accommodating, less revisionist Soviet behaviour. This was an especially important part of the 'structure of peace' that United States president Richard Nixon and his national security advisor Henry Kissinger conceived for managing the superpower relationship during the 1970s era of detente. This element of economic strategy was epitomised by 'Basket 2' of the 1975 Helsinki Final Act, which comprised trade and technology transfers that disproportionately benefitted the less efficient and less innovative economies of the Soviet Union and its Eastern European satellites.

The efficacy of sanctions during the Cold War was intrinsically limited, though, by the largely autarkic nature of the Soviet Union, whose economic ties with the capitalist West were rarely significant. Furthermore, the major exceptions – hydrocarbon exports, grain imports and Western loans – were rarely subjected to sanctions, and never for long. Sanctions could also prove divisive among Western allies, as with the open disagreements between the US and even its closest Western European security partners on the issue of the construction of a Soviet gas pipeline in the early 1980s.

The end of the Cold War, collapse of the Soviet bloc and disintegration of the Soviet Union in 1989–91 led to a fundamental change in Western economic strategy, as with every aspect of its policy towards the region. The West supported the transition of Soviet successor states from centrally planned authoritarian regimes to market democracies, and their integration into a wider security community. It lifted restrictions on trade and investment and encouraged accession to international economic and regulatory organisations, such as the World Trade Organization.

In the West many hopes drove deeper economic engagement: that Russia would become wealthier and thus more peaceful; that a richer, more market-oriented Russia would create a powerful domestic political constituency in favour of the rule of law; that thickening ties of interdependence with the West would create a stake in a stable and mutually beneficial relationship; that adoption of international standards of corporate and regulatory governance would make reform irreversible.

Western commercial interests also sought profitable access to Russia's huge natural resources and Russian markets – both the emerging middle class and the high-net-worth, increasingly globally mobile business-people who began to make fortunes during the transition. In short, by replacing Cold War sanctions and punishment with post-war engagement and integration, the West could both do well and do good.

This strategy was unequivocally successful only in the three Baltic states. These were the exception that proved the rule: as the last conquests of the Soviet Union, they more closely resembled the Eastern European bloc states that integrated fully into the European Union as stable market democracies than they did other Soviet successor states.

Outcomes were otherwise mixed. As Russia rapidly grew richer in the early 2000s, it became more, not less, authoritarian and adversarial. Yet even as the West's political and security relationship with Russia deteriorated, its economic and financial engagement deepened. As a consequence, by early 2014, when Russia began its first invasion of Ukraine, occupied Crimea and fomented unrest in the Donbas, the Russian-Western economic relationship was deeper, extended across more sectors and took a wider variety of forms than ever before. Flows from Western countries to Russia included portfolio and direct investment; provision of financial, consulting and other services, including 'oligarch valet services' to wealthy Russians who sought to protect their wealth and reputation, and the export of consumer products, capital goods and technology. Flows from Russia to the West overwhelmingly comprised the export of primary products, especially oil, gas, metals and diamonds – though major Russian companies had also begun buying Western companies and assets, notably in the energy industry.

Against the background of this flourishing economic relationship, Western states were innovating new forms of coercive economic statecraft against smaller targets. In particular, after the 9/11 attacks the US developed potent financial instruments against terrorist and organised criminal groups, and then against North Korea and Iran. As a consequence, when the West began to draw up its response to Russia's aggression, it could contemplate using new weapons against a wider spectrum of economic relations than ever before. Applying them to Russia, though, would be a new test of these weapons, and would also have to overcome resistance from Western interests invested in the existing profitable relationship.

The West's initial response to Russia's aggression in 2014 was limited. On the one hand, its imposition of sanctions on Russia marked a sharp reversal of the post Cold War policy of unconditionally supporting trade and investment. Having sought to influence Russia's domestic- and foreign-policy evolution by offering it the benefits of access to Western markets and capital, it now sought to punish Russia's violation of international norms by depriving it of some of these benefits. On the other hand, the measures were specific and targeted. In no sense did they amount to a comprehensive assault on Russia's economic and financial system. None of the most severe measures that were available to Western states – and that had recently been used against smaller targets – were applied. Western states and companies alike continued to support trade and investment with Russia in areas not subject to sanctions, and to make new commitments. Perhaps the most striking example was Germany's approval of the Nord Stream 2 gas pipeline in 2015. Had it become operational, it would have not only deepened the country's dependence on Russian gas by doubling the capacity of the Nord Stream system but also allowed more Russian gas exports to bypass rather than transit Belarus and Ukraine, thereby making those countries more vulnerable to future Russian pressure. Five major European energy companies contributed half of the project's financing.

The first wave of Western sanctions was applied to individuals and companies deemed responsible for Russia's unacceptable behaviour. Following debates about the appropriate extent and limits of wider measures, a novel kind of measure, the Sectoral Sanctions Identification (SSI) List, was designed and, after the shooting down of Malaysian airliner MH17 in July 2014, implemented by the US and its European partners. Targeting the energy and finance sectors, these prohibited specific kinds of transactions – all but very short-term financing, as well as participation in deep-water oil projects and Arctic offshore and shale exploration and production – while avoiding a general prohibition on doing business with these sectors.

Significant subsequent measures included the 2017 Countering America's Adversaries Through Sanctions Act (CAATSA), a response to Russian 'malign behaviour'. One of its most notable measures was to impose secondary sanctions on any violators of US sanctions related to the Russian-occupied areas of Ukraine, thereby enforcing these restrictions globally. After the Russian military-intelligence service (GRU) attack using the nerve agent Novichok in Salisbury in 2018, Western sanctions on individuals expanded beyond the political, military and administrative spheres to include oligarchs who personally benefitted from access to the West but played no formal role in making or implementing state policy.

The post-2014 sanctions marked a turning point. As they were designed to be specific in scope, so they were accordingly limited in effect. They dampened Russian growth, but not significantly. They put elites on notice that they could be targeted and deprived of access to the West and its services. Beyond this, their main effects were cumulative and longer term. They retarded development of the crucial oil and gas sector in ways that Russia struggled to adapt to. Foreign direct investment (FDI) into Russia more than halved, and capital outflows rose sharply. The shared Western hope was that these effects would in due course induce Russia to reach a stable and mutually acceptable settlement of Ukrainian security issues, and in particular to implement in full the Minsk-2 agreement signed in February 2015 that sought to lay the basis for a settlement of the conflict. In this the West failed. While large-scale fighting in eastern Ukraine subsided, deadly exchanges continued, and the security situation there remained inherently unstable.

Russia sought to adapt to Western sanctions in several ways, including implementing import-substitution policies (which were of limited efficacy); building an even bigger role for the state in the economy, especially the financial sector; and developing closer relations with non-Western economic partners. Russia also understood that it remained vulnerable to further measures. There are indications that Western countries privately warned Russia that they would impose far more severe sanctions if Russian and Russian-backed forces did not halt their advance on Mariupol in early 2015. This deterrent appears to have worked, and to have helped pave the way to Minsk-2. But Russia drew lessons from this episode. By building up its reserves with a conservative fiscal policy, reducing its dollar holdings and developing an alternative payments system to SWIFT (the global messaging system for financial transactions), it sought to protect itself against sanctions escalation.

The response to Russia's second invasion

In October 2021 Russia began a major build-up of forces on Ukraine's border. The West began to discuss further sanctions. Unlike in 2014, the US abandoned its incremental approach and began to pursue the strategy of 'start high, stay high'. The new sanctions policy was to find asymmetries where Western strengths intersected with Russian vulnerabilities, particularly Russia's dependency on high-end technology and foreign capital, as well as on currency trade. The architects behind the sanctions policy were Daleep Singh, then-deputy national security advisor for international economics in the Biden administration, and Deputy Secretary of the Treasury Wally Adeyemo.

As the US marshalled a major sanctions response with its European allies, it warned Russia that it faced 'massive consequences' if it undertook a second invasion of Ukraine. This deterrent failed. In the days following the invasion, the West made good on its threat and imposed sanctions that were unprecedented in their range of effects, speed of implementation and unity of purpose. Within a month, Russia had become the most sanctioned country in the world, superseding North Korea and Iran in terms of the number of measures imposed on it.

The new sanctions included severe measures previously imposed on much smaller targets. Several non-systemic banks were disconnected from SWIFT. Russia's largest financial institutions, such as Sberbank, VTB and Alfa Bank, were placed on the full blocking sanctions lists in the US and the UK. More than 1,000 Russian individuals, including many major oligarchs, were targeted across many jurisdictions. Severe financial sanctions were complemented with unprecedented export controls. A ban was imposed on the export of dual-use items and of luxury goods. The US expanded its dual-use restrictions and applied the so-called Foreign Direct Product (FDP) rule to Russia's defence, aerospace and maritime sectors, prohibiting the export of microchips and semiconductors of US origin.

Especially significant was the freezing of more than half of Russia's US$640 billion of foreign reserves. Sanctions on central-bank reserves had previously been applied only to rogue states such as Cuba, Iran, Syria and Venezuela. The tandem of Janet Yellen, the US Treasury secretary, and Italy's then-prime minister Mario Draghi pushed for the freezing of assets on both sides of the Atlantic. Closely guarded from any media leaks, the freeze left Moscow shocked and unprepared. Russian Foreign Minister Sergei Lavrov later acknowledged that 'nobody who was predicting what sanctions the West would pass could have pictured that. It's just thievery.'

One of the most remarkable developments was the Western corporate response to Russia's invasion of Ukraine. Within three months, over 1,000 international companies had announced plans to curtail or shut down their operations in Russia. They encompassed a full range of sectors, from oil and gas majors with fixed, immovable assets and decades-long time horizons, to the data giants of the 'weightless economy'. These 'self-sanctions', as they came to be called, went far beyond legal compliance with official state sanctions. They were largely driven by reputational risks – specifically, that continuing to work, trade or invest in Russia would incur severe and costly public criticism from Western civil society.

Effective preparatory diplomacy underlay transatlantic coordination. The Biden administration conducted more than 180 consultations with its allies. It held frequent conversations with Bjoern Seibert, the head of the cabinet of European Commission President Ursula von der Leyen, and G7 partners. Germany's decision to pause the certification of the Nord Stream 2 pipeline was vital in bringing other reluctant European countries on board.

The emerging impact of sanctions and export controls

Russia entered the war seemingly well prepared. The 'Fortress Russia' strategy that Moscow had developed since 2014 was intended to strengthen the country's ability to blunt any impact of sanctions. Sovereign debt was minimal and the public sector's finances were in surplus. Russia's diversification of foreign-currency reserves to euros, yen and pounds was meant to reduce exposure to the US dollar. Russia's economic interconnectedness with Europe was supposed to work as a shield. Due to the EU's financial exposure and close energy ties, Moscow believed that Brussels would be reluctant to trigger severe sanctions.

The sweeping measures imposed after the invasion showed the failure of these efforts to insulate the Russian economy from external pressure. The impact of economic and financial sanctions will be cumulative. Internal Russian government studies forecast a likely 7–12% fall in GDP. According to the World Bank's forecasts, export from and imports to Russia will fall by 31% and 35% respectively. More severe disruption underlay these head-line figures. Supply-chain problems began to spread across manufacturing sectors, laying bare the extent of Russia's dependence on value-adding imports. The stand-out example was car production, which fell by over 90%, but by summer 2022 other sectors had begun to suffer significant falls. A picture emerged of Russia as a country that struggled to turn its huge natural wealth into high-quality finished products without the use of foreign capital goods, the supply of which was being cut off.

As with the post-2014 sanctions, Russia responded to the new measures with a range of mitigation policies. The Central Bank of Russia raised interest rates to 20% and quickly introduced severe capital controls, obliging exporters to convert 80% of their hard currency into roubles. In an attempt to minimise capital flight, the authorities imposed restrictions on selling or withdrawing hard currency. The National Welfare Fund announced that it would allocate one trillion roubles for the capitalisation of the Russian banking system. The greatest effort was directed towards taming inflation and the currency volatility. By comparison, state support for small- and medium-sized businesses was modest and insufficient.

Export controls were expected to exert an impact only over the longer term, but began to do so much sooner. Several companies – including AvtoVAZ, Russia's largest carmaker; Sukhoi, which manufactures the Superjet short-haul passenger aircraft; and Uralvagonzavod, Russia's largest tank manufacturer – reported problems with procuring spare parts. This underlined Russia's high dependence on the import of Western items and technology, a vulnerability that the Kremlin's post-2014 import-substitution programme had failed to solve. As of 2020, Russia relied on imports for 75% of its non-food consumer items. To mitigate the loss of access to vital foreign parts for a range of sectors, Russia officially began to allow 'parallel import' of products without the permission of the trademark's holder. The practice of grey imports will require logistical changes in the affected supply chains, most likely via China, the Eurasian Economic Union (EAEU) and India.

A combination of unprecedented financial sanctions, export controls and de-risking behaviour by Western companies began to drive Russia's commercial, financial and technological decoupling from the West and from several major Indo-Pacific economies that also joined the international sanctions coalition. In response, Russia has sought to intensify its import-substitution policies (even as it moves towards a war economy), deepen its de-dollarisation of foreign economic relations and seek closer relations with non-Western countries, especially China and Middle Eastern states. However, attempting anything close to self-sufficiency in a highly integrated and technologically globalised world will force 'reverse industrialisation' – adoption of less advanced technologies and production processes – on Russia. Furthermore, new restrictions on access to public data – financial reporting, ownership structure, oil production and government debt – that have been adopted to further 'securitise' the economy are making Russia even less transparent.

The road ahead

The absence of energy sanctions constituted the major weakness of the initial coercive economic-statecraft regime imposed since February 2015. Russia continued receiving revenues of around US$1bn per day, capitalising on energy prices that rose in spring 2022. While Canada, the United Kingdom and the US banned the import of Russian hydrocarbons, the EU did not initially follow suit. Germany, which imported 55% of its gas and 25% of its oil from Russia in 2021, was the main opponent of a full immediate energy embargo, fearing this would trigger an economic recession. Without a European energy ban, Russia was projected to earn between US$240bn and US$320bn in windfall, an increase of more than a third from 2021, and an inflow that over time threatened to mitigate the freezing of much of Russia's hard-currency reserves.

But as the war continued, broader Western opinion shifted in favour of energy restrictions. This marked an expansion in the scope of sanctions from imports (and other inflows like direct investment and technology transfer) which sustain Russia's real economy, to exports which sustain its finances. As part of its sixth package of sanctions in June, the EU agreed to ban imports of seaborne Russian crude from 5 December 2022 and petroleum products from 5 February 2023. Together with a voluntary German and Polish ban on oil-pipeline imports, these measures will block 90% of Russian oil imports into the EU.

The EU also agreed to introduce a ban on shipping insurance for tankers carrying Russian oil. Building on this, in September the G7 countries – later joined by the EU itself – agreed an ambitious plan to impose a price cap on Russian oil above the marginal cost of production but well below current market price. Originally promoted by the Biden administration, this sought to keep oil flowing to global markets while reducing revenues to Russia. This will be implemented by amplifying the insurance ban and by prohibiting banks from financing Russian oil transactions. If successfully implemented, this will represent a formidable use of the West's near-monopoly in financial and related services to reshape real international economic flows.

Conclusions

Russia's invasion of Ukraine triggered the biggest European war since 1945. But the West's coercive economic response is no less significant. The urgent need to impose severe sanctions on a large, dangerous and resilient target has driven significant innovation in economic statecraft, and continues to do so. Together with the war itself, this is imposing more serious social and political strains than the Putin regime has ever faced. By restricting supplies of semiconductors and other components of high-precision weapons, sanctions are also increasingly hindering Russia's capacity to wage the war.

As Russia's stockpiles and spare parts dwindle, its import-substitution efforts flail and potent new weapons – like the oil-price cap – are deployed by the West, the effects of the sanctions are much more likely to intensify than ease with time. Russia's economy faces a bleak future. Together with military mobilisation, this means that neither Russia's elites nor its general population can ignore the war. On the home front as well as on the battlefield, Russia is becoming weaker, and its underlying weaknesses are being exposed.

CHAPTER 9

Middle East and North Africa

©IISS

Drivers of Strategic Change

REGIONAL SHARE OF GLOBAL POPULATION, GDP AND DEFENCE BUDGET

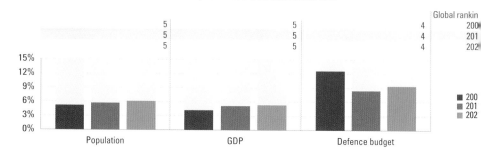

POPULATION

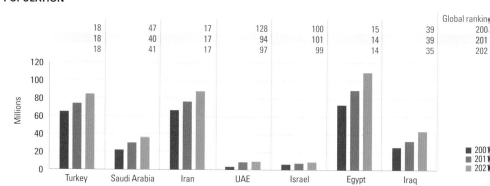

AGE STRUCTURE
(Percentage of national population)

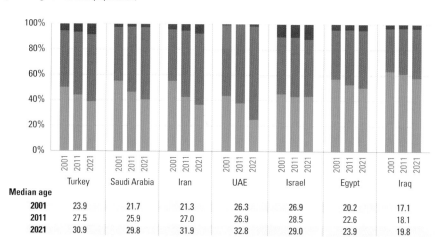

Median age	Turkey	Saudi Arabia	Iran	UAE	Israel	Egypt	Iraq
2001	23.9	21.7	21.3	26.3	26.9	20.2	17.1
2011	27.5	25.9	27.0	26.9	28.5	22.6	18.1
2021	30.9	29.8	31.9	32.8	29.0	23.9	19.8

Defence spending is high relative to population and GDP. Many countries face a potentially combustible mix of a young population, poor economic growth and (from already-low levels) declining freedom. Higher commodity prices due to the Russia–Ukraine war are a windfall for oil and gas exporters, but put food importers under greater strain.

GDP
(Constant 2010 US dollars)

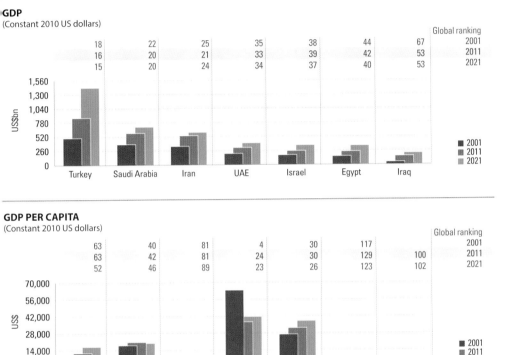

Global ranking

	Turkey	Saudi Arabia	Iran	UAE	Israel	Egypt	Iraq
2001	18	22	25	35	38	44	67
2011	16	20	21	33	39	42	53
2021	15	20	24	34	37	40	53

US$bn: 1,560 / 1,300 / 1,040 / 780 / 520 / 260 / 0

Legend: 2001, 2011, 2021

GDP PER CAPITA
(Constant 2010 US dollars)

Global ranking

	Turkey	Saudi Arabia	Iran	UAE	Israel	Egypt	Iraq*
2001	63	40	81	4	30	117	100
2011	63	42	81	24	30	129	100
2021	52	46	89	23	26	123	102

US$: 70,000 / 56,000 / 42,000 / 28,000 / 14,000 / 0

Legend: 2001, 2011, 2021

* No 2001 data available for Iraq

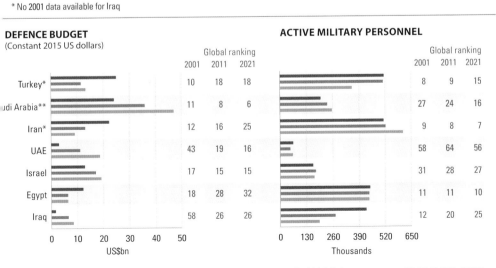

DEFENCE BUDGET
(Constant 2015 US dollars)

Global ranking

	2001	2011	2021
Turkey*	10	18	18
Saudi Arabia**	11	8	6
Iran*	12	16	25
UAE	43	19	16
Israel	17	15	15
Egypt	18	28	32
Iraq	58	26	26

US$bn: 0 10 20 30 40 50

ACTIVE MILITARY PERSONNEL

Global ranking

	2001	2011	2021
Turkey*	8	9	15
Saudi Arabia**	27	24	16
Iran*	9	8	7
UAE	58	64	56
Israel	31	28	27
Egypt	11	11	10
Iraq	12	20	25

Thousands: 0 130 260 390 520 650

*2001 defence budget values for Iran and Turkey are estimates, and may be distorted by high inflation rates.
**Defence budget only, security excluded.

Legend: 2001, 2011, 2021

For explanation of drivers and sources, see page 8

HUMAN DEVELOPMENT INDEX (HDI)
(Score between 0 and 1, where 0 denotes a low level of development and 1 a high level of development)

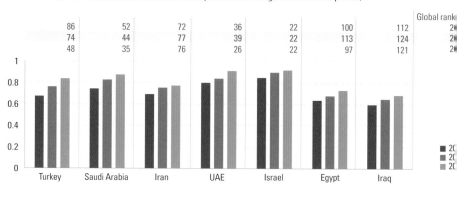

POLITICAL SYSTEM
(Score between 0 and 100, where 0 denotes no political freedom and 100 fully free)

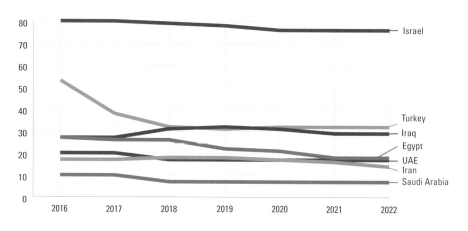

FISCAL BREAKEVEN OIL PRICES (2016–22)

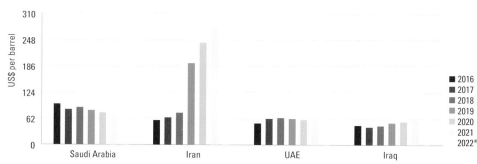

*Figures for 2022 are projections

Average spot crude price 2015–21, US$/barrel Dubai dated

2015	2016	2017	2018	2019	2020	2021
$51.20	$41.19	$53.13	$69.51	$63.43	$42.41	$68.91

2021–22 Review

The Middle East and North Africa region provided some cause for optimism during 2021–22. Rival powers, including Iran, Saudi Arabia, Turkey and the United Arab Emirates (UAE), engaged in constructive bilateral talks aimed at easing tensions and restoring diplomatic relations. In Yemen, warring parties agreed to a nationwide truce for the first time since the start of the war in 2014. Elections were held successfully in Lebanon and Iraq despite those countries' political and security challenges.

Against this hopeful background, however, international efforts in Vienna aimed at restoring an arms-control deal to curb Iran's nuclear programme were at risk of failing. In the absence of an arms-control deal, tensions between the United States and Iran look likely to rise, while Israel will likely continue to take covert unilateral action to slow Iran's nuclear progress. Meanwhile, the Islamic State (ISIS) regrouped for the first time since the fall of its proclaimed capital, Raqqa, in 2017 into an active insurgency in Iraq and Syria, complementing its presence in Nigeria and Afghanistan. The region also continued to suffer from the humanitarian consequences of the conflicts in Iraq, Libya, Syria and Yemen. The Russia–Ukraine war exacerbated the global rise in food and energy prices, placing fragile populations in the region at greater risk of famine.

The Russia–Ukraine war

The surge in food and energy prices, worsened by the Russia–Ukraine war, began to have widespread implications in the region. According to the IMF, global food prices, which had already increased by 28% on average in 2021, were expected to see an additional 14% increase in 2022 due largely to the war in Ukraine. Although global food prices fell significantly in July, according to data from the United Nations' Food and Agriculture Organization, this was accompanied by warnings of high fertiliser prices and a gloomy global economic outlook. Several economically vulnerable nations in the region source the bulk of their wheat imports from Russia and Ukraine, making them vulnerable to the price and supply shocks caused by the war. In 2021, Russia and Ukraine's share of total wheat imports stood at about 45% in Yemen and about 75% in Egypt and Lebanon. Rising energy prices caused Brent-crude spot prices to soar to over US$130 per barrel (bbl) in March 2022 and then stabilise at an average of US$112/bbl in July, worsening the import burden on these oil-importing states. The oil-exporting nations of the Gulf Cooperation Council (GCC), however, stood to accumulate greater earnings, helping them offset the budgetary impact of higher food prices.

Beyond its economic and humanitarian impact, the Russian invasion of Ukraine shed light on the changing nature of alliances and partnerships in the region. The UAE's decision to abstain on a UN Security Council resolution condemning the Russian invasion suggested that some of the United States' closest security partners in the region were reluctant to take its side. Other US partners in the Middle East, including Bahrain, Egypt, Jordan, Morocco and Saudi Arabia, took ambivalent positions, rejecting the use of military force in settling international disputes while shying away from pointing the finger at Russia. Nevertheless, with the exception of Morocco, which failed to attend the vote, all US partners in the region, including the UAE, voted in favour of the symbolic resolution at the UN General Assembly that called on Russia to withdraw unconditionally from Ukraine. Their reluctance to take a categorical position against Russia's assault on Ukraine may seem surprising given Russia's modest economic and military footprint in the region, notwithstanding Egypt and Algeria, which rely on Russian military equipment. This reflected frustration – especially in Riyadh and Abu Dhabi – with US policy in the Middle East, but did not imply that Russia's standing in the region had necessarily improved. Russia's attempt to link the easing of Western sanctions to the progress of the international talks in Vienna over Iran's nuclear programme was rejected by Iran and the West and ultimately failed. The strain of the war on Russian forces was felt in Syria, where Russia reportedly downsized its military presence to redirect troops to Ukraine.

Regional de-escalation

The region's de-escalatory trend largely continued. Saudi and Iranian security officials held five rounds of direct talks in Baghdad between April 2021 and April 2022. Saudi Foreign Minister Prince Faisal bin Farhan described the talks as 'cordial' whilst also highlighting their lack of substantive progress. Diplomatic momentum continued as both parties were rumoured to be preparing for a round of talks at the level of foreign ministers. Such a meeting would be the first of its kind since rioting mobs set fire to Saudi Arabia's diplomatic missions in Iran in January 2016.

Other Arab Gulf states continued to engage in high-level talks and visits with Iran. On 12 May 2022, the Emir of Qatar Prince Tamim bin Hamad Al Thani flew to Tehran in an attempt to play an informal mediating role in the stalled talks on Iran's nuclear programme. Following the death of UAE president Sheikh Khalifa bin Zayed Al Nahyan, Iran's Minister of Foreign Affairs Hossein Amir-Abdollahian travelled to Abu Dhabi on 16 May 2022 to pay his condolences to the ruler's brother and heir, Sheikh Mohammed bin Zayed. On 23 May 2022, Iranian President Ebrahim Raisi paid a one-day visit to Oman to discuss trade shortly after Iran's and Oman's oil ministers held talks to revive a proposal dating from 2003 to build an underwater gas pipeline. Iran's sustained diplomatic engagement with the Arab Gulf states was consistent with its stated objective of prioritising relations with its neighbours.

Turkey also sought to de-escalate tensions with Egypt, Israel, Saudi Arabia and the UAE. In April and May 2022, Turkish President Recep Tayyip Erdoğan paid visits to Abu Dhabi and Riyadh in a bid to improve ties. The thaw in Turkey's relations with Saudi Arabia and the UAE was expected to facilitate a normalisation of Turkey's relations with Egypt. Turkey's Minister of Treasury and Finance Nureddin Nebati visited Egypt in June to participate in the annual meeting of the Islamic Development Bank, ending a hiatus in diplomatic ties.

Turkey's relations with Israel also appeared to be improving. In March 2022, Israeli President Isaac Herzog met with Erdoğan in Ankara.

Turkey hopes to serve as a transit point for Israeli gas exports to Europe, especially as Europe faces potential gas shortages due to the war in Ukraine, though the project faced logistical and technical obstacles. In May 2022, Turkish Minister of Foreign Affairs Mevlüt Çavuşoğlu paid a visit to Israel in a bid to revive ties that have been tepid since the Israeli raid in 2010 on a Turkish ship, the *MV Mavi Marmara*, that was headed for Gaza.

Israel also sought to sustain the diplomatic momentum of the Abraham Accords. On 27–28 March 2022, Israel held the Negev Summit that brought together Bahrain, Egypt, Morocco, the UAE and the US. The objective of the summit, according to Israel's Foreign Affairs Minister Yair Lapid, was to build 'a new regional architecture that will deter Iran'. Absent from the summit was Jordan, whose monarch, King Abdullah II, chose to visit Palestinian Authority President Mahmoud Abbas in Ramallah instead, implying Jordan's displeasure with Israeli policies in Jerusalem and the Occupied Territories. Periodic clashes between Israelis and Palestinians slowed the pace of normalisation and invited calls for restraint even from Israel's new-found Arab partners.

By contrast, Israeli–Iranian relations continued to buck the region's de-escalatory trend. Israel and Iran remained engaged in a shadow war as international talks over Iran's nuclear programme continued to stall. On 13 March 2022, Iran fired missiles at a site in Erbil, Iraq, that it claimed was being used by the Israeli intelligence service Mossad. The attacks were an apparent response to earlier Israeli strikes targeting Islamic Revolutionary Guard Corps (IRGC) agents in Damascus and an Iranian uninhabited aerial vehicle (UAV) base operated by the IRGC in Mahidasht, Iran, in which hundreds of Iranian UAVs were reportedly destroyed. On 22 May 2022, assailants shot and killed a senior officer of the Quds Force, Colonel Hassan Sayad Khodayari, outside his home in Tehran. The IRGC blamed Mossad for the operation and vowed to exact revenge. Meanwhile, Israel sought to maintain pressure on the Biden administration to prevent it from making concessions to Iran. In particular, Israel opposes the de-listing of the IRGC from the US Foreign Terrorist Organizations (FTOs) list, arguing that a reversal of the Trump administration's decision to formally designate the IRGC as a terrorist entity would send the wrong signal about the United States' resolve to counter Iran's support for armed non-state actors in the region.

Difficult political transitions

Iraq, Lebanon and Tunisia remained mired in political and economic crises and faced obstacles on the road to smooth political transitions. Tunisia languished in a constitutional crisis that began on 25 July 2021, when President Kaïs Saïed invoked emergency powers to suspend parliament and dismiss the prime minister Hichem Mechichi. Tunisia's economy had been hit hard by the coronavirus pandemic, with real GDP contracting by 8.2% in 2020. It also faced a high unemployment rate and a soaring debt burden. While Saïed's opponents accused him of overstepping his constitutional limits, his supporters defended the move as a necessary response to Tunisia's political paralysis and governance failures. Tunisia's constitutional crisis took on a regional dimension as the president appears to enjoy the support of Egypt and the UAE. Meanwhile, Saïed's Islamist opponents, especially the Ennahda party, seem to be backed by Qatar and its media arm, Al-Jazeera. In December 2021, Saïed announced a road map involving online consultations on amending the constitution, a public referendum on the constitution in July 2022 and fresh elections in December 2022. Tunisia faces a mounting risk of defaulting on its debts, incurring a downgrade of its sovereign-debt rating by the rating agency Fitch Ratings. Tunisia was in talks with the IMF for a US$4 billion loan that would help finance its budget and avert the risk of default. Talks were paused in July, however, and the Tunisian government failed to convince the powerful UGTT trade union to support the far-reaching fiscal reforms necessary to unlock the IMF's assistance.

Similarly, Lebanon's chances of rescuing its economy hinged on whether its political system would stabilise. In September 2021, Najib Mikati, a businessman who had served as prime minister in the past, finally succeeded in forming a government after previous attempts had failed. Lebanon, which defaulted on its external debt in 2020, was engaged in talks with the IMF for a US$3bn rescue package. As with Tunisia, a key condition of accessing the loan was the passing of economic reforms, which had yet to be achieved by the end of July 2022. In May 2022, Lebanon held its first legislative elections since the August 2020 Beirut port explosion. The 41% turnout was low compared to previous elections. Although the Shi'ite parties Hizbullah and Amal retained their seats, the Hizbullah-led March 8 coalition, which comprises Christian and Druze groups, won only 61 out of 128 seats, a drop of ten seats from the previous elections. While the Hizbullah-led coalition lost its majority in parliament, the Lebanese Forces – a Christian group opposed to Hizbullah and backed by the Sunni-majority Saudi Arabia – and the independents were the elections' biggest winners. Nevertheless, the Hizbullah-led March 8 coalition managed to get its two candidates, veteran politician Nabih Berri and Elias Bou Saab, elected as speaker and deputy speaker of parliament respectively during the first session of parliament on 5 June 2022. Although the election of Berri to the post of speaker, which he has held since 1992, was expected, the contentious victory of Bou Saab, a former minister of education and defence and a member of the Hizbullah-aligned Free Patriotic Movement, suggested that Lebanon's established parties continued to hold sway over the country's political institutions.

In Iraq, the October 2021 elections, held under a new voting system, shifted the balance of power in parliament among Iraq's Shi'ite factions. The coalition led by cleric Moqtada al-Sadr, an Iraqi militia leader who opposed the United States' military presence in Iraq and a member of one of Iraq's most prominent Shi'ite clerical families, scored large gains as it climbed from 54 to 73 seats. Meanwhile, the al-Fatah coalition, composed of affiliates of the Popular Mobilisation Units (PMU) over which Iran holds sway, suffered significant losses and was reduced from 48 to 17 seats. The PMU rejected the results and accused the Iraqi government of fraud. They are widely suspected of standing behind an attempt on Prime Minister Mustafa al-Kadhimi's life in November 2021. The elections also ushered in new faces among both Arabs and Kurds, signalling a desire for change amongst Iraqis.

ISIS resurgence

ISIS witnessed a resurgence in Iraq and Syria. It launched an assault on Gweiran Prison, run by the US-backed, Kurdish-led Syrian Democratic Forces (SDF) in the governorate of al-Hasakah, on 20 January 2022. On the same day, it killed 11 Iraqi soldiers in an attack on Iraqi army barracks in the province of Diyala northeast of Baghdad. On 23 May 2022, it launched attacks in the Iraqi governorate of Kirkuk and province of Diyala under cover of sandstorms, killing 12 civilians. ISIS also claimed several attacks against Egyptian security forces in Sinai, including the killing of five soldiers on 25 January 2022 and 11 more in an attack on a water-pumping station east of the Suez Canal on 7 May 2022. ISIS also claimed responsibility for two deadly attacks by lone-wolf Palestinian militants inside Israel, including a knife attack in Beer Sheva and an attack with automatic weapons in Hadera in March 2022.

The divergent trajectories of Middle Eastern conflicts

While the conflict in Yemen saw signs of progress towards a political settlement, other conflicts in Libya and Syria continued with no end in sight. Yemen's first nationwide ceasefire since the outbreak of war in 2014 was fragile but still holding despite multiple reported violations. A two-month UN-brokered ceasefire, which came into force on 2 April 2022, led to the partial reopening of Sana'a International Airport, Hodeidah Port and of roads leading to the besieged southwestern city of Taiz. On 7 April 2022, Abd Rabbo Mansour Hadi resigned from the presidency, a post which he had held for about a decade, and ceded power to an eight-member Presidential Leadership Council brokered by Saudi Arabia and the UAE. The council, headed by Rashad al-Alimi, a former minister of the interior, included four northerners and four southerners, bringing together disparate groups and leaders of the various military factions in Yemen. This followed the stalemate between the Houthis and the coalition comprising local tribes, the UAE-backed Giants Brigades and forces loyal to the Yemeni government.

Meanwhile, a two-year-long effort led by the UN Mission in Libya to broker an end to Libya's conflict appeared to falter. Libya's legislative elections were postponed indefinitely shortly before they were to be held on 24 December 2021. With the House of Representatives in the east having appointed its own prime minister (Fathi Bashagha) in February 2022, Libya once again split into two rival administrations after the Government of National Unity had briefly succeeded in uniting the warring factions under a single political umbrella in 2021. The postponing of elections and renewed split in political authority in Libya suggested that the country was still far from reaching a political resolution to its civil war.

Syria's political and battlefield dynamics remained largely unchanged. Clashes between the Turkey-based Syrian National Army and the SDF, which is dominated by Kurds, continued in Syria's northeast. Due to setbacks in its war against Ukraine, Russia reportedly downsized its troop presence in Syria. Although the Russians are unlikely to depart from Syria fully, this force reduction is likely to be seized upon by Iran to widen its influence in Syria. This places the Syrian regime, which has relied on the Russian presence to counterbalance Iran and Turkey, in a difficult situation as it faces the prospect of further loss of autonomy to regional powers. Given the gains that Iran and the Lebanon-based Hizbullah are poised to make in Syria, Israel is also concerned about the implications for its own ability to operate in Syria. Russia said that military deconfliction with Israel, which allowed Israel to target IRGC facilities in Syria from the air with relative impunity, would continue.

Syria's humanitarian tragedy continues to unfold as 90% of the population lives below the poverty line and over 14 million Syrians rely on humanitarian aid to survive. The al-Hol detention camp in Syria's northeast, whose population stands at about 56,000 people, most of whom are women and children, stands out for its appalling conditions. The camp, which houses many families of foreign fighters and female ISIS recruits, illustrates the complexities of Syria's humanitarian situation, as other states remain wary of the security risk of repatriating their nationals from the Syrian conflict zone.

Desert Geopolitics
Will tensions in Western Sahara lead to war?

Introduction

Ever since the surprise December 2020 announcement that Morocco had joined the United States' Abraham Accords, diplomatic and security tensions between Rabat and Algiers have steadily escalated. For instance, Algeria has severed diplomatic ties with Morocco and in November 2021 an errant Moroccan drone strike killed three Algerian citizens. Both capitals feel aggrieved and there is no immediately apparent way to de-escalate the situation.

The Abraham Accords and Western Sahara

In December 2020, in the final days of former president Donald Trump's administration, the US announced that it was reversing its three-decade-old policy towards the disputed territory of Western Sahara (which is claimed by Morocco) and was now officially recognising Moroccan sovereignty over the territory. The change in US policy was driven by Morocco joining the Abraham Accords – a Middle Eastern initiative spearheaded by Trump's son-in-law Jared Kushner that promoted normalised diplomatic ties with Israel. Morocco effectively engaged in quid pro quo diplomacy: if Washington supported Morocco's policy objectives regarding Western Sahara, Rabat would support the United States' policy objectives in the Middle East.

Since 1975, Morocco has claimed the disputed territory of Western Sahara. The territory was a former Spanish colony. However, in 1975, Spain withdrew from the territory after fighting a two-year counter-insurgency against the Polisario Front (the Western Saharan independence movement). With Spain's withdrawal, Morocco's King Hassan II ordered the 'Green March', during which around 350,000 Moroccan civilians and soldiers marched into Western Saharan territory. The arrival of the Moroccan population, and Rabat's claims to the territory, incited a new war between the Polisario Front and Morocco. The Western Sahara War lasted from 1975–91 and produced more than 90,000 refugees who fled to Algeria. Algeria has hosted the refugee population ever since. As part of the truce that ended open conflict between Morocco and the Polisario Front, Morocco agreed to hold a referendum in Western Sahara to allow the Western Saharan population to determine whether it wanted to live under Moroccan sovereignty or to establish its own independent state. To date, no referendum has been held, but Morocco has proposed an alternative plan in which it would retain sovereignty over the territory and Western Saharans would benefit from a large degree of autonomy from Rabat. Algeria, which continues to support the Western Saharans, views Morocco's claims to Western Sahara as illegal. Although Algeria has no claims to the territory, it strongly supports Western Saharans' right to self-determination. This issue is at the heart of Algeria's grievances with Morocco.

For Morocco, joining the Abraham Accords was not as significant as it appeared at first blush. Morocco has long had informal diplomatic relations with Israel, and the Abraham Accords merely formalised these ties. But what it got in return – US recognition of its claims to Western Sahara – marked a diplomatic sea change for the country. The US also announced that it would open a consulate in the southern city of Dakhla, which is located in the disputed territory, and foster foreign direct investment in the territory. (However, there is a small but vocal US congressional caucus that supports Western Saharan independence, and no consulate has been opened because the US Congress has not approved funding for it.)

Although there were questions about whether the incoming administration of President Joe Biden would reverse the Trump administration's decision, it gradually became clear that Western Sahara policy was not high on the Biden administration's list of priorities. The Trump policy has remained in place. Morocco saw this decision to uphold the policy as a signal that European capitals would follow Washington's lead.

Algeria, on the other hand, which is one of Western Sahara's staunchest allies and hosts an estimated 173,000 refugees from Western Sahara, was blindsided by the Trump administration's recognition of

Moroccan and Polisario Front control of Western Sahara

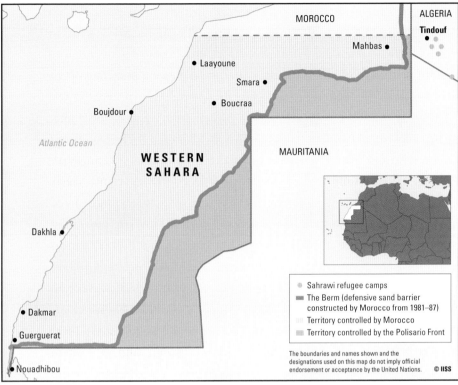

Source: UN Mission for the Referendum in Western Sahara

Moroccan sovereignty over the territory. Worse, it felt that the Biden administration's maintenance of the policy sabotaged relations between the two countries. In short, US recognition of Moroccan sovereignty over Western Sahara has fundamentally disrupted the diplomatic status quo in North Africa.

Morocco on the offensive

Since the United States' recognition of Moroccan sovereignty over the disputed territory, Morocco has adopted a more aggressive foreign policy aimed at building on the United States' new policy position. In the span of just two-and-a-half months in 2021, Morocco instigated two significant diplomatic actions. First, in March 2021, Morocco suspended contact with the German Embassy in Rabat after Germany made it clear that it would not follow the United States in recognising Moroccan sovereignty but instead maintain its position that the Western Sahara dispute should be resolved through the United Nations. Adding fuel to the fire, the German state of Bremen raised the Sahrawi flag over official buildings in recognition of the 45th anniversary of the founding of the Sahrawi state, the Sahrawi Arab Democratic Republic.

Then, in May 2021, Rabat recalled its ambassador to Madrid after Spain allowed Brahim Ghali, the former General Secretary of the Polisario Front and the current president of the Sahrawi Arab Democratic Republic, to be admitted to a Spanish hospital for COVID-19 treatment. Spain had already indicated that it would not follow the United States' lead and recognise Moroccan sovereignty over the disputed territory. Morocco accused Madrid of allowing a 'terrorist' to enter Spanish territory. But, despite having withdrawn its ambassador from Spain, Rabat did not suspend diplomatic ties. Instead, Morocco relaxed border controls outside the Spanish exclave of Ceuta, allowing thousands of immigrants to cross into the Spanish city, effectively weaponising illegal immigration to punish Madrid for its 'support' for the Sahrawi cause.

Morocco's forcefulness was driven by two sentiments. Firstly, Morocco felt that if it was able to convince the US to change its position on Western Sahara, then it could convince lesser diplomatic powers to do so as well. Secondly, Morocco was resentful that its normalisation of diplomatic ties with Israel did not garner it as much diplomatic credit in Europe as it had hoped.

Algeria on the defensive

Algeria, Morocco's long-time regional rival and the Sahrawis' main benefactor, was slow to react to the changing diplomatic landscape. Algiers had held out hope that the Biden administration would reverse the Trump administration's stance on Western Sahara. However, it gradually became resigned to the fact that the policy was here to stay. Algeria's slow reaction was likely due to three factors. Firstly, policymaking in Algeria is typically slow. Secondly, Algeria's domestic political circumstances slowed policymaking even further. Thirdly, Algeria's borders were sealed from March 2020 to July 2021 in order to mitigate the spread of COVID-19.

Algeria is an acutely risk-averse country. This means that it does not change policy positions easily. Instead, it prefers to hold its course, in the hope that events are cyclical. Algiers had hoped that maintaining its policy and not overreacting would leave it in a better position when the US eventually reversed its stance on Western Sahara.

Furthermore, policymaking in Algeria is the result of an informal consensus-building process. However, throughout 2020 and the first half of 2021, contested political power in Algeria meant that it was unclear who would participate in this consensus building. At that time, President Abdelmadjid Tebboune did not exert a monopoly on political power. Neither, however, did the powerful Chief of Staff of the People's National Army Saïd Chengriha. Even the roles of foreign ministers Sabri Boukadoum and Ramtane Lamamra were uncertain. In some periods, their influence in Algeria was strong; in others, they were marginalised by either the presidency or the Ministry of National Defence. This meant that even if Algeria was inclined to shift its policy in response to the United States' recognition of Moroccan sovereignty over Western Sahara, it would have been unable to do so.

Lastly, in response to the coronavirus pandemic, Algeria completely closed its land, sea and air borders. No Algerians were allowed out of the country, and even Algerians abroad could not return to their home-land. Algeria effectively cut itself off from the rest of the world. Making matters worse, President Tebboune himself was hospitalised with COVID-19 while in Germany in October 2020; he was only able to return to Algeria two months later. Algeria's diplomatic engagements were effectively suspended until the country's borders reopened in July 2021. But, by that time, the diplomatic playing field had shifted completely.

Morocco overplays its hand

Morocco's new foreign-policy stridency, however, eventually led it to overplay its hand, resulting in a sharp decline in its regional relations. In July 2021, the Pegasus Project, an international journalists' initiative, published the results of its investigation into various countries' use of the Pegasus cyber spyware developed by the Israeli NSO Group. One of the key findings was that Morocco had used the spyware to access the phones of opposition activists in Morocco, French government officials and nearly 6,000 Algerian officials including a former army chief of staff, a former foreign minister, and former president Abdelaziz Bouteflika's brother. In May 2022, it was revealed that Morocco also used the spyware to hack the phone of Spain's prime minister.

France expressed its frustration with Rabat, but it did not aggressively pursue the issue. Algeria, on the other hand, viewed the cyber espionage as a direct violation of Algeria's sovereignty. Worse, at about the same time (and potentially to deflect attention from the Pegasus scandal), Morocco's Ambassador to the UN Omar Hilal called for 'the independence of the Kabyle people' – an ethnic minority of Berbers living in northeastern Algeria who have their own language and regional homeland. Algiers interpreted the comments as an attempt by Rabat to interfere in Algeria's domestic affairs and sow division in Algeria.

Morocco, however, maintained its forceful foreign policy. It believed that it continued to enjoy broad US support and saw France's somewhat gentle reaction to the Pegasus scandal as a sign that Paris continued to favour Rabat as well. In November 2021, a drone strike killed three Algerian civilians in Sahrawi-controlled Western Sahara. Algeria blamed Morocco; Morocco refused to comment. Behind closed doors, however, Morocco acknowledged to its allies, including the US, that it was responsible for the drone strike but claimed this had been a targeting error. Meanwhile, Morocco ramped up its defence purchases, particularly from its new ally, Israel. In addition to new orders of Turkish *Bayraktar* drones, Rabat secured the Israeli *Skylock Dome* anti-drone system in November 2021.

Algeria gets in the game

Algeria was late to respond to the changing regional diplomatic milieu. However, it eventually did so, first by cutting diplomatic ties with Rabat and then by trying to undermine Morocco's energy security.

In July 2021, Algeria withdrew its ambassador to Morocco and in August cut diplomatic ties. In September 2021, Algeria closed its airspace to Moroccan aircraft, disrupting Moroccan flag-carrier flights to Tunisia, Egypt and elsewhere in the Middle East. President Tebboune subsequently threatened Morocco with armed conflict if Rabat's aggressions continued. The severing of diplomatic ties had a limited impact apart from stoking regional tensions. The land borders between Morocco and Algeria have been closed since 1994. Likewise, economic trade between the two countries is limited, although there is extensive illicit cross-border economic activity. The closure of Algerian airspace to Moroccan planes simply added distance to Moroccan flights, which were obliged to fly north to the Mediterranean before heading to points further east.

More important than these diplomatic measures was Algeria's refusal to renew the Maghreb–Europe Gas Pipeline (MEG). The MEG originates in Algeria, transits Morocco and ends in Spain where it feeds into the Spanish energy infrastructure. Under a contract that governed the MEG's operations, Morocco received volumes of natural gas in lieu of a transit fee. The natural gas that Morocco received from the MEG was Morocco's only source of gas, which it used to power roughly 18% of the country's electricity generation. The MEG contract was set to expire at the end of October 2021, and Algeria made it clear that it would not renew the contract and instead would shutter the pipeline. It assured Spain that it would be able to meet Spanish energy needs via the Medgaz pipeline, which directly links Algeria and Spain, and through increased liquefied natural gas (LNG) cargoes to Spanish regasification terminals.

On 1 November 2021, Algeria shut the pipeline down and Morocco lost its only source of natural gas. Morocco's energy minister announced in January 2022 that Rabat had completed feasibility studies for floating regasification terminals, but, since then, no construction contracts have been awarded. Subsequently, in April 2022, Spain announced that it would restart the MEG in reverse mode, feeding gas through Spanish networks back to Morocco. Algeria reacted immediately, asserting that if Spain reversed the flow of the MEG, it would suspend all gas supplies to Spain. Algeria argued that its supply contracts with Spain included end-user agreements that prevented Spain from re-exporting Algerian gas. Although Spain insisted that any gas it exported to Morocco would be taken from regasified LNG imports, Algeria argued that once gas was in the pipeline it was impossible to distinguish the country of origin and that Spain would therefore be unable to guarantee that gas exported to Morocco did not include gas from Algeria. The argument initially seemed to dissuade Spain from operating the MEG in reverse mode, but, in June 2022, Spain did in fact export gas through the pipeline to Morocco. This appears to have been a one-time event, however, with the pipeline being empty once again in July 2022.

Not only is Algeria determined to punish Morocco economically, it is also intensifying its war-footing rhetoric. Chengriha stated in a speech in April 2022 that Algeria was well aware of its territorial borders. This was both a jab at Morocco's continuing claims to Western Sahara and a warning that Algeria would steadfastly defend its own borders. There may have been a personal animus in this too: Chengriha had been captured by Moroccan forces and held as a prisoner of war during the First Battle of Amgala in 1976.

While Algeria may be simply sabre-rattling, it has a lot of sabres. Algeria had the fifth-largest defence budget as a percentage of GDP in the world in 2021, spending US$9.04 billion. It has an active force of 139,000 (along with 187,200 active gendarmerie and paramilitary) and an additional reserve force of 150,000, making it the largest military in Africa after Egypt. In short, it has ample military capability.

The current stand-off

Regardless of the risks posed by rising tensions, neither Morocco nor Algeria appears willing to take steps to de-escalate the stand-off. Morocco is determined to capitalise on US recognition of its sovereignty over Western Sahara. It refuses to cede any ground and is resolved to retaliate against countries that do not recognise its sovereignty claims. Algeria is digging in as well. It refuses to scale back its demands for Western Saharan self-determination. A post-colonial revolutionary ideology reinforces this: acknowledging Morocco's claims would betray the state's core ideological orientation. Morocco in turn has no incentive to undermine the achievement of US recognition of its sovereignty by compromising with Algeria. Given these two stances, neither side is currently willing to budge.

Consequences of the Russia–Ukraine war

Russia's invasion of Ukraine has added a new dynamic to this dispute. On the one hand, it has jeopardised Morocco's energy and food security. On the other hand, it has increased Algeria's importance as an alternative energy source for Europe. As a result, both countries are urgently intensifying their diplomacy with other states.

Morocco imports 90% of its energy needs. The bulk of its electricity production comes from imported coal, 87% of which is imported from Russia. Its 2021 coal bill of US$1.6bn could treble in 2022 as a result of Russia's invasion of Ukraine. In March 2022, thermal coal for power generation reached approximately US$435/tonne, the highest price ever. Secondly, around 18% of Morocco's electricity generation came from two natural-gas-powered facilities, which were supplied through the now-shuttered MEG. In order to make up for the lost natural-gas-powered electricity generation, Morocco needs to increase coal or heavy-fuel-oil imports. Morocco also imports two to three million tonnes of wheat per year in normal circumstances. Since domestic production has been hit by the worst drought in nearly three decades, it now needs to import more. But with Ukrainian wheat no longer available due to Russia's invasion and blockade, it must source this elsewhere at higher prices. Wheat spending is expected to rise nearly US$500m in 2022.

Capitulating on Western Sahara while simultaneously facing a worsening economic environment could signal twin setbacks for Rabat. As a result, Morocco's difficult economic trajectory makes it even less likely to seek a detente with Algeria. Morocco simply cannot entertain the prospect of back-to-back defeats.

By contrast, Algeria's economic outlook is better than it has been in more than a decade. This is due in no small part to rising energy prices as a result of Russia's invasion of Ukraine and Europe's search for alternatives to Russian energy supplies. Although Algeria cannot materially increase energy production in the short term due to lack of investment in the upstream over the last 20 years, it is still profiting from the current energy-price environment. Its 2022 budget crude-oil reference price is US$45 per barrel (bbl) and its fiscal breakeven price is US$72/bbl. Moreover, Algeria has marginally increased crude-oil production since the launch of the Russian invasion from 994,000 barrels per day (bpd) to 1.01m bpd. With Algeria's Sahara Blend crude oil trading at roughly US$123/bbl, Algeria is looking at a massive hard-currency windfall. This budgetary surplus will ease Algeria's perennial political tensions.

Algeria has also benefited diplomatically from Europe's quest for alternatives to Russian energy supplies. Since Russia's invasion of Ukraine began, Algeria has hosted foreign ministers and other high-level delegations from France, Italy, Qatar, Russia, Spain, Ukraine and the US. In addition, President Tebboune has made visits to Egypt, Italy and Turkey, and had planned an additional visit to Moscow for July 2022. While none of these visits has resulted in an outward expression of support for Algeria's Western Sahara stance, Algeria is making its case for Western Saharan self-determination. With its new economic bounty and diplomatic salience, Algeria sees no need to compromise with Morocco.

Given the current circumstances and future trajectories, direct armed confrontation between Algeria and Morocco cannot be ruled out. The regional dynamic has shifted. On the one hand, Morocco won, and Algeria lost, from the Trump administration's recognition of Moroccan sovereignty over Western Sahara. Morocco appeared ascendant, whereas Algeria's diplomatic influence seemed to be declining. On the other hand, Russia's invasion of Ukraine has flipped the circumstances. Algeria is becoming economically and diplomatically much stronger due to the threats the Russia–Ukraine war poses to European energy supplies. The conflict has also significantly weakened Morocco, dramatically raising its food and energy import bill.

This sharply swinging regional dynamic is what makes the prospect for conflict between the two countries more likely than it has been in recent years. Each side feels aggrieved and believes it is in the right. Likewise, each side senses an urgency to act. Morocco wants to claw back the diplomatic advantage it had in 2020 and 2021. Algeria wants to leverage current conditions before they dissipate. Moreover, Morocco feels that its allies would rush to its side were conflict to erupt, while Algeria also feels that the international community would support it as the aggrieved party. While neither is likely to be true, this misreading of the current broader diplomatic posture makes conflict even more likely.

Recalibrating Saudi Foreign Policy
How has MBS changed Saudi diplomacy, and can it support his modernisation drive?

After years of economic pain and political isolation from the West, Saudi Arabia has rebounded spectacularly. Energy-market turbulence has played a key role in this change in fortune: the Western scramble for oil and gas resulting from Russia's invasion of Ukraine has reminded the world of the kingdom's centrality to energy politics, and has improved the country's economic outlook by driving up oil prices and bringing back once-reticent businesses and investors.

Nothing exemplifies this shift as much as the visit to Jeddah of United States President Joe Biden in July 2022. As recently as 2019, then-presidential candidate Biden had described the kingdom as a 'pariah' state due to the ruthless leadership of Crown Prince Muhammad bin Salman bin Abdulaziz Al Saud (MBS). He then shunned it for the first year of his presidency before sharply changing tack. Saudi Arabia is clearly a pariah no longer.

However, the contribution of Riyadh's own policy recalibration to this turnaround in fortunes is often overlooked. Under MBS's stewardship, the Saudi monarchy has sought to recast itself as a modern global power. In line with his re-engineering of the country, the young prince has sought to question or jettison some of the previous assumptions and pillars of Saudi foreign policy, and transcend its traditional role as the self-declared champion of the Islamic and Arab worlds. As with many other MBS initiatives, this recalibration has yet to deliver tangible and durable results. But it has already shaken the country's diplomacy, creating trepidation as well as excitement inside and outside the kingdom.

Changing priorities and policies

MBS's frenetic modernisation drive, which has had dramatic effects at home, has extended into the realm of foreign policy. Crucially, he has been keen to reduce the ideological and geopolitical baggage that comes with Saudi Arabia's traditional claims to Islamic and Arab leadership, which he sees as convenient but also as limiting and costly. If this ambition were to be fully realised, considerations of Islamic and Arab solidarity would no longer routinely constrain Saudi policies. Traditional regions of Saudi interest could no longer expect automatic Saudi attention and largesse. Instead, Saudi Arabia would review its legacy entanglements, and prioritise its geo-economic and geopolitical interests in the service of the kingdom's transformation.

In this regard, MBS shapes but also reflects the priorities of a new generation of leaders that do not share attachments to issues that have consumed and frustrated their predecessors. For this new elite, the focus on regional relationships has been a waste of attention and resources. It has often been uncoordinated, with senior royals taking responsibility for separate portfolios with no integrated view of national interests. It created dependencies and expectations abroad, often miring the kingdom in reputation-damaging controversies. And it politicised (and sometimes radicalised) Saudi subjects more invested in regional conflicts than in embracing national identity and modernising their country.

There is an overwhelming sense in Riyadh that legacy relationships from Pakistan to Lebanon have not delivered the expected returns. Saudi largesse did not secure Egyptian or Pakistani participation when its campaign in Yemen began in 2015. Long the darling of Saudi leaders, Lebanon has become a source of disappointment and an exporter of threats to the kingdom with the rise of Hizbullah, the Shia militant group whose ideology and activities now target Saudi Arabia as much as Israel. Saudi Arabia was one of only three countries to recognise Taliban rule in Afghanistan in 1996, only to see al-Qaeda plotting operations against the royal family from Afghanistan. Saudi backing for Syrian rebels fighting President Bashar al-Assad generated accusations that the kingdom actively or complacently supported the Islamic State (ISIS). For MBS, even the imperative to intervene in Yemen could be traced to indecisive and unrealistic Saudi policy in previous years. And political and tribal leaders in Yemen that Riyadh cultivated at great cost proved fickle, weak and two-faced. In short, Saudi diplomacy until 2015 was often misguided and came at an exorbitant price.

Such thinking has had significant consequences, particularly in the Levant, where Saudi Arabia had long been a major actor. The kingdom's attachment to Jordan, Lebanon and Syria had been personal as well as strategic, with Saudi royals cultivating friendships with national leaders. In contrast, MBS came with an unsentimental view of these relationships. In his view, they did not serve the kingdom's interests: Saudi Arabia's friends and partners had underdelivered or underperformed. In Lebanon, the Saudi-backed Hariri political dynasty had weakened and failed to contain Hizbullah. As a result, Saudi Arabia has been effectively disengaged since 2016. Neighbouring Jordan, long dependent on Saudi largesse, also suffered from downgrading. The Hashemite kingdom was undercut by US president Donald Trump's rejection of the Israeli–Palestinian peace process and felt threatened by Saudi ambitions. Riyadh even toyed briefly with the idea of replacing Jordanian trusteeship of the Muslim religious sites in Jerusalem. Jordanian leaders complained that Saudi financial and energy assistance had dried up, causing major economic and budgetary damage. In Syria, the kingdom became disillusioned with its failure to unseat Assad and with the dominance of rivals Turkey and Iran there. Seeing no way to re-establish influence, MBS preferred to cut costs and extract Saudi Arabia from the Syrian crisis for the time being.

Elsewhere, Riyadh signalled that it would no longer automatically champion Muslim causes in its foreign-policy responses. When India altered the constitutional status of the disputed region of Kashmir in 2019, the Saudi response was relatively muted, drawing Pakistani ire. In a historic reversal, Riyadh prioritised the cultivation of economic and defence relations with a rising New Delhi over alignment with Islamabad, which had been a close if ambivalent and needy security partner for decades. No less revealing was Saudi Arabia's support for China over the fate of the Uighur community: in the face of Western criticism of China, Riyadh has backed Beijing's narrative of counter-terrorism and religious reform in Xinjiang, signing letters in 2019 at the United Nations to this effect. Once the Arab state most opposed to communism during the Cold War, Saudi Arabia now sees courting China as essential to its prosperity and security, and is eager to avoid being forced to choose between Washington and Beijing. In April 2022, MBS told Chinese President Xi Jinping that the kingdom would 'staunchly support China's legitimate position on such issues concerning core interests as Xinjiang, resolutely oppose any interference in China's internal affairs and firmly safeguard the rights of all countries to choose their own political and human rights paths independently'.

In its immediate neighbourhood, the kingdom started paying more attention to the Red Sea region, which it had previously largely ignored. For Riyadh, which had long prioritised development in the Najd hinterland and on the Gulf coast, the Red Sea coast now appears secure and economically promising. The most grandiose of MBS's projects is the US$500 billion new city of NEOM on the northwest coast, but there has also been infrastructure development – including pipelines, railways, tourist facilities and ports – along the littoral. To secure this shift, Saudi Arabia recovered the islands of Tiran and Sanafir from Egypt and established a Red Sea Council to bring together littoral states. This ambition has unnerved out-of-region states such as Turkey and the United Arab Emirates (UAE), but also Egypt, the Arab state once dominant in the area. In parallel, Saudi Arabia has cultivated good relations with Ethiopia despite the latter's dispute with Egypt over the construction of the Grand Ethiopian Renaissance Dam (GERD), which will significantly affect downstream Nile River water flows into Egypt.

Domestically, tighter control of religious organisations and the promotion of a more tolerant brand of Islam were deemed essential to MBS's modernisation plans. A wide crackdown on clerics with radical or reformist inclinations who had been tolerated in the past and who could challenge MBS's views ensued. This recalibration was equally important as a means to burnish the kingdom's international image and credibility, which had suffered ever since the 11 September 2001 attacks. Consequently, government spending for proselytising abroad has been slashed and Saudi religious leaders have pursued outreach to non-Islamic faiths. The head of the World Muslim League, the organisation once in charge of propagating Salafi-Wahhabi teachings worldwide, has held meetings with Christian, Jewish, Hindu and other religious figures to promote a message of tolerance.

Recasting the kingdom, and surviving ostracism

The crown prince has strived to position Saudi Arabia as a modern nation keen to deploy geo-economic and geopolitical power globally. In his view, instead of being a leader of poor, weak and dependent countries, Saudi Arabia should be an equal to First World nations. Prioritising relations with leading economies not only makes geopolitical sense but is also essential to the fulfilment of the kingdom's ambitions. No forum could provide better validation of Saudi Arabia's new ambitions than the G20, the gathering of the world's 20 largest economies.

The success of Vision 2030, MBS's grandiose transformation plan, depends on not only an overhaul of the Saudi economy but also a significant upgrading of political and economic relations with major powers. Instead of being merely an exporter of commodities and an importer of high-value consumer goods, the kingdom now aspires to become an economic power that is embedded in global supply chains as both a manufacturer and a logistical hub; a producer of both traditional and renewable energies; a destination for foreign investment; an allocator of capital to key sectors; and a partner of choice for major companies.

Developing such relations has required the kingdom to conduct more sophisticated statecraft than in the past, when energy was the Saudi card. Having concentrated power in his hands to an unprecedented degree, MBS is forcing greater alignment of the kingdom's foreign, defence and economic policies. For example, the establishment of a production line for Chinese uninhabited aerial vehicles (UAVs) in Saudi Arabia is meant not only to advance defence cooperation with Beijing, but also to foster the development of an indigenous defence industry, secure technology transfers and eventually allow the kingdom to become an exporter of weapons systems, as detailed in a recent IISS study entitled 'The Defence Policy and Economics of the Middle East and North Africa'. Crucially,

MBS transformed the once-sleepy Public Investment Fund (PIF) into a driver of domestic economic development as well as an instrument of international investment and influence.

Such an expansive and transformative plan has necessitated, to an extent, a retooling of Saudi diplomacy. Coincidently, Prince Saud al-Faisal, the formidable foreign minister who embodied Saudi diplomacy for 40 years, died in 2015, a few months after relinquishing his position. In 2018, his successor, Adel al-Jubeir, a protégé of the late King Abdallah bin Abdulaziz Al Saud associated with 'old' diplomacy, was demoted from his job as foreign minister and replaced with Ibrahim al-Assaf, a veteran economist who had served as finance minister. A year later, al-Assaf himself was replaced by Prince Faisal bin Farhan, a young prince aligned with MBS. While the management of the crucial US–Saudi relationship has remained in the hands of MBS and his brother Prince Khaled, Prince Faisal has been charged with diversifying Saudi relations. Saudi ambassadors in major capitals were tasked with more aggressive economic outreach. Tellingly, Khalid al-Falih, the investment minister who previously served as CEO of state-owned oil company Saudi Aramco and as energy minister, became the point man for key relationships such as with China and Japan, the country most involved in the implementation of Vision 2030. In early 2020, Japan's then-prime minister Abe Shinzo was the first leader of a G7 country to visit Riyadh since the assassination of Saudi journalist-turned-dissident Jamal Khashoggi, for which US intelligence blamed MBS.

Importantly, MBS has revamped Saudi energy policy, establishing royal control over a sector that had been left to bureaucrats for decades. In 2015, MBS was appointed chair of the Supreme Council of Saudi Aramco; the company had been mostly shielded from royal interference in the past. MBS also installed Yasir al-Rumayyan, the head of the PIF and his right-hand man, as Saudi Aramco chair. In 2019, Prince Abdulaziz bin Salman, a half-brother of MBS, became the first royal to head the energy ministry. The public listing of Saudi Aramco, which MBS hoped would be in London, New York or Tokyo but ultimately occurred in Riyadh in 2019, was a statement of power as well as an essential element of his economic plan.

MBS has appeared willing to use oil production as an instrument of influence. The goal of Saudi policy since the 2000s had been to stabilise energy markets by ensuring that oil prices did not climb to a degree that would dampen or destroy demand, thus jeopardising the main source of Saudi income in the long term. Instead, operating on a shorter time frame, MBS has proved more willing to prioritise economic interests (the listing of Saudi Aramco) or strategic objectives (upholding the OPEC+ agreement to cut oil production despite Western demands for greater production after the peak of the coronavirus pandemic). Saudi Arabia has been more assertive in the defence of its energy interests, whether against the US shale-oil industry or against Russia's attempt in 2020 to compel it to cut its production amid falling demand at the beginning of the pandemic.

This new global positioning was already under way when, in 2018, MBS-led Saudi Arabia faced the biggest setback to its efforts. The widespread perception of Saudi aggressiveness and overreach, already fuelled by the calamitous war in Yemen, seemed to be vindicated with the Khashoggi assassination. The resulting spotlight on the kingdom cast a shadow on MBS's modernising efforts. Significant camps in the US sought to isolate him: progressives on the left, diplomats, intelligence professionals and others.

To survive ostracism by the West, Saudi Arabia sought to consolidate power at home by cracking down on dissent. Notwithstanding the hopes of many in Western capitals that another prince could replace him, the message was that there was no alternative to MBS. The young prince was destined to become king (with a shot at being the longest-serving monarch) regardless of Western concerns. Similarly important was the closing of ranks among Arab powers. Riyadh secured the support of Egypt, the UAE and other Arab nations that were also displeased with US policy.

Importantly, MBS doubled down on strategic diversification. Calculating that only Western leaders would isolate him to placate public opinion, he sought closer relationships with autocratic and populist leaders in China, India, Russia and elsewhere. Conveniently, the

2018 G20 summit in Argentina allowed a then-ostracised MBS to mingle, if uncomfortably, with international leaders. Fittingly, Saudi Arabia was slated to host the G20 summit in 2020. This prospect had caused headaches in Western capitals intent on shunning the young prince for his excesses. The pandemic brought a fortuitous result in this regard, however: the global suspension of travel meant that international leaders could no longer visit the kingdom, while Saudi Arabia dodged the embarrassment of more junior delegations attending. The ongoing pandemic meant that the focus at the summit (held virtually) was on the management of the pandemic and the economic recovery, relatively safe topics for all concerned.

Ups and downs with the US

Of the many relationships MBS sought to transform and solidify, the one with the US was central. Relatively unknown in Washington when he emerged in 2015, he was seen by some as the moderniser that the kingdom dearly needed to escape its social conservatism and revamp its economy. Others, notably in the intelligence community, preferred the then-crown prince Mohamed bin Nayef, who had proven a reliable counter-terrorism partner.

Unlike his older half-brothers and some of his siblings, MBS had not studied in Western countries and had minimal contacts there. But his fascination with the US was on display when he embarked on a three-week tour in 2018, during which he visited Hollywood and Silicon Valley and met US economic, cultural and political elites. In contrast, his visits to China, India and Russia only lasted days.

Strategically, however, MBS saw the US under president Barack Obama as an ungrateful and wobbly partner. Its hesitant support in Yemen, its eager diplomacy with Iran, its pivot to Asia and its dithering in Syria suggested that Saudi dependence on Washington was too risky and that accelerating strategic diversification was necessary.

The surprise victory of Trump in 2016 gave rise to optimism in Riyadh that US policy could be shaped to Saudi desires. Active courtship of Trump delivered a spectacular first visit to Riyadh in 2017 and apparent alignment on a host of regional issues. These hopes were dashed when it became clear that US policy would not necessarily reflect the preferences of Trump (as was the case with the crisis with Qatar) and, strikingly, when the US declined to retaliate after the 2019 Iranian drone attacks on major Saudi oil facilities.

By late 2020, Saudi Arabia was failing to achieve important goals. Oil prices hovered below US$45 a barrel (bbl), under the fiscal breakeven point for the kingdom. US attempts to exert maximum pressure on Iran, a strategy which the kingdom eagerly supported, did not deliver the crushing blows that the Trump administration had promised. The Saudi-led boycott of Qatar had failed to weaken the small emirate. The Houthi insurgency in Yemen was making military gains even as the political, military and reputational costs for Saudi Arabia steadily mounted. The election of Biden, amid intensifying criticism of the country in US media and across the political spectrum, seemed to guarantee tense relations. Biden had promised to revive diplomacy with Iran, to treat the kingdom as a pariah, to pressure countries over their ties with Russia and China and to promote human rights.

Estrangement from the US had a practical cost for the kingdom. The intensification of Houthi aerial attacks from Yemen exposed Saudi physical vulnerabilities. The only defensive response was US-provided intelligence, surveillance and reconnaissance (ISR) and defence systems. These, however, arrived in limited numbers, and US redeployment of assets out of the region heightened concerns in the kingdom about US reliability.

Demonstrating flexibility, MBS changed tack, pursuing a less belli-cose agenda that prioritised economic modernisation. The reconciliation with Qatar occurred during a summit in Saudi Arabia in early 2021, with political and economic normalisation proceeding briskly. In the spring of 2021, Riyadh began a dialogue with Tehran in Baghdad. Ostensibly intended to de-escalate the conflict in Yemen, this track was also meant to demonstrate to Washington that Riyadh was less inflexible than por-trayed. In Yemen, Saudi Arabia was eager to appear as the flexible party, if only to reduce its involvement in this protracted conflict. Hoping to reduce its exposure in Yemen, Riyadh worked with US and UN envoys to reach a ceasefire, even pushing aside in 2022 its main Yemeni client, the ineffectual and controversial president Abd Rabbo Mansour Hadi.

All these moves relieved pressure on the kingdom but failed to sway the US. Biden maintained a tough line, refusing to talk to MBS and delegating the management of the relationship to his secretaries of state and defence, and other advisers. The Russian invasion of Ukraine dramatically changed this dynamic. Saudi Arabia's reluctance to support Western diplomacy and to break the OPEC+ agreement enraged Western officials. As oil prices increased from US$60/bbl in April 2021 to US$120/bbl a year later, generating enormous revenues for the kingdom after years of low income, Saudi Arabia refused to be the swing state, in contrast to its response to the oil price peak in 2008. Riyadh only agreed to small production increases in line with the OPEC+ agreement and in line with its own spare capacity, which appeared to be more limited than expected. The resulting tensions on the oil market were useful in that they demonstrated the enduring pivotal role of Saudi Arabia to its traditional partners. Riyadh relished the sight of the then-prime minister of the United Kingdom Boris Johnson, French President Emmanuel Macron and Biden courting him in the hope of greater production levels; importantly, all three appeared resigned to the fact that MBS would not distance himself from Russian President Vladimir Putin.

After months of diplomacy, Biden came to the realisation that US interests demanded a detente with the kingdom. He flew to Jeddah with low expectations. The visit was meant to reassure US partners in the Middle East that American military power would still underpin regional security. If the visit rehabilitated the Saudi leadership, it also served as a reminder that despite any aspirations for autonomy from its major Western partner and desire to diversify relations, Riyadh still remained eager for US attention and protection.

Conclusion

MBS has been able to articulate a foreign policy that is more independent of the interests of Saudi Arabia's traditional partners and less constrained domestically. He has done so in a context of American retrenchment and contested geopolitics and in the name of his modernisation project.

But his recalibration has not been wholly successful. The constraints on Saudi policy have remained significant. His attempt to build closer relations with Israel, which Trump encouraged and which culminated in a secret trip by then-prime minister Benjamin Netanyahu to NEOM in 2020, was checked by King Salman bin Abdulaziz Al Saud's continued attachment to the Palestinian cause and Jerusalem. The price that Saudi leaders attach to an eventual recognition of Israel is considerably higher than the one placed by the Emirati and Bahraini leaderships who agreed to normalise relations in 2020.

It is also unclear whether Saudi Arabia's new orientation can mitigate the effects of the Iranian challenge, which Saudi officials insist is the gravest the country faces. Most of the countries Riyadh is courting are unwilling or unable to act as security providers and are averse to taking sides. This only emphasises Saudi reliance on its traditional Western partners: at its moment of extreme vulnerability after the 2019 attacks, only the US and France could send defensive systems.

Fundamentally, Saudi Arabia's claim to the leadership of the Arab and Islamic worlds is central to its global standing. It confers heavy responsibilities and obligations on Saudi policy, but ensures the attention and courtship of foreign powers. And relationships with dependent countries have come in handy: in 2018, when Western elites boycotted the annual economic conference he organises, MBS was able to compel the attendance of the prime minister of Lebanon and presidents of African countries as well as Gulf leaders.

Requiem for the Iran Nuclear Deal
Is there any other way to constrain Iran's nuclear hedging?

Failed diplomacy

On the presidential campaign trail in 2020, Joe Biden pledged, if elected, to restore the 2015 Iran nuclear deal, officially called the Joint Comprehensive Plan of Action (JCPOA), which had provided sanctions relief in exchange for strict limits on Iran's nuclear programme and enhanced verification by the International Atomic Energy Agency (IAEA). In May 2018, then-president Donald Trump had pulled the United States out of the deal, reimposing sanctions that had been lifted under the accord and adding new economic penalties. A year later Iran began to undo nuclear limits, responding to Trump's policy of 'maximum pressure' with 'maximum resistance'. Iran's estimated 'breakout period' – the time it would need to produce a weapon's worth of highly enriched uranium – which had been at least 12 months under the JCPOA, was steadily reduced.

Taking office in 2021, Biden looked set to achieve his election promise to resume the status quo ante, even though negotiations did not begin until that April. Because Iran refused to meet directly with the US as long as sanctions remained in place, the European Union and the other five parties to the JCPOA – China, France, Germany, Russia and the United Kingdom – acted as intermediaries in what were called 'proximity talks'. Largely setting aside additional demands, the US and Iran focused on a mutual goal of 'compliance for compliance', under which both would return to their commitments. Amongst other advantages, keeping strictly to the conditions of the JCPOA would give Biden a better chance of avoiding the need for new congressional review. For over a year, however, Iran and the US could not fully agree on what those commitments were. By June 2022, the talks were hopelessly stalled, and the US, in concert with Israel and the other states most concerned about Iran, considered 'Plan B' options for preventing Iran from acquiring nuclear weapons.

The Islamic Revolutionary Guard Corps

The key impediment concerned Trump's April 2019 designation of the Islamic Revolutionary Guard Corps (IRGC) as a foreign terrorist organization (FTO). Iran demanded that this be lifted unconditionally. Although the IRGC was blacklisted as a tactic to block a future president's ability to restore the JCPOA, that is, as a cornerstone of Trump's 'sanctions wall', the Biden team was technically correct in arguing that this sanction was outside the purview of the accord, which had left non-nuclear penalties in place. Under bipartisan political pressure not to appear to condone IRGC-abetted terrorist actions, the Biden administration was willing to remove the designation only if Iran took compensatory action to assuage security concerns outside the JCPOA. If the IRGC were to be de-designated, Iran would have to demonstrate diminution of the group's terrorist activity. Amongst other ways Iran could do so would be by calling off its vendetta targeting former US officials whom it deemed to be involved in the January 2020 killing of General Qasem Soleimani, commander of the IRGC Quds Force, Iran's primary instrument for external military engagement. Among those targeted were Trump's secretary of state Mike Pompeo and special representative for Iran Brian Hook, both of whom faced 'serious and credible' threats, according to the US government, and for whom 24-hour security protection was costing more than US$2 million a month.

Such a trade-off, which could be called off if either party reneged, would need to be formalised in a separate bilateral understanding. Iran insisted that, on principle, it could not forgo bringing justice to those responsible for the murder of a beloved general whom many regarded as the second-most powerful and popular person in the country (after Supreme Leader Ayatollah Ali Khamenei). 'Certain issues that have to do with our national heroes are non-negotiable', declared Iran's Foreign Minister Hossein Amir-Abdollahian in March 2022. Negotiators left the proximity talks in Vienna early that month and subsequent shuttle diplomacy by EU senior official Enrique Mora and others, who proposed, inter alia, that Iran agree to follow-on talks on regional issues in exchange for removing the FTO designation, failed to break the impasse.

For this issue to block an agreement that all parties professed to be in their national interest defies pragmatism. Removing the FTO designation would make no difference to Iran's economy, since over a dozen other remaining US sanctions block foreign firms and banks from engaging in any trade involving the IRGC. The only economic case that JCPOA critics can make is that the FTO label heightens the criminal liability for foreign entities that do business involving the IRGC and makes it somewhat easier for American victims of Iran-related terrorism to recover damages from outstanding legal judgments against Iran. Nor does the designation limit the IRGC's regional activity; according to the US, the number of attacks from Iran-backed groups increased fourfold in the year after the IRGC was so designated.

Yet the blacklisting carries immense political and symbolic importance to both sides. For Tehran, the IRGC is a key organ of the state, constitutionally mandated with protecting the revolutionary order, and which also has a large stake in the economy. It is the only government entity in the world to be harnessed as an FTO under a US regulation designed for non-state actors. Iran sees the blacklisting as having given the US a legal basis for the Soleimani assassination. The designation also applies to over 11m citizens who were conscripted into the corps, thereby prohibiting their travel to the US.

For Washington, the IRGC is considered responsible for the deaths of and injury to hundreds of US citizens and others over the years and for arming proxy forces throughout the region. When the IRGC launched 12 missiles against an Israeli facility in Erbil in the Kurdistan Region of Iraq on 12 March 2022, injuring two people and coming perilously close to a US military base and a US consulate under construction, consideration of removing the terrorist designation became all the more fraught.

Israel's then-prime minister, Naftali Bennett, and Minister of Foreign Affairs Yair Lapid weighed in strongly against de-designation, as did Bahrain, Saudi Arabia and the United Arab Emirates (UAE), with whom relations with Biden were already strained. Most importantly, a solid majority of the US Senate, including nearly one-third of the Democratic senators, joined a non-binding resolution calling on the president not to remove the FTO label. The Department of Defense argued against delisting, and ultimately the White House did as well.

Compromises to date

All other issues appeared to have been settled in a draft agreement of roughly 27 pages, with technical details on how the two parties would come back into compliance in stages. The US stopped insisting that Iran agree to follow-on talks to extend the nuclear limits beyond 2031 and to address concerns about Iran's missile programme and involvement in nearby states. The US also repeatedly extended its stated February 2022 deadline for completion of the talks. Iran stopped insisting that the US move first in lifting sanctions.

Iranian maximalist demands

The Vienna negotiations had been difficult anyway. Iran put the talks on hold for five months after the June 2021 election of hardliner President Ebrahim Raisi. For foreign minister, he appointed a JCPOA sceptic, Hossein Amir-Abdollahian, who, when talks resumed in November, presented maximalist demands that exceeded the positions taken by his predecessor, Mohammad Javad Zarif. Iran demanded compensation for the billions of dollars of trade lost to US sanctions, verification of sanctions removal before observing Iran's own JCPOA obligations and a guarantee that the US would not again withdraw from the deal. In addition, Iran insisted on an end to all 1,600 Trump-era designations of Iranian individuals and entities. Many of those sanctions had been imposed purposely to prevent a future president from restoring the JCPOA, but other measures, for example, those over human-rights violations and interference in US elections, had no connection to the deal and would not impede its implementation – a condition the US had set for determining which sanctions to lift.

For a week in early March 2022, talks appeared to be imperilled by Russian demands to exempt trade with Iran from Western sanctions over its invasion of Ukraine. Talks in Vienna were immediately broken off. When Amir-Abdollahian hastily visited Moscow, however,

Russia clarified that its position required only an exemption for nuclear cooperation with Iran. Since such trade was spelled out in the JCPOA, the US readily complied, prompting a mood of optimism that the talks soon would succeed. But as weeks went by, it became more and more apparent that the IRGC issue was insurmountable.

Failure to restore the JCPOA meant that four American–Iranian dual citizens detained under dubious charges continued to be denied freedom. Their families were optimistic when two British-Iranian political prisoners, Nazanin Zaghari-Ratcliffe and Anousheh Ashouri, left Iran on 16 March 2022 after serving lengthy sentences. In exchange, the UK paid Iran a £390m debt over the shah's purchase of British *Chieftain* tanks in the 1970s that were never delivered. News reports predicted that the four American detainees – 84-year-old Baquer Namazi and his businessman son Siamak, businessman Emad Shargi and environmentalist Morad Tahbaz, who is also a British citizen – would similarly be released upon the unfreezing of a portion of Iran's blocked assets in South Korea and release of several Iranians jailed in the US for sanctions violations. These hopes proved to be false. It appeared that release of the detainees and Iran's blocked oil revenue would only come in connection with agreement to restore the JCPOA.

Implications

Restoring the JCPOA would free up about US$100 billion in Iranian oil-sale revenue frozen in foreign banks due to the prohibition on using the US financial system for trade with Iran, although not all of this amount would be readily accessible or convertible. It would also allow unfettered Iranian export of petroleum products, including up to 170m barrels stored on land and at sea. Experts predicted that restoration of the JCPOA could see Iranian oil exports increase by 1.3m barrels per day (bpd) by the end of 2022. Each month that the accord remained in limbo, Iran was estimated to lose out on US$4bn in potential oil revenue.

These lost sales meant less to Iran when the Russia–Ukraine war bumped oil prices above US$100 per barrel. In addition, gradual evasion of sanctions allowed Iran already to sell more barrels, even though it had to do so at a discount. Oil exports (including condensates) of 400,000 bpd in 2020 climbed to 1–1.2m bpd in December 2021. Overall, the Iranian economy was not in the dire straits often painted by its detractors. While inflation and unemployment remain high, at close to 40% and over 10% respectively, Iran's GDP grew at an average of 3% in 2020 and 2021 and may exceed that in 2022 in light of the high oil prices. Further reducing incentives to compromise, the economic benefits from restoring the JCPOA would be short-lived if a Republican were to return to the White House in 2025, as Biden's low popularity ratings seem to forecast will be the case. Iranian sceptics argued it would not be worth giving up nuclear leverage and managing the double dislocation to the economy of first re-entering the deal and then departing from it again in two to three years' time.

Nuclear progress

For the US and its European partners, the implications of not restoring the JCPOA are arguably worse. On the economic front, there would be no return of Iranian oil exports to world markets, which could help stabilise oil prices. More importantly, the non-proliferation benefits of the deal would be lost. By late May 2022, Iran's nuclear breakout time was calculated to be approximately two weeks or less. Iran had stockpiled enough enriched uranium to provide the fissile material for up to four nuclear weapons if further enriched. The stockpile included over 40 kilograms of uranium enriched to 60% U-235, a short step away from weapons grade (92%). Iran's enrichment capacity increased with the installation of several versions of advanced centrifuges which operate at greater efficiency.

Timely inspections are the best guarantee against breakout. Without the JCPOA, those concerned about Iran's nuclear programme were deprived of the enhanced IAEA monitoring that many analysts saw as the most beneficial element of the accord. From February 2021, Iran denied the IAEA these additional monitoring rights. In addition to lacking access to the data from online enrichment monitors and monitoring of uranium conversion, the agency was not allowed to monitor a centrifuge-production workshop at Karaj which was damaged by a drone attack in June 2021 attributed to Israel. Iran permitted IAEA cameras at the site but would not grant access to camera footage as long as the JCPOA was not restored. The same conditions applied to a new workshop at Esfahan to which the previous work at Karaj was transferred. Without this access, the agency cannot determine whether any centrifuge components have been diverted to military use elsewhere.

Although Tehran continued to grant the IAEA access to conduct normal verification under its full-scope safeguards agreement, Iran was cagey about addressing IAEA questions that arose from the discovery of uranium particles at three previously undeclared sites in Iran in 2019. The agency wanted to know if the uranium was related to past nuclear-weapons-related activities, work that Iran has consistently denied, despite the massive cache of evidence uncovered by a Mossad raid on an atomic archive in Tehran in January 2018. Investigation of anomalous activity at a fourth site, Lavizan-Shian, finished in March 2022 and concluded that Iran had not abided by its safeguards agreement by not reporting the possession and processing of a uranium-metal disc there in 2003. In March 2022, Mohammad Eslami, the head of the civilian Atomic Energy Organization of Iran, and IAEA Director General Rafael Grossi reached an agreement that Iran would present documents and written explanations aimed at resolving outstanding issues concerning the sites in question. When those explanations proved to be unsatisfactory, on 8 June 2022 the IAEA Board of Governors passed a mildly critical resolution calling on Iran to fully cooperate. Iran's response was to turn off all remaining monitoring equipment installed under the JCPOA.

The investigation of past unreported nuclear activity is separate from the talks on restoring the JCPOA, but putting IAEA questions to rest was deemed by some diplomats to be a requisite condition for implementation of any restoration deal. This is because not reporting nuclear activity violates Iran's safeguards agreement, potentially repeating the nuclear crisis that began in 2002 when the IAEA confirmed undisclosed uranium imports.

Looking ahead

As the stalemate dragged into summer 2022, neither side wanted to admit diplomatic failure and to be seen as responsible for it. Although the US had said in February that the non-proliferation benefits of a restored deal would soon dissipate, the alternative of no deal – an unconstrained, less transparent Iranian nuclear programme – still looked worse. Iranian commentators mooted the possibility of Iran leaving the Nuclear Non-Proliferation Treaty, discarding all international monitoring. This would significantly increase the risk of conflict over efforts to prevent Iran from following North Korea's path towards producing nuclear weapons. Meanwhile, Iran seemed to have concluded that time was on its side. The situation was thus set to drift.

Partial delisting of the IRGC continued to be seen as a possible compromise, for example, keeping the Quds Force designated as an FTO. This would make sense, as the rest of the IRGC is not directly involved in lethal activities outside Iran, which are the cause of concern. For even partial delisting, however, the US, for political reasons, still would need compensatory Iranian concessions on issues extraneous to the JCPOA.

If negotiations were to succeed in restoring the JCPOA, it would be less beneficial on non-proliferation grounds than the original accord. Even if all other limits on enrichment stockpiles and production were restored, unfettered Iranian advances in nuclear R&D since the US withdrew from the deal mean that it would not be possible to return to a 12-month breakout period. Estimates are fuzzy, but six to nine months might be the best achievable benchmark. Half a year would be far better, of course, than the two-week breakout period estimated in spring 2022. And all breakout-time estimates must acknowledge that fissile-material accumulation is only one step in bomb production. Israeli experts predicted that another two years would be required for Iran to weaponise the highly enriched uranium and produce a bomb that could be carried by its missiles.

The default plan B is to ramp up sanctions. New multilateral penalties backed by the United Nations Security Council are off the table, given the breakdown in great-power relations due to Russia's invasion of

Ukraine and to China–US tensions. This leaves unilateral measures. The US could exact more pressure by enforcing Trump-era sanctions against buyers of Iranian oil. This would primarily apply to China, which gradually increased purchases in 2021, eventually exceeding the 623,000 bpd peak recorded in 2017. Chinese imports exceeded 700,000 bpd in January 2022. Squeezing these imports, however, would cause a further spike in oil prices that were already inflated by Western efforts to take Russian oil off the market. Higher petroleum prices at the pump would reverberate badly on Biden in the run-up to midterm congressional elections in November 2022. And there is no reason to think that additional sanctions would fare any better than Trump's policy of maximum pressure to force a change in Iran's policies.

If diplomacy does not constrain Iran's nuclear capability, Israel is likely to employ kinetic and cyber means to try to do so. Recent sabotage attacks attributed to Israel – at Natanz in April 2021 and July 2020, and the November 2020 assassination of top nuclear-weapons scientist Mohsen Fakhrizadeh – only temporarily delayed Iran's progress while provoking it to further exceed JCPOA limits. Notwithstanding the disappointing results of previous covert actions, the Israel Defense Forces have reportedly been preparing military options to strike key Iranian nuclear facilities with more force. Whether a US green light would be given or even needed is uncertain. What does seem certain is that Iran could rebuild nuclear facilities after any attack and would do so without any international monitoring.

The best plan B options thus remain in the diplomatic realm. If the JCPOA cannot be restored, the US and its allies may be inclined to seek a partial restoration, or the elusive 'longer, stronger' deal, extending the time limits of the JCPOA and addressing non-nuclear concerns in exchange for more benefits for Iran, including access to US markets. Given the complexity of restoring a limited deal, however, the prospects for a better deal appear unrealistically optimistic.

CHAPTER 10

Sub-Saharan Africa

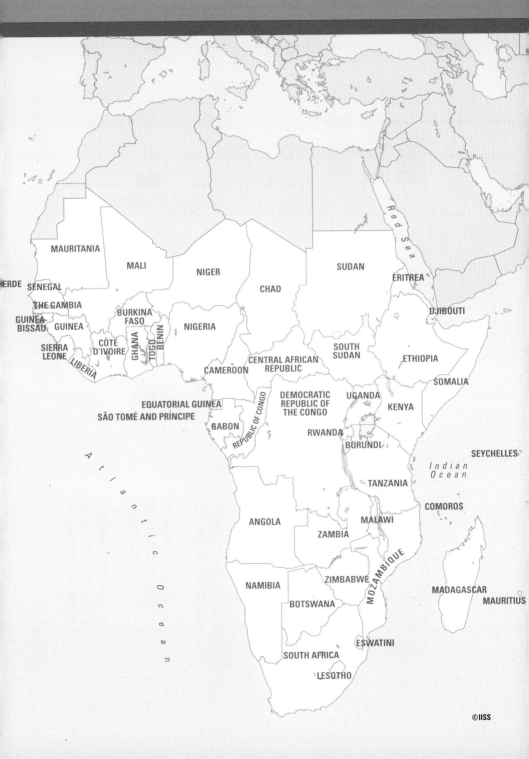

MAURITANIA

MALI

NIGER

SUDAN

ERITREA

CHAD

DJIBOUTI

ERDE SENEGAL

THE GAMBIA

GUINEA-
BISSAU GUINEA

BURKINA
FASO

NIGERIA

SIERRA
LEONE

CÔTE
D'IVOIRE

GHANA

TOGO

BENIN

LIBERIA

CAMEROON

CENTRAL AFRICAN
REPUBLIC

SOUTH
SUDAN

ETHIOPIA

SOMALIA

EQUATORIAL GUINEA

SÃO TOMÉ AND PRÍNCIPE

GABON

REPUBLIC OF CONGO

DEMOCRATIC
REPUBLIC OF
THE CONGO

UGANDA

KENYA

RWANDA

BURUNDI

TANZANIA

SEYCHELLES

*Indian
Ocean*

COMOROS

ANGOLA

ZAMBIA

MALAWI

MOZAMBIQUE

NAMIBIA

ZIMBABWE

BOTSWANA

MADAGASCAR

MAURITIUS

ESWATINI

SOUTH AFRICA

LESOTHO

Red Sea

A t l a n t i c   O c e a n

©IISS

Drivers of Strategic Change

REGIONAL SHARE OF GLOBAL POPULATION, GDP AND DEFENCE BUDGET

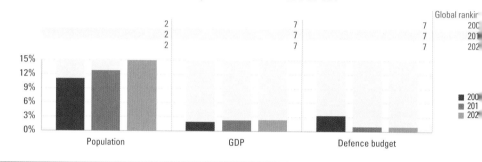

POPULATION

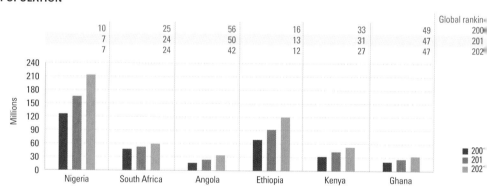

AGE STRUCTURE
(Percentage of national population)

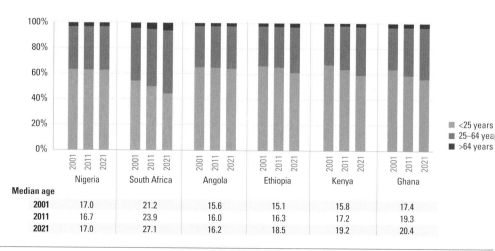

Median age	Nigeria	South Africa	Angola	Ethiopia	Kenya	Ghana
2001	17.0	21.2	15.6	15.1	15.8	17.4
2011	16.7	23.9	16.0	16.3	17.2	19.3
2021	17.0	27.1	16.2	18.5	19.2	20.4

Sub-Saharan Africa's large, young population has the potential to fuel a 'demographic dividend' of growth, or the 'youth bulge' associated with a higher risk of conflict. Large economies like South Africa and Nigeria have struggled to raise living standards. The rapid growth of mobile-money payments – sub-Saharan Africa accounts for two-thirds of all such transactions – can help drive growth and support financial resilience.

GDP
(Constant 2010 US dollars)

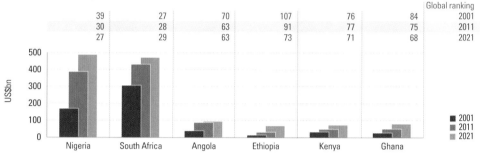

						Global ranking
39	27	70	107	76	84	2001
30	28	63	91	77	75	2011
27	29	63	73	71	68	2021

US$bn — Nigeria, South Africa, Angola, Ethiopia, Kenya, Ghana (2001, 2011, 2021)

GDP PER CAPITA
(Constant 2010 US dollars)

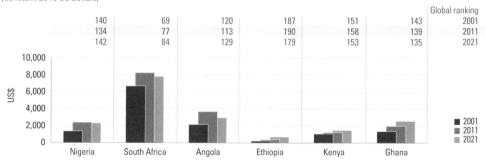

						Global ranking
140	69	120	187	151	143	2001
134	77	113	190	158	139	2011
142	84	129	179	153	135	2021

US$ — Nigeria, South Africa, Angola, Ethiopia, Kenya, Ghana (2001, 2011, 2021)

DEFENCE BUDGET
(Constant 2015 US dollars)

ACTIVE MILITARY PERSONNEL

DEFENCE BUDGET — Global ranking

	2001	2011	2021
Nigeria	53	54	53
South Africa	36	41	55
Angola*	16	46	67
Ethiopia	41	85	98
Kenya	86	71	77
Ghana	95	123	103

US$bn

ACTIVE MILITARY PERSONNEL — Global ranking

	2001	2011	2021
Nigeria	51	49	36
South Africa	60	59	50
Angola*	37	45	45
Ethiopia	22	36	38
Kenya	94	88	91
Ghana	133	100	105

Thousands

*2001 defence budget value for Angola is an estimate, and may be distorted by high inflation rates.

2001 2011 2021

HUMAN DEVELOPMENT INDEX (HDI)
(Score between 0 and 1, where 0 denotes a low level of development and 1 a high level of development)

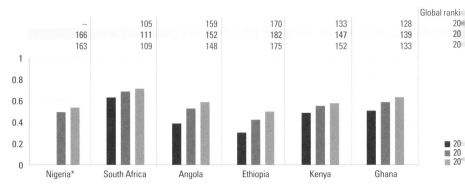

*No 2001 data available for Nigeria

POLITICAL SYSTEM
(Score between 0 and 100, where 0 denotes no political freedom and 100 fully free)

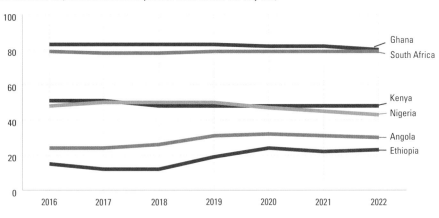

PERCENTAGE OF ADULTS WITH A MOBILE-MONEY ACCOUNT

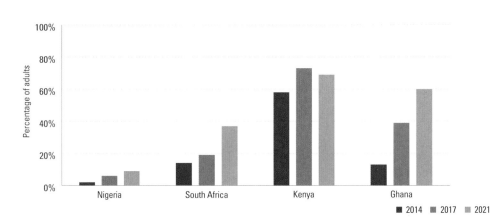

For explanation of drivers and sources, see page ✱

2021–22 Review

A step back for democracy?

Over the past year, elevated insecurity, including a high number of attempted and successful coups, has characterised sub-Saharan Africa. In September 2021, Guinea's increasingly authoritarian president, Alpha Condé, was overthrown in a coup led by Colonel Mamady Doumbouya, the head of the country's special forces. Condé had faced an increasing number of protests after altering the country's constitution to allow himself a third term in office, and his government's crackdowns on protesters had become progressively more violent. Burkina Faso experienced two military coups in 2022: in January, a junta led by Lieutenant-Colonel Paul-Henri Damiba seized power in the wake of escalating anti-government protests before Damiba himself was removed in September and replaced by Captain Ibrahim Traore. In February 2022, there was an attempted coup in Guinea-Bissau, which President Umaro Sissoco Embaló claimed may have been linked to the drug trade.

Coups were not restricted to West Africa during this period. In October 2021, Sudanese military forces dissolved the country's transitional government after detaining the civilian leadership, including the prime minister, Abdalla Hamdok. The dissolution of the civilian government followed an attempted coup the previous month and occurred only a few weeks before the military was due to hand over the leadership of the Sovereign Council – formed in 2019 after the ousting of the former dictator, Omar al-Bashir – to its civilian elements. The takeover by General Abdel Fattah al-Burhan prompted widespread domestic protests and the suspension of Western financial assistance, exacerbating economic instability. Following this takeover, Burhan agreed to form an independent civilian government of technocrats (appointing 15 ministers to a new government in January 2022) and launch a comprehensive national dialogue with pro-democracy groups. However, protests persisted, and in the face of these, Burhan announced in July 2022 that the military would withdraw from national talks facilitated by the African Union (AU), the Intergovernmental Authority on Development, and the

United Nations Integrated Transition Assistance Mission in Sudan and 'make room for political and revolutionary forces and other national factions' to form a civilian government. The announcement was a significant concession by the military and should go some way towards easing the long-standing political crisis in Sudan. That said, distrust of the military remains high, and protests over elevated inflation and poor living standards are likely to persist.

At the same time, there were ongoing insurgencies in the Sahel (underscoring the weakness of state institutions in the region), and Tigrayan forces in Ethiopia staged a counter-offensive against the Ethiopian military, retaking the city of Mekelle in June 2021. By November 2021, rebel forces had captured Dessie and Kombolcha, just 160 miles northeast of the capital, prompting Abiy Ahmed's government to announce a six-month state of emergency. Subsequently, however, the Ethiopian military retook substantial amounts of territory, and in June 2022, Abiy announced that the government had established a seven-member committee led by Deputy Prime Minister Demeke Mekonnen that will handle negotiations (perceived as de facto peace talks) with the Tigrayan ruling party. This process may prove challenging given reports of ongoing human-rights abuses, including alleged massacres of civilians in Oromia.

More positively, in August 2021, there was a democratic transition of power in Zambia, where the incumbent Edgar Lungu and the Patriotic Front (PF) were defeated in a free election by Hakainde Hichilema and the United Party for National Development. Lungu, who had become increasingly unpopular (in part because of a significant rise in public debt), initially indicated that he intended to refuse to accept the results. However, given the scale of the opposition victory – Hichilema won 59.0% of the presidential vote, while Lungu only won 38.7% – he backtracked.

Chinese retrenchment from Africa?

In November 2021, Senegal hosted the Eighth Ministerial Conference of the Forum on China–Africa Cooperation (FOCAC), the triennial summit between China and African states at which the Chinese government traditionally makes major announcements about its policy towards the continent. While the official theme of the meeting was 'Deepen China–Africa Partnership and Promote Sustainable Development to Build a China–Africa Community with a Shared Future in the New Era', the conference prompted international speculation that China was retrenching from the continent. China appeared to be significantly scaling back planned activities in a variety of areas. For example, it committed to only ten projects, compared to 50 in 2018, in each of the following areas: agricultural assistance, climate and environment, health, peace and security, and trade promotion. However, the main reason for the international speculation was the reduction in China's headline financial pledge to Africa, from US\$60 billion in 2018 to US\$40bn in 2021. This was the first reduction in China's financial commitment to African states in the history of the summit. The changes in the composition of the funding – with a sharp reduction in credit lines and grants and an increased focus on corporate investment, trade finance and the allocation of IMF Special Drawing Rights – also suggested that, at the very least, China was seeking to reduce its exposure to higher-risk mega-projects. Notably, there was no overt reference to infrastructure, whereas, in the 2018 FOCAC commitment, connectivity infrastructure was listed as the second among eight 'action plans'.

China has faced consistent criticism from the West for its alleged debt-trap diplomacy. The difficulty that some African governments faced in meeting debt repayments led to speculation that China would take control of Entebbe airport in Uganda or Mombasa port in Kenya. China has rebuffed such criticism, but there is little doubt that some large-scale projects have faced opposition from local governments and civil-society groups because of concerns about their budgetary implications or social or environmental impact. For example, the US\$14.4bn Lagos–Calabar Coastal Railway project in Nigeria, due to be built and partly funded by Chinese interests, attracted significant public criticism and appears to be on hold. Concern over financial sustainability is apparent on both sides. Chinese lenders are taking a more selective approach to large-scale infrastructure projects in the region in light of white-elephant projects such as Kenya's standard-gauge railway. China's own efforts to move towards more sustainable domestic growth are also prompting greater caution in providing finance.

'Peace and security' was the last of nine programmes set out by President Xi Jinping at the 2021 FOCAC meeting. He pledged that China would undertake ten such projects for Africa, continue to deliver military assistance to the AU, support African efforts to maintain regional security and fight terrorism, continue to cooperate on the control of small arms and light weaponry, and conduct joint exercises and on-site training. Despite the relatively little attention given to security in the FOCAC announcement, however, there are signs that China is continuing to seek to consolidate a pan-African security architecture focused on protecting its interests in the ongoing Belt and Road Initiative (BRI). For example, in December 2021, classified United States intelligence reports suggested that China was aiming to establish a permanent military installation in Equatorial Guinea – its first permanent military presence on the Atlantic Ocean.

Such reports are unconfirmed but are in line with long-standing US speculation about Chinese plans for a second African base. For example, in 2021, a Department of Defense report stated that China 'likely considered' 13 different countries for military installations, with potential sites including Angola, Kenya, the Seychelles and Tanzania. However, speculation has focused on Equatorial Guinea, with the head of US Africa Command (AFRICOM), General Stephen Townsend, stating in early 2022 that this was 'the place that they've got traction right now'. Proponents of this view point to several factors: China's role as Equatorial Guinea's key development partner; Equatorial Guinea's high levels of debt exposure (a September 2021 report suggested that the country's sovereign and hidden debt exposure to China amounts to 49.7% of GDP); China's construction of a deep-sea port in Bata that can accommodate both commercial and military vessels; and the possibility that, as with its base in Djibouti, China could portray the construction of this port as providing support for multilateral anti-piracy activities. However, China has avoided West African pressure to become more involved in peacekeeping in the subregion. The January 2022 African tour by Chinese Foreign Minister Wang Yi focused on Comoros, Eritrea and Kenya, suggesting stronger Chinese interest in the northern Indian Ocean than the Atlantic.

European aims complicated by West African coups

The European Union held its own triennial meeting with African states – the sixth EU–AU Summit (the first since 2017 because of coronavirus-pandemic-related postponements) – in February 2022, at the end of which the two sides issued a Joint Vision for 2030, focusing on the creation of 'a space of solidarity, security, peace and sustainable prosperity'. The Joint Vision for 2030 concentrates on renewed cooperation for peace and security, a commitment to multilateralism and the integration of Africa into the EU's Global Gateway initiative, which aims to dispense up to €300bn in investments around the world by 2027 to support infrastructure development. At the summit, half of the overall Global Gateway total was pledged to the Africa–Europe Investment Package in an effort to bolster the claim by European Commission President Ursula von der Leyen that Europe was Africa's 'most reliable partner'. The investment package targets efforts to accelerate the green and digital transitions in Africa, bolster sustainable growth and the creation of decent jobs, strengthen healthcare systems and improve education and training.

However, the EU has failed to fully honour past financial pledges, and the commitments announced at the summit have been criticised as repackaged initiatives or as impractical. For instance, €135bn of Global Gateway's overall funding will come from the already dedicated European Fund for Sustainable Development Plus, and there are plans to incorporate and repackage other existing EU initiatives under the Global Gateway banner. Likewise, some of the commitments have been labelled impractical either because they lack an actionable plan or because of disagreements among EU member states and African partners concerning what projects to fund.

Moreover, tackling the EU's main area of concern – migration flows, notably those resulting from instability in the Sahel – has been further complicated by the coups in Mali and Burkina Faso. Many migrants coming to the EU are either from, or transit through, the Sahel. European governments remain wary of a repeat of the refugee and migration crisis of 2014–15, not least because some 2.6 million people in the Sahel are already internally displaced, according to the UN High Commissioner for Refugees. However, due to the coups in their countries, the heads of state of Mali and Burkina Faso were not invited to the EU–AU summit. Meanwhile French President Emmanuel Macron announced the withdrawal of French and European troops from Mali, putting an end to *Operation Barkhane*, the French-led counter-insurgency mission that has been in operation since 2014. Though many troops have been relocated to Niger, the end of *Operation Barkhane* and Mali's subsequent withdrawal from the Group of Five for the Sahel (G5-Sahel) threatens to increase insecurity in northern Mali and thus exacerbate migration flows. The aid packages announced are unlikely to be sufficient to address conflict in the Sahel or incentivise local populations to stay in the area.

Russia's unconventional Africa strategy to persist

Russia's invasion of Ukraine, which began a week after the summit, is also likely to complicate EU–African relations, since African states maintaining relations with Russia could be caught up in Western sanctions. Russia has expanded its influence in Africa over the past decade, pledging US$20bn in investment (with no conditionalities attached) at its first Russia–Africa summit in 2019, and the impact of its increased engagement was apparent in the wake of the invasion. While African states are not providing direct military assistance – although a small number of fighters from the Central African Republic (CAR) are believed to be participating – African states were notable abstainers in the UN vote on its invasion of Ukraine. Although only one sub-Saharan African state (Eritrea) voted against the resolution demanding that Russia immediately withdraw its forces, 16 (including South Africa) abstained, and others (including Cameroon and Ethiopia) did not participate. This is likely a reflection of Russia's ongoing efforts to protect ruling elites in states such as CAR, Libya, Madagascar, Mali, Mozambique and Sudan, as well as other measures of support. Following the Malian coup in

May 2021, for example, Russia voted against a UN Security Council measure to support Economic Community of West African States (ECOWAS) sanctions.

The second Russia–Africa summit is due to be held in St Petersburg in mid-2023, and it will likely see a continuation of Russian efforts to create a post-liberal international order that validates governance models other than democracy and to expand its global influence via the use of unconventional tactics. In its relations with sub-Saharan Africa, Russia has tended not to rely on conventional statecraft measures such as official security assistance, foreign direct investment and trade links (according to the UN Conference on Trade and Development, Russia accounted for only around 3% of Africa's international goods trade between 2016 and 2020). Instead, it will continue to rely on extra-legal measures including electoral 'support' for fragile regimes, arms-for-resources deals and the deployment of so-called 'private military companies' (PMCs). This last measure risks exacerbating insecurity; the Russia-based Wagner Group, for instance, has been accused of perpetrating human-rights abuses in Mali, CAR and elsewhere, potentially contributing to increased local support for insurgents.

A modest African return for the US

Although the optics of current US engagement with Africa are substantially more positive than under the Trump administration, there have been few signs yet of the 'bold strategy' for Africa promised by President Joe Biden when he was running for the presidency. For example, while Secretary of State Antony Blinken announced in November 2021 that Biden would host a US–Africa leaders' summit (only the second such gathering and the first since 2014) some time in 2022, it took until July 2022 for the summit dates and agenda to be announced, with the crisis in Ukraine dominating diplomatic attention. Equally, the Global Posture Review, released by the Pentagon in November 2021, was vague on the issue of future US troop levels in Africa, stating merely that these were subject to 'several ongoing interagency reviews'. That said, there are a few signs of re-engagement in some areas. Notably, in May 2022,

Biden authorised the deployment of around 500 troops to Somalia to 're-establish a small, persistent US military presence', thus reversing former president Donald Trump's December 2020 decision to with-draw around 700 special forces that had been deployed to work with the Somali military. Trump's decision had been criticised by AFRICOM head General Townsend, who stated that it 'caused new challenges and risks for our troops' and enabled al-Shabaab to increase its activities. While US troops will continue to perform the same tasks, they will no longer have to 'commute' to the country. Likewise, their presence will potentially provide additional support for new Somali President Hassan Sheikh Mohamud, who beat the incumbent, Mohamed Abdullahi Mohamed (Farmaajo), in May 2022 and has prioritised tackling insurgency.

However, while there is little in the way of fresh, direct US engage-ment with sub-Saharan Africa, American politicians remain keen to counteract Chinese and Russian influence in the region. In April 2022 remarks to the House Committee on Appropriations, Townsend warned that 'China's heavy investment in Africa as its "second continent"… is fuelling Chinese economic growth, outpacing the US, and allowing it to exploit opportunities to their benefit'. Furthermore, military sources have suggested that Africa could serve as a forward base for China to project power directly towards North America and Europe.

Meanwhile, in April 2022, the House Foreign Affairs Committee advanced a bill giving the State Department 90 days to develop a strategy to counter the 'malign influence and activities' of Russia and its proxies in Africa. This calls for the strengthening of democratic institutions and anti-corruption initiatives in sub-Saharan Africa, the monitoring of natural resources and extractive industries (similar to the Extractive Industries Transparency Initiative), and the tracking of Russia's political influence, disinformation campaigns and military operations.

Given the overwhelming bipartisan support for the bill when it came to the House of Representatives, it appears probable that the proposed legislation will be passed in the Senate as well. But the bill will likely face pushback from some African governments, not least because the measure also seeks to hold accountable African officials 'facilitating the

Russian Federation's malign activities'. At a summit of the Southern African Development Community (SADC) in August 2022, leaders of the member states expressed their dissatisfaction with the bill's 'punitive measures'. Governments that are heavily reliant on Russia for political assistance are likely to portray the US legislation as imperialist.

ECOWAS: Problems and Prospects
Can this major regional body meet growing economic and military challenges?

The Economic Community of West African States (ECOWAS) is struggling to respond to growing security, political and economic challenges within the West African subregion. There have been four successful coups, and two failed putsches, in ECOWAS member states since August 2020, and the regional body's response has had little practical impact thus far. In part this reflects weakness in Nigeria – which, as the continent's largest economy (and with the subregion's strongest military), has very substantial influence within ECOWAS.

Several other ECOWAS members are affected by instability. While ECOWAS played a key role in the establishment of the Group of Five for the Sahel (G5-Sahel) – which seeks to tackle insecurity in Burkina Faso, Chad, Mali, Mauritania and Niger – it has largely failed to address the weak governance, muted economic growth, poverty and corruption that are driving insecurity. Moreover, since it is primarily an economic body, it lacks effective mechanisms by which to drive a return to civilian rule, with sanctions often proving unpopular with local people and enforcement remaining patchy. While the election of a new president in Nigeria in early 2023 could potentially see this subregional hegemon play a more active role, West Africa's security and development environment looks likely to remain challenging over the medium term.

ECOWAS's goals

ECOWAS was established in 1975 with the broad aim of promoting the economic integration and shared development of its 15 member states – Benin, Burkina Faso, Cabo Verde, Côte d'Ivoire, The Gambia, Ghana, Guinea, Guinea-Bissau, Liberia, Mali, Niger, Nigeria, Senegal, Sierra Leone and Togo. The establishing treaty focused primarily on economic development and did not include any overt mechanism to deal with conflict management. This was partially addressed in the 1980s, with the signing of a Protocol on Mutual Assistance in Defence that provided for the setting up of an Allied Armed Forces of the Community if needed. However, the establishment of the Economic Community of West African States Monitoring Group (ECOMOG) in 1990 was controversial, since it was set up by anglophone members of ECOWAS to intervene in the civil war in Liberia, a move that was opposed by several francophone states. It was not until 1993 that a revised treaty provided for the maintenance of regional peace, stability and security so as to accelerate the integration process and improve living standards across the subregion.

ECOWAS has had some security successes. No two sovereign member states have ever gone to war, and ECOMOG played an important role in the first Liberian civil war (1989–97), where it negotiated peace accords and ceasefires, disarmed rebels and helped to create the conditions for reasonably transparent elections. It also successfully intervened in The Gambia in 2016, when the then-president, Yahya Jammeh, refused to step down after losing the presidential election to Adama Barrow. However, it has proved far less effective at tackling insurgencies in the subregion, or the factors underlying the spread of such unrest. These include poor governance, high levels of corruption among the elites, elevated inequality (as the benefits of economic growth are not evenly divided among the population), rapid population growth, increasing competition for land and other natural resources, and climate change.

Contagious coups

The apparent inability of central governments to quash insurrections has eroded public and military trust in state institutions and led to further instability, with no fewer than five successful coups (and two failed putsches) led in ECOWAS member states since August 2020. The first of these was in Mali, when elements of the military, headed by Colonel Assimi Goïta, took power following months of civil protests, political deadlock and growing military discontent over the government's handling of insecurity in the north and centre of the country, forcing the president, Ibrahim Boubacar Keïta, to resign and dismiss the government. However, just as a previous (2012) coup exacerbated existing political fragility (and in effect enabled insurgents to increase their territorial control in the north), the 2020 putsch did not lead to any improvement in overall security conditions. Indeed, having nominally handed over power to a civilian-led transitional administration (while retaining the position of vice-president), Goïta seized power again in May 2021 after the transitional administration announced a cabinet reshuffle, removing the defence and internal-security portfolios from members of the military junta that staged the August 2020 coup.

Similarly, in January 2022 a junta led by Lieutenant-Colonel Paul-Henri Damiba seized power in Burkina Faso and dissolved the previously elected government and legislature. Eight months later, Damiba was overthrown and replaced by Captain Ibrahim Traore, who dissolved the constitution. As in Mali, the first coup followed months of anti-government protests and a growing perception among the military that the civilian authorities were incapable of restoring national security in the face of an escalating Islamist insurgency. As in Mali, the first coup exacerbated the security situation, with attacks by armed groups increasing during Damiba's time in power; Traore cited the worsening security situation as the reason for Damiba's ousting.

Waning confidence in civilian institutions is a clear theme in recent coups and coup attempts. For example, the September 2021 coup in Guinea – when Colonel Mamady Doumbouya, the head of the country's special forces, announced the dissolution of the government, the suspension of the constitution and detention of the president, Alpha Condé – took place in the wake of protests at president Conde's scrapping of the two-term presidential limit. Doumbouya stated that 'the personalisation of political life is over. We will no longer entrust politics to one man. We will entrust it to the people', underscoring the way in which the military was able to use genuine civic discontent over constitutional issues, poverty and endemic corruption to justify its unconstitutional seizure of power.

Military disaffection and a worsening jihadi insurgency were also factors in the attempted coup in Niger in March 2021 – although this appears to have been a relatively small-scale attempt involving only junior officers. The attempted putsch in Guinea-Bissau in February 2022 took place in the context of persistent political fragility, with President Umaro Sissoco Embaló threatening to dissolve parliament on several occasions. In both cases, the governments remain highly vulnerable to intervention by frustrated elements of the military.

ECOWAS's response has failed to produce results so far

ECOWAS has strongly condemned the various military takeovers but has so far failed to roll them back. Moreover, it has not taken a consistent approach to the various military governments and has faced pushback from populations in the countries affected, as well as the courts and some civil-society organisations, likely diluting the strength of its response. It promptly suspended Burkina Faso, Guinea and Mali from ECOWAS membership in the wake of their coups, but it has subsequently taken a different approach to each country. It has yet to impose any financial or economic sanctions against Burkina Faso. Instead it has urged both Damiba and Traore to honour a pledge made by the former that the country would hold an election by mid-2024. After the second coup, a mediator sent by ECOWAS to the country said that the bloc would 'remain with the people of Burkina Faso ... and the difficult challenge they face.' It has taken a somewhat stronger line against Guinea, maintaining targeted personal sanctions against key members of the regime and threatening further sanctions in September, when Guinea had not presented a plan for a return to civilian rule since missing the 25 April deadline.

However, ECOWAS steadily ramped up measures against the Mali putschists for failing to hold democratic elections by the end of February 2022. On top of targeted sanctions, the regional body imposed measures including the closure of land and air borders; the suspension of all commercial and financial transactions except for food products, pharmaceutical goods, medical supplies, and petroleum products and electricity; the freezing of Malian assets in ECOWAS central banks; and the suspension of all financial assistance.

The relative severity of the sanctions on Mali was in part a function of timing, as the Malian coup occurred much earlier than the putsches in Guinea and Burkina Faso and the military authorities had much longer to prepare a plan for a return to civilian rule. However, ECOWAS also sees the transition in Mali as a key test of its commitment to safeguarding the relative democratic progress made in West and Central Africa since the 1990s, when there were some 25 coups or attempted coups (including three successful coups in Sierra Leone alone). In addition, ECOWAS has made considerable diplomatic investment in Mali since the March 2012 coup and subsequent signing of the 2015 Algiers Agreement.

However, the more severe sanctions were heavily criticised as a blunt instrument that would inflict more harm on the Malian population than on the coup leaders. The Malian government's response – that ECOWAS was being 'exploited by extra-regional powers with ulterior motives' (i.e., the former colonial power, France) – was unsurprising. But its call for public protests against the 'extreme and inhumane' sanctions led to demonstrations by thousands of people. In March 2022 the Court of Justice of the West African Economic and Monetary Union (UEMOA) ordered the suspension of sanctions. And in April, several civil-society organisations and the Open Society Initiative for West Africa called for the lifting of measures in Burkina Faso, Guinea and Mali, arguing that these were unlikely to resolve the problems they were intended to address. At a meeting in July, ECOWAS leaders agreed to lift sanctions against Mali but did not end the country's suspension from the bloc.

The belief held by citizens in target countries and beyond that economic sanctions are attacks on the people has bolstered popular support for the nationalist rhetoric of coup leaders. Critics also suggest that ECOWAS is guilty of double standards, applying sanctions in the case of miliary takeovers but failing to act against 'constitutional' coups, where long-serving rulers remove or otherwise circumvent presidential term limits in order to hang on to power, as former president Condé did in Guinea. The organisation thus faces growing difficulties both in persuading military regimes to cede power and in preventing similar instability in other regional states.

Nigeria's problematic role

A crucial issue is the role played by Nigeria, the largest economy in Africa. This has both an economic and a political dimension. As the West African hegemon, Nigeria is in theory well placed to drive economic progress, but it has largely failed to do so, opting for protectionism rather than the trade liberalisation that could potentially help fellow ECOWAS members develop. For example, Nigeria closed its land borders with Benin, Cameroon, Chad and Niger in August 2019, citing alleged smuggling of food items which, the government stated, was undermining local agricultural businesses. A February 2020 meeting of finance and trade ministers convened by ECOWAS failed to resolve the situation, and borders were not reopened until December 2020. While Nigeria has not subsequently resorted to border closures, it has continued to adopt policies that disadvantage neighbouring (and less developed) states, including increasing tariffs on imported rice, banning the import of sugar and derivatives from its free-trade zones, and imposing systems of quotas, local-content laws and restrictions on the use of foreign exchange to import certain items. Thus, Nigeria has not only itself underperformed – average annual real GDP growth was 3.8% in the decade to 2019, according to IMF data, as against an average annual expansion of 6.7% in Ghana, which is of a similar level of development – it has also acted as a drag on overall ECOWAS expansion.

Politically, too, Nigeria – which has the strongest military in the region, ranking 35th out of 142 states in the 2022 Global Firepower index – is proving increasingly problematic. Nigeria played a leading role in the establishment of ECOWAS in 1975 and later played a positive role following its return to civilian rule in 1999, reflecting president Olusegun Obasanjo's Afrocentrist approach to regional security and other issues. In São Tomé and Príncipe, for example, Obasanjo ensured the reinstatement of president Fradique de Menezes following a military coup in 2003, while he also played key roles in ending the civil war in Liberia and in the transition to democratic rule that saw Ellen Johnson Sirleaf elected president of Sierra Leone in 2006. However, subsequent presidents have adopted a more domestic focus, and in recent years

Nigeria has become increasingly unable to provide political and security leadership given worsening instability at home. While the current head of state, President Muhammadu Buhari, pledged to end insecurity in the north of the country, conflict with Boko Haram and Islamic State West Africa Province (ISWAP) in the northeast has continued, while banditry in the northwest has arguably worsened. In March 2022, for example, at least eight people were killed and some 168 were reported missing (potentially kidnapped for ransom) when bandits blew up a section of railway track between Abuja and the northern city of Kaduna and attacked a passenger train. The domestic security situation is highly unlikely to improve in the short term, not least because Nigerian politicians are expected to focus chiefly on the February 2023 presidential elections in the coming months, while disputes over the sharing of power between candidates from the mainly Muslim north and chiefly Christian south (under an informal system in which power rotates between north and south) will likely fuel ethnic and religious tensions still further.

Insecurity in Nigeria is particularly problematic given its geographic location and the porous nature of its borders – it shares land borders with Benin, Cameroon, Chad and Niger, and is in close maritime proximity to São Tomé and Príncipe and Equatorial Guinea. In a January 2022 report, Nigeria's auditor-general stated that 178,459 weapons had 'disappeared' from police armouries as of January 2020, while the United Nations Office on Drugs and Crime suggests that tens of thousands of firearms from the Gadhafi regime in Libya are in circulation and are being sold at low cost to armed non-state groups in northern Mali, to secessionist groups in northern Niger and in the Casamance region of Senegal, as well as to Boko Haram and forces loyal to the former Ivoirian president Laurent Gbagbo. Other member states have struggled to prevent the passage of armed groups across their borders, and ECOWAS itself does not have the capacity to tackle the issue.

Prospects for ECOWAS and West Africa

There are unlikely to be rapid or straightforward solutions to the problems facing ECOWAS, or West Africa more generally. In theory, a new

Nigerian president could adopt a more Afrocentrist approach, leading to greater engagement in ECOWAS, but this appears unlikely, certainly in the short term. In June 2022 the ruling All Progressives Congress party selected Bola Tinubu, a former governor of Lagos State, as its presidential candidate, while the People's Democratic Party will field Atiku Abubakar, a two-time former presidential candidate. Tinubu is likely best placed to win, given the party's incumbency. But whoever is elected in February 2023 is likely to focus initially on embedding their own group of supporters in key positions and – as with successive presidents – is likely to struggle to solve the unrest in the north. Most other ECOWAS members are poorly placed to take a leading role, and the two largest economies after Nigeria – Ghana and Senegal – have shown little interest in doing so (Senegal is facing its own insurgency in the anglophone regions, and while Ghana is an active participant in ECOWAS, it is relatively insulated from Sahelian insurgency and faces substantial political and fiscal challenges at home).

The role of external actors is also problematic. France has played a leading role in the Sahel. But it faces growing public hostility, in part because of its position as the former colonial ruler of many ECOWAS member states, and in part because of local objections to the presence of foreign troops. France is also re-evaluating its position in Africa, ending its counter-insurgency campaign, *Operation Barkhane*, in February 2022 and redeploying French forces from Mali to Niger as part of a larger international mission. Equally, while the sixth European Union–African Union (AU) summit, held in Brussels in February, pledged new funding, including a €150 billion investment package for Africa, as a whole, financial and military aid remains insufficient to address issues in the Sahel.

Fundamentally, ECOWAS is not well placed to tackle the deep-seated causes of conflict in the Sahel and broader regional insurgency, which in turn is driving popular unrest, disillusionment with democratic institutions and thus military takeovers. Issues at stake include competition over dwindling natural resources in rural areas, poor political representation in post-colonial states and poor economic prospects. These are likely to become more challenging over time as climate change tightens resource constraints and youthful populations – around 65% of the combined populations of Burkina Faso, Chad, Mali, Mauritania and Niger are aged under 30 – increasingly demand better jobs, social services and basic infrastructure. All of this suggests that the security and development environment in the Sahel and West Africa more broadly will remain challenging over the medium term.

Finally, the advent of the African Continental Free Trade Area (AfCFTA) raises questions about the long-term role of ECOWAS and other regional economic communities. While the legal framework of the AfCFTA was signed in March 2018, implementation has been substantially delayed, in part due to COVID-19. In theory, AfCFTA will bring together 54 out of 55 AU states in one of the world's largest free-trade areas. As of May 2022, 12 out of the 15 ECOWAS members had deposited their instruments of AfCFTA ratification. Should AfCFTA take off, it is doubtful whether member states will want to incur the costs of balancing competing AfCFTA and ECOWAS regulations. AfCFTA's rise may therefore put ECOWAS's future in doubt.

Russia's Military Activity in Africa
What does a decade of deepening involvement presage?

Since 2015, Russia's military activity in sub-Saharan Africa has precipitously increased. After striking a military-cooperation agreement with Cameroon in April 2015, Russia signed 18 similar pacts with other African countries. These agreements encompass armed-forces training, counter-terrorism assistance and anti-piracy support. Russia has also deployed the Wagner Group, a so-called private military company (PMC), to conduct counter-insurgency operations in the Central African Republic (CAR), Mali and Mozambique, guard vital Russian economic assets in Sudan and Guinea, and facilitate military cooperation with the Democratic Republic of the Congo. The success of these operations has varied greatly. Nonetheless, Russia has leveraged its military cooperation with African countries to gain political influence and secure lucrative mining and energy contracts.

Russia's February 2022 invasion of Ukraine has so far not reversed this positive trajectory. Russian PMCs remain stationed in CAR, Mali and Sudan, and Russia has upgraded its military cooperation with Cameroon. The war could motivate Russia to expand its ambitions in Africa, but also tighten constraints on realising them.

The evolution of Russia's military presence in Africa

During the first two decades after the collapse of the Soviet Union in 1991, Russia's military presence in Africa was negligible and almost exclusively confined to transactional linkages, such as arms sales. The marginalisation of Russia as a military actor in Africa contrasted markedly with the diverse array of Soviet-era training programmes and reflected Moscow's broader divestment from the continent during the 1990s. The ascension of Dmitry Medvedev to the presidency in 2008 caused Russia to pay increased attention to African affairs and fuelled its resurgence as a military actor. Maritime security served as Russia's gateway to a military presence in Africa. The Somali piracy crisis, which escalated in the second half of 2008, provided Russia with an opportunity to collaborate with NATO on maritime security and de-escalate tensions with the West over the Georgian War. The collaboration of the missile frigate *Neustrashimy* with Britain's HMS *Cumberland* to prevent the seizure of a Danish vessel in November 2008 was a particularly noteworthy example of Russian assertiveness in the maritime security space. The Moran Security Group, which focused on the maritime domain, established a role for Russian PMCs in Africa. But a criminal case brought against its operations in Nigeria from 2012–13 restricted its influence.

After a brief lull in activity following the annexation of Crimea in 2014 and military intervention in Syria in 2015, Russia resurfaced as a counter-insurgency partner for African countries. It became involved in operations to fight rebel groups in CAR, suppress popular unrest in Sudan and combat transnational terrorism in Mozambique. After the suspension of *Operation Sangaris,* France's counter-insurgency operation, in 2016, Russia emerged as CAR's main foreign backer against the threat of the ex-Seleka rebels. In 2018, Russia expanded its contingent of military instructors in CAR from 175 to 235 personnel, and subsequently added 300 more personnel before President Faustin-Archange Touadéra's re-election in December 2020. These 'instructors', which is the Kremlin's terminology for members of the Wagner Group, trained 1,000 CAR military personnel during the first months of their deployment. Russia also dispatched nine tranches of military equipment to CAR. Touadéra's March 2018 appointment of retired Russian military intelligence official Valery Zakharov as national-security adviser has deepened the Wagner Group's influence.

Russia's hostile attitude to the second wave of Arab uprisings from 2018–19 contributed to its military intervention in Sudan. As mass protests against president Omar al-Bashir's regime gained momentum in December 2018, Russian PMCs began training Sudan's National Intelligence and Security Services (NISS). Yevgeny Prigozhin, the oligarch known as 'Putin's chef' who reportedly finances the Wagner Group, received two Russian Tu-154M airliners to expand Wagner's presence in Sudan. Wagner advised the Sudanese authorities on counter-revolutionary strategies, which included delegitimising the Forces of Freedom and Change (FFC)

protesters as stooges of Israel, but Bashir largely ignored its recommendations. The Wagner Group found a more receptive partner in General Abdel
Fattah al-Burhan, who seized power through a *coup d'état* in April 2019.
But the June 2019 Khartoum massacre and Sudan's transition to democracy
derailed Wagner's autocracy-promotion goals.

Russia's desire to expand its economic presence in southern Africa,
evinced by Foreign Minister Sergei Lavrov's 2018 tour of the region,
prompted its counter-terrorism role in Mozambique. In September 2019,
160 Wagner Group personnel arrived in northern Mozambique's Cabo
Delgado province to carry out counter-terrorism operations against the
Islamic State (ISIS) and Ansar al-Sunnah (known locally as al-Shabaab).
Russia viewed these operations as a gateway for access to natural-gas
reserves in Cabo Delgado, but the killing of seven Wagner Group personnel and 20 Mozambican special forces in October 2019 caused it to
suspend its military operations in the country. The failure reflected
Russia's inexperience in Mozambique's terrain and poor relations
between the Wagner Group and local officers.

Russia's inefficacy elsewhere in Africa, and the centrality of Central
and West Africa to its continental strategy, has led it to focus on counter-
insurgency and counter-terrorism campaigns in CAR and Mali. This has
so far produced few tangible results and led to extensive human-rights
abuses. During the 2020 presidential elections in CAR, Russia focused
on thwarting the political ambitions of former president François Bozizé.
With military support from Rwanda, Russia prevented Bozizé from
staging a coup with the support of ex-Seleka rebels. On 25 January 2021,
the Wagner Group carried out an operation with CAR military outside
Bangui that killed 44 militants. Since early 2021, the Wagner Group has
achieved no significant military successes in CAR and has faced fierce
criticism for its perpetration of egregious human-rights abuses. Atrocities
such as the July 2021 Bossangoa massacre, which resulted in the deaths
of at least 12 unarmed men, led the African Union (AU) to call for the
complete removal of foreign mercenaries from Africa.

Despite international criticism, the Wagner Group has continued its
indiscriminate targeting of civilians in rebel strongholds. From 16–17

January 2022, Wagner Group personnel killed dozens of civilians in Aigbado, which is located near a hub for the rebel group Union for Peace in the Central African Republic, and from 11–12 April it collaborated with CAR armed forces in killing between ten and 15 civilians in Gordile and Ndah villages. Despite mounting discontent with Russia's actions, which was augmented further by an April 2022 assault on mining sites in Kouki, CAR civil-society groups have not supported the Wagner Group's expulsion, and Touadéra honoured the Wagner-aligned 7th Territorial Infantry Battalion in February 2022. This underscores the resilience of the Wagner Group's presence in CAR, which has been enhanced by state capture, cultural diplomacy and Russian-language education.

Following the May 2021 coup in Mali, which reinstated Colonel Assimi Goïta as president, the country's security partnership with France atrophied and Russia became the principal beneficiary. In September 2021, the Malian junta struck a security agreement with the Wagner Group for the deployment of 1,000 personnel in Mali at a monthly cost of US$10.8 million. On 1 October, Russia delivered a cargo plane to Mali containing Mi-171Sh and M-17V5 helicopters, weapons and ammunition, which were reportedly 'gifts' pledged in a December 2020 Moscow–Bamako defence deal. To justify soliciting Russian military trainers, the Malian authorities highlighted the relatively low cost and France's refusal to consult with the junta on counter-terrorism. Despite mounting criticisms from Western countries and the threat of sanctions, 500 Wagner Group personnel arrived in Mali in December 2021. By 7 January, they had established a military foothold in Timbuktu, embarked on counter-insurgency operations in central Mali and displaced French forces from bases used for *Operation Barkhane* missions.

However, in 2022, the Wagner Group's counter-terrorism performance has been underwhelming, and Russian PMCs have been implicated in massacres of civilians that dwarf those witnessed in CAR. For example, Wagner's migration from Timbuktu to central Mali has been ineffective in stemming the activities of al-Qaeda-linked Jama'at Nasr al-Islam wal-Muslimin (JNIM) fighters and communal militias. And due to stricter government regulations than in CAR, and anti-Russian sentiment among non-state actors in northern Mali like Coordination des mouvements de l'Azawad, Wagner has not consolidated control over gold mines that would finance its operations. The Wagner Group's ground presence is Russia's only realistic route to consolidate control over these gold reserves, as Soviet-era investments in southwestern Mali's Kalana gold project were supplanted by British capital during the 1990s.

The Wagner Group and the Malian junta have resorted to collective punishment of the Fulani population, who are often recruited by al-Qaeda in the Islamic Maghreb (AQIM) and Islamic State in the Greater Sahara (ISGS). The Wagner Group's 27–31 March 2022 killing of over 300 civilian Fulani men in Moura was described by Human Rights Watch as the single-worst atrocity in Mali's decade-long conflict. Despite its well-documented record of violence, and Ukraine-war-related equipment shortages, Russia has continued to transfer military hardware to Mali, including Mi-35M attack helicopters and advanced radar systems. Russia is also leveraging its economic ties with the Malian junta, which include wheat and petroleum shipments, to try to use Mali as a long-term power-projection foothold in West Africa.

Russia's appeal as a security partner for African countries

Russia's current military power projection in Africa consists of four pillars: arms exports, counter-insurgency assistance, special-forces and police training, and asset guardianship. Although Russia's democratic experiment and foreign minister Andrei Kozyrev's pro-Western outlook discouraged arms sales to authoritarian regimes in the early 1990s, Moscow established itself as a human-rights-blind vendor of weapons to African countries later in the decade. Russia's simultaneous arms deals with Ethiopia and Eritrea during the war over Badme from 1998–2000, and exports to sanctioned regimes, such as Bashir's Sudan during the conflict in Darfur, reflect this trend. After the United States rejected Nigeria's request for *Cobra* helicopters in 2014 over concerns about human-rights violations, Russia stepped in with Mi-17 and Mi-35 helicopters. Russia's increased prestige as a counter-insurgency partner has also yielded benefits for its arms exports and training programmes. This trend mirrors the expansion of Russia's defence ties in the Middle East and North Africa (MENA) region. From 2017–21 Russia accounted for 44% of Africa's arms purchases, compared to 17% for the US, 10% for China and 6.1% for France. Although Algeria and Egypt are Russia's largest arms markets in Africa, sub-Saharan African countries such as Angola, Ethiopia, Nigeria and Sudan are also key purchasers of Russian weapons.

The proliferation of transnational terrorist networks in Africa over the past decade explains Russia's growing appeal as a counter-insurgency partner. After the March 2012 coup in Mali, Russia criticised Western counter-terrorism policy and used information warfare to bolster its soft power, claiming that France's *Operation Serval* and *Operation Barkhane* were smokescreens for capturing Malian gold and uranium reserves. Russia also blamed regional disorder in Mali on the 2011 NATO military intervention in Libya. Russia's military intervention in Syria, which entrenched Bashar al-Assad's hold on power and allowed him to defeat rebel groups in major cities like Aleppo, burnished its prestige as a counter-insurgency partner for African countries. Russia's 'Syrian model' of counter-insurgency was especially appealing for authoritarian regimes and countries with poor human-rights records, as it abetted their policy of targeting opposition groups in the name of counter-terrorism.

Russian PMCs deployed in counter-insurgency operations provide African partners with political as well as military benefits. Due to its close cooperation with 'political technologists' – Russian advisers on political strategy – the Wagner Group combines counter-insurgency operations with election interference and disinformation to further the agendas of its clients. Although it works closely with Russia's military-intelligence directorate, its operations are independently financed by external donors, such as the United Arab Emirates (UAE) for operations in Libya, and the sale of mineral deposits and oil reserves. While Wagner is the main PMC for Russia's African missions, smaller so-called 'private security companies' such as Patriot and Shield also have a presence.

To ensure that its military doctrine proliferates in Africa without a long-term ground presence, Russia has invested significantly in special forces and police training. In 2014, Russia trained special forces in northern Nigeria's Borno and Adamawa regions to fight against the Islamic terrorist organisation Boko Haram, while Wagner has provided training for the CAR presidential guard. Due to its military-training roles in both countries, Russia signed comprehensive military-cooperation agreements with CAR in 2018 and Nigeria in 2021.

To ensure the profitability of its operations and to evade Western sanctions, Russia has also invested significantly in asset guardianship. A 5 June *New York Times* report on the so-called 'Russian company' which processes gold 300 kilometres north of Khartoum, and Russian military operations in the CAR–Sudan border region, point to the Wagner Group's continued presence in Sudan. The Wagner Group's involvement in Sudan is shrouded in uncertainty. Due to concerns about secondary sanctions that could impact the financial interests of Sovereign Council Deputy Chairman Mohamed Hamdan 'Hemedti' Dagalo, the Sudanese Foreign Ministry denies the Wagner Group's presence. Russian PMCs also engaged in a smaller-scale mission of uncertain duration in Guinea, which possesses extensive bauxite reserves owned by Russian aluminium producer Rusal.

The Russia–Ukraine war's impact on Russia's security policy towards Africa

Although the Russia–Ukraine war has not discernibly affected Russia's military activities in Africa, it could have long-term implications for the Wagner Group's presence. On the one hand, some African operations could prove even more attractive to Russia as it seeks to escape diplomatic isolation. In addition, as sanctions tighten Russia's budgetary pressures, the self-financing character of the Wagner Group's operations could prove increasingly appealing. Its involvement in gold smuggling in Sudan underscores its ability to enrich the Russian state with little prospect of retributive sanctions.

On the other hand, the Wagner Group has not only proved inconsistent in its military performance in Africa, but has also suffered significant losses in Russia's war against Ukraine. Russia is urgently seeking more infantry to replenish manpower it has lost in its invasion, and is going to great lengths to avoid mass conscription. More Wagner personnel may therefore be sent to Ukraine, as regular armed forces deployed beyond Russia's borders have been.

African states will watch these developments as they decide how much engagement, and in what forms, they seek from Russia. Although Russia's military intervention in Mali has provoked criticism from Sahel countries such as Niger and Chad, West Africa remains a fertile ground for the Wagner Group to expand its operations. Burkina Faso is especially likely to become a new frontier of the Wagner Group's operations, as the architect of the January 2022 coup Lieutenant-Colonel Paul-Henri Damiba solicited Russian assistance in the months leading up to his rise to power. Soon after the September 2022 coup that saw Captain Ibrahim Traore overthrow Damiba, Prigozhin described Traore as 'a truly courageous son of the motherland.'

As Sudan's relations with Russia demonstrate, African views can shift. Russia's aspiration to build a naval base in Sudan was set back by Khartoum's suspension of their agreement on this in April 2021. Since the October 2021 coup in Sudan, the new military government appears to be looking more favourably on this again, especially following Hemedti's week-long visit to Moscow that began on the eve of Russia's invasion of Ukraine – though there remains much uncertainty. Russia could also seek to consolidate its foothold in CAR through the construction of a base there, a possibility repeatedly broached by Touadéra's government since 2018. All signs are that Russia is working hard to deepen its military, as well as diplomatic and economic, presence in Africa.

Fuelling Insurgency in Mozambique
Does Southern Africa face a broader front of Islamic militancy?

Islamist militants remain active in Mozambique's northern Cabo Delgado province, where more than 4,000 people have died (and some 850,000 have been internally displaced) since October 2017, when militants and jihadists attempting to establish an Islamic state in the region mounted raids on three police stations in Mocímboa da Praia, killing 17 people. The insurgents claim that Islam in Mozambique has been corrupted and needs to return to the teachings of the Prophet Muhammad. They reject state healthcare and education, refuse to pay taxes and want to establish an Islamic state with sharia law. Insurgency in the area has effectively delayed the development of the country's liquefied natural gas (LNG) sector, but the security situation is gradually improving with support from foreign troops. The Mozambican domestic security services have fairly limited operational capacity, despite support from both the United States and European Union. Improvement in the security situation since the second half of 2021 is largely due to the deployment of external troops (notably from Rwanda), which have had more success than previous counter-insurgency operations, including by Russia's Wagner Group.

However, territorial gains by government and allied troops – including Mocímboa da Praia, the insurgents' de facto capital – have chiefly resulted from militants abandoning positions rather than successful military action. There are signs that militants have been regrouping and spreading across both Cabo Delgado and neighbouring Niassa province. Attacks on towns and villages in the area are likely to continue, and there is a risk that militants will be able to use challenging social and economic conditions to recruit more fighters and entrench unrest in the north of the country. Thus, concerns will persist among neighbouring states that the conflict will affect other parts of Southern Africa, through population displacement and the spread of extremist ideologies.

Roots of the insurgency

The Mozambican government has sought to portray the insurgency in Cabo Delgado province as 'external aggression perpetrated by terrorists' and 'pure banditry driven by others' greed'. But it has multiple causes, including social and economic marginalisation, and radicalisation (of young people in particular) by domestic and foreign Islamist extremists. Some 53% of the province's population was aged under 18 in 2017 (according to that year's census, the most recent available), and illiteracy and poverty levels are high. According to Cabo Delgado's governor, Valige Tauabo, the illiteracy rate in the province was around 53.5% in the second half of 2021 (he claimed that this would be reduced to 39.0% by 2024 thanks to a series of literacy programmes). Meanwhile, according to the International Wealth Index (IWI), in 2014, 94.7% of households in Cabo Delgado had a value of less than 35, where 0 means no measured consumer durables and the lowest-quality housing, and 100 all assets and the highest-quality housing. This is the highest percentage of any province, and well above the Mozambican average of 78.6%.

Despite the discovery of substantial natural resources including rubies and natural gas, the continued economic exclusion of most of the local population and, among the Mwani and Makua minorities, the perceived economic dominance of President Filipe Nyusi's Makonde ethnic group has exacerbated discontent with the central government. Extremist groups have been able to capitalise on this. The key player is a jihadist group known by several names, including Ansar al-Sunnah and Ahlu al-Sunnah wal-Jamaah. Locally it is known as al-Shabaab but it has no formal connection to the Somali group of the same name. Islamic State (ISIS) claims to be behind the local groups and has branded the Mozambican (and Tanzanian) groups as Islamic State Central Africa Province (ISCAP). However, while in December 2020 Nathan Sales, the then-coordinator for counter-terrorism in the US, stated that the militants were part of a 'committed ISIS affiliate that embraces the ISIS ideology', the US State Department considers the Mozambican group to be a 'distinct entity' with a broadly Salafist orientation (in contrast to the Sufi orders that traditionally dominated in the area) and partly inspired by Aboud Rogo Mohammed, the main ideological leader of a radical Kenyan group, al-Hijra, who was assassinated in 2012.

The domestic response

The national security services have struggled to respond effectively to militant attacks. This reflects decades of underinvestment and, until mid-2021, the simultaneous need to tackle an insurgency by dissident members of the opposition Mozambican National Resistance (Renamo) in Sofala and Manica provinces. In October 2021 the leader of the Renamo Military Junta (RMJ) – a splinter group that rejected a 2019 peace deal – was killed by government forces, and in December the UN envoy, Mirko Manzoni, stated that the remaining members of the RMJ had laid down their arms. However, lack of capacity among the local military remains a serious issue.

Mozambique ranks 116th out of 142 countries in the 2022 Global Firepower index. The Mozambican Defence Armed Forces (FADM) has 11,200 personnel – only around one-third of the level suggested following the 1992 peace accords that ended the country's civil war – with no reserve personnel or paramilitary. In addition, it has reportedly been infiltrated by al-Shabaab intelligence cells, and it lacks equipment – with only 417 armoured vehicles and 60 tanks, for example. Military spending remains low, at 0.89% of GDP in 2021 – in comparison, Burkina Faso and Mali, which are also tackling Islamist insurgencies, spent a respective 2.4% and 4.4%. As a result much of the FADM's stock is in a poor state of repair. The Rapid Intervention Unit (UIR), affiliated with the national police, has higher levels of funding and equipment and was therefore at the forefront of efforts to combat militants when the insurgency developed. However, it is headed by the police commander, Bernardino Rafael, who is of Makonde ethnicity, and this has served to reinforce local perceptions of the political dominance of the Makonde.

In apparent recognition of the poor performance of the counter-insurgency campaign in Cabo Delgado in November 2021, President Nyusi appointed new security-sector ministers, with Cristóvão Chume becoming defence minister and Arsénia Massingue minister of the interior. Chume, a former head of the army, replaced Jaime Neto, a civilian who had struggled to improve standards in the military, while Massingue previously served as a provincial police commander in the Inhambane, Manica and Nampula provinces. The changes appear designed to give the army a larger role in Cabo Delgado and to tackle a protracted period of inter-service rivalry and competition for resources, with the UIR having trouble securing ammunition and logistical support from the FADM, for example. However, improving the operational capacity of the domestic security services is unlikely to be straightforward or rapid, suggesting that there will be a continued role for external actors, whether in training or combat, for some time.

The conflict privatised …

External military forces have been involved in tackling the Cabo Delgado insurgency since at least 2019. This initially took the form of private military companies (PMCs), with mixed success. The Wagner Group, a PMC allegedly headed by Yevgeny Prigozhin, a close friend of Russian President Vladimir Putin, deployed to Cabo Delgado in September 2019, with the Mozambican authorities reportedly choosing Wagner over a US PMC as a relatively low-cost option. The legacy of the Soviet Union's role in aiding Mozambique's independence movement, and Russia's 2017 decision to forgive US$40 million of Mozambican debt, are also likely to have been factors. Wagner deployed around 200 personnel but failed to cooperate with the local military – in part because of language differences – and struggled to adapt to the bush warfare being used by insurgents. Challenging local terrain with only limited basic infrastructure favours ambushes. Seven Wagner Group personnel were killed in two separate attacks in October 2019. Wagner withdrew from Cabo Delgado a month later.

Despite this, the Mozambican government continued to rule out the deployment of foreign government troops and instead persisted with PMCs, including South Africa-based Dyck Advisory Group, which provided air support for local security forces. However, this also proved controversial, with Dyck being accused by the international non-governmental organisation Amnesty International of indiscriminately firing into groups of civilians and attacking civilian infrastructure. In addition, while Dyck air support helped stop an insurgent advance in July 2020 that posed a potential threat to Pemba, the provincial capital of Cabo Delgado, it was unable to play a similar role in August, when insurgents took control of the strategic port town of Mocímboa da Praia, inflicting heavy casualties and forcing Mozambican government troops to escape the area by boat. Dyck was reportedly unable to resupply Mozambican forces with enough ammunition as its helicopters had to fly too far to refuel. Dyck's contract ended in April 2021; a company executive told South African media that government officials had decided not to renew it.

... and further internationalised

The insurgents' capture of Mocímboa da Praia, and the inability of government troops to retake the town, added to the pressure on President Nyusi to accept external-troop deployment. Despite the worsening situation in Cabo Delgado, the president continued to insist that the counter-insurgency campaign be led domestically – perhaps because the authorities feared that deployment of foreign troops within Mozambique could expose the weakness of domestic military capabilities, or could undermine the narrative that the insurgents were largely foreign-born terrorists linked to ISIS, rather than domestic militants. However, pressure intensified further in March 2021 when the militants launched an attack near the Afungi Peninsula – the location of the Area 1 LNG project being developed by France's TotalEnergies. The company subsequently suspended construction activity, withdrew all staff and stated that it would not resume construction activity at the site until the security situation improved substantially.

With development of the natural-gas sector a crucial element of the government's 2015–35 development strategy, and casualties and internal displacements continuing to mount, President Nyusi appeared to accept the need for substantial numbers of foreign troops (on top of small numbers of European soldiers deployed to train local forces and gather intelligence). Following talks with Rwandan President Paul Kagame in

April 2021, a 1,000-strong contingent of the Rwanda Defence Force (RDF) was deployed in July (and subsequently doubled in size), while members of the Southern African Development Community (SADC) announced in June the formation of the Southern African Development Community Mission in Mozambique (SAMIM). SAMIM comprises troops from eight SADC states – Angola, Botswana, the Democratic Republic of the Congo, Lesotho, Malawi, South Africa, Tanzania and Zambia – with the South African National Defence Force pledging up to 1,495 personnel, Botswana around 300 and Tanzania some 275.

These troops have had considerable successes. Just a month after being deployed, Rwandan forces operating with the FADM recaptured Mocímboa da Praia – the only district capital held by insurgents, and a strategically significant town whose port and airport could be logistically important to reviving TotalEnergies' multibillion-dollar LNG project in Palma. Meanwhile, SAMIM troops based in central Cabo Delgado and towards Pemba, as well as in Nangade district near the border with Tanzania, have managed to dislodge insurgents from some of their strongholds. However, most major territorial gains, including Mocímboa da Praia, have been the result of militants abandoning positions rather than successful military action, and there are few signs as yet that ISCAP and al-Shabaab have been defeated. Rather, local reports suggest that militants have scattered south to Macomia district (South Africa's operational zone) and northwest to Nangade (a Tanzanian operational zone). Bonomade Machude Omar, designated by the US as a 'specially designated global terrorist', is believed to be based in Macomia, and insurgents have increased their attacks in the district, targeting locations including Chai, Nova Zambézia and Quinto Congresso, while in Nangade the United Nations High Commissioner for Refugees estimated that 24,000 people in the district were displaced by violence in the period between January and March 2022 alone.

The spreading out of the insurgents and ongoing adoption of hit-and-run tactics have tested the logistical capacities of both SAMIM and Rwandan forces. The South African military has long complained that it is inadequately funded, and it has yet to reach its promised force level, so far offering mainly air support (although it is reported to be seeking to boost troop numbers in the area). Moreover, ongoing instability in Nangade has prompted speculation that the Tanzanian military is primarily focused on preventing insurgent groups from gaining a foothold in Tanzania's southern Mtwara region, rather than on stabilising Cabo Delgado. There are substantial numbers of Makua (and a smaller Mwani community) in southern Tanzania, and the Tanzanian authorities are reportedly wary of infiltration of the area, particularly given that Abu Yasir Hassan – one of the insurgents' main spiritual and political leaders – is a Tanzanian national.

Meanwhile, US and European support remains focused on training existing troops, potentially because more direct involvement could attract additional Islamic fighters from other parts of Africa, as well as the Middle East and even South Asia, seeking to attack Western troops. Training is chiefly located at military bases in the south of the country – well away from front-line military operations – and does not appear to involve significant intelligence-sharing. It has not so far resulted in a significant change in the operational capability of Mozambique's armed forces.

Mission changing for SADC

Despite these challenges, there are signs that the SADC mission in Mozambique is shifting focus. In January 2022, SADC states agreed to extend SAMIM's mandate (which had been due to end on 15 January) for a further three months. A further three-month extension was subsequently agreed in April but will involve de-escalation from 'full enforcement' to a peacekeeping operation, with increased intelligence-gathering using a Regional Counter-Terrorism Centre inaugurated in Tanzania in February 2022.

De-escalation has some advantages for both SADC and the Mozambican government. SADC states are probably keen to avoid being entangled in a likely long-running insurgency where they may struggle to define success. The Mozambican authorities have had an ambivalent attitude to the presence of SADC forces, since this brings greater scrutiny

Conflict and displacement in Cabo Delgado

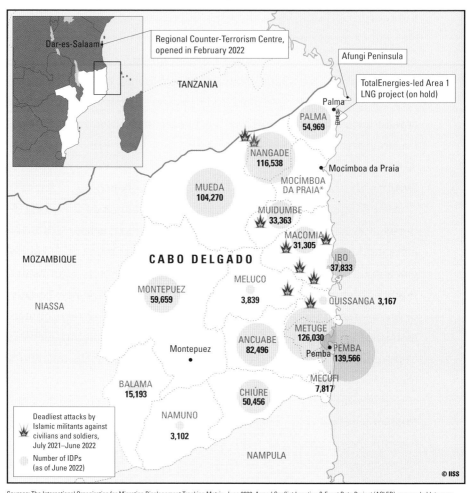

Sources: The International Organization for Migration Displacement Tracking Matrix, June 2022; Armed Conflict Location & Event Data Project (ACLED), www.acleddata.com
*No data available for number of IDPs

of the local human-rights record and quality of governance. There have also been tensions between Rwandan and SADC leaders, with then-defence minister of South Africa Nosiviwe Mapisa-Nqakula making it clear in July 2021 that South Africa did not welcome Rwanda deploying its military in Cabo Delgado before SADC did. This appears to have led to a failure to coordinate. In January 2022, President Nyusi held separate meetings with President Kagame in Kigali and with SADC leaders in Lilongwe, Malawi. This prompted Adriano Nuvunga, executive director of Mozambique's Centre for Democracy and Development, to state that the failure of the SADC to engage Kagame, and of the Mozambican authorities to reveal the terms of their agreement with Rwanda, were prompting concern about human-rights accountability and the precise nature of Rwanda's responsibilities. Furthermore, de-escalation calls into question SADC's potential role if – as seems likely – the insurgency spreads across Southern African borders or poses a threat to regional transport infrastructure.

Doubts about the government's financial approach

Concerns about the future trajectory of the insurgency are likely to persist. Crucially, while the Mozambican government is keen to avoid a protracted conflict, it has not thus far sought to use short-term territorial gains to seek negotiations, or to implement the governance reforms that might address some of the underlying causes of the insurgency. Equally, questions remain over the roll-out and likely efficacy of development assistance to improve humanitarian and socio-economic conditions in Cabo Delgado. The five-year Resilience and Development Strategy for the North (RDSN), due to be approved by the cabinet by mid-2022, is the first official document to recognise the role of domestic factors in the Cabo Delgado insurgency. It is designed to mobilise funding – with financing of up to US$700m expected from donors including the World Bank, UN, EU and the African Development Bank – to prevent and counter violent extremism in Cabo Delgado, Niassa and Nampula. It aims to do so by:

- supporting the construction of peace, security and social cohesion;
- rebuilding the social contract between the state and the population, including by ensuring fair access to public services, tackling corruption, and ensuring redistribution and fiscal transparency; and
- focusing on 'recovery economics' and resilience, by repairing the damage caused to livelihoods, particularly in the agricultural, fisheries and forestry sectors, supporting the private sector in areas including tourism, and rebuilding infrastructure.

However, it remains to be seen whether the ruling Mozambique Liberation Front (Frelimo) and President Nyusi – himself born in Cabo Delgado – will in practice be prepared to tackle the poor governance and self-enrichment by the governing elite that has played a key role in generating and sustaining inequality, exclusion and thus radicalisation in Cabo Delgado and elsewhere. The risk is that the RDSN will bring in substantial external resources that will be used primarily for the benefit of local elites rather than marginalised communities. This could prove particularly inflammatory given that the Mozambican population faces declining living standards due to the impact of Russia's invasion of Ukraine on international food and fuel prices. In May the energy regulatory authority announced a 6% rise in the price of cooking gas, on top of a 13.3% rise in March, and while the government will maintain subsidies for some essential foods, it will not be able to substantially increase social spending given its fragile fiscal position, likely translating into a rise in poverty.

There is little to suggest that disenfranchised communities will be given the opportunity to effect change through the ballot box. In March 2022, the government announced that municipal elections would be held in October 2023. Along with the election of provincial governors, municipal polls formed a key part of decentralisation reforms included in the 2019 peace agreement between Frelimo and Renamo. However, the 2018 municipal vote was marred by opposition allegations of widespread irregularities, and Frelimo won 44 out of 53 municipalities. The ruling party is likely to similarly dominate the 2023 vote, while regional governors are likely to continue to have only limited autonomy.

In late April 2022 Ugandan President Yoweri Museveni suggested that substantial numbers of Ugandan troops may be deployed to help fight the insurgency. Overall, however, there is a high risk that the conflict in Cabo Delgado will evolve into a long-term stalemate in which neither insurgents nor the government and allied troops are able to gain a decisive victory. Southern Africa may then become a broader front for insurgent attacks.

BERMUDA

BAHAMAS

MEXICO

CUBA

DOMINICAN
REPUBLIC

HAITI

BELIZE

JAMAICA

PUERTO RICO

GUATEMALA

HONDURAS

DOMINICA

EL SALVADOR

NICARAGUA

BARBADOS

COSTA RICA

TRINIDAD AND TOBAGO

PANAMA

VENEZUELA

COLOMBIA

GUYANA

SURINAME

FRENCH GUIANA

ECUADOR

PERU

BRAZIL

BOLIVIA

PARAGUAY

CHILE

URUGUAY

ARGENTINA

Falkland Islands

©IISS

South Georgia

Drivers of Strategic Change

REGIONAL SHARE OF GLOBAL POPULATION, GDP AND DEFENCE BUDGET

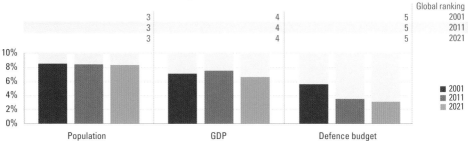

	Global ranking
	2001
	2011
	2021

Population — 3, 3, 3
GDP — 4, 4, 4
Defence budget — 5, 5, 5

Legend: 2001, 2011, 2021

POPULATION

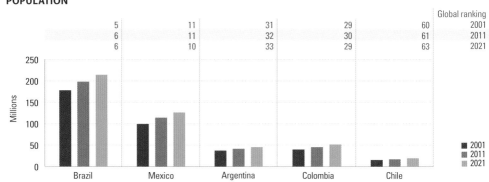

	Global ranking
	2001
	2011
	2021

Brazil — 5, 6, 6
Mexico — 11, 11, 10
Argentina — 31, 32, 33
Colombia — 29, 30, 29
Chile — 60, 61, 63

Legend: 2001, 2011, 2021

AGE STRUCTURE
(Percentage of national population)

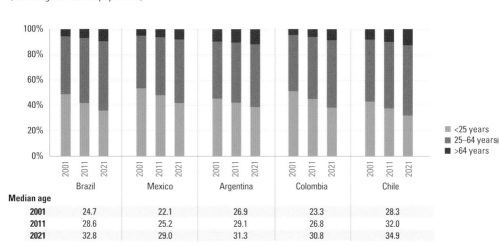

Legend: <25 years, 25–64 years, >64 years

Median age	Brazil	Mexico	Argentina	Colombia	Chile
2001	24.7	22.1	26.9	23.3	28.3
2011	28.6	25.2	29.1	26.8	32.0
2021	32.8	29.0	31.3	30.8	34.9

Latin America exhibits greater continuity than any other region. Most countries show little variation in their relative level of key power resources over the past 20 years. Some defence budgets have fallen in real as well as relative terms, with Colombia the major exception. Despite this, Brazil's armed forces have grown significantly. Trust in government remains low in major countries.

GDP
(Constant 2010 US dollars)

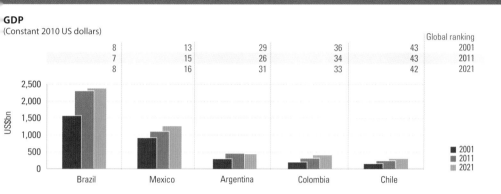

GDP PER CAPITA
(Constant 2010 US dollars)

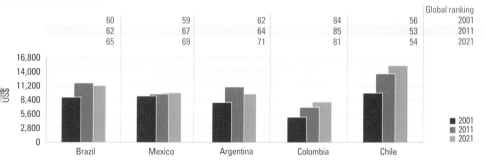

DEFENCE BUDGET
(Constant 2015 US dollars)

ACTIVE MILITARY PERSONNEL

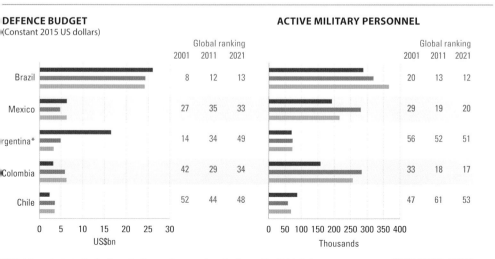

*2001 defence budget value for Argentina is an estimate, and may be distorted by high inflation rates.

■ 2001 ■ 2011 ■ 2021

For explanation of drivers and sources, see page 8

HUMAN DEVELOPMENT INDEX (HDI)
(Score between 0 and 1, where 0 denotes a low level of development and 1 a high level of development)

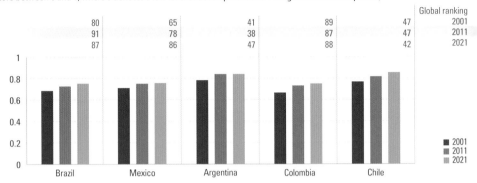

	Brazil	Mexico	Argentina	Colombia	Chile	Global ranking
	80	65	41	89	47	2001
	91	78	38	87	47	2011
	87	86	47	88	42	2021

■ 2001 ■ 2011 ■ 2021

POLITICAL SYSTEM
(Score between 0 and 100, where 0 denotes no political freedom and 100 fully free)

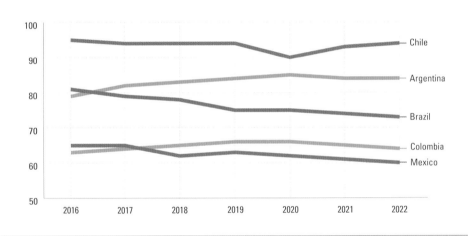

TRUST IN GOVERNMENT
(Average level of trust)

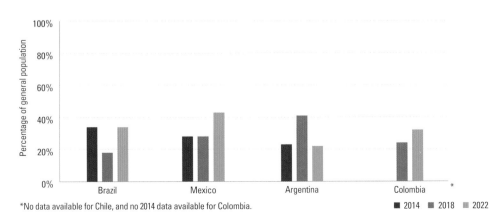

*No data available for Chile, and no 2014 data available for Colombia.

■ 2014 ■ 2018 ■ 2022

For explanation of drivers and sources, see page

2021–22 Review

While the severity of the coronavirus pandemic started to decrease in Latin America amid an impressive vaccine roll-out in the second half of 2021, the regional outlook remained fraught with risks. Although GDP rebounded by 6.8% in 2021 (reversing a 7% contraction in 2020), endemic socio-economic and institutional fragilities appeared to have massively deteriorated against a backdrop of heightened political volatility, weakened macroeconomic fundamentals and rising insecurity. The election super-cycle in the region, which had started in late 2019, continued throughout the review period, with rising polarisation and rejection of both the status quo and traditional politics in full display. This often resulted in increased ungovernability amid dysfunctional and fragmented congresses in many countries across the region.

Ensuing domestic instability often spilled into regional crises and tensions over migration flows, which resumed in earnest once COVID-19 restrictions were lifted and were also driven by misguided expectations of a more liberal United States migration policy under the presidency of Joe Biden. External headwinds, including Russia's war in Ukraine, complicated domestic woes, further fuelling inflation trends that had negative impacts on economic and social stability in the region.

A complicated socio-economic picture

Latin America was arguably the worst-hit region in the world by the coronavirus pandemic. But a speedy COVID-19 vaccine roll-out in the second half of 2021, coupled with a favourable external environment and pent-up domestic demand, supported a strong recovery that year. Momentum appeared to wane in 2022, however, with forecast GDP growth falling to only 2.5% amid chronic competitiveness, bottlenecks and growing global uncertainties.

Even before the global shock of higher agricultural and energy prices caused by Russia's war in Ukraine, inflation had resurfaced, driven by post-pandemic worldwide supply-chain shortages and historical currency depreciation. This prompted the tightening of monetary policy

Table 1: **The macroeconomic picture of Latin America and the Caribbean**

	2019	2020	2021	2022	2023	2024	2025	2026	2027
GDP growth (% change)	0.1	-7.0	6.8	2.6	2.5	2.5	2.4	2.4	2.4
Inflation, average consumer prices (% change)	7.7	6.4	9.8	11.2	8.0	6.6	6.1	5.4	5.0
General government gross debt (% of GDP)	68.1	77.4	72.0	71.3	71.4	71.4	71.1	70.6	69.8
External debt (% of GDP)	47.8	55.5	51.8	48.0	46.9	n/a	n/a	n/a	n/a

Source: IMF, World Economic Outlook Database, April 2022

across the region, further constraining growth. Brazil was a case in point, raising its Selic benchmark interest rate 12 times in a row from 2% (in March 2021) to 13.75% (in August 2022) in one of the most aggressive tightening cycles among major economies in recent memory.

Weaker fiscal fundamentals across the region added to macroeconomic woes; government debt as a percentage of GDP increased by almost ten percentage points from 68.07% in 2019 to 77.38% in 2020 (a record by recent regional standards), amid extensive emergency stimulus programmes. Even excluding the clear outlier of Venezuela (304.13%), debt levels appeared particularly unsustainable for countries such as Argentina (102.79%), Brazil (98.68%) and El Salvador (89.16%) in 2020. Given lacklustre growth, the only way to lower sovereign risk will be fiscal consolidation – itself an additional headwind to growth prospects.

The social needs of a region left poorer and more unequal by the coronavirus pandemic intensified these problems of macroeconomic fragility. Despite economic recovery, rates of poverty and extreme poverty in 2021 remained higher than in 2019, with an additional five million people falling into extreme poverty. The region also suffered its highest rates of food insecurity in over 15 years, with the combined rate of severe and moderate food insecurity reaching 40.6% in 2021. Rising inflation further curtailed access to basic products and services, reinforcing poverty and food-insecurity trends as well as social discontent.

More political instability

The coronavirus pandemic's disastrous socio-economic legacy laid bare the many flaws and entrenched institutional fragilities of the prevailing regional economic model, fuelling demands for more inclusive societies, better governance standards and more efficient governments. Social dissatisfaction resulted in several episodes of unrest, most notably protracted protests in Colombia against a deeply unpopular tax reform from April–July 2021. Argentina, Bolivia, Brazil, Mexico, Peru and even El Salvador (under the presidency of arguably the most popular leader in the region, Nayib Bukele) also saw mobilisation and protests.

Social malaise continued to drive the rejection of mainstream political parties and politics along with political polarisation and fragmentation. These trends were on full display in the presidential-election victories of several 'outsiders': Pedro Castillo in Peru (June 2021), Gabriel Boric in Chile (December 2021) and Rodrigo Chaves in Costa Rica (April 2022). Many presidential run-offs featured candidates at the very opposite ends of the political spectrum, which also resulted in fragmented and dysfunctional legislatures. Peru's permanent institutional crisis was a glaring example of this trend; in less than one year in power, Castillo had to appoint four prime ministers as well as endure repeated ministerial resignations and a number of impeachment attempts, amid frequent U-turns in policies and corruption scandals.

Former student leader Boric, who ran on a 'new left' platform that prominently featured environmental and inclusivity issues, already faced huge governability challenges a few months into his term, with difficulties securing support in a fragmented congress in which he did not have a majority. Boric's troubles were no doubt aggravated by the momentous challenges of the slowing Chilean economy, rising inflation and an intractable conflict in the south of the country around indigenous rights and autonomy. But they also exemplified the difficulties that 'outsider' leaders face in delivering on their promise of radical change and more inclusive and transparent development models, given the limited tools at their disposal, especially in a post-COVID-19 world.

The continued appetite for anti/non-establishment leaders and new ways to address old problems also evoked concerns about the strength of democracy in the region. The sustained popularity of leaders such as El Salvador's Bukele or Mexico's Andrés Manuel López Obrador, who share an unorthodox governing style, suggested that achieving quick results could be a more important consideration in the eyes of many voters than complying with all democratic forms and procedures.

Another concerning dimension related to the erosion of democracy in the region has been the growing strength of criminal governance associated with drug-trafficking groups in the Northern Triangle of Central America and beyond. The arrest and extradition to the US of former Honduran president Juan Orlando Hernández on trafficking charges was a vivid example. At the same time, elections in Honduras in November 2021 were won by Xiomara Castro from the leftist Libre party, who ran on an anti-corruption platform. This gave some reason for optimism despite concerns regarding old corruption allegations against Castro's husband and former president Manuel Zelaya (who had been ousted in 2009 by a *coup d'état*) and other members of her family.

Regional security tested

Organised criminal violence continued as changes in drug-trafficking routes and product mix (notably the rising significance of synthetic drugs) were exacerbated by the coronavirus pandemic. Ecuador, previously only marginally affected, has seen six large-scale prison massacres associated with gang rivalries since the beginning of 2021, leading the government to impose a state of emergency several times. In Haiti, the assassination of president Jovenel Moïse in July 2021, and a major earthquake a month later, led to a spiralling political and economic crisis that allowed criminal gangs to challenge what was left of the state and exercise criminal governance in many parts of the island.

Venezuela remained mired in a constitutional crisis with two parallel governments. By providing a safe haven for Colombia's non-state armed groups and other illicit actors, it also continued to drive regional instability and criminal violence. Negotiations between President Nicolás Maduro and the opposition collapsed after a month in October 2021, having made little progress towards making the regional and municipal elections in November free and fair. A rapprochement of sorts between Maduro and the US that included the easing of some sanctions in May 2022 was accelerated by the Russia–Ukraine war and related energy-security concerns, and had the potential to lead to a restarting of the negotiations.

The past year saw successive migration crises. At the border between Mexico and the US, migration flows were at a record high in 2021 (with a notable increase in unaccompanied minors) and showed no sign of easing in the first few months of 2022. US Customs and Border Protection apprehended over 220,000 migrants in March 2022 alone, a 33% increase from February 2022 and the highest monthly figure in over 20 years. The record numbers have been driven by much-deteriorated socio-economic and security conditions in countries of origin (El Salvador, Guatemala and Honduras, but also increasingly Nicaragua and Cuba) but also by hopes of a more liberal immigration policy under Biden. The latest Haitian migration crisis in September 2021 was a case in point; it involved mainly Haitians who had migrated to South America in the aftermath of the disastrous 2010 earthquake on the island. Faced with post-pandemic rising poverty and unemployment in their countries of adoption, they decided to make the perilous journey to the US, also enticed by the understanding that the US would grant Temporary Protected Status to any Haitian on its soil.

In South America, the Venezuela crisis continued to drive migration flows to neighbouring countries, creating additional strains on social and health systems already massively stretched by the coronavirus pandemic and fuelling xenophobic sentiment against migrants. This also added to the appeal of hard-line discourses and politicians, which was demonstrated by the unexpected success of extreme-right candidate José Antonio Kast in the first round of Chile's presidential elections.

Still not top of the US foreign-policy agenda

Expectations that the Biden administration would mark an inflection point in bilateral relations, after years of progressive US disengagement from the region (culminating under Donald Trump), did not materialise in the review period. The region remained relatively low in the United States' list of foreign-policy priorities with no major departure from previous policies. The Biden administration's focus on promoting democracy and the rule of law in Central America, while addressing the root causes of migration (with US$4 billion earmarked for the region over four years), did not yield significant progress amid frictions with governments in the Northern Triangle over governance practices. Castro's victory in Honduras was a welcome development, as shown by her government's collaboration in extraditing former president Hernández to the US.

Regarding Venezuela, there was little change in practice from the United States' previous stance. The Biden administration kept Trump-era sanctions in place and continued to recognise Juan Guaidó as the legitimate president, although it supported the last round of negotiations in October 2021.

Likewise, regarding Cuba, there has been no return to former president Barack Obama's normalisation steps. This has had ripple effects on progress on the Venezuela crisis, given the importance of Havana's intelligence and support for the Maduro regime. A timid easing of sanctions towards Cuba was announced in May 2022, together with similar measures for Venezuela.

The Summit of the Americas, a triennial gathering of member states of the Organization of American States, which the US hosted in June 2022 for the first time since 1994, did not produce any significant outcomes (bar some limited commitment on migration and economic support) due to poor planning and its boycott by the presidents of Bolivia, El Salvador, Guatemala, Honduras and Mexico (over the exclusion of Cuba, Nicaragua and Venezuela from the invitee list). This reflected the low priority assigned by the US to the region as well as America's waning influence and importance in the eyes of many Latin American countries, which are increasingly looking east for support and opportunities.

Looking ahead

A number of developments are likely to have important repercussions for Latin America's short-term prospects. Russia's war in Ukraine will continue to complicate regional policymakers' efforts to put their macroeconomic houses in order, with potential implications for social stability as well. As for the rest of the world, the war's net impact will depend on a given country's access to and the availability of agricultural staples and energy, given Russia's and Ukraine's importance for the global supply of energy (notably oil), food and agricultural goods, and fertilisers. Latin America is home to both large oil producers such as Colombia, Mexico and Venezuela and oil importers such as Peru and Chile. It also features large food and agricultural exporters including Argentina, Brazil and Mexico together with countries which are net food importers, including most Caribbean states.

The sanctions imposed on Russia and the disruptions of supply chains due to the Russia–Ukraine war will keep energy and agricultural prices high, potentially benefitting Latin American exporters of these commodities by providing them with new market shares. This will depend, however, on whether agricultural exporters manage to secure access to fertilisers, for which they are heavily reliant on imports, since a large chunk of the global production of fertilisers comes from Belarus, Russia and Ukraine.

The war will accentuate existing inflationary pressures and monetary tightening across the region. Considering food prices represent around a quarter of the average regional consumption basket, their increase will further strain the ever-fragile socio-economic fabric of the region, with potential knock-on effects on stability through new waves of social unrest.

On a more positive note, recent easing of US sanctions against Venezuela may lead to a revival in negotiations between Maduro and the opposition and headway towards breaking the country's political impasse, potentially heralding some progress towards free and fair elections. There are many downsides and risks to this scenario, but concomitant steps towards a normalisation of US relations with Cuba could improve its odds.

On the domestic front, two elections could have regional and pan-regional implications. The victory of former guerrilla member and left-wing politician Gustavo Petro in Colombia's presidential elections in

June 2022 marked a political watershed in the country's history and could lead to significant changes in Colombia's drugs policy and approach to organised crime and violence. Regarding Colombia's drugs policy, Petro will likely abandon the current hard-line approach sponsored by the US, which focuses on fumigation of coca crops and the criminalisation of drugs, in favour of policies targeting development and land redistribution. Regarding organised crime and violence, Petro has committed to the full implementation of the peace agreement (which had lagged under the current administration) signed in 2016 with the Revolutionary Armed Forces of Colombia (FARC) and to initiating a comprehensive peace process with all non-state armed groups operating in the country. Given Colombia's role as the main coca grower and cocaine producer in the region, changes in its security and drugs policies will be monitored closely by the US and could create momentum for a pan-regional discussion on the merits of the prevailing strategy, which has not been effective at curbing illicit economies and related violence in the region.

In Brazil's general election in October 2022, the incumbent right-wing populist Jair Bolsonaro performed better than expected, denying his leading opponent, centre-left former president Luiz Inácio 'Lula' da Silva, an outright victory in the first round. A Lula victory, although not a concern for the markets given Lula's sound economic track record when in power, would reinforce the pink tide in the region and stoke fears that Brazil may move even closer to China (which is already a major player in the region). However, judging by some of his campaign actions (including his efforts to discredit electronic voting), Bolsonaro could reject an adverse election result. This would lead to social unrest, further polarisation and political instability.

Chile's Struggle for a More Inclusive Developmental Model
Why was the new constitution defeated, and what next?

After the restoration of democracy in 1990 Chile enjoyed three decades of respectable economic growth under generally stable macroeconomic and financial conditions and external economic openness. But economic progress came along with high inequality of income and wealth, de-industrialisation and strains on the environment due to resource-intensive development. Over time, social and political contradictions mounted, and a range of social groups – students, environmentalists, feminists, a workers' movement for the de-privatisation of the pension system and others – began to contest the prevailing institutional framework. In late 2019, a growing crisis of political representation and challenging of economic inequities erupted in massive protests at the national level. In response to this wave of social unrest, a political agreement among various political forces was forged.

A central part of this agreement was the adoption of a new constitution to replace the current one adopted in 1980 under the rule of Augusto Pinochet. The new constitution was to be drafted by an elected constitutional convention and to be subject to ratification by a nationwide referendum in which citizens were legally obliged to vote. A novel feature of the constitutional convention was gender parity and guaranteed representation of indigenous population groups. Dissatisfaction with the prevailing economic model and mainstream politics also resulted in the election in December 2021 of a centre-left coalition, headed by 36-year-old former student leader Gabriel Boric. The new government took office in March 2022 with an ambitious progressive agenda, which included addressing inequalities and promoting social rights and sustainability. It threw its weight behind the proposed new constitution in the run-up to the referendum which took place on 4 September 2022. The emphatic rejection of the new constitution by 62% of voters (vs 38% in favour) highlighted the many shortcomings of the constitutional process and its final outcome, as well as disgruntlement with the Boric government. However, considering most recent polls, and the clear mandate to rewrite the constitution given by 80% of the electorate in the 2020 plebiscite which started the constitutional process, it is clear that a new constitution remains on the cards. Less clear is how the country will get there and whether the final charter would deliver on the changes for which the constitutional process started in the first place.

Economic and political development from independence to 1973

Historically, Chile has been reliant on natural resources for its economic development, such as a nitrate commodity cycle that started in approximately 1880 after the seizure of vast territories in the north of the country in the wake of the War of the Pacific until its eventual decline in the early 1930s; and a copper cycle that started in the 1930s and has largely prevailed since then. Chile was hit very hard by the Great Depression of the 1930s, with GDP contracting by 46% between 1929 and 1932. After recovering from the Depression, Chile, like other Latin American countries, embarked on an import-substitution industrialisation (ISI) strategy to reduce external dependence and promote domestic industrialisation. The state created public enterprises in energy, telecommunications and other sectors, and protected domestic industry through tariff quotas and preferential import arrangements for intermediate inputs and capital equipment. The manufacturing sector grew more important, but dependency on imports of capital goods and inputs remained high. The agricultural sector did not grow more dynamic and Chile continued to depend on food imports. An agrarian elite benefitted from large landholdings, although a process of agrarian reform took place between the mid-1960s and 1973 that redistributed land to small agrarian producers and peasants. Provision of social services, such as public education, public health, housing and social-security schemes, became more widespread. At the same time, this period registered expanded trade-union membership in the public and industrial sectors. The trade unions were particularly active in the 1950s and 1960s, and their actions were oriented to protect the purchasing power of wages eroded by chronic double-digit inflation.

A period of transition to democratic socialism (1970–73) under president Salvador Allende stimulated aggregate demand, saw the implementation of nationalisation policies and accelerated agrarian reform. Domestic economic elites opposed these policies, and American companies with investments in the Chilean extractives sector were dissatisfied with the government's nationalisation terms. President Richard Nixon and secretary of state Henry Kissinger cut multilateral funding to Chile through the IMF and the World Bank and engaged in covert economic and political de-stabilisation tactics against Chile. The Popular Unity government, which had the support of the worker and student movements, the peasantry and sectors of the middle class, struggled to control a severe economic crisis, resulting in high inflation, food shortages, strikes and stalled growth. This created social divisions and confrontations with economic elites and upper-middle-income groups. On 11 September 1973 the head of the army, General Augusto Pinochet, led a military coup that ousted the Allende government.

Free-market economics and dictatorship: the Pinochet era

The new military junta closed parliament, restricted trade unions, banned political activities, suspended civil rights and imposed tight censorship. It persecuted and imprisoned political opponents and labour leaders and committed other severe violations of human rights.

At the same time, authoritarian politics was complemented by a free-market economic agenda that deregulated prices, returned nationalised enterprises to their previous owners and privatised other public enterprises, reduced import tariffs and liberalised financial flows from abroad. These neoliberal policies had the support of a class of new owners who acquired public enterprises at low cost, with financial intermediaries obtaining big profits from banking deregulation. Workers could not effectively oppose privatisation policies, and massive layoffs occurred in the public sector. The new price incentives following trade liberalisation promoted forestry, fishing and fruit agroindustry for export.

In the early 1980s the Pinochet regime also launched a set of so-called 'market-oriented social policies' in which social services traditionally provided by the state began to be delivered by the private sector. New laws allowed for-profit providers to operate in the education, health, housing and pension-fund sectors. In 1982–83, a serious economic and financial crisis led to large cuts in output and employment. This crisis and the lack of civil liberties incubated serious, sometimes violent social protests that cornered the military regime. As a way out of an increasingly untenable situation, in 1988 the regime agreed to hold a national referendum on its future. A majority of the population voted against the regime. The military called a general election for the following year, which was won by a centre-left coalition.

The return to democracy in 1990: economic continuity and the resilience of the 1980 constitution

After the restoration of democracy in 1990, the constitution of 1980 was maintained with some amendments. Subsequent civilian governments continued the free-market, pro-business policies of General Pinochet, albeit in a more pragmatic fashion. The minimum wage increased, and public investment and social-sector spending, which had been neglected by the military regime, grew. Nonetheless, the new governments abstained from progressive redistribution policies, the non-transparent privatisation of public enterprises of the late 1980s was not revised and private economic conglomerates expanded their control of financial and natural resources, consolidating their political influence over the new civilian governments. Further privatisation took place during the post-Pinochet democratic period, including of water provision to large cities during the government of president Eduardo Frei Ruiz-Tagle (1994–2000). Coal mining in the historic Lota area in the south of the country was closed. Social services such as education, health, housing and pension administration continued to be delivered for profit, and accessing them remains dependent on users' ability to pay. The economy continues to depend on mining and the services sector, while the importance of the manufacturing sector has declined over time. Until 2021, macroeconomic management was characterised by moderately low inflation rates, a fiscal rule restricting deficit financing (the fiscal rule consists of linking increases of long-run public spending to permanent sources of revenue, such as trends in GDP growth and copper prices), free-floating exchange rates and an open capital account governing inflows and outflows of financial capital.

Social conflict and the unequal distribution of the fruits of development

The current Chilean economic-development model has led to high inequality. The gross income Gini coefficient is around 50 but the wealth Gini is much higher, reaching over 80 (with 100 denoting maximum possible inequality). The gap between the top deciles and bottom deciles is over 35 times and the income share of the wealthiest 1% of the population is close to 30%. Measured multidimensional poverty, which tracks access to social services, is twice as high as income poverty. Indices of educational attainment, unemployment, labour-market informality, quality of housing and access to health services are systematically lower for the poor in urban and rural areas.

Persistently high inequality in Chile is a consequence of several factors. Firstly, the concentration of productive wealth among small elites, historically high in Chile, was reinforced by the privatisation of public assets undertaken between the mid-1970s and late 1990s and by the financialisation of pension-fund management. Secondly, labour's share of national income (the proportion of total wage payments in national income) fell after the introduction of Pinochet's neoliberal model due to the weakening of trade unions and the adoption of pro-business labour legislation that impaired labour's ability to negotiate better wages and more favourable working conditions. Thirdly, the tax system is not progressive and thus does not correct gross inequalities. Fourthly, public education, a traditional mechanism of social mobility and broader access to opportunities, has steadily deteriorated. Finally, economic conglomerates have captured significant economic rents (profits above the competitive rate of return on capital) in a range of non-competitive sectors, chiefly natural resources and the financial sector.

Constitutions in the nineteenth and twentieth centuries

Since achieving independence from the Spanish Crown in the second decade of the nineteenth century, Chile has had eight constitutions (this also includes the draft constitution for a federal state in 1826). The three most long-lasting ones were the constitutions of 1833, 1925 and 1980. None of these were written by a constitutional convention, but rather by small commissions appointed by the executive. All were approved by a small number of voters. At the time of the ratification plebiscite for the 1980 constitution Chile was ruled by a military junta and lacked a free press and basic democratic guarantees.

The 1833 constitution consolidated centralised conservative power and ushered in several decades of relative political stability and economic growth, within a context of low popular participation and restricted voting. The first three decades of the twentieth century were affected by various degrees of political instability and social unrest. As a response to growing social demands for more inclusion and economic security, the 1925 constitution was reformist and incorporated new social and labour rights. This constitution, with some amendments, lasted until the military coup in 1973. Pinochet's 1980 constitution entrenched military oversight of the civilian political system and consolidated a neoliberal economic regime around deregulated markets and a very limited role for the state. The prevalence of the Pinochet constitution over more than three decades of civilian rule has been a permanent source of unease in Chilean society. But it took the wave of violent social unrest and massive protests in late 2019 for the political establishment to open the door to a process aimed to replace Pinochet's charter with a new one.

The proposed constitution and its main features

The new constitution text, approved in plenary by the constitutional convention and presented in July 2022, was a major departure from Pinochet's charter in content and approach. While the latter gave primacy to private-property rights of productive wealth over labour and social rights, enshrined a 'minimal state' doctrine and centralised decision-making under a strong president, the new text reflected long-standing demands for greater political participation and inclusion, decentralisation, protection of the environment and natural resources, and a more equitable distribution of national income. However, the radical tilt of the constitutional convention and attempts to incorporate many specific partisan and one-issue agendas resulted in a record 162-page-long document legislating on a disparate range of issues in often too confusing or radical terms for most voters (see Box 1).

Box 1: Main provisions of the new constitution

The new constitution included the following main principles:

a) The Chilean republic will be a plurinational, multicultural and regional state, encompassing several nationalities each with their own language, historic and ethnic identity and cultural traits; the proposed new constitution provides indigenous communities, such as the Aymara, Mapuche, Quechua, Rapa Nui and others, an equal footing in terms of rights and obligations in Chilean society.

b) The state will guarantee respect of basic political freedoms (of association, free speech, free press, formation of political parties and so on), respect for human rights and the protection and respect of nature and the environment.

c) Chile will be a 'democratic social state of rights' ensuring egalitarian access to basic social services such as education, health, housing, social security, and care for the whole population including children and the elderly.

d) The new legislative power will be composed of a chamber of deputies of 155 members and a regional chamber (a deliberative body of representatives from the regions representing gender parity and multiculturalism). The current branch of Congress (upper chamber) will be phased out after a transition period.

e) The judiciary system recognises an administration of justice in the territories lived in by indigenous communities according to their ancestral rules. Both a People's Ombudsman, with a mandate to promote and protect human rights, and a Nature's Ombudsman, to protect nature and ecosystems, will be created.

f) Chile will be a regional state within an overall unitary state framework (non-federal), composed of autonomous regions, counties, indigenous territories and special zones endowed with legal autonomy and independent patrimony.

g) Citizens will be able to initiate new laws provided 3% of the electorate support the initiative. A request to phase out existing laws requires the support of 5% of the electorate. These are considered elements of participatory and direct democracy.

h) Rights of access to water and common resources will be guaranteed, and privatisation of water resources will be phased out.

i) Property rights are fully recognised but will be subject to limitations relating to the upholding of public interest and access to common resources.

j) Trade agreements and foreign investment will incorporate in their design stringent environmental considerations and dispute-resolution mechanisms as well as promote technology transfer from abroad and respect for labour rights.

The referendum setback

The issues with the new text became increasingly apparent in the weeks preceding the 4 September referendum, with polls pointing to the *rechazo* ('reject') front having a significant lead on the *apruebo* ('approve'). Acknowledging the text's shortcomings, parties from the governing coalition committed on 11 August to undertake major revisions to the most controversial provisions regarding plurinationalism, social rights, law and order, as well as the legislative and justice system, if the constitution was approved. The above notwithstanding, the sheer size of the rejection vote surprised most. With 68% of the votes, the *rechazo* option won in all of Chile's 16 regions and all but eight of the municipal districts as well as in almost all demographic segments, including those that supposedly stood to benefit from the new constitution, such as indigenous communities.

A number of reasons possibly explain this outcome, including the well-organised and -funded *rechazo* campaign, which adopted a moderate tone and skilfully exploited ambiguities and vagueness in the constitution to spread alarming messages on radical changes the constitution would have ushered in (including on separate justice systems and autonomous governance for indigenous communities). The many instances of histrionic and unprofessional behaviour by members of the constitutional convention added to voters' disgruntlement with the process, while the referendum was also used by many to express disapproval with the new administration and the state of the economy. Indeed, Boric seemed to have had only a very brief honeymoon period after taking office in March, with his approval rates hovering below 40% from April onwards (and falling to 33% after the referendum) amid a sharp deceleration of the economy and rising inflation.

More fundamentally, it appeared the agenda espoused by the proposed constitution was too radical for most: while the 2020 vote which launched the constitutional process saw a 7.5 million turnout, 13m people cast their vote in the September referendum, arguably a more diverse (and complete) sample of the Chilean population. The constitution's maximalist approach and attempt to substantially reform institutions (eliminating the senate and changing the justice system, among others) and the state itself (with plurinationalism), as well as its proposed weakening of property rights (notably on minerals and water), went too far for the moderate majority. However, the demands which drove the constitutional process in the first place, centred around a more inclusive economic model, remain as potent as ever, especially amid a deteriorating socio-economic outlook. Although the constitution's rejection means the 1980 charter should remain in place, there is broad agreement across the political spectrum and public opinion on the need for a new charter, and discussions have already started on the mechanisms to get there.

What next?

The rejection of the constitution was a major defeat for the composite, broadly left-leaning, movement which emerged from the 2019 protests and particularly for the Boric government, already in a delicate position amid the many economic, security and social challenges Chile currently faces, and the unruly coalition supporting it. Boric responded to the events with a major reshuffle of his cabinet. This notably saw the replacement of close allies of his holding the Interior Ministry and the General Secretariat of the Presidency with seasoned centre-left politicians, in an effort to improve relations with Congress and ease the passage of his ambitious legislative agenda. Boric also suggested that Congress should lead on the next steps for a new charter. The two options under discussion are for Congress to significantly re-work the rejected text, amending it as needed, or to choose a new constitutional convention, elected according to new rules which would likely restrict the number of independent candidates, or at least lean on independent experts.

Both options present their own challenges. In the first case, favoured by the opposition, it is not clear how Congress could decide and agree on changes to be made in the current polarised climate. In the second case, supported by Boric, the additional time required for the setting up of a new convention and for it to carry out its work may stretch voters' patience and the public budget too far.

On a more positive side, Boric's response to the referendum setback suggests he is willing to listen to voters and moderate his agenda accordingly, in a way that could facilitate consensus building in Congress. The likely outcome will be a new charter which, while not radically changing the economic and institutional model, makes it more inclusive and sustainable. The main challenge will then be to operationalise the changes in the context of a much more limited fiscal space and a contracting (or at best, stagnating) economy. Macroeconomic and fiscal reforms will be on the cards to raise the extra revenue needed for the new constitution to succeed.

US–China Rivalry in Latin America
Who is winning the geostrategic contest?

China's rise as a global power has seen its influence spread into Latin America, where it now challenges the historical dominance of the United States in key areas such as trade and finance. China's economic presence in the region has also come with growing political and military clout, which risks putting it on a collision course with the US in a region that the latter has traditionally considered its sphere of influence. The regional rivalry between these two countries is set to intensify over the next few decades following the introduction of ambitious global infrastructure plans with which they will attempt to woo Latin American governments into their respective orbits. But while China's economic ambitions are clear-cut, the extent to which the Asian giant can flex its political muscles in a region where it lacks both historical and cultural linkages as well as significant power projection remains questionable.

One of the most important elements of China's involvement in Latin America is its attempt to embrace even those countries that are more closely aligned within the United States' orbit but whose economic interests square with China's. China has designated seven major countries in the region as 'comprehensive strategic partners', which includes traditional US ally Mexico. Although the US has acknowledged the geopolitical rivalry it has with China in the region, it has also not opposed it and has openly stated that Chinese economic involvement is beneficial insofar as it serves development needs. Nevertheless, China has shown a clear interest in maintaining strong ties with certain countries that have antagonistic relationships with the US, such as Venezuela, which is the largest recipient of Chinese lending in Latin America and also a major buyer of Chinese arms. As a result, the rivalry between the two powers does not come without risks.

The economics of rivalry

China's economic presence in Latin America has grown enormously since the 1990s, particularly in South America, where it has overtaken

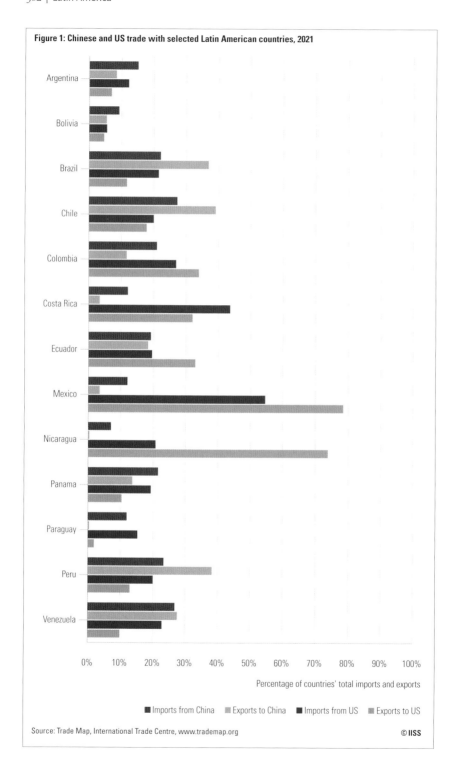

Figure 1: Chinese and US trade with selected Latin American countries, 2021

Percentage of countries' total imports and exports

■ Imports from China ■ Exports to China ■ Imports from US ■ Exports to US

Source: Trade Map, International Trade Centre, www.trademap.org   © IISS

the US as the continent's main trading partner. This has been the result of China's massive demand for natural resources and commodities to fuel its industrialisation and urbanisation drives. China, for example, imports the bulk of Chile's copper, Brazil's soybean and iron, and Argentina's and Uruguay's beef. In exchange, it supplies Latin America with intermediate and capital goods. This has fuelled concerns over unequal trade relations, as the region exports low-value-added commodities but imports high-value-added manufacturing goods. China has also achieved some degree of export success with countries whose trade relationship with the US is stronger. For example, in absolute terms China exports more to Mexico than to any other country in the region and runs a significant trade surplus.

China has also considerably stepped up its foreign direct investment (FDI) in the region over the past decade. Data on Chinese FDI is notoriously inconsistent, not least because a significant amount is channelled through offshore tax havens as well as Hong Kong. According to official data, around 11% of Latin America's stock of FDI has come from China and is heavily concentrated in a sector that corresponds to its main source of imports from the region: basic materials and energy (US$44 billion or 59% of all mergers and acquisitions [M&A] reported between 2001 and 2018). There is a significant presence in utilities (US$18bn or 25%) as well. China's strategic goal of acquiring key productive assets in the region needed for domestic consumption and investment may drive this. There is also demand for Chinese FDI from Latin American countries to address existing investment gaps, particularly in infrastructure. Chinese FDI has also been focused more on cross-border M&A (around two-thirds of its total) rather than on new investment projects. In terms of M&A alone, in 2020 China was the largest investor in the region, although when all types of FDI are tallied China still trails the US and, to a lesser extent, Spain.

China's investment binge in Latin America has been complemented by a massive increase in financing, which now exceeds that of the region's two main multilateral lenders, the World Bank and the Inter-American Development Bank (IADB). Financing to the region from

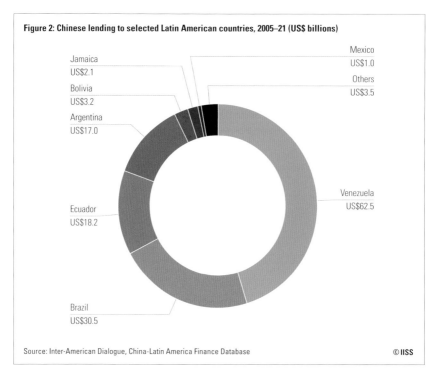

Figure 2: Chinese lending to selected Latin American countries, 2005–21 (US$ billions)

Jamaica US$2.1

Bolivia US$3.2

Argentina US$17.0

Ecuador US$18.2

Brazil US$30.5

Mexico US$1.0

Others US$3.5

Venezuela US$62.5

Source: Inter-American Dialogue, China-Latin America Finance Database   © IISS

the China Development Bank (CDB) and China Export–Import Bank (Ex–Im Bank) since 2005 is estimated to amount to US$138bn, and three regional funds have been established to channel these resources. This surge in Chinese financing has proved difficult for the US to compete against due to the fact that China's lending typically comes with fewer strings attached. China has had no qualms about lending to regional governments with questionable democratic and human-rights records, and has imposed less stringent conditions with regard to environmental standards, macroeconomic-policy requirements or transparency in its contracts. This has made Chinese lending much more attractive and affordable than what the US and the multilateral agencies can offer.

Chinese projects, however, have not been free from scandal, with numerous instances of corruption and bribery reported. For example, a US$3.75bn high-speed rail line in Mexico was cancelled in 2014 amid concerns about the transparency of the bidding process, while the construction of a hydroelectric dam in Ecuador (financed by a US$1.7bn loan) led to numerous convictions for bribery. Additionally, while the conditions to China's loans may appear more lax than those of their Western counterparts, the loans still often come with notable requirements, such as guaranteed commodity sales and purchases of Chinese equipment. Analysts have warned that this could simply add another dimension to the region's foreign dependency. China has also made some questionable decisions about the scope of its lending. Venezuela has been the main recipient of Chinese loans since 2005, accounting for US$62.5bn (more than twice as much as the next highest, Brazil). However, the country's severe economic crisis since 2014 has raised concerns over whether these loans will be repaid. Tellingly, China has offered no new loans to Venezuela since 2016. US agencies have also tried to capitalise on Latin America's increased indebtedness to China. For example, the US International Development Finance Corporation (DFC) agreed a US$2.8bn loan package to Ecuador for infrastructure in 2021 that could also be used to 'refinance predatory Chinese debt'. The package came with considerable strings attached.

China's most recent instrument for deepening its economic ties with Latin America is the Belt and Road Initiative (BRI), an ambitious global investment and lending programme that has been incorporating Latin American countries since 2018, five years after its initial announcement (Panama joined a year earlier). In 2022, a total of 21 countries in Latin America and the Caribbean have joined the BRI, though many of the region's largest economies have so far opted out, including Brazil, Colombia and Mexico. The BRI has not fundamentally changed China's priorities. Still relatively new, and disrupted by the pandemic, it has to date had little impact on the patterns of China's economic relations with the region, nor is there evidence that it has intensified trade, investment and lending beyond what would have been expected from existing trends.

The BRI has nevertheless prompted the US to respond with a similar global infrastructure programme of its own, known as the Build Back Better World (B3W) initiative, which is to be undertaken in partnership with the G7. The Trump administration's answer to the BRI, an initiative known as 'América Crece' [Growth in the Americas], never gained much traction and was quietly shelved at the end of Donald Trump's term. Announced in June 2021, B3W has yet to be formally launched. The B3W is clearly set up to be an alternative to the BRI, with the objective of tapping into the assessed US$40 trillion of infrastructure needs in the developing world. It sets itself apart from the BRI by emphasising its 'values-driven' approach based on the Blue Dot Network (BDN), a multi-stakeholder initiative led by Australia, Japan and the US that provides assessment and certification of infrastructure on numerous measures, including transparency and inclusivity as well as environmental and social sustainability. The B3W is also designed with a heavy focus on mobilising private capital. But the role of private companies in B3W runs the risk that Chinese state-owned firms outbid them above market prices, or that they may simply not find key development sectors lucrative enough to invest in at all.

With the B3W yet to be launched, it is too early to tell whether it will present a viable alternative to the BRI. Thus far, the sole discussion of B3W in Latin America has been a three-country listening tour to Colombia, Ecuador and Panama led by Daleep Singh, deputy national security advisor for international economics, when some financing commitments were made. Although the geostrategic stakes of their respective initiatives are obvious, both US and Chinese officials have emphasised their complementarities and it does not appear that commitments to either programme will necessarily preclude cooperation with the other (countries like Panama and Ecuador may end up joining both). This is already evident from patterns of Chinese lending in Brazil, which, despite not joining the BRI, is the second-biggest recipient of lending from the CDB and the Ex–Im Bank in the region. China has been increasingly open about permitting non-Chinese participants in BRI projects, particularly in areas (such as tourism infrastructure) where they are likely to have advantages, and it is likely that the US will also remain relatively permissive (with possible exceptions arising in areas perceived to represent national-security risks, such as energy grids or 5G networks). That may change under future administrations, however, as evidenced by the Trump administration strong-arming Panama's government to abandon numerous projects with China after it gave diplomatic recognition to the mainland over Taiwan in 2017.

In the end, the attractiveness of the BRI and B3W will depend on each recipient country's individual investment needs as well as the track record of previous deals with the US and China. As such, it is unlikely that either of the two initiatives can win out over the other. The consistency of Chinese policy does, however, give a long-term advantage to the BRI compared to the B3W, particularly if future US administrations lose interest in regaining their regional influence through investment. The Biden administration's mixed success with infrastructure at home (its original Build Back Better agenda was sharply diluted and its largest component failed to pass in the Senate) also does not bode well for a more ambitious global effort.

The military question

China's military ties with Latin America closely follow its political ones and are mostly limited to weapons sales, training, joint exercises and personnel exchanges. Although these ties are strongest with the countries and governments with which it is more closely aligned, they are not exclusive to them. China's military activities in the region have been dwarfed by those of Russia, which has been more openly collaborative with regional allies like Venezuela and has made far more provocative moves, such as repeatedly flying Tu-160 nuclear-capable bombers (most recently in 2018) to Venezuelan territory and sending the guided-missile battlecruiser *Pyotr Veliky* for exercises in the Caribbean in 2008.

In contrast to Russia's sabre-rattling, China has taken a restrained approach that broadly follows the tone of its regional collaboration in other areas of policy. Its 2016 White Paper on Latin America covers military cooperation in a single paragraph and is focused on policy dialogue and professional exchanges as well as issues such as peacekeeping, humanitarian relief and counter-terrorism. Trade in weapons and technology transfers is mentioned almost in passing, although this is likely a deliberate understatement of their importance given how active China has been over the past decade and a half in attempting to break into the regional market. China also has no stated intention of establishing a permanent military presence in the region and its sole intervention has been as part of the (concluded)

MINUSTAH peacekeeping operation in Haiti, which involved a contingent of civilian riot police rather than actual military personnel.

The arms trade is another area of rivalry. China's exports to Latin America have increased substantially since 2005, yet they remain considerably smaller than those of Russia, the US and many European countries, including Germany, France, the Netherlands and Spain. They are almost entirely concentrated on a single country, Venezuela: the US$629 million-worth of arms sales to Venezuela between 2005 and 2021 represents 87% of its regional total, with Bolivia, Peru and Trinidad and Tobago accounting for most of the remainder. Latin America also represents a small fraction of China's global arms exports, just 3.3% since 2005, though this is not dissimilar to Russian and US shares due to the region's relatively low overall spending. This could preclude greater interest in penetrating the local market given the strong competition China faces, particularly from European arms makers, which collectively account for the largest share of Latin American arms imports.

China's main exports have comprised personnel equipment, combat and internal-security vehicles, and surveillance systems, as well as a handful of transport aircraft, helicopters and trainer/light attack aircraft. Sales of high-end weaponry, such as fighter aircraft or tanks, have eluded it. The closest a deal came to completion was in 2015, when Argentina was evaluating purchasing up to 20 FC-1/JF-17 fighters. The deal failed to materialise, although a visit to Pakistan in June 2022 by the head of Argentina's joint military staff fuelled speculation that a deal may be reached in the future; officials reportedly discussed a plan that would see the JF-17 being assembled in Argentina, with China and Pakistan supplying parts. China is also said to have offered Argentina a loan to help with the acquisition. Earlier, a planned sale of Chinese MBT-2000/Type-90-IIM tanks to Peru in 2011 also collapsed due to failure to obtain an export licence for the tanks' Ukrainian-made engines. China has also struggled to maintain a reputation for quality. Bolivian authorities were reportedly disappointed with the performance of their H425 *Panther* helicopters, as was Argentina with its WZ-551B1 armoured personnel carriers (APCs).

China has no stated ambition to establish a permanent military presence in the region, which would prove highly contentious with the US (whose own presence has been vastly reduced since the end of the Cold War), particularly if it were to involve the stationing of offensive weaponry that could be used to attack the US. But with China controlling strategic assets of ever-increasing value in the region, such as infrastructure and natural resources, there will be a corresponding need to ensure their security as well as that of communications routes to and from the region. If a permanent Chinese presence were to materialise, it would therefore likely be under the guise of facilities protection or logistics bases. The People's Liberation Army's (PLA) 'support base' in Djibouti, its only major military facility outside China's borders, could be a blueprint for how such a presence could take shape.

After COVID-19

The coronavirus pandemic has been another opportunity for China to expand its soft power in Latin America. Whereas US and European vaccine makers showed a preference for supplying their domestic markets first, Chinese vaccines were exported in large numbers in early 2021 and filled important global supply gaps before Western vaccines were made available in larger quantities. Among the regional countries with domestic vaccine-manufacturing capabilities, Brazil established an agreement with Sinovac in September 2020 to produce its CoronaVac vaccine via its Butantan state-owned laboratory, while Chile secured priority access to orders from the same company by allowing extensive clinical trials. Mexico has also been a significant user of Chinese vaccines, with an order for 22m doses placed in March 2021 following delays in its Pfizer orders that set back the country's vaccination programme during January–February.

Chinese vaccines therefore fulfilled an important role during the crucial early months of 2021 and helped some countries like Chile achieve some of the quickest levels of vaccine protection in the world. But questions over Chinese vaccine efficacy began to emerge later that year as many of them were shown to be less effective against more contagious variants, such as Delta and Omicron, compared to Western

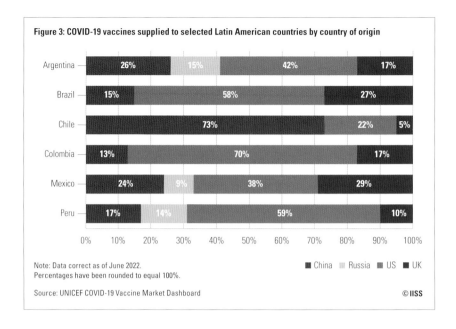

Figure 3: COVID-19 vaccines supplied to selected Latin American countries by country of origin

Note: Data correct as of June 2022.
Percentages have been rounded to equal 100%.

■ China ■ Russia ■ US ■ UK

Source: UNICEF COVID-19 Vaccine Market Dashboard

© IISS

vaccines (or even Russia's Sputnik V, which also saw widespread use in Latin America). Despite its eagerness to show off its prowess in high-technology industries such as medical research, the mixed success of its vaccines unfortunately demonstrated that China still has some catching up to do with more established countries in these fields. This could make potential clients apprehensive about adopting Chinese technology until there is more convincing evidence of its effectiveness. It also made clear that the US and Europe will continue to enjoy a comparative advantage over China in sectors related to high-technology, which are likely to increase in importance as an investment need over the next decades.

Who will win the rivalry?

Despite the United States' support of Ukraine against Russia's invasion, the 2022 National Defense Strategy reiterated that China remained the country's 'most consequential strategic competitor'. The US maintains a dominant political, cultural and military presence in Latin America, and remains its main foreign investor. But in the realms of trade and financing, China has managed to equal or exceed it. Nevertheless, elements of this rivalry have all too frequently featured alarmist overtones, particularly in the military sphere, where China's influence is often greatly overstated. China is also unlikely to attach as much importance to Latin America as it does to more proximate regions like Eurasia and Africa. This could help reduce the risk of the region becoming a potential powder keg for conflict, as China will be hesitant to challenge the US in the event of a serious clash of interests. But China may nonetheless gain from deepening ties with Latin America. Should the US and China engage in open conflict in the future, a region torn between the two sides may well choose to sit it out and declare its neutrality, thereby denying or restricting key hemispheric support to the US.

The tendency to see this rivalry through the lens of Beijing's and Washington's interests obscures Latin America's own role in shaping outcomes. The success of either side in advancing its agenda will depend substantially on its ability to adapt to regional interests and sensitivities. This is particularly true of the US, given the considerable resentment that remains over US interventionism in the past. Although the Biden administration's regional foreign policy has been far more tactful and cooperative than that of its predecessor, recent remarks by President Joe Biden claiming that Latin America was the United States' 'front yard' rather than backyard are unlikely to go down well in a region whose members hope to be seen and treated as equals by Washington. But while many Latin Americans see the emergence of a multipolar world in a positive light, attitudes towards China are not fundamentally more favourable than they are towards the US: of the 18 countries covered in the Latinobarómetro survey, only Venezuela showed higher net approval for China than for the US in 2020. China's approval ratings could deteriorate if countries where corruption is a major voter concern opt for less-transparent Chinese loans and investments.

Shifting dynamics of global power suggest China will manage to maintain its existing advantages in Latin America while making further inroads in areas where the US remains dominant. But it is unlikely ever to replace the US as the region's most influential external power. Rather, the real winner of this contest may well be Latin

America itself. Insofar as regional governments can take the best from both sides, they will be better able to fill much-needed gaps in their development and security agendas given the resource, technology and skill constraints that many of these countries, particularly smaller ones, face. A wealthier and more secure Latin America may ultimately be the major outcome of growing US–China rivalry.

Index